The Perfect Baby Name

THE
PERFECT
BABY NAME

■ *Finding the Name* ■
that Sounds Just Right

WHITNEY WALKER AND **ERIC REYES**

BERKLEY BOOKS
NEW YORK

The Berkley Publishing Group
Published by the Penguin Group
Penguin Group (USA) Inc.
375 Hudson Street, New York, New York 10014, USA

Penguin Group (Canada), 10 Alcorn Avenue, Toronto, Ontario M4V 3B2, Canada
   (a division of Pearson Penguin Canada Inc.)

Penguin Books Ltd., 80 Strand, London WC2R 0RL, England

Penguin Group Ireland, 25 St. Stephen's Green, Dublin 2, Ireland
   (a division of Penguin Books Ltd.)

Penguin Group (Australia), 250 Camberwell Road, Camberwell, Victoria 3124, Australia
   (a division of Pearson Australia Group Pty. Ltd.)

Penguin Books India Pvt. Ltd., 11 Community Centre, Panchsheel Park, New Delhi—110 017, India

Penguin Group (NZ), cnr Airborne and Rosedale Roads, Albany, Auckland 1310, New Zealand
   (a division of Pearson New Zealand Ltd.)

Penguin Books (South Africa) (Pty.) Ltd., 24 Sturdee Avenue, Rosebank, Johannesburg 2196, South Africa

Penguin Books Ltd., Registered Offices: 80 Strand, London WC2R 0RL, England

The publisher does not have any control over and does not assume any responsibility for author or
third-party websites or their content.

PRINTING HISTORY
Berkley trade paperback edition / July 2005

Library of Congress Cataloging-in-Publication Data
Walker, Whitney.
   The perfect baby name : finding the name that sounds just right /
   Whitney Walker and Eric Reyes.—Berkley trade pbk. ed.
     p. cm.
   ISBN 0-425-20265-8
   1. Names, Personal. I. Reyes, Eric. I. Title.

CS2377.W36 2005
929.4'4—dc22

                            2004065596

PRINTED IN THE UNITED STATES OF AMERICA
10 9 8 7 6 5 4

To our sons, Gabriel and Jasper, for inspiring us to write this book.
And to our friends and family for helping us complete it.

ACKNOWLEDGMENTS

We owe a debt of gratitude to all of the parents and children named in this book—thank you for sharing your stories with us.

We want to thank Sharon Brown, a speech language pathologist, for advising us so thoroughly on the phonetics chapter, and Sandra McPherson, English professor at the University of California at Davis, for consulting on the poetry chapter. We also had two terrific researchers—Moya Stone and Sarah Stevenson—who tracked down pronunciations and helped compile our additional resources list.

Our editor, Allison McCabe, lent us her precision with words and helped us bake a coherent whole out of an overflowing feast. Our agents, Renee Zuckerbrot and Martha Kaplan, supplied encouragement and numerous insights along the way.

Finally, we'd like to thank all of the professors and foreign-language speakers who helped us compile pronunciations for our name lists:

Moradewun Adejunmobi, program director of African-American studies and African studies, University of California at Davis; Naheed Attari; Joel Baum and Pamela Wool; Sharon Brown; Cari Bilyeu Clark; Maiheng Dietrich, Ph.D., foreign language professor at the University of Pennsylvania; Cleveland Kent Evans, psychology professor, Bellevue University; Candelas Gala, Ph.D., Chair of the Department of Romance Languages, Wake Forest University; Anna Katz; Ravi Mallikarjunan; Susan McDonic, Ph.D., cultural anthropology lecturer at Duke University; Michael and Yoriko Mikesell; Wellington W. Nyangoni, chair of African and Afro-American studies, Brandeis University; Terrence Potter, Ph.D., associate professor of Arabic at Georgetown University; Faisal Rana; M. Dolores Ruiz-Rothhammer; Alex and Ruth Reyes; Peggy Sandel, Ph.D. in Jewish Studies; Hiroko K. Sherry, foreign language lecturer at the University of Pennsylvania; Giovanna Queeto; Jeannie Wilson, director of the Daraja Project at Chabot College; Deborah Wool; Hadi Zamrik; Leslie Salmon-Zhu and Dave Zhu.

CONTENTS

INTRODUCTION

People dream about it. Family feuds have been started over it. Some want to keep it a secret until the big day. Others want to tell the world as soon as they know. It is a question that can test marriages and make grown-ups cry.

What to name the baby?

Whatever you decide will be your child's label forever. But hey, no pressure!

A name creates the first impression that others develop about you, *especially* if they hear your name before they meet you. Parents scan the Internet and interrogate preschool teachers looking for the perfect name for their child. But they often focus only on first and middle names that sound good together, not realizing that the *last* name is just as important. When your children become adults, they will introduce themselves by both first and last names—that's how people are known in both the business world and in social circles. That's why it's crucial to consider your surname when choosing first names for your children. We believe that when a person has a good combination of first and last name—one that is memorable and pleasing to the ear—she or he has confidence about introducing themselves to others. Therefore, it follows that a well chosen name helps form a positive self-identity.

The Perfect Baby Name is a guide for custom-picking the name that suits your child best. Unlike other books that overwhelm you with endless alphabetical lists and name definitions, *The Perfect Baby Name* is the first book to offer a systematic process for choosing a first name that sounds good with your last name. Our method works with any surname—and it's easy to learn. We're not talking about simple alliteration (Roy Rogers) or rhyming (Ronald McDonald). Instead, using the most basic rules of phonetics and poetry, our system explains how to break down a surname by consonants and vowel sounds, number of syllables, and accents. Once you have learned these simple techniques, you can turn to the end of this book, where we provide lists of first names (with pronunciations, but no definitions!) that are organized by prominent sounds and rhythms. Parents can use these lists to match first names up to their last names. The lists are sorted by similar sounds (rather than alphabetically) so that, for example, every name with a D sound in it (Darius, Addison, Benedict) appears in the same list. We also teach parents to listen to the way names sound, to determine which combinations are most pleasing. Which is the more prominent sound in your surname—the vowels or the consonants? Is the accent on the first or second syllable? Once you've answered those questions, you're ready to look for a first name that matches. *The Perfect Baby Name* also covers how to choose a matching middle name, create your own name, and name siblings so that their names go well together without sounding too much alike.

Name combinations that are pleasing to the ear are also inherently easier to remember. If people remember your name, they tend to think of you first for party invitations, job referrals, and social introductions. Your name can give you an edge, can even make you more popular and successful. There aren't any scientific studies to prove this theory; it's something we came up with as parents trying to name our own children. We noticed that certain names sound good and others don't. What we realized was that names with repeating sounds are more pleasing, at least to our ears. We discovered that we especially like names with rhyming vowel sounds, like Elvis Presley (short E), Muhammad Ali (short O), and Gabriel Reyes (long A), our first son's name. As we shared these ideas with our friends, we discovered that lots of other parents wanted to find a systematic approach for choosing a first name that sounds good with their surnames. These folks became our case studies. We ended up helping lots of friends (and friends of friends) break down the sounds in their surnames and find matching first names. And now we hope to help you!

Before You Begin

Take a long hard look at your own name—first, middle, and last. What do you like and dislike about it? Do you like the sound combinations? Do your names flow well together? Does your first name match your surname phonetically (see Chapter 1) or rhythmically (see Chapter 2)? Is your last name short or long, plain, or unusual—and how does that jibe with your first name (see Chapter 3)? Is your first name traditional or unconventional, common or unique? Is it a family name, a name that reflects your cultural background (see Chapter 4)? Do you find yourself repeating your name for others, correcting misspellings and mispronunciations? Once you have the answer to all of these questions, you'll be ready to determine what you want for your own child.

fast match

At the end of each chapter, we'll have a little box like this one that summarizes what you just learned. These Fast Match boxes can be like *Cliff's Notes* if you don't have time to read the whole chapter. Yes, choosing a name for your child can be an agonizing process . . . but now it doesn't have to be!

BREAKING DOWN THE SOUNDS

CONSIDER YOUR LAST name. Whether it is Green, Chu, or Martinez, it is made up of a variety of sounds. In this chapter, we'll use a simple tool you probably learned in high school—phonetics—to show you how to break apart your last name and determine which sounds are important. Then we'll explain how to match your surname sounds with complementary sounds in a first name, ensuring a combination that's pleasing to the ear. As we explained in the Introduction, names that sound good together are easier to remember and can help make a person (in this case, your child!) more popular and successful in life. Think of memorable celebrity names like Lucy Liu, Wayne Brady, and Elvis Presley. These names sound good together because they repeat similar sounds:

L and OO in Lucy and Liu
Long A in Wayne and Brady
L, S and short E in Elvis and Presley

Those repeating sounds create what we call a "phonetic echo," a kind of muscle memory for your brain that helps you remember the name combination. In other words, those celebrity names "match," and so can your child's name.

Every name (and every spoken word) consists of different sounds called phonemes. Here's how it works with the surname Green. Break down the sounds: G, R, long E, and N. Those are the four different sounds (or phonemes) in that name. Now go to those four different lists in the back of this book.

The G list has names like Hugo and Morgan that contain the G sound.
The R list has Rex and Aurora.
The long E list, Eli and Alicia.
The N list, Nathaniel and Lindy.

All of these names sound good with the surname Green. Once you break down your surname in this way, you can then scan the lists at the end of this book for the name you like best and choose the name you like best—your perfect match. The names in this book are drawn in part from the Social Security Administration's list of the 1,000 most popular names from the last one hundred years. We've broken down the sounds in each name and categorized them phonetically. Some dictionaries may list more phonemes than others, just as people with different accents will pronounce names in different ways. For the purposes of this book we stick to phonemes that are commonly used in names, and group together anything that sounds similar. For example, the vowels in Claudia and Molly sound different in Boston, but pretty much the same in California. Since they both feature the AW sound (think "Aw, shucks!") and sound good with surnames like Johnson and Dawson, we've grouped them together on the Short O list. Below are the phonemes we use in this book, along with the phonetic spellings we intend to use for each one in parentheses.

PHONEME LIST

• VOWELS •

Long A (AY) as in Jada (JAY-duh) and Aidan (AY-den)
Short A (A) as in Alice (AL-liss) and Samson (SAM-sun)
AIR as in Erica (AIR-rik-uh) and Perry (PAIR-ee)
AR as in Darlene (dar-LEEN) and Charlie (CHAR-lee)
Long E (EE) as in Frida (FREE-duh) and Eli (EE-ly)
Short E (EH or E) as in Stella (STEL-luh) and Henry (HEN-ree)
Long I (EYE or Y) as in Lila (LY-luh) and Isaac (EYE-zek)
Short I (I) as in Ilsa (ILL-suh) and William (WILL-yum)
Long O (OH) as in Sophie (SOH-fee) and Owen (OH-wen)

• CONSONANTS •

B (Ruby, Ben)
CH (Chelsea, Mitchell)
D (Deirdre, Cody)
F (Farrah, Raphael)
G (Greta, Angus)
H (Hannah, Alejandro)
J (Angela, Ajax)
K (Kylee, Declan)
L (Lucy, Dylan)
M (Emma, Matthew)
N/NG (Anna, Irving)
P (Pippin, Oprah)
Q (KW) (Shaniqua, Quentin)
R (Aurora, Wren, Harry, Riordan)
S (Tess, Sam)
SH/ZH (Asia, Lucian)
T (Octavia, Thomas)
TH (Aretha, Theodore)

• **VOWELS** •

Short O (AW) as in Molly (MAW-lee) and Dawson (DAW-sun)

OI as in Moira (MOI-ruh) and Troy (TROI)

OR as in Rory (ROR-ee) and Jordan (JOR-den)

OW as in Howard (HOW-wurd) and Paola (POW-luh)

OO as in Ruth (ROOTH) and Woody (WOOD-dee)

Short U (UH or U) as in Justine (juss-TEEN) and Gulliver (GULL-liv-ur)

UR as in Pearl (PURL) and Herb (HURB)

• **CONSONANTS** •

V (Olivia, Xavier)

W (Willa, Noah)

X (KS) (Roxanne, Alex)

Y (Y) (Yasmine, Gabriel)

Z (Jasmine, Xena, Cosmo, Zane)

Finding Phonemes

The first step in finding the phonemes in your surname is to listen to the different sounds, paying close attention to the way your mouth, tongue, and teeth move together to pronounce each separate piece—those are the phonemes. Write down a literal spelling for each sound in your name, especially for long surnames. Here are some examples:

Chu—CH-OO
Fresco—F-R-short E-S-K-long O
Price—P-R-long I-S
Phelan (FAY-len)—F-long A-L-short E-N
Juarez (WAR-ez)—W-AR-short E-Z
Rogers—R-short O-J-UR-Z
Newbury (NOO-bair-ee)—N-OO-B-AIR-long E
Reyes (RAY-yes)—R-long A-YE-short E-S
Martinez (mar-TEE-nez)—M-AR-T-long E-N-short E-Z

Remember that this process focuses on the way you *pronounce* names, so the hard C in Fresco is actually the K phoneme, whereas the soft C in Price is the S phoneme. Likewise, the soft G in Rogers makes a J sound and the hard S makes a Z sound. The PH in Phelan makes an F sound, the J in Juarez makes a W ("wuh") sound, the Y in Newbury makes long E sound, and the Y in Reyes makes a consonant Y ("yuh") sound.

As we mentioned at the beginning of this chapter, the Greens would look at four phoneme lists (G, R, long E, and N), while the Chus would look at two (CH and OO). If those don't generate enough names to choose from, they might then look at other similar-sounding phonemes.

Notice how your mouth, teeth, and tongue move to say different sounds and you'll see that some phonemes are pronounced practically the same way. Try it with G and K by saying "guh" and "kuh" several times quickly: The back of your tongue hits the roof of your mouth with both sounds, creating that muscle memory that makes your brain think it's hearing the same sound. When you say them together in a name like Gwen Keaton, the phonetic echo is just as strong as if you'd said Kim Keaton. So if Greg sounds good with your surname, so will Craig. And vice versa—if you have a G sound in your surname (like Gonzalez), you might want to check the K list for first names (like Jacqueline), too.

Besides G and K, other partners include:

S and Z (Chase and Chaz)
D and T (Adella and Estella)
B and P (Barry and Perry)
F and V (Farrah and Vera)
J-CH-SH-ZH (Jessie, Chelsea, Shelly, Zsa-Zsa)

In phonetics, groupings of similar consonants have different terms—paired cognates, fricatives, glottal stops—but we don't need all that terminology. For our purposes, we call them all "partner phonemes." Again, they're different sounds, but they're similar enough to be interchangeable. When you start consulting name lists, you'll notice that NG names like Domingo and Sterling appear on the N list, simply because N is the dominant sound (and there aren't that many NG names). There are also two combination phonemes:

Q (phoneme KW) makes a "kwuh" sound combining K and W
(so Q names will appear on both the K and W lists).

X (phoneme KS) makes an "eks" sound combining K and S
(so X names will appear on the K and S lists).

Some vowels are also partners because they incorporate parts of the same sound, like OO and UR (if Ruby sounds good with your surname, so will Pearl), AW-AR-OW (Oliver, Charlie, and Howard), OI and EE (Roy and Reese), and OH-OR-OI (Toni, Tori, and Troy). So now the

Chus can check the J-CH-SH-ZH, OO, and UR lists, and the Greens can consult the G, K-Q-X, R, Long E, OI, and N lists.

Don't worry—you don't need to remember all of these groupings. When you start looking at the name lists, we'll remind you about all these partner phonemes, but we thought we'd mention it up front to lay the groundwork for the rest of what you read.

Making a Match

Now you're ready to make your match. Here's how we did it: The last name of our children is Reyes (pronounced RAY-yes), so the phonemes are R, long A, YE, short E, S. When you say the name, you stress the first syllable, making the long A sound the most prominent. So we started looking at first names with prominent long A sounds to match. For our first son, we chose the name Gabriel (GAY-bree-yell). Say it out loud and you can hear that long A stands out in both Gabriel and Reyes, and they also share the R and YE sounds. It's a match!

Notice which part of your name you stress to determine which syllable has the accent. The vowel sound in the accented syllable usually stands out most, like the long A in Reyes. Your perfect match can often be found among first names with that same prominent vowel, so start there. Consider these celebrity endorsements for that concept: Pamela Anderson (short A), Mike Myers (long I), Clay Aiken (long A), and Elvis Presley (short E).

While writing this book, we worked with several expectant couples trying to choose names. They became our case studies, and we provided them with customized phonetic lists of names—rudimentary versions of the lists you now see in this book. For Nate and Meliss Grover, we provided a Long O list that featured several names they liked: Nolan, Owen, and their ultimate choice, Beau, all sound great with Grover because the dominant sounds match. From the phonetic lists that we gave Amy and John West, at first they liked the sound of Stella West, which has matching S, T, and prominent Short E sounds. But as the due date drew near, they started hearing about so many celebrity babies named Stella that they were afraid it was getting too popular. So they went back and found Scarlett on the same three phoneme lists, S, T, and Short E. Though AR is the prominent phoneme in Scarlett, short E is the secondary vowel sound. And on the Short A list, Noel and Frank Gallagher found two of their favorite family names, Kathleen and Daniel, so when they had a girl they named her Kathleen: The secondary short A in Kathleen matches the primary short A in Gallagher.

If you don't find anything you like on your prominent vowel list, simply move on to other sounds in your surname. Linda Behla (BAY-luh) and Jeff Davis decided to use Jeff's last name for their son's surname and Linda's last name for his middle name. We gave them a list of long A names like Raymond, Clayton, and Jake, but since Behla and Davis both feature prominent long A sounds, they decided that they didn't want a first name with that same sound. So we turned to the other phonemes in Davis—D/T, V/F, short I, and S/Z/X (remember about those partner phonemes that are pronounced almost the same way). Then, like many couples, Linda and Jeff each wrote down a list of names they liked and compared them. We pointed out that the ones that overlapped—Nicholas, Phillip, Oliver, and William—happened to match the L in Behla and the short I in Davis. When their son was born, "he just looked like a Will," Jeff said, so William Behla Davis it was. Tori Amos (OR/long O), Gwen Stefani (short E), and Lily Tomlin (short I) are all celebrities whose first names match the secondary vowels in their last names.

Other couples found themselves drawn to matching the consonants rather than the vowels in their surnames. For their daughter, Lynn Kusnierz and Mark Compton (who used Mark's last name, pronounced KAWMP-ten, for their kids) looked at K (Clarissa), M (Emma), and T (Stella) names before deciding on Eleanor (N). Ricki and Ethan Klos (pronounced KLOHS like Glenn Close) were particularly interested in X names to match the K and S sounds in Klos, so they came up with the name Bixby for their son. And after looking at M, G/K/Q/X, and N names, Naheed Attari and Kevin McGahan (who use Kevin's surname, pronounced mik-GAN, for their kids) chose Declan (DEK-len) for their son, matching the K and N sounds in Declan with the G and N sounds in McGahan. Stars with matching consonants in their names include Demi Moore (M), and Marilyn Monroe (M, R, N).

GREAT MATCHES

Still not clear on what makes a good match?
Here are some more excellent examples.

Jason Bateman, actor (long A)
Halle Berry, actress (short A/AIR)
Jackie Chan, actor (short A)
Elvis Costello, singer (short E, L, S)
Phyllis Diller, comedian (short I, L)
Robert Frost, poet (short O)
Cary Grant, actor (short A/AIR)
Samuel L. Jackson, actor (short A, S)
Angelina Jolie, actress (J, L, long E)
Orlando Jones, actor (long O)
Alicia Keys, musician (long E, SH-Z)
Nicole Kidman, actress (short I, K)
Bruno Kirby, actor (OO-UR)
Nathan Lane, actor (long A)
Elmore Leonard, author (short E, L)
Debra Messing, actress (short E)
Rosie O'Donnell, comedian (long O)
Keanu Reeves, actor (long E)
Will Smith, actor (short I)
Amber Tamblyn, actress (short A, M, B)

handwritten: Greta Recht n
short E, R, T

Allowing for Alliteration

When a first and last name both start with the same letter, that's alliteration; it can be an excellent way of making your child's name stand out.
Think of Lucy Liu, Nick Nolte, Roy Rogers, and even Whitney Walker
(if you don't recognize that last name, check out the cover of this book).
Surnames that start with strong consonants like D, K, M, N, R, S, and T
tend to stand up to alliteration; others can sound a little cartoonish as in
Penelope Pittstop. Vowels generally aren't well suited to alliteration
either, but of course, it's all a matter of personal preference. Some people love alliterative names, and some don't. If you're on the fence, check

the list of names for the first letter in your surname and see what you think—you may be pleasantly surprised with a good match.

Partner phonemes offer an alternative to alliteration; certain letters produce such similar sounds they can trick the listener into hearing alliteration without using the same initials. We call that "near alliteration," and it offers another way to create a name with similar sounds. That's what Frank and Noel Gallagher did when they named their daughter Kathleen (since K and G are partners), as did Andi and Colin Botto when they chose Piper for their daughter (since P and B are partners). Near alliteration will only work with certain vowels and consonants.

SOUNDS THE SAME

There's more than one kind of alliteration. The traditional way, of course, is when the first and last name both start with the same letter and create the same sound, as in Ansel Adams. Alliteration also works with names that have different letters but produce the same sounds, like George Jefferson and Cecil Smith. Then there's what we're calling near alliteration, when partner phonemes produce similar sounds, as in Garrison Keillor, Cary Grant, Tommy Dorsey. Here are some other (made-up) examples:

Oliver Austin
Charlotte Sherwood
Finneas Vincent
Theresa Davis
Benjamin Peters
Eric Adams

Alliteration can work the other way, too—that is, you can use the same initials with different sounds. Here are some examples:

George Gray
Cecilia Crawford
Theodore Tollen
Peter Phillips
Alice Abrams

Ending Where You Start

You may have heard that a child's first name should not end in the same letter that the last name starts with because it will be a burden to pronounce. Jennifer and Paul Vetter decided they wouldn't name their child Olive for that reason, and Rand and Allison Singer had to rule out Grace, as well. Try to pronounce "Olive Vetter" and "Grace Singer" and you'll see why: Your lips, teeth, and tongue have to work hard to repeat the V and S phonemes. (Instead, the Vetters named their sons Kurtis and Milo, and the Singers went with Ruby and Avlyn for their daughters.)

Some consonants butt up against each other in a cumbersome way, like B, D, G, L, M, N, P, S, and T. Names like Greg Garrett and Sam Martin are tough to articulate clearly without letting the Gs and Ms run together (our apologies to the Greg Garretts and Sam Martins out there). And yet, Lyle Lovett made it work for him! Other consonants don't seem to have that problem, like the hard C at the end of Eric and the soft CH sound at the beginning of Cheever. The "-er" ending (phoneme UR) in Jasper makes your mouth pucker slightly, while the "re-" beginning in Reyes stretches your mouth into a smile. We decided that the combination was not difficult to pronounce, giving Jasper (and any other "-er" name) the green light for us.

In general, surnames that start with a vowel should not be paired with first names that end in a vowel, unless the sounds are different, as in Stella Adler and Flannery O'Connor. Stacy Thurm and Antonio Izzo chose the name Ari for their second son, which works because the I in Ari (AR-ee) is a long E sound, whereas the I in Izzo (EYE-zoh) is a long I sound. The letters are the same but the sounds are different, so it's not difficult to pronounce. Again, if you're considering a name that ends in the same letter or sound as your surname, simply listen to the combination and decide whether it sounds good to you.

By that same token, consider the suffix of your surname. For instance, Victoria Tollen says she's always loved the names Carson and Austin, "but not with Tollen—the double '-en' endings are too rhyming." The Vetters weren't too keen on Oliver because the double "-er" endings sounded choppy to them. However, Denise and Markus Kemper fell in love with the name Ryder and decided that they didn't mind the repeat endings. Repetition can help make a name memorable: Think of TV's Jennifer Garner and children's book author Mercer Mayer, both with double "-er" endings.

Matching the Middle

Don't forget the middle name! It's a crucial element, because when a middle name complements both the first and last name, it enhances the sound and rhythm of the entire string. Your child's middle name can phonetically match her first name, her surname, or both. Often it makes sense to wait until you've settled on a first name that sounds good alone with your surname. Then you can choose one or two phonemes from either the first or last name to find a middle name.

We liked the name Jasper for our second son, even though the short A sound doesn't match the long A sound in Reyes. So we did what Diane Keaton did when she named her daughter Dexter Dean Keaton—chose a matching middle name to tie them all together. James matches the J in Jasper and the long A in Reyes, so now Jasper James Reyes (JJ for short) sounds good. Julia and Larry Chambers fell in love with the first name Penelope for their daughter and wanted a somewhat unconventional, one-syllable middle name to offset her longer, more traditional first and last names. They considered Rain (matching the R and long A in Chambers), Leigh (repeating the L and long E in Penelope), and Lane (L in Penelope and long A in Chambers) before settling on Blu (echoing the P/B sounds in Penelope and Chambers and the L in Penelope).

However, sometimes parents know which middle name they'll use before deciding on a first name. The Comptons wanted their daughter to carry the middle name Irene for grandmothers on both sides, but they were at a loss for her first name. They were drawn to names like Eva and Ella but didn't like the way they sounded with their middle name choice, Irene. The "-a" ending butted up against the opening vowel I, making Ella Irene cumbersome to pronounce. That meant ruling out Bella, Emma, Ada, and other "-a" ending names. But what about Bellamy, Ellery, or Hillary, which still have the "-el" and "-la" sounds but end in "-y"? Or Maybelle, Mirabelle, and Isabel, which end in "-el"? After scanning the lists to match the sounds in their surname, they also looked at the Long I, R, and Long E lists to find names to match their middle name choice. In the end they settled on Eleanor Irene Compton, which features R in Eleanor and Irene and N in all three names. Plus, they can still call her Elle or Ella for short.

Predicting Nicknames

To some parents, the nickname is just as important as what's written on the birth certificate, so consider the phonetics of every version of your child's name. Which will your child go by most often—his given name or his nickname? Is it likely to change when he's an adult? That's probably the one that should be a phonetic match.

Sometimes, a nickname can help push a name to the top of your list or bring it down a notch or two. As soon as we heard the name Jasper, we fell in love with the idea of calling our son Jazz. But if you name your son James, he will someday be called Jim, Jimmy, or even Jimbo. Unless you select very carefully, most every child gets a nickname at one time or another, so you might as well choose one you like from the start—but also face up to the fact that your child may determine his own nickname some day.

A Word about Mispronunciations

One family we know of loved the name Axel for their new baby, but they had second thoughts when their toddler tried to say Axel and it came out as "Ass-hell." Most two- and three-year-olds have some speech problems that they eventually outgrow. (In fact, you'll hardly ever hear a three-year-old say he's three—he's always "free.") Still, since we're talking about phonetics in this book, it seems prudent to get you thinking about how your child might say his own name, once he starts to talk. Indeed, before naming your child, it's wise to consider any inevitable mispronunciations that your offspring will have to endure.

It's very common for young kids to drop letters and mix up sounds, particularly M for N, Y or W for L, W for R and V, and F for S and TH, but some kids replace G and K with D and T, too. That's too many variables to avoid, and really no name is totally safe, so don't even try to pick something that can't be mispronounced. Just take note that if you name your son Theodore, you'd better like the sound of FEE-dor. Rest assured, though, that speech impediments are rarely hereditary and the majority of these verbal boo-boos will fade by kindergarten. In fact, parents should cherish (and record!) them before they're gone. Besides, your child may say his name just fine. Little Axel did!

fast match

To **break down** your surname, first say it out loud slowly and listen to the different sounds. Pay attention to your pronunciation and determine which sounds are most prominent. Write them down. Then check out the lists of names that match those phonemes. They will all match your surname, so as soon as you find a name you like, the rest is up to you. Whether you choose to mix and match vowel sounds, modify the name, or use alliteration is a simple matter of personal preference. You can use the same technique to choose a matching middle name, or nickname.

FEEL THE RHYTHM

WE'VE TOLD YOU names that match phonetically are more memorable and pleasing to the ear. But what about Abraham Lincoln, Johnny Cash, and Audrey Hepburn? Those are certainly good, distinctive names, even though they don't repeat any sounds. That's where rhythm comes into play.

When parents say they want their child's name to have a nice "flow" to it, what they're really looking for are first and last names that create a pleasing rhythm when strung together. That can be achieved by following the basic rules of poetics. So let us give you a little poetry lesson that you can apply to naming your baby.

Poetry is very much about hearing the music in words. When you say a name out loud, you stress one syllable more than another. That's the accent. String two names together and you can hear how the accents work with each other, like beats in music. Where the beats fall in a name determines whether it is music to the ear or not. Once you know the *rhythm* of your surname, you can choose a first name to match.

Let's take a look at a famous name as an example. Hepburn is two syllables long with the stress on the first: HEP-burn. Audrey is also two syllables and also stresses the first syllable—AUD-rey—so the full name has a pleasing rhythm to it: DA-da DA-da. Of course, that other famous Hepburn sounds good, too, even though Katharine is a three-syllable name. The accent is still on the first syllable—KATH-a-rine—so you get two unstressed syllables in between the accents: DA-da-da

DA-da. Poets would say that those names "scan," which means that they sound good together, because the beats fall roughly every other syllable. Hannah and Martin Wolf wanted their kids' names to scan. So they alternated two- and three-syllable first and middle names to go with their one-syllable surname, choosing Isabel Kathryn Wolf (DA-da-da DA-da DA) for their daughter and Philip Frederick Wolf (DA-da DA-da-da DA) for their son.

Rhythm Section

To get the hang of it, try this little exercise. Look at these first and last names in the columns below. Just by their rhythm, judge which first names sound best with which last names.

Eric	Walker
Jerome	Kawabata
Elisa	Jones
Monique	O'Connor
Lee	DeJohnette

If you matched every first name on this list with every last name, you came up with a variety of sounds. Eric Walker sounds good because it has that nice DA-da DA-da we talked about. Elisa O'Connor sounds nice because the stress comes in the middle of two unstressed syllables: da-DA-da da-DA-da. What about Lee Jones? It may sound weird to some people because it is two heavily stressed, single-syllable words. But, to others, that makes it strong and distinctive. Think of John Wayne, James Dean, Bruce Lee, Tom Cruise, and Ice-T, to name just a few.

So take a look at your own surname. Say it out loud slowly and pay attention to where the beats fall. Write it down, if that helps. Is it one, two, three, or more syllables? Does the accent fall on the first or last syllable, or somewhere in between? That's the rhythm of your name, and now you can classify it.

Dactyls and Trochees and Iambs—Oh My!

This terminology may put images of prehistoric birds in your head, but these are the actual terms the poets use:

○ **Trochee (TROH-kee):** One heavily stressed syllable followed by one unstressed, as in Walker and Reyes, Whitney and Eric. Many English names, first and last, happen to be trochees.

○ **Iamb (EYE-yam):** One unstressed syllable followed by a heavy stress, as in Camus and Marquez, Nicole and Denzel. Many French, Middle Eastern, and African-American names are iambs.

○ **Dactyl (DAK-til):** One heavily stressed syllable followed by two unstressed, as in Carpenter and Anderson, Gabriel and Hillary.

○ **Anapest (ANN-uh-pest):** Two unstressed syllables followed by one heavy stress, as in DeJohnette, Dominique, Gabrielle, and a hyphenated surname like Salmon-Zhu. Again, French-derived names are often anapests.

○ **Spondee (SPAWN-dee):** Two heavily stressed syllables next to each other, such as George Bush and John Wayne.

○ **Middle stresses:** There's no poetic term for this, but many three-syllable first names have an unstressed syllable followed by a heavy stress followed by another unstressed syllable, as in O'Connor and Delillo, Elisa and Elijah. There are also two kinds of four-syllable middle stresses: da-da-DA-da as in Kurasawa and Angelina and da-DA-da-da as in Penelope and the famous surname of Laurence Olivier.

You don't have to say to yourself every time you read the back of a soup can, "Oh, there's a double dactyl in that recipe." But thinking of everyday speech as a form of poetry will help you appreciate other people's names, the names of brands you see in the store, and even the names of cars on the road. And it will train your ear to find the perfect name for your baby.

Playing with Matches

Now that you know what type of surname you have, you can choose a first name to match. Play with the columns of names in the preceding section again. Add your own surname, or those of family and friends—even a hyphenated name, if you choose. Add some of the first names you're considering for your baby, too. If you apply this little poetry lesson to the names around you, some will undoubtedly sound better to your ear than others. Recognizing where the beats fall in different combinations will help you to choose a good poetic match for your surname. Only you can decide what sounds best to you, but here are some general guidelines to follow:

○ If your surname is a **trochee** (DA-da), match it with another trochee, a dactyl, or a three- or four-syllable name accented in the middle. Nina Canter and Rob Fresco went with a trochee for their first son, David Fresco (DA-da DA-da), and a middle-accented, three-syllable name, Elijah, for their second son (da-DA-da DA-da).

○ If your surname is an **iamb** (da-DA), it will work with any type of first name. Naheed Attari and Kevin McGahan (who used Kevin's last name, pronounced mik-GAN, for their kids) decided on the middle-accented Persian name Parisa for their daughter (da-DA-da da-DA) and the trochaic Irish name Declan for their son (DA-da da-DA).

○ If your surname is a **dactyl** (DA-da-da), pair it with a trochee, another dactyl, or a three- or four-syllable name accented in the middle. Elisa and Andres Alvarez chose Madeline, another dactyl, for their first child (DA-da-da DA-da-da), and Lily, a trochee, for their second (DA-da DA-da-da).

○ If your surname is an **anapest** (da-da-DA), match it with an iamb, a trochee, another anapest, or a one, three-, or four-syllable name accented in the middle. Leslie Salmon and David Zhu combined their surnames when they married, creating an anapest with the accent on the last syllable: sa-mun-JOO. They assigned trochees to both their daughters, Maya and Bella (DA-da da-da-DA).

○ If your surname is **one syllable**, you can give your child a spondee with two equal heavy stresses by choosing a one-syllable first name, as John and Amy West did when they named their son Scout West (DA DA). Ricki and Ethan Klos, however, preferred trochees and named their children Sadie and Bixby Klos (DA-da DA), while Matt and Laurie Light preferred the middle-accented Savannah (da-DA-da DA). One-syllable surnames also pair well with dactyls, anapest, or three- or four-syllable names accented in the middle.

○ If your surname is a **middle stress**, it will sound good with anything. So, to match their middle-stressed surname of

Cometa (ko-MET-uh), Katy and Tom chose one-syllable Max for their firstborn (DA da-DA-da) and the three-syllable dactyl Madeline for their daughter (DA-da-da da-DA-da).

Exceptions to the Rule

As we mentioned, you may find that names scan better when you stress every other syllable, but poets intentionally break these rules sometimes, and so can you. Names that match phonetically can often get away with two heavy stresses in a row, as in Nicole Kidman (matching short I and K), Renée Zellweger (matching short E), and Bill Clinton (short I and L). You have to work a little harder to pronounce those double stresses, but perhaps that makes the names even more distinctive. It's all up to you, so experiment with the sounds and accents in several types of name combinations to find the match you like best.

Different cultures may find different sounds more pleasing. In English, many first names are trochees, but many French-derived names are accented on the second syllable, as in Nicole (nih-KOHL) and Michelle (mih-SHELL). And in Spanish, an accent on the second-to-last syllable is more common, as in Diego (dee-AY-goh) and Maria (mah-REE-ah). African-American names often combine iambic first names with anapest or trochee last names, as in Denzel Washington and Montel Williams. Your cultural background or international heritage may influence the type of name combinations you like, and indeed, you may want to match your surname with a first name from the same background. You should also consider whether your surname has any other unique characteristics and whether there are other naming factors in your family tradition. Chapters 4 and 5 can help with all of that, but first check out Chapter 3 to see if you want to make any modifications to the phonetic- or poetic-matching process you just learned.

New Name, New Rhythm

Any time you add a new name, it changes the rhythm of the combination. It's a good rule of thumb that first and middle names flow best together when they have different rhythms. Julie and Darrin Vinall (vih-NAWL) were going to name their daughter Chloe Linda (two trochees) for her mother, but decided that Chloe Elizabeth (a trochee and a dactyl) created a prettier string with their surname. There are a variety of syllables and accents in all three names, but the L sound is the common denominator that ties them all together.

Sometimes, two two-syllable names can sound choppy together, and you need to mix it up. That's why the Hammons went with Logan Augusta for their first daughter and Miranda Kay for their second. Likewise, Lynn Kusnierz and Mark Compton already had Irene, a trochee, picked out for their daughter's middle name, so they chose Eleanor, a dactyl, for her first name. They also liked the nickname Ellie, a trochee, which works just as well with her surname, Compton, also a trochee. That's not always the case, though. The Kloses chose two trochees for their children's first and middle names—Sadie Parker and Bixby Eli—to complement their one-syllable surname.

Parents often like to pair multi-syllabic first names with one-syllable middle names, as we did with Gabriel Rush and Jasper James. Technically, those one-syllable middle names butt up against our trochee last name, Reyes, but the heavy stress in the middle name creates a natural stopping point, like a period on a sentence. This can be an effective way of breaking the rules to make your name stand out even more.

If you plan to hyphenate your child's surname, that will change its rhythm, too. Pam Wool and Joel Baum both have spondee names, but when they combined their surnames for their son, it became a trochee, Wool-Baum (WOOL-bowm). They chose a trochaic first name, Jonah, to match (DA-da DA-da). Mona Molarsky has a middle-accented surname, but when paired with her husband Frank's surname of Beck, it makes two iambs: mo-LAR-skee BEK. They chose a middle-accented first name, Marina (da-DA-da da-DA-da-DA). And when Julie Felner and Amy Harrison decided to have a baby, they struggled with how to combine their surnames and finally agreed to put the longer one first, creating a dactyl-trochee. Since Harrison-Felner is a pretty long last name, they picked short first and middle names, Cleo Joan, for their daughter. The whole string breaks down rhythmically like this: DA-da DA DA-da-da-DA-da.

BEAT THAT!

If you're still not clear on what makes a good match, here are some excellent examples using the names of celebrities:

- ◆ Dudley Dooright (DA-da DA-da) is two trochees.
- ◆ Elijah Wood (uh-LY-juh WOOD) (da-DA-da DA) is a middle-stressed three-syllable first name paired with a one-syllable surname, making two iambs.
- ◆ Jennifer Aniston (JEN-ih-fur ANN-iss-ton) (DA-da-da DA-da-da) is two dactyls. So is Englebert Humperdink, by the way, not that we're suggesting that name for your new baby!
- ◆ Penelope Cruz (da-DA-da-da DA) makes an iamb and an anapest.
- ◆ Angelina Jolie (da-da-DA-da DA-da) is an anapest and a trochee and a stray unstressed syllable.

Scansion Screening

Here's your chance to prove to yourself you can find the beats, or meter, in some real poetry. This exercise is called scansion and it is the way the poets read the beats in their verse and evaluate the rhythm in other poetry. Scanning is a matter of taking a sentence and marking it with an apostrophe over a stressed syllable or a short line over an unstressed syllable. You can also put longer hash lines between each syllable to help you keep track of the breaks. Let's try it on a sentence:

"Shall I compare thee to a summer's day?"
Say it out loud and notice where the accents fall:
shall-**I**-com-**PARE**-thee-**TO**-a-**SUM**-mer's-**DAY**
Now write out the scansion:
__ ' __ ' __ ' __ ' __ '

That's the first line of William Shakespeare's Sonnet 18 and a famous first line at that. Notice the perfectly stressed/unstressed syllable pattern. Recognize the iambic form in the beats. There are five of them. That is called iambic pentameter—a five-foot beat line done entirely in iambs. For our purposes, a five-syllable combination of names that stresses every other syllable makes a virtual line of poetry in the Shakespearean tradition—as in Patricia Heaton (puh-TRISH-uh HEEton), Miranda Hammon (mi-RAN-duh HAM-men), and Diego Reyes (dee-AY-go RAY-yes). If you're into poetry, that's just cool.

Go back to that list of names a few pages back. Scan some of them and see what kind of patterns you get. The ones with the patterns that kind of look like the heartbeats on a cardiograph have the best potential to sound good together.

Monique O'Connor	moh-NEEK oh-KAW-nor	—'—'—
Jerome DeJohnette	juh-ROME dee-jaw-NET	—'— —'
Elisa Kawabata	uh-LEE-suh kow-uh-BOT-uh	—'— — —'—

Your newfound scansion skills can help you find the rhythm in words and understand how names compliment each other. You can practice scanning poetry (or street signs, cereal boxes, newspaper articles, or whatever you enjoy reading) until you get really good at it. Then you will be able to instinctively evaluate potential baby names that have a good beat to them.

fast match

Poetry isn't just about rhyming "cat" and "hat." It's a simple process of understanding the language you use every day. Saying names out loud lets you hear the beats. Is the accent in the first part of a name or at the end? Putting terms to the patterns of stresses can help you find the poetic beats in all names, and then you can determine whether a name sounds good with your surname. As you get better at scanning names, you'll find yourself instinctively scanning everything around you.

BENDING THE RULES

NOW THAT YOU know the rules, here's how to break them. Armed with your newfound knowledge of phonetic structure, rhythm and poetry you can now start improvising as if you were a jazz musician. In the end, your composition will be a mellifluous string of names that sound great together. Your baby's perfect name will make you want to sing! We'll show you how to look beyond the sounds and accents you've identified in your surname, and how to mix vowels and cross-match consonants in order to find unique name combinations. We'll show you how to examine first names for common roots, add different prefixes and suffixes to first names, and how to change the rhythm of a name to create a better match. We'll also discuss hard-to-match surnames—be they short, long, hyphenated, or simply unusual.

Name Riffing

When a jazz musician riffs on a melody, it leads to a new tune that departs from, but still echoes, the original song. You can riff on names, too. Just take the root of the name you like and start improvising, adding new prefixes or suffixes, combining elements of other names you like. Once you know that you like names with a particular vowel combination or rhythmic structure, try some out with your surname by saying them out loud together. Do you like the way it sounds? If so, great—you can narrow your search field to that type of name. If not, try to figure out why you don't like it and look for similar names that might provide a better match. Don't be afraid to focus only on your favorite phoneme lists and ignore the others.

For example, Laurie and Matt Light scanned the Long I list to match the vowel in their surname. They liked Delilah and Skylar, but when paired with Light, the double Is seemed "over-the-top," Laurie said. But since Delilah and Skylar both have Ls in them, they tried L names and found Sterling, Alexandria, Noelle, and Lucy. Laurie had always liked the double L sound of her own name, so she kept going back to Lucy Light, and that is what they named their daughter.

Poetic Assonance

The simple truth is that some people don't like the way certain sounds repeat.

Knowing when *not* to match can be just as important as knowing when to match. Luckily, you can *mix* sounds in complementary ways, too. In poetry, there is a technique called assonance that depends on the similarities of some pairs of vowel sounds. Famously, Irish poet William B. Yeats in 1919 rhymed "stones" with "swans" in his poem "The Wild Swans at Coole":

> *Upon the Brimming water among the stones*
> *Are Nine-and-fifty swans.*

The long O in "stones" and the short O in "swans" are so closely related in the way they sound and the shape your mouth makes to form them that they create a "near rhyme." Yeats's technique adds dramatic emphasis and makes for a deeper emotional reaction than if the line was a true rhyme such as "stones" and "bones."

In phonetic name matching, you can do the same thing by combining near rhyme vowels:

Delia (long E) works with Iverson (long I)
Stella (short E) matches Hicks (short I)
Rory (OR) goes with Thurman (UR)

You can come up with your own near rhymes, too, of course, just by listening to which sounds are similar to your ear. Katie and Graham

Wadsworth did that successfully with their children, pairing AIR (Derek) and OR (Laura) names with the UR in Wadsworth.

Consonants that are pronounced similarly can match, too, so the Comptons and Kloses both considered K names like Kate and Michael, as well as X (phoneme KS) and Q (phoneme KW) names like Roxanne and Quinn. As we mentioned in Chapter 1, D and T are partner phonemes, as are B and P, G and K, F and V, Q and W, S-Z-X, and J-CH-SH-ZH. That's because they sound similar and your mouth makes almost the same formation to pronounce them. You may want to consider D and J names as partners, as well, since you say "duh" to pronounce J ("djuh"). Likewise, S/SH and H/TH sound similar to many ears, although your mouth makes different movements to pronounce them. Think about how little kids mispronounce words before they learn the difference between sounds and you may think of some more partners, like M and N, F and S, L and Y, R and W, and B and V. Once you discover that you like certain sound combinations, simply consult those lists and choose a name you like.

Working with Short Surnames

Short surnames like West, Held, Katz, or Zhu all feature a single heavy stress. You can pair these striking names with another one-syllable first name to create a spondee. Amy and John West did that with their son Scout West, as did Ivan and Patricia Held with their son, George Held. The force of two heavy accents next to each other can make the whole name more memorable.

On the other hand, Josh and Anna Katz liked the melodious rhythm of a three-syllable first name paired with their one-syllable surname. The middle syllable in Sophia is stressed, bracketed by two unstressed syllables and followed up by the one-syllable, stressed last name, Katz, creating a da-DA-da DA beat. Two iambic feet that would make any poet proud. Whereas Dave Zhu and Leslie Salmon-Zhu, who used Dave's surname (pronounced JOO) for their daughters, went with two two-syllable first names, Maya and Bella, to make a DA-da DA rhythm. In short, almost any beat works with a short surname.

Tackling Long Surnames

With a long surname, the good news is that the more phonemes you have, the more choices you have. Take Wojciehowicz. Looks intimidating, right? But let's do it together: woh-joh-HO-wits. Break down the sounds and it's:

W
long O
J
long O
H
long O
W
short I
T
S

Seven phonemes total. And poetically, any type of first name will work, since it's a middle-stressed surname. Rose and Coleman Wojciehowicz sound just as good as Fernando, Jasmine, Delaney, Roxie, Isaac, and Odalys. The long O in Rose, Coleman, Fernando, and Odalys all match the long O sound in Wojciehowicz. The Z in Jasmine and Isaac and the X in Roxie echo the S phoneme. The D in Fernando, Delaney, and Odalys sounds similar to the T and J sounds, since you say "djuh" to pronounce J. If your surname is Wojciehowicz, all these names would be on your lists, so now you just have to choose the one you like best.

But, of course, if your surname is three or more syllables and adds up to six or more phonemes, that becomes a huge list of names to go through. The Alvarezes got ten (short A, L, V-F, short U, R, short E, and Z-S-X). If you would rather narrow things down in a hurry, choose one phoneme you like and start with that list. If none of those names lights a fire in you, then move on to other sounds. When Elisa and Andres Alvarezes were trying to name their third child, we noticed that their first two girls, Madeline and Lily, both have Ls in their names to match Alvarez. So we told them to start with the L list to guarantee that they'd find a name that not only sounds good with their last name, but also sounds good among all three siblings. From the L list, they liked Violet for a girl, and Eliot for a boy. Then they mentioned that they were gravitating towards more unusual names the third time around, so we also encouraged them to pay attention to the V and Z lists, where they found Enzo, Octavio, Eva, and Violet again.

Also, feel free to ignore less prominent phonemes in your last name. For instance, if you flip to the back of this book, you will see that the N list is very long, since many first names have Ns in them. But N is not a phoneme that tends to stand out in most surnames. Take Hammon, Compton, and even Johnston—the N practically falls silent. So unless your last name is Ennis or Nelson, where N is one of the foremost sounds, you might just as well skip the N list altogether. Likewise, many girl names end in "-a," resulting in an "uh" sound. There's a very minor "uh" in Alvarez, so they didn't need the Short U list.

Handling Hyphenations

If you plan to hyphenate your child's surname, that will change its sound and rhythm, as well. Pam Wool and Joel Baum are both spondee names—one syllable each—but when they combined their surnames, it became a trochee, Wool-Baum (WOOL-bowm). Although neither of them wanted to give up their last name, they worried that Wool-Baum would be a mouthful for their son. But when we helped them break down the sounds in each name, they realized that a hyphenated name can actually offer more naming choices. Just like multi-syllabic surnames, you have more syllables and phonemes to work with. They chose trochaic first and middle names to match the trochaic last name, and so Jonah Sanford Wool-Baum creates three trochees in a row: DA-da DA-da Da-da. Plus, the long O in Jonah is similar to the OR in Sanford and the OO in Wool. If they have a girl next, they like Ruby, another trochee that echoes the OO in Wool and the B in Baum.

Unusual Surnames

Perhaps your surname includes a distinctive combination of phonemes that would sound silly to repeat in a first name. If you've got an unusual surname, try matching just one or two phonemes, instead of several, and concentrate on the secondary vowels and consonants instead of the prominent ones.

Andi and Colin Botto (BAW-toh) thought we would suggest names like Otto or Cosmo that rhyme with their surname. Some people might like those true rhyme combinations, but to the Bottos, they just sounded silly. Instead, we offered names that match either the short O or long O sounds in Botto—but not both. Two- and three-syllable names like Walker, Owen, and Oliver compliment Botto, without sounding over the top. Even a one-syllable name like Rose Botto works because it repeats the unstressed long O sound, whereas Sol Botto might seem to rhyme too much because it repeats the stressed short O sound. We also came up with names that concentrated on the secondary B and T sounds, like Libby and Abraham, Trudy and Ty. They considered Delaney, which sounds good with Botto because D and T are similar, and finally settled on Piper Botto, which matches because B and P are similar.

On the other hand, Lenore Skenazy (ski-NAY-zee) and Joe Kolman (KOHL-men) like rhyming names, so they sought them out. They named their first son Morris after Joe's grandfather and gave him the middle name Tsipouras (pronounced sip-OR-us) for the geneticist who helped them conceive. Not only do they love the fact that Morris Tsipouras rhymes, but the OR in Morris (or Morry, as they call him) matches the long O in his surname, Kolman. For their second son, they went with Isaac after Lenore's father and call him Izzy. Then, they gave him Lenore's surname, so Izzy Skenazy matches, too.

CHOOSING A SURNAME

If you think you're stuck with your last name, think again. Nowadays, with more and more women keeping their surnames after marriage, it's becoming common to pick and choose the last name for a child, as well as the first. One idea is to alternate surnames between siblings. Another option is to use both surnames, with or without hyphenation. And if your surnames share similar phonemes, you can combine them into one word: Walkereyes (Walker and Reyes.)

Naming Baby Number Two

Siblings present a unique challenge. Remember, you'll be saying your kids' names in the same breath for years, so you want them to sound like they belong together. But you probably don't want to pick monikers that are too similar, like Eric and Derrick or Whitney and Brittany. It's a common problem: Once you fall in love with your first child's name, you're probably going to be drawn to similar sounds for your second child's name. Nate and Meliss Grover liked Jane for a girl, but realized that if anyone called her Janie, it would rhyme too closely with their first son's name, Chaney (CHAY-nee). Amy and John West named their children Scout and Scarlett without considering the phonetic similarities: Both names start with SC and end in T, not something the Wests did intentionally. "A lot of the sounds that worked the first time just sound right again the second time," Amy explains. But since Scout is one syllable and Scarlett is two, they come across as different and complementary.

Boys and girls get away with similar-sounding names better, as do first and third children or siblings with a great age span between them, but consider your family dynamics when choosing rhyming names. The good news is, if you've already chosen a name that goes well with your surname, you can employ the same tactics for naming a sibling. Since we matched the long A in Gabriel and Reyes for our first son, we liked Nathan and Diego for our second son. Both names feature the same long A sound, but they don't rhyme with Gabriel. Kate Kerner and Tom Cometa gave both their kids M names (Max and Madeline), matching the M in Tom's surname. Martin and Hannah Wolf matched the L in Wolf with Isabel and Phillip. Michael and Yoriko Mikesell chose Jasmine for their first daughter and Sienna for their second, both matching the S in Mikesell.

Another option is to focus on a different phoneme from your surname to match to your second child's name—perhaps even making a different match with your first child's name. We chose Jasper for the S sound in Reyes, but the P is similar to the B in Gabriel. Now when we say "our boys, Gabriel and Jasper . . . "—which we do nearly every day!—it has a nice ring to it.

fast match

Feel **free** to experiment with phonemes and beats. Once you know how to match sounds and recognize stresses, you start to really have fun playing around with different combinations of root names, prefixes, and suffixes. Make modifications, bend the rules—break them even. Don't be afraid to decide you hate the names that are supposed to sound best with your last name. Mix and match phonemes and accents to see what you like best. No matter how short or long your surname is—whether it's just a single beat or multiple syllables—this method can be adapted to work for you.

FAMILY TIES

IS AUNT PHILOMENA making it her personal mission to get you to name a kid after her? Has the firstborn son in your family *always* been named John Jacob as far back as anyone can remember?

Family influence, as we all know, is not an easily dismissed source of pull. While it's a noble desire to honor a relative, follow a family tradition, or even reflect your background or heritage in your child's name, no one wants to get stuck with a dud name just to "keep it in the family." In this chapter, we'll help you process all the potential names for your child by showing you how to get creative about looking for cultural and family names. You'll learn to scan your family tree and other sources and adapt names that aren't an exact match.

Great Expectations

For our second son, one set of grandparents wanted a name drawn from their Mexican heritage, another set wanted to honor relatives, and an aunt wanted us to follow a family pattern of giving cousins matching names. Meanwhile, we had four or five names we definitely liked, but we couldn't agree on a single one. In the end, we decided to choose the name we kept coming back to (Jasper), to honor a great-grandfather with a middle name (James), and to use a nickname (JJ) with the long A sound to match the cousin's names (Faelan and Taye). We then told the Mexican side of the family that they could call the child by the Spanish equivalent of James, Diego, which was our second choice, but so far that nickname hasn't stuck. Yeah, it's a bit convoluted and it didn't totally satisfy everyone, but at least we tried. And that's the point: You can't make everyone happy.

Though even if you can't please *every* relative, do read on.

You'll learn several ways to offer an olive branch to family factions who take a serious interest in your baby-naming process.

Climbing Your Family Tree

When considering family names, go back as far as you can. If mom and dad's names don't tickle your fancy, climb farther up their branches of the family tree to find something you like better. You may discover a wealth of names hidden in the memories of your great uncle Mordecai, and Aunt Hilda will be just as pleased to hear that you're naming your daughter for her great-great-grandmother Tillie than after her, directly. Until we asked, we had no idea that our own family trees had such interesting names. Eric's father always claimed he didn't have a middle name, but when we asked for details for our sons' baby books, he admitted that it's Crispin—a name we loved (but Eric's father obviously didn't). Going through family photos, Eric found wonderful old snapshots of his grandma Tomasa and her sisters, Luz and Romana. We considered all three names for girls.

With nine months to pick a name, you can interview grandparents, aunts and uncles, second cousins, and close friends of the family until the eleventh hour, and become more connected to all the people who have helped you become you, either through influence or ancestry. Then you can truly say, "Everyone in my entire family helped us name this child."

Branching Out

By turning over every leaf on your family tree, you might discover some wonderful middle, maiden, and last names that you love, too. Nate and Meliss Grover wanted to "use a family name in an interesting way," so they named their first son Chaney, the surname of Nate's grandfather. For their second son, they chose the first name Beau for a dear family friend and used McCoy, Meliss's grandma's maiden name, as the middle name. You can also change the spelling to reflect other cultural factors. Ashley Walker was living in Scotland when she had her first child and named him Faelan, a Celtic version of Phelan—a family name from six generations back.

The middle name can be a great spot for paying tribute to family. Katie and Graham Wadsworth both had grandfathers and uncles named Clifford, which wasn't their ideal choice for a first name. Instead, they went with Derek for their son, but used Clifford as a middle name, as a way of keeping it in the family. Julie and Darin Vinall wanted to name their daughter Chloe Linda for Julie's mom, but didn't like the sound of those two trochees next to each other. So they went one generation back and discovered that Julie's grandmother, Elizabeth, offered a prettier alternative, Chloe Elizabeth. "It thrilled my mom for us to use her mom's name as our daughter's middle name," says Julie, "and it made us feel better since we didn't use Linda!"

On the other hand, many kids go only by their middle names, especially when the first name is one that's already used by someone else in the family. Hernan and Michelle Luna chose her grandmother's maiden name, Blake, as their son's first name, but since it's also her uncle's name, they call their son by his middle name, Zachary. "My uncle Blake's first name is James (his father's name), so we're also following a bit of a tradition by calling Zachary by his second name," Michelle says. They also like the way the three names work phonetically and rhythmically: The K in Blake matches the K in Zachary and the L in Blake matches the L in Luna; plus, Zachary Luna flows well on its own, and by putting Blake first, it has a more unconventional ring to it.

Great Adaptations

Are there any names that you like but feel you "can't" use? If there are two Rubys in your neighborhood already, you don't want to look like a copycat. And if a cousin also has a Julian, it can make things awkward. Or maybe there's a long list of ex-girlfriends and ex-boyfriends, whose names just can't be considered. Don't give up! You can always *adapt* the name, keeping the sounds or rhythms that you like, changing it enough to be different from the off-limits version.

First, sound out the name in question and try to determine what it *is* that you like or dislike about it. Look for substitutes that are similar, but offer different sounds and rhythms that work with your surname. The short I in William doesn't match the surname Reese, but the long E in Liam does. The short E in Leonard becomes a long E/long O combo with Leo, while the OR phoneme in one-syllable George can be two syllables with Geo (GEE-yoh). And it works the other way, too—if you like the nickname Finn, you could use several long versions: Finnegan, Finian, Phineas, or even Phileas.

Another handy adaptation tip from the Hebrew naming tradition is to honor relatives by first letter only, and honor Uncle Alvin with names like Alastair or Arabella, and Grandma Dolores with Dorit or Delano. Aunt Alfreda begets Frida or even Freya and cousin Eunice sounds cute as Eulalie or Eugenie. It's hard to break with tradition if the firstborn son has been John Jr. for generations, but perhaps you can satisfy the family with a variation like Jack, Jake, or Jonah.

Lynn and Jim Drogo wanted to give their daughter Kadence a middle name that paid tribute to Jim's grandmother, Willamina Petranella. A great long name like that can yield dozens of shorter names, like Willa, Mina, Minna, Petra, Nell, and Nellie. From Lynn's side of the family, the Drogos liked Von for her mother (Yvonne) and Raine for Lynn's own middle name (Lorraine). Finally, they chose two of these contemporary versions of old family favorites to reflect both sides: Petra (PAY-truh) and Raine, which both have the long A sound to match Kadence and the R sound to match Drogo. We tried this technique with Whitney's mother's name, Maedell. Actually, she was named for an aunt, Mary Adella, who simply nicknamed herself Maedell and Whitney's mom shortened that to Mae. If we'd had a girl, we thought of changing that to Adela Mae.

Familial Places

Place names like Austin, Madison, Jackson, and Brooklyn make trendy baby names these days, and will mean something special to your child if your family has ties to that namesake place. Parents love place names, as long as they're not too close to home. The Tollens and the Kloses, both originally from Austin, TX, considered the name Austin for their offspring, but thought that if they ever moved back, their offspring wouldn't like having the same name as the town where they lived. But Ashley Walker and Martin Westhead named their second son Taye after a Scottish loch they loved to visit. A place that bears some connection to your roots—the town where you grew up, met your spouse, or honeymooned, for instance—makes a great name for your child.

If you still live in your hometown (or might again someday), simply go farther back and pore over maps of the town where your parents were born, or the country your ancestors came from. Here's how it might have worked for us: Whitney's mother grew up in Dunedin, Florida, and her father in High Point, North Carolina. Carolina is already a girl's name, and Dunedin (dun-EE-din) could work for either gender. Eric's mother was born in Azuza, CA, and his father's side of the family comes from Jalisco, Mexico. Azuza (uh-ZOO-zuh) makes a cute girl's name, with the nickname Zuzu, like the little girl in the beloved Jimmy Stewart movie, *It's a Wonderful Life*. Jalisco (haw-LEES-koh) sounds like a great boy's name.

Going Global

Another way to honor family, even when every relative's name does nothing for you, is to think internationally. *If only your great uncle James had a more interesting name*, you say to yourself. Why not try the Spanish equivalents of James—Diego, Santiago, Jaime? Or the Irish Seamus, Scottish Hamish, or Portuguese Xanti? Too many Alexanders in your family—go for Alejandro (Spanish), Xander (Greek), Sandro (Italian), or Sasha (Russian). Beatrice gets a European/Scandinavian twist as Beatrix and a Spanish flair as Beatriz.

That's how Rezsin Jaulus and Mark Gonzalez came up with Erzsabet, a respelling of the Hungarian version of Elizabeth. They also could have gone with Liz-like version in French (Babette), Scandinavian (Elsa), or Hebrew (Lisbet). Sticking with Hungarian names, there's also Ilona, Lilike, and Zsa-Zsa, or for a boy Dezso, Laszlo, and Vidor.

Using other languages to help name your child can open up a world of naming alternatives, offering a great way to match your cultural background and pay tribute to a family member at the same time. It's also a way of finding more matching options for your surname. If Mary doesn't match, try Amara (Greek), Marlo (English), Mei (Chinese), Mai (Vietnamese), or Mairwen (Welsh). A Jewish-Hispanic marriage could produce a child with the name Josue, which is Spanish for Joshua, a traditional Hebrew name. If the names themselves are too limiting, then translate the meaning of the name and see what you get. In Hebrew, Nathan means "gift of god," as does Makaio in Hawaiian and Tedros in Ethiopian. And if you shorten that to just "gift," you'll find close to a hundred names, like Tudor (Welsh), Shaun (Gaelic), Mattox (English), and Hercules (Greek). (Check the list of additional resources at the back of this book to learn more about finding international names and meanings online.)

fast match

Y **ou can find** a lot of great names in your family if you dig a little—beyond Uncle Hal and Aunt Shirley. Interview members of both sides of your family, including your spouse's side of the family for inspiration. A first, maiden, or middle name of a relative may be the one. Appease family by choosing a name that means Fred in Greek or Spanish or Hebrew. Go back in your family as far as possible.

USING THE LISTS

O **N THE FOLLOWING** pages you'll find more than 3,500 names—roughly 1,600 for boys, 1,700 for girls. They are grouped into fifty-five lists organized by major phonetic sounds, rhythms, and themes. That includes thirty-nine phonetic lists (all the consonant and vowel sounds), as well as six poetic lists broken down by accents and rhythms, and one crossover list. Because they are grouped by categories that you can match up to your surname, you will only need to scrutinize a fraction of the names. That makes your job of picking the perfect baby name that much easier, so let's get to work.

How Are the Lists Organized?

The first names on our lists are taken in part from the U.S. Social Security Administration's tally of the 1,000 most popular names from the last one hundred years. In addition, we added all the names used (or even contemplated) by our case study couples, so if you came across a name you liked in the previous chapters, you'll find it on our lists. Then, we broke down each name phonetically and rhythmically according to the way it sounds. Since every name contains a vowel sound, we only included pronunciations and alternate spellings in the lists of vowel names. (Otherwise this book would have been too heavy to lift.) So if you come across the name Lizbeth on the B list and want to see the alternate spellings and pronunciations for that name, simply refer to the short I list where you'll find:

Lizbeth (LIZ-beth, liz-BETH; see also Lisbet)
Alternate spellings: Lisbeth

Or, log on to our website, *www.theperfectbabyname.com*, where you'll find the complete consonant and rhythm lists with pronunciations and alternate spellings.

This is one of the few baby name books to provide pronunciations; and now we know why—it's not easy! The way a name is said in California might be different from the way it's said in Alabama or New York—or if you happen to be Puerto Rican, Israeli, or Syrian. If we didn't know how to pronounce a name, we tried to find someone who did. We talked to speakers of various languages—Hebrew, Arabic, Spanish, Cantonese and Mandarin, Japanese, Korean, Italian, French, German, Greek, Hindu, Persian. They offered different ways to say some of the names on our list and suggested variations, which we added to the list, too. We did not focus on the origins and meanings of the names (there are plenty of other books for that); we simply tried to zero in on whether any names would be pronounced differently when they're used by different cultures.

We also figured that parents should know how their baby's name sounds in different languages, so they can be sure that all the variations sound good with their surname. Or perhaps you will decide that the way a name is said in Italian doesn't really matter much to your Wisconsin-born baby. That's fine, too. Bear in mind, though, that we had a lot of cultural ground to cover in this book, so we couldn't delve too deeply into the names of any one particular culture or language. If you're looking specifically for a Hebrew name, for instance, this book may help you with some common pronunciations, but you're probably going to want to consult a Hebrew baby name book to look for a greater variety of names.

As you will soon see, there really is no one true and definitive way to say some names. In fact, for many names, the phonetic possibilities seem endless. Cecilio could be sess-SEE-lee-yoh or the-THEE-lee-yoh (in Spain) or che-CHEE-lee-yoh (in Italy). The dialectical differences stemming from geography may mean there are several ways a Spanish or Italian speaker could pronounce it. We listed as many different pronunciations as we could find. (Whenever possible, we put the pronunciation that's more commonly used in the United States first.)

Next to each name on the vowel lists we offer a key to let you know which language pronounces it that way. When we could, we indicated how alternate spellings would match up with different pronunciations, but sometimes there was too much overlap to make any clear distinction. We hope these groupings help you choose the pronunciation and spelling you like best. When you see [HEB] or [IT] or [FR] next to a name, it is simply an indication of how that name is commonly pronounced within that particular culture. It does not necessarily mean that the name originates in Israel or Italy or France, and it certainly does not mean that you must be Jewish or Italian or French in order to use it. Parents borrow names from other cultures all the time, so go for it!

Take Aaliyah: It's pronounced as uh-LEE-yuh in the African-American community, but it was probably borrowed from the Arabic/Hebrew name, which is pronounced AW-lee-yuh. So you'll see [AA] next to the first pronunciation and [HEB] and [AR] next to the second. And just as the pronunciation of a name may change in another language, so might the spellings. Whereas Aliya or Aliyah is recognized as the English spelling for the Hebrew name, Aaliyah would probably be more popular with Arabic and African-American parents. We list Aaliyah first because it is now the most popular spelling of this name, but you'll see the alternate spellings underneath it: Aliyah, Aliya, Aleah*, and Alia. (The asterisk [*] next to Aleah indicates that it also has its own entry on the list because it could be pronounced as uh-LAY-yuh.)

About Phonetic Spellings

We searched high and low for a source that would help us deliver consistent, easy-to-read written phonetic spellings. We hated those dictionary-style pronunciation keys, which force you to decipher upside-down Es, apostrophes, and umlauts. So, for the names in this book we looked at each one and tried to come up with the *simplest* phonetic spelling on a case-by-case basis. You'll see that we use AW (as in "aw, shucks") for the short O sound, so John is spelled phonetically as JAWN. But when we got to Walter, the AW in WAWL-tur just looked too weird, so we used a word with the short O sound that everyone knows how to pronounce and gave Walter the phonetic spelling WALL-tur.

Of course, some elements of speech are practically impossible to convey in written form—such as the guttural CH sound in Hebrew, the pronounced H in Arabic, the sustained N in French, and the rolled R in Spanish. We noted those wherever possible (with three Rs in a row for a rolled R, as in RRROH-suh [SP]).

Speaking of Rs, you'll notice that the R list only includes names with hard Rs in them. The name Theodore (THEE-yoh-dor) appears on the OR list, whereas Theodora (thee-yoh-DOR-ruh) has that extra "ruh" suffix, and so it appears on both the OR and R lists. Other names on the R list include Richard (RICH-urd) and Gregory (GREG-or-ree), Roxanne (rok-SAN) and Maria (muh-REE-yuh). But you'll find Marge (MARJ) and Argus (AR-gus) on the AR list, Piper (PY-pur) and Jasper (JAS-pur) on the UR list, Lourdes (LOR-dess) and Lorne (LORN) on the OR list.

Confused? Don't worry.

If you don't see a name you're looking for on the R list, we'll remind you to check those other phonemes, too.

We also discovered that the short vowel sounds in some name suffixes are practically indistinguishable. Is Benson pronounced BEN-sen, BEN-sin, or BEN-sun? It seemed like a toss-up to us, especially when that last unstressed syllable is said quickly. Or what about the "a" ending in many girls' names (Adella, Maria, Sylvia)? Speakers of other languages sometimes insisted on a short A sound (as in "pat") or a short O (as in "pot"), but when we heard them say the names out loud, they mostly sounded like the Short U sound ("putt") to our ears. So for consistency, we used "uh" as a phonetic spelling for the "a" suffix, but we did not include those names on the Short U list since there were so many of them. These subtle distinctions shouldn't upset the phonetic balance of your baby's name. You probably wouldn't use short throwaway syllables to match sounds in your surname anyway, and any name that's really a perfect match is likely to appear on more than one phonetic list.

Finally, you might find it odd that we put Ys in the phonetic spellings of Gabriel (GAY-bree-yell) and Naomi (nay-YOH-mee), for instance, or Ws in the phonetic spellings of Joey (JOH-wee) and Noelle (noh-WELL). But if you say the names slowly, those consonant sounds are evident. In some cultures, though, there is a break between syllables, so that Gabriel is gaw-vree-ELL in Hebrew and Naomi is NAW-oh-mee in Japanese. Again, if you have a different pronunciation (or you simply don't agree with our phonetic spellings), that's okay. Feel free to make up your own.

And please, when naming your child, try to account for dialectical differences. In an English accent, Blanche is BLAWNCH and Natasha is nuh-TASH-uh (rhymes with window sash). But in a Southern drawl, it's more like BLAY-ench, and in the Midwest, you might hear nuh-TAR-sha. That's something to consider when choosing a name, especially if you don't like the predominant pronunciation in your place of residence. For example, an Australian friend of ours living in California pronounced Graham as two syllables (GRAY-ham) and refused to give his son that name because he insisted that Americans said it wrong as one syllable (GRAM).

Making a Sound Match

Remember from Chapter 1 that all names have at least two or three phonetic sounds, so you may come across the same names on several lists. Theoretically, a name that appears on more than one list will sound best with your surname.

Of course, it could be bad if a name appears on *too* many lists. For example, the first name David matches four out of five phonemes in the surname Davis, but David Davis is like having the same first and last name. Now, some people may think that's cool—rock star David Bowie deliberately chose to name his son Zowie Bowie because he liked the way it rhymed, but now the lad goes by Duncan Jones. Our first son's name, Gabriel Reyes, echoes four out of five phonemes, though—R, long A, Y, and short E—just not in the same order, and we love the way it sounds. Again, it's all a matter of figuring out what works for you. Perhaps you will like a name that matches several phonemes, or just one, or none at all. Listening to the pulse and music of your last name will help guide you to the best first name.

In addition to the phonemes in your surname, there are also partner phonemes that you may choose to consult. As we promised, you'll find reminders about those at the top of each name list. So the J list will refer you to the CH and SH/ZH lists, the Long O list will refer you to the OR and OI lists, and so on.

Remember that these lists are organized by phonemes, not by spelling. (However, within the phoneme groups we list the names alphabetically.) Although the Social Security lists include multiple spellings of the same names (Kaitlyn, Caitlin, Katelynn), as long as the pronunciations are the same (KAYT-lin), we group them together under the most popular spelling (which in this case happens to be Kaitlyn) with all the alternate spellings underneath it. If the pronunciations are even slightly different (Kiara can be kee-YAR-ruh, Kira can be KEER-ruh, and Kierra can be kee-YAIR-ruh) then they will each have their own entries.

Furthermore, hard C names like Caitlin will appear on the K list along with Kiara, whereas soft C names like Celia will be on the S list along with Samantha. The G list features names with hard G sounds like Gregory, but soft G names like George will appear on the J list along with James. Similarly, Phelan can be found on the F list, Yvonne on the Short I list, and Joaquin on the W list. Names with multiple pronunciations will appear on multiple lists, so Xavier does double duty on the X and Z lists, depending on whether you pronounce it eks-ZAY-vee-ur or simply ZAY-vee-er.

Making a Rhythm Match

You may also choose to match your surname rhythmically, and so we've included six lists of names broken down by syllables and accents and categorized by poetic terminology (see Chapter 2). If your surname is Johnson, a trochee, and you want to pair it with a trochaic first name, you'll find Ingrid and Jada, Lucas and Milo on the trochee list. If your last name is Smith and you want to give your child a short first name to create a spondee, you'll find Rose and Scout, Eve and Ned on the one-syllable list. We'll remind you about which names sound good with different types of surnames when you get to the poetic lists.

These lists are also helpful for choosing middle names, so you can break up the rhythm of the name you give your child. If you've gone with a multi-syllabic first name like Penelope, you may want to use a one-syllable middle name like Blu. On the other hand, if you've chosen a short first name like Blake, you might prefer a long dactyl like Zachary. The choice is all yours.

We've tried to second-guess all possible accent placements for the names at the back of the book, so Adrian is a dactyl in English (AY-dree-yen), but an anapest in French (ad-ree-YAW) and a middle-stressed name in Spanish (aw-DREE-yawn). Adrian appears on all three of those rhythm lists, but you'll need to check the pertinent vowel lists to see all of those pronunciations. Phonetics and scansion are not exact sciences, so you may find that you place the accent somewhere other than where we've indicated it to be. For instance, we found it simplest to attribute only one accent per name, so Angelina is an-juh-LEE-nuh and Kurasawa is koo-ruh-SAW-wuh. If you prefer to attribute primary and secondary accents to long names (as in AN-juh-LEE-nuh and KOO-ruh-SAW-wuh), be our guest. The techniques we've described here for matching up first and last names will still work even if you reclassify the pronunciations to your own liking.

Making a Crossover Match

And finally, if you want a name with international flavor or you're trying to pay tribute to a variety of ethnic backgrounds, check out the Crossovers list. Here you'll find names that are recognized by more than one culture but are often pronounced differently in each language.

fast match

Giving you a list of names is one thing, but here we tell you how to use it. This chapter tells you how we organized the lists and explains our pronunciation keys and phonetic spellings. We compiled our name lists from many sources and drew pronunciations from as many cultures as we could. Finally, we recap how to make a match by sound and rhythm. Remember, you can pronounce a name any way you like, no matter what this book says.

PRONUNCIATION KEY

Nationality Attribution Codes

[AA] African-American
[AR] Arabic
[BIB] Biblical, specifically New Testament
[BR] British
[CG] Celtic/Gaelic
[CH] Chinese
[EGY] Egyptian
[EI] East Indian
[FR] French
[GER] German
[GRK] Greek
[HW] Hawaiian
[HEB] Hebrew
[HUN] Hungarian
[IR] Irish
[IT] Italian
[JAP] Japanese
[KOR] Korean
[NA] Native American
[PER] Persian
[RUS] Russian
[SCAN] Scandinavian
[SCOT] Scottish
[SP] Spanish
[VI] Vietnamese
[WL] Welsh

* Asterisk indicates that an alternate spelling can be found as its own entry.
   RRR indicates rolled R.

Phonetic Lists

Vowels

Long A (AY) as in **Jada** (JAY-duh) and **Aidan** (AY-den)

Short A (A) as in **Alice** (AL-liss) and **Samson** (SAM-sun)

AIR as in **Erica** (AIR-rik-uh) and **Perry** (PAIR-ee)

AR as in **Darlene** (dar-LEEN) and **Charlie** (CHAR-lee)

Long E (EE) as in **Frida** (FREE-duh) and **Eli** (EE-ly)

Short E (EH or E) as in **Stella** (STEL-luh) and **Henry** (HEN-ree)

Long I (EYE or Y) as in **Lila** (LY-luh) and **Isaac** (EYE-zek)

Short I (I) as in **Ilsa** (ILL-suh) and **William** (WILL-yum)

Long O (OH) as in **Sophie** (SOH-fee) and **Owen** (OH-wen)

Short O (AW) as in **Molly** (MAW-lee) and **Dawson** (DAW-sun)

OI as in **Moira** (MOI-ruh) and **Troy** (TROI)

OR as in **Rory** (ROR-ee) and **Jordan** (JOR-den)

OW as in **Howard** (HOW-wurd) and **Paola** (POW-luh)

OO as in **Ruth** (ROOTH) and **Woody** (WOOD-dee)

Short U (UH or U) as in **Justine** (juss-TEEN) and **Gulliver** (GULL-liv-ur)

UR as in **Pearl** (PURL) and **Herb** (HURB)

Consonants

B (**Ruby, Ben**)

CH (**Chelsea, Mitchell**)

D (**Deirdre, Cody**)

F (**Farrah, Raphael**)

G (**Greta, Angus**)

H (**Hannah, Alejandro**)

J (**Angela, Ajax**)

K (**Kylee, Declan**)

L (**Lucy, Dylan**)

M (**Emma, Matthew**)

N/NG (**Anna, Irving**)

P (**Pippin, Oprah**)

Q (KW) (**Shaniqua, Quentin**)

R (**Aurora, Wren, Harry, Riordan**)

S (**Tess, Sam**)

SH/ZH (**Asia, Lucian**)

T (**Octavia, Thomas**)

TH (**Aretha, Theodore**)
V (**Olivia, Xavier**)
W (**Willa, Noah**)
X (KS) (**Roxanne, Alex**)
Y (Y) (**Yasmine, Gabriel**)
Z (**Jasmine, Xena, Cosmo, Zane**)

VOWEL NAMES FOR GIRLS

Long A (AY); Short A (A); AIR; AR; Long E (EE); Short E (EH or E); Long I (EYE or Y); Short I (I); Long O (OH); Short O (AW); Short U (UH or U); UR, OI; OR; OO

■ LONG A (AY) ■

PARTNER POINTER:
Check out the AIR list, too.

Abigail (AB-big-ayl, aw-vee-GYL [HEB])
 Alternate spellings: Abbigail, Abigayle, Abigale, Abagail, Avigayil [HEB]
Acacia (uh-KAY-shuh)
Ada (AY-duh [HEB/GER], ADD-uh [IT])
 Alternate spellings: Aida*, Adah, Eda*
Adelaida (add-uh-LAY-duh)
Adelaide (ADD-uh-layd [GER], add-eh-LED or uh-dell-uh-EED [FR])
Adrian (AY-dree-yen)
 Alternate spellings: Adriane
Adriana (ay-dree-YAWN-uh, aw-dree-YAWN-uh [SP])
Adrianna (ay-dree-YAN-uh)
Adrienne (ay-dree-YAN, ay-dree-YEN with sustained N [FR])
 Alternate spellings: Adriane
Aida (eye-YEE-duh [AR], aw-YEE-duh, EYE-duh, AY-duh)
 Alternate spellings: Ada*, Adah, Eda*
Aileen (AY-leen [IR], eye-LEEN)
 Alternate spellings: Eileen*, Ilene, Aline*, Allene, Alene
Ainsley (AYNZ-lee)
Alani (uh-LAW-nee, uh-LAN-nee, uh-LAY-nee)
Aleah (uh-LAY-yuh, uh-LEE-yuh, AW-lee-yuh [AR/HEB])
 Alternate spellings: Aaliyah*, Aliyah, Aliya, Alia
Alfreda (al-FRAY-duh, al-FRED-uh [IT])
Almeda (al-MAY-duh, al-MEE-duh)
 Alternate spellings: Almeta
Amelie (aw-may-LEE [FR]; see also Emilie)
Amy (AY-mee)
 Alternate spellings: Aimee, Ami*, Amie*
Anastasia (aw-naw-STAW-zee-yuh or aw-naw-STAW-zhuh [RUS], ann-uh-STAY-shuh, aw-naw-STAW-see-yuh [IT], aw-naw-staw-SEE-yuh [GRK])
 Alternate spellings: Anastacia
Andrea (ANN-dree-yuh, ann-DRAY-yuh [IT], awn-DRAY-yuh [SP])
 Alternate spellings: Andria
Angel (AYN-jell, AWN-hell [SP])
Annamae (ANN-uh-may)
April (AYP-rill)
Asia (AY-zhuh [AA], AW-see-yuh with pronounced H at end [AR])
 Alternate spellings: Aja, Eja
Aurea (OR-ree-yuh, or-RAY-yuh, ow-REE-yuh or ow-RAY-yuh [SP])
Ava (AY-vuh, AW-vuh)
 Alternate spellings: Eva*
Avery (AY-vur-ree)
Avis (AY-viss)
Ayanna (ay-YAWN-uh, eye-YAN-uh)
 Alternate spellings: Ayana, Aiyana
Ayla (AY-luh, EYE-luh)
Aylin (AY-lin, EYE-lin)

Bailey (BAY-lee)
 Alternate spellings: Baylee, Bailee
Beatrice (BEE-yuh-triss, bay-yuh-TREES [FR/SP], vay-yuh-TRITH [SP])
 Alternate spellings: Beatriz [SP]
Beatrix (BEE-yuh-triks [GER/SCAN], bay-yuh-TREEKS [IT])

Cadence (KAY-dens)
 Alternate spellings: Kadence, Kaydence
Casey (KAY-see)
 Alternate spellings: Kasey, Kacie, Kaci, Casie, Kacy
Cecile (sess-SEEL, say-SEEL [FR])
 Alternate spellings: Cécile [FR]
Celeste (sell-EST, chell-ESS-teh [IT], say-LEST [FR])
 Alternate spellings: Céleste [FR]

Celestine (sell-ess-TEEN, say-less-TEEN [FR])
　Alternate spellings: Célestine [FR]
Celine (sell-EEN, say-LEEN [FR])
　Alternate spellings: Céline [FR]
Chana (CHAW-naw with guttural CH [HEB],
　SHAW-nuh, SHAY-nuh, SHAN-nuh)
　Alternate spellings: Hannah*, Hanna,
　Hana, Hanaa, Shawna*, Shauna,
　Shonna, Shayna*, Shana, Shanna
Charmaine (shar-MAYN [FR])
Chloë (KLOH-wee [GRK], kloh-WAY [FR])
　Alternate spellings: Chloé
Cleo (KLEE-yoh, KLAY-oh [FR])
　Alternate spellings: Cléo
Consuelo (kohn-SWAY-loh or
　kohn-THWAY-loh [SP])

Daisy (DAY-zee)
Dale (DAYL, DAY-yell [GER])
Dana (DAY-nuh, DAWN-uh [HEB])
　Alternate spellings: Dayna, Dena,
　Danna*
Dania (DAN-ee-yuh, DAY-nee-yuh,
　duh-NEE-yuh or duh-NY-yuh [AA],
　DAWN-yuh or DAW-nee-yuh [HEB])
　Alternate spellings: Daniya, Danya
Dasia (DAY-zhuh [AA], DAY-shuh [GRK/RUS],
　DAY-see-yuh)
Dayana (DAY-yaw-nuh [AA], dy-YAN-nuh)
　Alternate spellings: Diana*, Dianna
Deasia (dee-YAY-zhuh, dee-YAY-see-yuh)
Déja (DAY-zhaw [FR])
Delaney (del-AY-nee)

Eda (ED-duh, EE-duh, AY-duh)
　Alternate spellings: Ada*
Elaine (ee-LAYN)
　Alternate spellings: Elayne
Eleanor (EL-len-nor, el-lay-yoh-NOR [FR])
　Alternate spellings: Eleanore, Elinor,
　Elinore, Elenor, Eléonore [FR]
Eleanora (el-len-NOR-ruh,
　el-lee-yuh-NOR-ruh,
　eh-lay-oh-NOR-uh [IT/SP])
　Alternate spellings: Elenora,
　Eleonora [IT/SP] (see also Elnora)
Elena (uh-LAY-nuh, ell-LAY-nuh [SP],
　ELL-en-uh [IT]; see also Helena)
　Alternate spellings: Alaina, Alayna,
　Elaina, Alena, Alayna, Alaina
Elise (ee-LEES, el-LEES [GER], ay-LEEZ [FR])
　Alternate spellings: Elyse, Elease,
　Élise [FR]
Ellamae (EL-luh-may)

Eloise (EL-oh-weez, el-oh-WEEZ,
　ay-loh-WEEZ [FR])
　Alternate spellings: Elouise, Elois*,
　Éloise [FR]
Étienne (ay-tee-YEN [FR])
Eugenia (yoo-JEE-nee-yuh,
　yoo-JAY-nee-yuh, oo-JEN-ee-yuh [IT],
　ay-yoo-HAY-nee-yuh [SP])
Eugenie (yoo-JEE-nee, yoo-JAY-nee,
　ay-yoo-HAY-nee [SP], oo-zhay-NEE [FR])
　Alternate spellings: Eugénie [FR]
Eulalia (yoo-LAY-lee-yuh,
　ay-yoo-LAW-lee-yuh [SP])
Eulalie (yoo-LAY-lee, oo-law-LEE [FR])
Eva (EE-vuh, EV-uh [IT], AY-vuh [SP])
　Alternate spellings: Ava*, Iva*
Evangelina (ev-van-jell-LEE-nuh [IT],
　ay-vawn-hell-LEE-nuh [SP])

Faith (FAYTH)
Faye (FAY)
　Alternate spellings: Fay, Fae
Frankie (FRAYN-kee)
Freya (FRAY-yuh or FRY-yuh [SCAN])
　Alternate spellings: Freja

Gabriel (GAY-bree-yell, gaw-bree-ELL or
　gaw-vree-ELL [HEB], gab-brrree-YELL
　[FR/SP/IT])
　Alternate spellings: Gavriel [HEB]
Gail (GAYL, GAY-yell [IR])
　Alternate spellings: Gayle, Gale
Gay (GAY)
　Alternate spellings: Gaye
Gayla (GAY-luh)
Gaynell (gay-NELL [AA])
Genoveva (jen-oh-VEE-vuh,
　jen-oh-VAY-vuh)
Germaine (jur-MAYN, zhair-MAYN with
　sustained N [FR])
Giada (JAW-duh [IT], jee-YAW-duh,
　JAY-duh)
　Alternate spellings: Jada*, Jayda,
　Jaida
Grace (GRAYS)
　Alternate spellings: Grayce
Gracie (GRAY-see)

Hailey (HAY-lee)
　Alternate spellings: Haley, Hayley,
　Haylee, Hailee, Haleigh, Hailie, Haylie,
　Halie, Hali, Hayleigh
Haven (HAY-ven)
Haydee (HAY-dee)

Hayden (HAY-den)
Hazel (HAY-zull [CG], HAW-zell)
Alternate spellings: Hazle
Helena (hell-AY-nuh, HELL-en-uh; see also Elena)
Helene (hel-LEEN, ay-LEN with sustained N [FR])
Alternate spellings: Hélène

Jada (JAY-duh [AA], YAY-duh or YAW-duh [HEB])
Alternate spellings: Jayda, Jaida, Giada*, Yada [HEB]
Jade (JAYD)
Alternate spellings: Jayde
Jaden (JAY-den)
Alternate spellings: Jayden, Jaiden, Jaidyn
Jaelyn (JAY-len)
Alternate spellings: Jaylin, Jalyn, Jaylynn, Jailyn, Jalynn, Jaylyn
Jakayla (juh-KAY-luh [AA])
James (JAYMZ)
Jamie (JAY-mee)
Alternate spellings: Jaime, Jami, Jaimie, Jayme, Jammie
Jana (JAY-nuh, JAN-uh, JAW-nuh)
Alternate spellings: Janna, Gianna*, Giana, Johnna, Jonna
Janae (jan-NAY)
Alternate spellings: Janay
Jane (JAYN)
Alternate spellings: Jayne
Janie (JAY-nee)
Jayla (JAY-luh)
Jaylene (jay-LEEN)

Kaitlyn (KAYT-lin [IR])
Alternate spellings: Katelyn, Caitlin, Caitlyn, Kaitlin, Katelynn, Kaitlynn, Katelin, Katlin*, Katlyn , Katlynn
Kala (KAL-uh, KAY-luh)
Alternate spellings: Kayla*
Kalyn (KAL-in, KAY-lin)
Alternate spellings: Kaylin*
Kate (KAYT [CG])
Kay (KAY)
Alternate spellings: Kaye
Kayden (KAY-den)
Kayla (KAY-luh or KY-luh [IR])
Alternate spellings: Kaila, Cayla [HEB], Keyla, Kaylah, Kaela, Keila, Kala, Kyla*, Keilah [HEB], Khayla*
Kaylee (KAY-lee)

Kailey, Kayleigh, Kaylie, Kaleigh, Kaley, Kailee, Kayley, Kayli, Kali, Caleigh, Keli [HW]
Kaylin (KAY-lin [IR])
Alternate spellings: Kaylyn, Kaelyn, Kailyn, Kaylynn, Kalyn*, Kaylen
Keiki (KAY-kee or kay-YEE-kee [HW])
Keiko (KAY-koh [JAP])
Khayla (CHAY-luh with guttural CH at beginning and pronounced H at end [AR], KAY-luh)
Alternate spellings: Kayla*, Kaila, Cayla [HEB], Keyla, Kaylah, Kaela, Keila, Kala, Kyla*, Keilah [HEB]
Kiele (kee-YAY-lay [HW], KEE-lee)
Alternate spellings: Keely*, Keeley

Laney (LAY-nee)
Laura (LOR-ruh, LOW-ruh [IT], LOR-ray [FR], law-OO-raw [SP])
Alternate spellings: Lora
Lavada (luh-VAY-duh)
Layla (LAY-luh, LY-luh [HEB], LY-luh with pronounced H at end [AR])
Alternate spellings: Laila, Leila*, Leyla, Lela, Lelah, Lila*, Lyla, Lilah
Leanne (lee-YAN, lay-YAW with short N [FR])
Alternate spellings: Leeann, Leann
Leatrice (LEE-yuh-triss, LAY-yuh-triss, lee-yuh-TREES, lay-uh-TREES)
Lei (LAY [CH])
Leila (LEE-luh, LAY-luh [AR/HEB/PER])
Alternate spellings: Laila, Leila, Layla*, Lela, Lelah, Lyla
Leilani (lay-LAWN-ee [HW])
Lelia (LEE-lee-yuh, LAY-lee-yuh, LEL-ee-yuh [IT])
Leola (lee-YOH-luh, lay-YOH-luh)
Leona (lee-YOH-nuh, lay-YOH-nuh)
Leone (lee-YOH-nee [GER], lay-yoh-NEE [FR])
Alternate spellings: Léonie [FR]
Leonora (lee-yoh-NOR-ruh, lay-oh-NOR-uh [IT/SP])
Alternate spellings: Eleonora [IT/SP], Lenora*
Lorena (lor-RAY-nuh, lor-REE-nuh, lor-REN-uh [IT/SP])
Lorene (lor-REEN, LOR-ren, lor-RAYN [FR])
Alternate spellings: Laureen, Loreen, Lorine, Laurine, Lauren*, Lauryn, Loren, Lorraine*
Lorraine (lor-RAYN, lor-REN [FR])

Alternate spellings: Loraine, Laraine, Lorene*
Luvenia (loo-VEN-nee-yuh, loo-VAY-nee-yuh; see also Lavinia)
Alternate spellings: Louvenia

Mabel (MAY-bull)
Alternate spellings: Mable
Macy (MAY-see)
Alternate spellings: Macie, Macey, Maci
Maddalena (mad-duh-LAY-nuh [IT])
Mae (MAY [CG])
Alternate spellings: Maye, May, Mei [CH/HW], Mai*
Maeve (MAYV [IR])
Magdalena (mag-duh-LAY-nuh [SP])
Makayla (muh-KAY-luh or mak-KAY-luh [CG/SP])
Alternate spellings: Mikayla, Michaela*, McKayla, Mikaela, Micaela, Makaila, Mikala
Maleah (maw-LAY-yuh [HW], muh-LEE-yuh)
Mamie (MAY-mee)
Alternate spellings: Maymie
Marlena (mar-LAY-nuh, mar-LEN-uh; see also Marilena)
Maryjane (mair-ree-JAYN)
Maryjo (mair-ree-JOH)
Marylou (mair-ree-LOO)
Alternate spellings: Marilou
Mavis (MAY-viss)
Maybelle (may-BELL)
Alternate spellings: Maybell
Mayme (MAYM)
Mayra (MAY-ruh, MY-ruh)
Alternate spellings: Maira, Myra*, Mira
Mazie (MAY-zee)
Megan (MAY-gen [IR/CG], MEG-en, MEE-gen)
Alternate spellings: Meghan, Meagan, Maegan, Meaghan, Meghann
Melanie (MEL-en-ee, may-lan-NEE [FR])
Alternate spellings: Melany, Melonie, Mélanie
Melissa (muh-LISS-uh, mel-LISS-uh, may-lee-SAW [FR])
Alternate spellings: Melisa*, Mellissa, Malissa, Mellisa, Mélissa
Mercedes (mur-SAY-deez, mair-SED-ess or mair-THED-eth [SP])
Michaela (mik-ELL-uh or mik-y-YELL-uh [IT], muh-KAY-luh, mee-chy-ELL-uh with guttural CH [HEB])

Alternate spellings: Makayla*, Mikayla, Mckayla, Mikaela, Micaela, Makaila, Mikala

Nadine (nay-DEEN, nad-EEN with sustained N [FR])
Naoma (nay-YOH-muh)
Alternate spellings: Neoma*
Naomi (nay-YOH-mee or NOH-mee [HEB], ny-YOH-mee, NAW-oh-mee [JAP])
Nayeli (ny-YELL-ee, naw-YELL-ee [SP], NY-yell-ee, NAY-yell-ee)
Alternate spellings: Nayely, Nayelli
Neoma (nee-YOH-muh, nay-YOH-muh)
Alternate spellings: Naoma*
Nereida (nair-RAY-duh [SP/GRK])
Alternate spellings: Nereyda
Neva (NEE-vuh, NAY-vuh, NEV-uh)
Nevaeh (nev-AY-yuh, nev-VY-yuh)
Neyla (NY-luh [AR], NAY-luh, NEE-luh [IR])
Alternate spellings: Nila, Nyla*, Neala or Neila [IR]
Noemi (no-WEM-ee, noh-WAY-mee [IT/SP], noh-way-MEE [FR])
Alternate spellings: Noémie
Nyasia (ny-YAY-zhuh, ny-YAY-see-yuh, nee-YAY-zhuh)

Octavia (awk-TAY-vee-yaw, awk-TAW-vee-yaw or ohk-TAW-bee-yaw [SP])
Omayra (oh-MY-ruh, oh-MAY-ruh)

Paige (PAYJ)
Patience (PAY-shens)
Payton (PAY-ten)
Alternate spellings: Peyton
Penelope (pen-NELL-oh-pee, pay-nay-LOHP)
Alternate spellings: Pénélope
Petra (PAY-truh [GRK/HUN], PET-ruh)
Petranella (pay-truh-NELL-uh)

Rachel (RAY-chell, ruh-CHELL with guttural CH [HEB], raw-SHELL [FR])
Alternate spellings: Rachael, Racheal
Rae (RAY [GER])
Alternate spellings: Ray, Rey
Rafaela (raff-ay-YELL-uh, raff-eye-ELL-uh [IT], raw-fuh-ELL-uh [HEB/SP])
Ramonita (ray-moh-NEE-tuh)
Raven (RAY-ven [AA])
Rayna (RAW-haw-naw [AR], RAY-nuh)

Alternate spellings: Raina, Reina,
Reyna*
Reagan (RAY-gen, REE-gen [IR])
Alternate spellings: Raegan, Regan
Rebecca (reb-EK-uh, RIV-kuh [HEB],
rrreb-AY-kuh [SP])
Alternate spellings: Rebekah, Rebeca,
Rivka* or Rivke [HEB]
Rena (REE-nuh [HEB], ren-NAY)
Alternate spellings: Renae, Rene,
Renee*, Renea*, Ranee*
Renea (ren-NAY-yuh, ren-NAY)
Alternate spellings: Renee*
Renee (ren-NAY, rrren-NAY [FR])
Alternate spellings: Renée [FR], Renae,
Rene, Rena*, Renea*, Ranee*
Renita (ray-NEE-taw [SP])
Reyna (RAY-nuh [SP])
Alternate spellings: Raina, Reina,
Rayna*
Rhea (REE-yuh [GRK], RAY-yuh)
Alternate spellings: Reia, Reya [SP]
Romaine (roh-MAYN, rrroh-MEN [FR])

Sade (shaw-DAY [AA])
Sadie (SAY-dee)
Alternate spellings: Sadye
Sage (SAYJ)
Alternate spellings: Saige
Sailor (SAY-lur)
Salome (sal-LOH-mee,
SAW-loh-may, suh-LOHM,
SAL-loh-may [BR], saw-loh-MAY [FR],
shaw-LOHM [HEB])
Alternate spellings: Salomé [FR],
Shalom [HEB]
Shanta (SHAWN-tuh [EI], SHAN-tuh,
shawn-TAY [AA])
Alternate spellings: Shante*, Shantay
Shante (shawn-TAY [AA], shaw-TAY with
short N [FR])
Alternate spellings: Shanta*, Shantay,
Chante [FR]
Shayla (SHAY-luh [AA/CG], SHY-luh)
Alternate spellings: Shaila [EI], Sheila*
Shaylee (SHAY-lee [AA/CG>])
Shayna (SHAY-nuh [HEB])
Alternate spellings: Shaina, Shana,
Chana*
Shea (SHAY [CG])
Sheila (SHEE-luh [CG], SHAY-hell-uh [PER],
SHAY-luh, SHY-luh)
Alternate spellings: Shiela, Shaila [EI]
Sienna (see-YEN-uh, shee-YAY-nuh [JAP])

Soheila (soh-HAY-luh [PER])
Stacia (STAY-shuh, STAY-see-yuh,
STAW-zee-yuh [RUS])
Alternate spellings: Stasia [RUS]
Stacy (STAY-see)
Alternate spellings: Stacey, Stacie,
Staci

Tatum (TAY-tem)
Taya (TAY-yuh, TY-yuh)
Alternate spellings: Tea, Thea*
Taylor (TAY-lur)
Alternate spellings: Tayler
Teagan (TEE-gen [IR], TAY-gen)
Thea (THEE-yuh, TAY-yuh)
Alternate spellings: Taya*, Tea
Theda (THAY-duh)
Theo (THEE-yoh, TAY-yoh [FR])
Alternate spellings: Théo [FR]
Theodora (thee-yuh-DOR-ruh,
tay-oh-DOR-ruh [IT])
Alternate spellings: Teodora [IT]
Therese (tur-REES, tay-REZ [FR])
Alternate spellings: Terese, Thérèse
Tracy (TRAY-see)
Alternate spellings: Traci, Tracey
Tracie
Treva (TREE-vuh, TRAY-vuh)

Veda (VEE-duh, VAY-duh)
Alternate spellings: Vada*, Vida*

Wava (WAY-vuh)
Wei (WAY [CH])

Zaida (ZAY-duh, zy-YEE-duh, zaw-HED-uh
with pronounced H at end [AR])
Zöe (ZOH-wee [GRK/HEB], zoh-WAY [FR])
Alternate spellings: Zoey, Zoie, Zoé [FR]
Zoraida (zoh-RAY-duh with pronounced
H at end [AR], zor-RY-duh [SP])

■ SHORT A (A) ■

PARTNER POINTER:
Check out the AIR list, too.

Abby (AB-bee)
Alternate spellings: Abbey, Abbie
Abigail (AB-big-ayl, aw-vee-GYL [HEB])
Alternate spellings: Abbigail, Abbigayle,
Abigale, Abagail, Avigayil [HEB]
Abrianna (ab-ree-YAWN-uh)

Abril (AB-rill, AY-brill, aw-BREEL [AR/SP],
    awv-REEL [SP])
Ada (AY-duh [HEB/GER], ADD-uh [IT])
    Alternate spellings: Aida*, Adah, Eda
Addie (ADD-ee)
Addison (ADD-iss-un)
Adelaida (add-uh-LAY-duh)
Adelaide (ADD-uh-layd [GER], add-eh-LED
    or uh-dell-uh-EED [FR])
Adele (uh-DELL [GER], ad-DEL)
    Alternate spellings: Adell, Adelle
Adelina (ad-uh-LEE-nuh,
    aw-dell-LEE-nuh [IT/SP])
Adeline (AD-uh-lin, ADD-uh-lyn,
    ad-dell-LEEN with sustained N [FR])
    Alternate spellings: Adaline
Adrianna (ay-dree-YAN-uh)
Adrienne (ay-dree-YAN, ay-dree-YEN
    with sustained N [FR])
    Alternate spellings: Adriane
Afton (AF-tun [IR])
Agatha (AG-uh-thuh, AW-guh-tuh [IT],
    ag-GAT [FR])
    Alternate spellings: Agathe [FR]
Agnes (AG-ness, an-YES [FR])
Agnese (an-YEZ-eh or an-YEZ [FR])
Agostina (ag-oh-STEEN-uh [IT])
Agustina (ag-uh-STEE-nuh,
    aw-goos-TEEN-uh or
    aw-gooth-TEEN-uh [SP])
Aisling (ASH-leeng [IR])
Alani (uh-LAW-nee, uh-LAN-nee,
    uh-LAY-nee)
Alanis (uh-LAW-niss, uh-LAN-niss)
Alanna (uh-LAN-nuh, uh-LAW-nuh)
    Alternate spellings: Alana*, Elana*,
    Ilana*
Alba (AL-buh, AWL-baw [IT/SP],
    AWL-vaw [SP])
Alberta (al-BUR-tuh, al-BAIR-tuh [IT/SP],
    al-VAIR-tuh [SP])
Albertha (al-BURTH-uh)
Albertine (al-bur-TEEN, awl-bair-TEEN
    with sustained N [FR])
Albina (al-BEE-nuh [IT])
Alda (AL-duh, AWL-duh)
Alex (AL-eks)
Alexandra (al-eks-ZAN-druh,
    al-eks-ZAWN-druh)
Alexandria (al-eks-ZAN-dree-yuh)
    Alternate spellings: Alexandrea
Alexandrie (al-ek-sawn-DREE with short
    N [FR]
Alexia (uh-LEK-see-yuh, al-LEK-see-uh [IT])

Alfreda (al-FRAY-duh, al-FRED-uh [IT])
Ali (aw-LEE, AL-ee)
    Alternate spellings: Allie*, Ally
Alice (AL-liss, al-LEES [FR])
    Alternate spellings: Alyce
Alize (uh-LEEZ, aw-LEEZ [FR],
    al-LEE-zay)
Allie (AL-lee)
    Alternate spellings: Ally, Ali
Allison (AL-liss-sun, al-lee-SAW
    with short N [FR])
    Alternate spellings: Alison, Allyson,
    Alyson
Almeda (al-MAY-duh, al-MEE-duh)
    Alternate spellings: Almeta
Alpha (AL-fuh)
Altha (AL-thuh)
Althea (al-THEE-yuh)
Alva (AL-vuh, AWL-vaw)
Alvera (al-VEER-ruh, al-VAIR-ruh)
Alverta (al-VUR-tuh)
Alvina (al-VEE-nuh)
    Alternate spellings: Alvena
Amanda (uh-MAN-duh,
    aw-MAWN-duh [SP])
Amaris (AM-ur-riss, uh-MAIR-riss)
Amaryllis (am-uh-RILL-iss)
Amber (AM-bur, AWM-bur [AR])
Anahi (ann-AW-hee [SP])
Anaïs (aw-naw-EES [FR], ann-NY-yiss)
Anastasia (aw-naw-STAW-zee-yuh or
    aw-naw-STAW-zhuh [RUS],
    ann-uh-STAY-shuh,
    aw-naw-STAW-see-yuh [IT],
    aw-naw-staw-SEE-yuh [GRK])
    Alternate spellings: Anastacia
Anastasie (ann-aw-staw-ZEE [FR])
Andrea (ANN-dree-yuh, ann-DRAY-yuh
    [IT], awn-DRAY-yuh [SP])
    Alternate spellings: Andria
Angela (ANN-jell-uh, AWN-jell-uh [IT],
    AWN-hell-uh or awn-HELL-uh [SP])
Angeles (ANN-jell-ess, ANN-jell-eez,
    AWN-hell-ess or awn-HELL-eth [SP])
Angelia (ann-JELL-ee-yuh,
    awn-JELL-ee-yuh [IT])
Angélica (ann-JELL-ik-uh,
    awn-jell-EEK-uh, awn-HELL-ee-kuh [SP])
    Alternate spellings: Anjelica
Angelina (ann-jell-EE-nuh,
    awn-jell-EE-nuh [IT],
    awn-hell-LEE-nuh [SP])
Angeline (ann-jell-EEN, ann-zhe-LEEN
    with sustained N [FR])

Angelique (ann-jell-LEEK, ann-zhe-LEEK
  [FR])
Angelita (ann-jell-LEE-tuh,
  awn-hell-LEE-tuh [SP])
Angie (ANN-jee)
Anjanette (ann-juh-NET)
Anna (ANN-uh, AW-nuh)
  Alternate spellings: Ana [SP]
Annabella (ann-uh-BELL-uh)
  Alternate spellings: Anabela [IT]
Annabelle (ANN-uh-bell, ann-uh-BELL [FR])
  Alternate spellings: Annabel, Anabel,
  Annabell
Annalise (ann-uh-LEES [GER/FR])
  Alternate spellings: Analise, Annelise
Annamae (ANN-uh-may)
Annamarie (ann-uh-muh-REE,
  aw-nuh-maw-REE [FR])
Anne (ANN)
  Alternate spellings: Ann
Annetta (ann-NET-uh)
Annette (ann-NET)
Annie (ANN-ee)
Annika (AW-nik-uh or ANN-ik-uh [SCAN],
  aw-NEE-kuh [AA] with pronounced H
  at end [AR])
  Alternate spellings: Anika
Annis (ANN-iss, aw-NEES)
Annmarie (ann-muh-REE)
Antoinette (ann-twah-NET [FR])
Antonetta (ann-toh-NET-uh)
Antonette (ann-toh-NET)
Antonia (ann-TOH-nee-yuh,
  awn-TOH-nee-yaw [IT/SP])
Antonietta (an-toh-nee-ETT-uh [IT])
Antonina (an-toh-NEE-nuh [IT])
Ansley (ANZ-lee)
Apple (APP-pull)
Arianna (ar-ree-YAN-uh)
  Alternate spellings: Aryanna
Ashley (ASH-lee)
  Alternate spellings: Ashleigh, Ashlee,
  Ashly, Ashely , Ashli, Ashlie, Ashely
Ashlyn (ASH-lin)
  Alternate spellings: Ashlynn
Ashton (ASH-ten)
  Alternate spellings: Ashtyn
Aspen (ASS-pen)
Astrid (AST-rid [BR/SCAN])
Avlyn (AV-lin)
Ayanna (ay-YAN-uh, eye-YAN-uh)
  Alternate spellings: Iyanna

Babette (bab-BET [FR])

Bambi (BAM-bee)
Blanche (BLANCH, BLAWNSH [FR])
  Alternate spellings: Blanch
Brandon (BRAN-den)
Brandy (BRAN-dee)
  Alternate spellings: Brandie, Brandi,
  Brandee [SCAN]
Brianna (bree-YAN-nuh or
  bree-YAWN-uh [IR])
  Alternate spellings: Briana, Breanna,
  Bryanna, Breana, Bryana, Breonna,
  Brionna
Brianne (bree-YAN, bree-YAWN [FR])
  Alternate spellings: Breanne, Breann,
  Briann

Callie (KAL-ee)
  Alternate spellings: Cali, Kali, Kallie,
  Caleigh
Cameron (KAM-ur-en)
  Alternate spellings: Camryn, Kamryn
Camilla (kam-MILL-luh, kaw-MEE-luh [IT/SP])
  Alternate spellings: Camila
Camille (kam-MEEL [FR])
Campbell (KAM-bell)
Camry (KAM-ree)
Candace (KAN-dess)
  Alternate spellings: Candice, Kandice,
  Kandace, Candis
Cándida (KAWN-did-uh [SP], kan-DEE-duh)
Candy (KAN-dee)
  Alternate spellings: Candi, Kandi,
  Kandy
Carolann (kair-rull-ANN)
Cassandra (kuh-SAN-druh [GRK],
  kaw-SAWN-draw or
  kaw-THAWN-draw [SP])
  Alternate spellings: Kassandra,
  Casandra, Kasandra
Cassidy (KASS-sid-ee [IR])
  Alternate spellings: Kassidy
Cassie (KASS-ee)
  Alternate spellings: Kassie
Catalina (kat-uh-LEE-nuh,
  kaw-taw-LEE-nuh [SP])
Catherine (KATH-ur-rin, kat-REEN [FR];
  see also Kathrine)
  Alternate spellings: Katheryn,
  Katharine, Catharine
Catina (kat-EE-nuh)
Chana (CHAW-naw with guttural CH [HEB],
  SHAW-nuh, SHAY-nuh, SHAN-nuh)
  Alternate spellings: Hannah*, Hanna,
  Hana, Hanaa, Shawna*, Shauna,

Shonna, Shayna*, Shana, Shanna
Chanda (CHAWN-duh [EI], SHAN-duh,
    SHAWN-duh)
    Alternate spellings: Shanda*
Chandler (CHAND-lur)
Chanel (shan-NELL [FR])
    Alternate spellings: Chanelle
Chantal (shawn-TAWL,
    shaw-TAL with short N [FR])
Chantel (shawn-TELL, shan-TELL [AA/FR])
    Alternate spellings: Shantel,
    Chantelle , Shantell
Chasity (CHAS-sit-ee)
Chastity (CHAS-tit-ee)
Cheyenne (shy-ANN)
    Alternate spellings: Cheyanne,
    Shyanne, Shyann
Christian (KRISS-chen, kree-stee-YAN [FR])
    Alternate spellings: Kristian,
    Christiane [FR]

Dagmar (DAG-mar [SCAN])
Dagny (DAG-nee)
Dalia (DAW-lee-yuh [HEB], DAL-lee-yuh
    [SCAN])
    Alternate spellings: Dahlia, Daliah,
    Daliya or Dalya [HEB]
Dallas (DAL-liss)
Damaris (DAM-ur-riss)
Danelle (dan-NELL [FR], daw-NELL [HEB])
Danette (dan-NETT [FR])
Dania (DAN-ee-yuh, DAY-nee-yuh, duh-
    NEE-yuh or duh-NY-yuh [AA], DAWN-
    yuh or DAW-nee-yuh [HEB])
    Alternate spellings: Daniya, Danya
Danica (DAN-ik-uh)
Daniela (dan-YELL-uh [IT], dawn-YELL-uh
    [HEB/SP])
    Alternate spellings: Daniella
Danielle (dan-YELL [FR], dawn-YELL [HEB])
    Alternate spellings: Danyelle
Danna (DAN-nuh, DAW-nuh [HEB])
    Alternate spellings: Dayna, Dena,
    Dana*Daphne (DAF-nee)
Davin (DAV-in [IR])
Dayana (DAY-yaw-nuh [AA], dy-YAN-nuh)
    Alternate spellings: Diana*, Dianna
Deanna (dee-YAN-uh)
    Alternate spellings: Deana
Diana (dy-YAN-uh, dee-YAWN-uh [IT/SP])
    Alternate spellings: Dayana*, Dianna
Diane (dy-YAN, dee-YAN [FR])
    Alternate spellings: Diann, Dianne,
    Dian, Deann*, Deanne, Dionne*

Emmanuela (em-man-WELL-uh [IT];
    see also Manuela)
Esmeralda (ez-mur-RAWL-duh,
    ess-mair-RAL-duh or
    eth-mair-RAL-duh [SP])
Esmerelda (ez-mur-RELL-duh,
    ess-mair-RAL-duh or
    eth-mair-RAL-duh [SP])
Evangelina (ee-van-jell-LEE-nuh [IT],
    ay-vawn-hell-LEE-nuh [SP])
Evangeline (ee-van-jell-LEEN with
    sustained N [FR])

Fabiola (fab-ee-YOH-luh)
Fallon (FAL-lun [GG])
Fannie (FAN-ee)
    Alternate spellings: Fanny
Fatima (FAW-tim-uh or FAWT-muh [AR],
    fat-EE-muh [IT])
Fernanda (fur-NAN-duh [IT],
    fair-NAWN-duh [SP])
Fran (FRAN)
Frances (FRAN-sess)
    Alternate spellings: Francis
Francesca (fran-CHESS-kuh [IT],
    fran-SESS-kuh)
    Alternate spellings: Franchesca,
    Francheska
Francine (fran-SEEN, frawn-SEEN with
    sustained N [FR])
Francisca (fran-SIS-kuh, fran-SEES-kuh
    or fran-THEETH-kuh [SP])

Gabriela (gaw-bree-YELL-uh [SP],
    gab-ree-YELL-uh,
    gaw-vree-ELL-uh [HEB])
    Alternate spellings: Gabriella*,
    Gavriela [HEB]
Gabriella (gab-ree-YELL-uh [IT],
    gaw-vree-ELL-uh [HEB])
    Alternate spellings: Gabriela*,
    Gavriela [HEB]
Gabrielle (gab-ree-YELL [FR])
Galilea (gal-ee-LAY-yuh,
    gal-ee-LEE-yuh)
Georgiana (jor-jee-YAN-nuh)
    Alternate spellings: Georgianna
Georgianne (jor-jee-YAN,
    zhor-zhee-YAW with short N [FR])
    Alternate spellings: Georgiane
Gladys (GLAD-iss)
    Alternate spellings: Gladyce [WL]

Hadley (HAD-lee)

Hallie (HAL-ee)
Alternate spellings: Halle [SCAN],
Haleigh, Halie, Hali
Hannah (HAN-nuh, HAW-nuh,
CHAW-naw with guttural CH [HEB],
hen-NUH with pronounced H at end
[AR])
Alternate spellings: Hanna, Hana [JAP],
Hanaa, Chana [HEB]
Hassie (HAS-see)
Hattie (HAD-ee)

Jackie (JAK-ee)
Alternate spellings: Jacque*
Jaclyn (JAK-lin)
Alternate spellings: Jacklyn
Jacqueline (JAK-uh-lin, JAK-well-lin,
jak-LEEN, zhawk-uh-LEEN with
sustained N [FR])
Alternate spellings: Jaqueline,
Jaquelyn, Jackeline, Jaquelin,
Jacquline, Jacalyn
Jan (JAN)
Alternate spellings: Jann
Jana (JAY-nuh, JAN-uh, JAW-nuh)
Alternate spellings: Janna, Gianna*,
Giana, Johnna, Jonna
Janae (jan-NAY)
Alternate spellings: Janay
Janelle (jan-NELL)
Alternate spellings: Janell, Janel ,
Jenelle
Janessa (jan-NESS-uh [AA])
Janet (JAN-net)
Janice (JAN-iss, juh-NEES [AA])
Alternate spellings: Janis
Janine (jan-NEEN)
Janiya (jan-NY-yuh, jan-NEE-yuh [AR])
Alternate spellings: Janiyah
Jannie (JAN-nee)
Jasmine (JAZ-min, jass-MEEN,
JAS-oo-meen [JAP]), yaz-MEEN [AR],
yass-MEEN [HEB/PER])
Alternate spellings: Jasmin, Jazmin,
Jazmine, Jazmyn, Jasmyn, Jazmyne,
Yasmin*, Yazmin, Yasmine*, Yasmeen
Jazlyn (JAZZ-lin)
Jean (JEEN [CG], ZHAN [FR])
Alternate spellings: Jeanne [FR],
Gene, Jeane
Jeanette (jen-NET [CG], zhan-NET [FR])
Alternate spellings: Janette, Jannette
Jeanine (jen-NEEN [CG], zhan-NEEN [FR])
Alternate spellings: Janeen

Joanna (joh-WAN-uh, joh-WAH-nuh)
Alternate spellings: Joana, Johana
Johanna (joh-HAN-uh, joh-HAW-nuh,
joh-WAN-uh, yo-HAW-nuh [GER],
yoh-CHAW-nuh with guttural CH [HEB])
Alternate spellings: Johana, Yochana
[HEB]
Juliana (joo-lee-YAWN-uh [IT],
joo-lee-YAN-uh, hoo-lee-YAWN-uh [SP],
yoo-lee-YAWN-nuh [SP/RUS])
Alternate spellings: Julianna, Giuliana
[IT], Yuliana* [RUS]
Julianne (joo-lee-YAN, zhoo-lee-YEN [FR])
Alternate spellings: Juliann, Julienne
[FR]

Kala (KAL-uh, KAY-luh)
Alternate spellings: Kayla*
Kalyn (KAL-in, KAY-lin)
Alternate spellings: Kaylin*
Kami (KAM-ee)
Kathaleen (kath-uh-LEEN)
Katharina (kath-ur-REE-nuh,
kat-uh-REE-nuh
Alternate spellings: Katarina*, Katerina
Kathleen (kath-LEEN [CG])
Alternate spellings: Cathleen
Kathlyn (KATH-lin)
Kathrine (KATH-rin, kath-REEN;
see also Catherine)
Alternate spellings: Cathryn,
Cathrine, Kathryn [CG], Kathryne
Kathy (KATH-ee [CG])
Alternate spellings: Cathy, Kathi,
Kathie, Cathie, Cathey, Cathi
Katlin (KAT-lin, KAYT-lin)
Alternate spellings: Katlyn , Katlynn,
Kaitlyn*
Katrina (kat-REE-nuh or kaw-TREE-nuh
[GER])
Alternate spellings: Catrina
Kattie (KAT-ee)

Lana (LAW-nuh or LAN-uh [CG])
Alternate spellings: Lona*, Lonna
Lanette (lan-NET; see also Lynette)
Lashanda (luh-SHAWN-duh or luh-
SHAN-duh [AA])
Alternate spellings: Lashonda
Latanya (luh-TAWN-yuh or luh-TAN-yuh
[AA])
Alternate spellings: Latonya*
Latasha (luh-TAW-shuh or luh-TASH-uh
[AA])

Alternate spellings: Latosha
Leandra (lee-YAN-druh, lee-YAWN-druh)
Leanna (lee-YAN-nuh, lee-YAW-nuh [IT])
 Alternate spellings: Liana [IT]
Leanne (lee-YAN, lay-YAW with short N
 [FR])
 Alternate spellings: Leeann, Leann
Loriann (lor-ree-YAN)
Luana (loo-WAH-nuh [GER/HW],
 loo-WAN-uh [IT])
 Alternate spellings: Louanna
Luann (loo-WAN)
 Alternate spellings: Luanne, Louann
Lucienne (loo-see-YAN, loo-see-YEN
 with sustained N [FR])

Mackenzie (muh-KEN-zee, mik-KEN-zee,
 mak-KEN-zee)
 Alternate spellings: Mckenzie,
 Makenzie
Maddalena (mad-duh-LAY-nuh [IT])
Madelena (mad-uh-LEN-uh [IT])
Madeline (MAD-uh-lin, MAD-uh-lyn,
 MAD-lin, mad-dell-LYN or
 mad-dell-LEN with sustained N [FR])
 Alternate spellings: Madelyn,
 Madeleine, Madalyn, Madelynn,
 Madilyn, Madalynn, Madaline
Madge (MAJ)
Madie (MAY-dee, MAD-ee)
 Alternate spellings: Maddie, Maddy,
 Mattie
Madison (MAD-iss-un)
 Alternate spellings: Madisyn,
 Madyson, Maddison, Madisen
Madonna (muh-DAWN-uh,
 mad-OH-nuh [IT])
Mafalda (maf-FAWL-duh [IT])
Magdalen (MAG-duh-len)
 Alternate spellings: Magdalene*
Magdalena (mag-duh-LAY-nuh [SP])
Magdalene (mag-duh-LEEN,
 MAG-duh-len)
 Alternate spellings: Magdalen*
Maggie (MAG-ee [CG])
Magnolia (mag-NOH-lee-yuh)
Makayla (muh-KAY-luh or
 mak-KAY-luh [CG/SP])
 Alternate spellings: Mikayla,
 Michaela*, McKayla, Mikaela, Micaela,
 Makaila, Mikala
Malika (MEL-ik-uh or mal-EE-kuh [AR],
 MAW-lee-kuh [EI/HUN], muh-LY-kuh [AA])
 Alternate spellings: Mallika [EI],

Malikah, Milika, Mylika
Mallory (MAL-or-ree)
Malvina (mal-VEE-nuh [SP])
Mammie (MAM-ee)
Mandy (MAN-dee)
Manuela (man-WELL-uh [SP]; see also
 Emmanuela)
Marianne (mair-ree-YAN)
 Alternate spellings: Maryann,
 Maryanne, Mariann
Masako (MAW-sak-oh [JAP])
Matilda (muh-TIL-duh [GER],
 mat-TEEL-deh [IT])
 Alternate spellings: Matilde*, Mathilda
Matilde (muh-TIL-dee, mat-TEELD [FR],
 mat-TEEL-day [SP], mat-TIL-duh [GER])
 Alternate spellings: Matilda*,
 Mathilda, Mathilde [FR]
Maxie (MAK-see)
Maxine (mak-SEEN [FR])
Miranda (mur-RAN-duh,
 meer-RAN-daw [SP])
 Alternate spellings: Meranda,
 Myranda, Maranda
Montana (mawn-TAN-uh)

Nadia (NAW-dee-yuh, NAW-dee-yah
 with pronounced H at end [AR],
 NAD-ee-yuh [IT])
 Alternate spellings: Nadje [GER],
 Nadya [RUS]
Nadine (nay-DEEN, nad-EEN with
 sustained N [FR])
Nan (NAN)
Nancy (NAN-see)
 Alternate spellings: Nanci, Nancie
Nanette (nan-NET [FR])
 Alternate spellings: Nannette
Nannie (NAN-ee)
Natalia (nat-TAW-lee-yuh,
 nat-taw-LEE-yuh [IT])
 Alternate spellings: Natalya, Nathalia
Natalie (NAD-uh-lee, naw-taw-LEE [HEB],
 nat-tal-LEE [FR])
 Alternate spellings: Nataly, Nathalie
 [FR], Natalee
Natasha (nat-TAW-shuh)
 Alternate spellings: Natosha
Natsumi (NAT-soo-mee [JAP])

Oralia (or-RAL-lee-yuh [SP])

Pam (PAM)
Pamela (PAM-el-uh)

Alternate spellings: Pamala

Pamella (pam-ELL-uh [IT])

Pansy (PAN-zee)

Pat (PAT)

Patrica (pat-TREE-suh)

Patrice (pat-REES [FR])

Patricia (pat-RISH-uh, pat-REES-ee-yuh
   [FR/SP], pat-REE-thee-yuh [SP])

Patrizia (pat-REET-zee-yuh [IT])

Patsy (PAT-see)

Patty (PAT-ee, PAD-ee)
   Alternate spellings: Patti, Pattie

Rafaela (raff-ay-YELL-uh,
   raff-eye-ELL-uh [IT],
   raw-fuh-ELL-uh [HEB/SP])

Ramona (ram-OH-nuh,
   rrraw-MOH-naw [SP])
   Alternate spellings: Romona

Randi (RAN-dee)
   Alternate spellings: Randy

Rhiannon (ree-YAN-nun [WL], REE-yen-en)

Rianna (ree-YAN-uh)
   Alternate spellings: Reanna

Rolanda (roh-LAWN-duh,
   roh-LAN-duh [IT])

Rosanna (roh-ZAN-uh, roh-SAW-nuh [IT]
   Alternate spellings: Roseanna,
   Rossanna, Rossana

Roseann (roh-ZAN)
   Alternate spellings: Rosanne,
   Roseanne, Rosann

Roxana (rawk-SAW-nuh, rawk-SAN-nuh,
   rohk-SAW-naw or rohk-THAW-naw
   [SP], ruk-SAW-nah with pronounced H
   at end [AR])
   Alternate spellings: Roxanna

Roxanne (rawk-SAN, rohk-SAW with
   short N [FR])
   Alternate spellings: Roxann, Roxane

Ruthann (roo-THAN)

Sabina (sab-BEE-nuh)

Sabine (sab-BEEN with sustained N [FR])

Sabrina (sab-BREE-nuh [IT])

Sally (SAL-ee)
   Alternate spellings: Sallie

Salma (SAL-muh, SAWL-maw [HEB/SP],
   THAWL-maw [SP], SUL-mah with
   pronounced H at end [AR])

Salome (sal-LOH-mee, SAW-loh-may,
   suh-LOHM, SAL-loh-may [BR],
   saw-loh-MAY [FR], shaw-LOHM [HEB])
   Alternate spellings: Salomé [FR],

Shalom [HEB]

Samantha (sam-MAN-thuh)

Sammie (SAM-ee)

Sandra (SAND-ruh [IT], SAWN-draw or
   THAWN-draw [SP])
   Alternate spellings: Sondra*, Saundra

Sandy (SAN-dee)
   Alternate spellings: Sandi

Saniya (suh-NY-yuh or suh-NEE-yuh [AA],
   san-NY-yuh [AR], SAWN-yuh [SP])
   Alternate spellings: Saniyya [AR],
   Sanya*, Sonia*, Sonya

Santa (SAWN-taw or THAWN-taw [SP])

Santana (sawn-TAW-naw or
   thawn-TAW-naw [SP], san-TAN-nuh)

Santina (san-TEE-nuh [IT])

Sasha (SAW-shuh [GER/RUS], SASH-uh)
   Alternate spellings: Sacha, Sascha

Satchel (SACH-ell)

Savannah (suh-VAN-uh)
   Alternate spellings: Savanna,
   Savanah, Savana

Shakira (shuh-KEER-ruh [AA],
   SHAW-keer-ruh or SHAK-eer-ruh [AR])

Shana (SHAWN-nuh, SHAN-nuh [AA])
   Alternate spellings: Shawna*, Shanna,
   Shauna, Chana*, Shonna

Shanda (SHAN-duh or SHAWN-duh [AA])
   Alternate spellings: Chanda*

Shannon (SHAN-en [IR])
   Alternate spellings: Shannan, Shanon

Shanta (SHAWN-tuh [EI], SHAN-tuh,
   shawn-TAY [AA])
   Alternate spellings: Shante*, Shantay

Shasta (SHAS-tuh)

Susana (soo-ZAN-uh, soo-ZAW-nuh [IT],
   soo-SAW-naw or
   thoo-THAW-naw [SP])
   Alternate spellings: Susanna,
   Suzanna (see also Shoshana)

Suzanne (soo-ZAN [FR])
   Alternate spellings: Susanne, Suzann,
   Susann (see also Shoshana)

Tabitha (TAB-ith-uh)
   Alternate spellings: Tabatha

Tamara (TAM-uh-ruh, tuh-MAR-ruh [AR/EI],
   tuh-MAIR-ruh [AA], tuh-MAR [HEB],
   TAW-mar-ruh [RUS])
   Alternate spellings: Tamera, Tamar
   [HEB], Tamarah [AR]

Tamatha (TAM-uth-uh)
   Alternate spellings: Tamitha

Tamela (TAM-el-uh or tam-ELL-uh [AA])

Alternate spellings: Tamala
Tami (TAM-ee)
 Alternate spellings: Tammie, Tamie,
 Tammi
Tamia (TAM-ee-yuh, TAWM-yuh)
 Alternate spellings: Tamya
Tamika (tam-EE-kuh [AA])
 Alternate spellings: Tameka,
 Tomeka*, Tomika
Tamiko (TAM-ee-koh [JAP])
Tamra (TAM-ruh)
Tana (TAN-uh)
Tangela (TAN-jell-uh)
Tania (TAWN-yuh, TAN-yuh [IT],
 tuh-NEE-yuh [AA])
 Alternate spellings: Tanya, Taniya,
 Tawnya, Tonya*, Tonja, Tonia
Tiana (tee-YAWN-uh, tee-YAN-nuh)
 Alternate spellings: Tianna
Trinidad (TRIN-id-add, tree-nee-DAD [SP])

Valencia (val-LEN-see-yuh,
 vuh-LEN-chuh [IT], vaw-LEN-see-yaw
 or baw-LEN-thee-yaw [SP])
Valentina (val-en-TEEN-uh [IT/SP])
Valentine (VAL-en-tyn, val-en-TEEN with
 sustained N [FR])
Valeria (val-ur-REE-yuh, val-AIR-ee-yuh
 [IT])
Valerie (VAL-ur-ree, vaw-lair-REE [FR])
 Alternate spellings: Valarie, Valorie
Vallie (VAL-ee)
Vanessa (van-NESS-suh)
 Alternate spellings: Vanesa, Venessa
Vivienne (viv-ee-YAN, vee-vee-YENN [FR])
 Alternate spellings: Vivien

Yadira (yad-DEER-ruh [HEB/SP])
Yanira (yan-NEER-raw [AA/GRK/HEB/SP])
Yasmin (YAZ-min, yass-MEEN [HEB/PER])
 Alternate spellings: Yazmin,
 Yasmine*, Yasmeen, Jasmine*,
 Jasmin, Jazmin, Jazmine, Jazmyn,
 Jasmyn, Jazmyne
Yasmine (yaz-MEEN [AR], yass-MEEN [HEB])
 Alternate spellings: Yazmin, Yasmin*,
 Yasmeen, Jasmine*, Jasmin, Jazmin,
 Jazmine, Jazmyn, Jasmyn, Jazmyne
Yolanda (yoh-LAWN-daw [SP],
 yoh-LAN-duh [IT])
 Alternate spellings: Yolonda, Iolanda [IT]

■ **AIR** ■

PARTNER POINTER:
**Check out the long A and short A
lists, too.**

Alberta (al-BUR-tuh, al-BAIR-tuh [IT/SP],
 al-VAIR-tuh [SP])
Albertine (al-bur-TEEN, awl-bair-TEEN
 with sustained N [FR])
Alvera (al-VEER-ruh, al-VAIR-ruh)
Amaris (AM-ur-riss, uh-MAIR-riss,
 uh-MAR-riss)
America (uh-MAIR-rik-uh,
 aw-MAIR-ree-kuh [IT])
Ara (AR-uh, AIR-ruh)
 Alternate spellings: Era*
Arabella (air-ruh-BELL-uh)
Araceli (air-ruh-SELL-ee, ar-raw-SELL-ee
 or ar-raw-THEL-ee [SP])
 Alternate spellings: Aracely
Arely (AIR-ruh-lee, AR-ruh-lee,
 uh-RELL-ee)
 Alternate spellings: Areli
Ariel (AIR-ree-yell, AR-ree-yell,
 ar-ree-YELL [HEB])
Arielle (air-ree-YELL, ar-ree-YELL [FR])

Bernadette (bur-nuh-DET, bair-nuh-DET
 [FR])
Bernardine (bur-nuh-DEEN,
 bair-nar-DEEN [FR])
 Alternate spellings: Bernadine
Bernita (bair-NEE-tuh or vair-NEE-tuh [SP])
Berta (BUR-tuh, BAIR-tuh [IT/SP],
 VAIR-tuh [SP])
Beryl (BAIR-rill)
Blair (BLAIR)

Carol (KAIR-rull)
 Alternate spellings: Carole, Karol,
 Caryl, Carroll, Carrol
Carolann (kair-rull-ANN)
Carolee (KAIR-oh-lee)
Carolina (kair-oh-LY-nuh,
 kar-oh-LEE-nuh [GER/IT/SP])
Caroline (KAIR-oh-lin, kair-oh-LYN,
 kar-oh-LEEN [FR])
 Alternate spellings: Carolyn,
 Karolyn, Carolynn
Carrie (KAIR-ree)
 Alternate spellings: Kerri, Kerry, Kari*,
 Cari , Carey, Karrie, Karie, Carie, Cary,
 Carri, Kerrie

Carys (KAR-ris [WL], KAIR-ris)
Ceres (SEER-reez, sair-REES [FR])
  Alternate spellings: Cerise [FR]
Charisse (shuh-REES, shair-RRREEZ [FR])
  Alternate spellings: Cherise
Charity (CHAIR-rit-ee)
Cherie (shair-REE [FR], SHAIR-ree, shu-
  REE, CHAIR-ree)
  Alternate spellings: Cheri, Sheree*,
  Sherrie, Sherie Cherry*, Sherry*)
Cherish (CHAIR-rish)
Cherry (CHAIR-ree, SHAIR-ree)
  Alternate spellings: Cherie*, Cheri,
  Sherry*, Sherrie, Sherie
Cheryl (SHAIR-rill)
  Alternate spellings: Sheryl, Cheryle,
  Sherrill, Sherryl
Claire (KLAIR [IR], KLAIRRR [FR])
  Alternate spellings: Clare
Clara (KLAIR-ruh, KLAR-ruh [IT/SP])
Clarabelle (KLAIR-ruh-bell,
  klar-ruh-BELL [FR])
  Alternate spellings: Claribel
Clarice (klair-REES, klar-REES [FR])
Clarine (klair-REEN, klar-REEN [FR])
Clarissa (klair-RISS-uh)

Damaris (DAM-ur-riss, duh-MAIR-ris,
  duh-MAR-ris)
Darian (DAIR-ree-yen)
Daryl (DAIR-rill)
Deirdre (DEER-druh or DAIR-druh [IR])

Elvera (el-VEER-ruh [IT], el-VAIR-ruh)
Era (EER-ruh, AIR-ruh)
  Alternate spellings: Ara*
Erica (AIR-rik-uh [SCAN], AIR-ree-kuh [IT])
  Alternate spellings: Erika, Ericka
Erin (AIR-rin [CG])
Eris (AIR-riss)
Erlinda (ur-LIN-duh, air-LEEN-duh [SP])
Ermina (ur-MEE-nuh, air-MEE-nuh [SP];
  see also Hermina)
Erna (UR-nuh, AIR-nuh)
Ernestina (ur-ness-TEE-nuh,
  air-ness-TEE-nuh [IT])
Erzsebet (AIR-zhuh-bet [HUN])
  Alternate spellings: Erzsabet
Esmeralda (ez-mur-RAWL-duh,
  ess-mair-RAL-duh or
  eth-mair-RAL-duh [SP])
Esmerelda (ez-mur-RELL-duh,
  ess-mair-RAL-duh or
  eth-mair-RAL-duh [SP])

Esperanza (ess-pair-AWN-suh or
  eth-pair-AWN-suh [SP];
  see also Speranza)
Esther (ESS-tur, ess-TAIR [FR/HEB])
  Alternate spellings: Ester

Fairy (FAIR-ree)
Farrah (FAIR-ruh, FAR-rah or far-RAH
  with pronounced H at end [AR])
  Alternate spellings: Farah
Fernanda (fur-NAN-duh [IT],
  fair-NAWN-duh [SP])

Geraldine (jair-rull-DEEN)
  Alternate spellings: Jeraldine
Geralyn (JAIR-rull-lin)
  Alternate spellings: Jerilyn
Germaine (jur-MAYN, zhair-MAYN with
  sustained N [FR])
Guillermina (yair-MEE-nuh [SP])

Harriet (HAIR-ree-yet [GER])
  Alternate spellings: Harriett, Harriette
Hermina (hur-MEE-nuh, air-MEE-nuh [SP];
  see also Ermina)
Herminia (her-MIN-ee-yuh, her-MEE-
  nee-yuh, air-MEE-nee-yuh [SP])

Jennifer (JEN-nif-ur [WL], zheh-nee-FAIR
  [FR])
  Alternate spellings: Jenifer, Genifer
Jeri (JAIR-ree)
  Alternate spellings: Jerri, Geri, Gerri,
  Jerry, Gerry, Jerrie
Jerrica (JAIR-rik-uh)

Kara (KAIR-ruh [IR], KAR-ruh)
  Alternate spellings: Cara [IT]
Karen (KAIR-ren)
  Alternate spellings: Karin, Caryn,
  Caren, Karyn, Karon, Karan, Caron,
  Karren
Kari (KAR-ree, KAIR-ree)
  Alternate spellings: Carrie*, Cari,
  Karie, Carie, Cary, Carri
Kierra (kee-YAIR-ruh)

Lara (LAW-ruh [IT/SP], LAIR-ruh)
  Alternate spellings: Lera
Lucero (loo-SAIR-roh or loo-THAIR-roh
  [SP])

Mairwen (MY-yur-wen or MYR-wen [WL],
  MAIR-wen)

Mara (MAR-raw [HEB/IT], MAIR-ruh)
  Alternate spellings: Maira, Marah
Mari (MAR-ree [SP], MAIR-ree)
  Alternate spellings: Mary*, Maree
Mariam (MAIR-ree-yum, MAR-ree-yum [AR])
  Alternate spellings: Maryam
Marian (MAIR-ree-yen)
  Alternate spellings: Marion
Marianne (mair-ree-YAN)
  Alternate spellings: Maryann,
  Maryanne, Mariann
Maribel (MAIR-rib-bell, mair-ee-BELL [FR])
  Alternate spellings: Marybelle
Marie (mar-REE, mair-RHEE [FR])
  Alternate spellings: Maree
Mariel (MAIR-ree-yell, MAR-ree-yell [GER],
  mair-ree-YELL [FR])
  Alternate spellings: Marielle [FR]
Mariella (mair-ree-YELL-uh,
  mar-ree-YELL-uh [SP])
  Alternate spellings: Mariela
Marietta (mair-ree-YET-uh,
  mar-ree-YET-uh [IT])
Marilee (MAIR-ril-lee)
Marilyn (MAIR-ril-lin)
  Alternate spellings: Marilynn, Marylin,
  Marylyn, Merilyn
Mary (MAIR-ree)
  Alternate spellings: Mari*, Merry
Marybeth (mair-ree-BETH)
  Alternate spellings: Maribeth
Maryellen (mair-ree-YELL-en)
Maryjane (mair-ree-JAYN)
Maryjo (mair-ree-JOH)
Marylou (mair-ree-LOO)
  Alternate spellings: Marilou
Mercedes (mur-SAY-deez, mair-SED-ess
  or mair-THED-eth [SP])
Meredith (MAIR-ruh-dith)

Nereida (nair-RAY-duh [SP/GRK])
  Alternate spellings: Nereyda

Paris (PAIR-riss, pair-RRREE [FR])
Parisa (puh-REE-suh, pair-ree-SUH [PER])
Perla (PUR-luh, PAIR-luh [IT/SP])

Rosemarie (rohz-mair-REE [FR])
Rosemary (ROHZ-mair-ree)

Samara (suh-MAR-ruh, suh-MAIR-ruh,
  suh-MARRR-ruh with pronounced H
  at end [AR])
  Alternate spellings: Samarrah

Sarah (SAIR-ruh, SAR-ruh [HEB],
  SARRR-rah with pronounced H at
  end [AR])
  Alternate spellings: Sara
Shara (SHAR-ruh, SHAIR-ruh)
Sharon (SHAIR-ren, shar-ROHN [HEB])
  Alternate spellings: Sharron, Sharyn,
  Sharen, Sheron, Sherron
Sherlyn (SHAIR-lin)
  Alternate spellings: Cherlyn
Sherry (SHAIR-ree)
  Alternate spellings: Cherie*, Cheri,
  Sheree*, Sherrie, Cherry*, Sherri,
  Shari*, Sherie
Sierra (see-YAIR-ruh)
  Alternate spellings: Cierra, Ciera
Speranza (spair-RAWN-zuh [IT]; see also
  Esperanza)

Tamara (TAM-uh-ruh, tuh-MAR-ruh [AR/EI],
  tuh-MAIR-ruh [AA], tuh-MAR [HEB],
  TAW-mar-ruh [RUS])
  Alternate spellings: Tamera, Tamar
  [HEB], Tamarah [AR]
Tara (TAR-ruh [IR/CG], TAIR-ruh,
  TARRR-raw [EI])
  Alternate spellings: Terra, Tera, Tarah
Taryn (TAIR-rin [CG])
Teresa (tur-REE-suh, tair-REZ-uh [IT],
  tair-RESS-suh or tair-RETH-uh [SP])
  Alternate spellings: Theresa, Teressa
  (see also Tressa)
Teresita (tair-ress-SEE-taw or
  tair-ress-THEE-taw [SP])
Teri (TAIR-ree)
  Alternate spellings: Terry, Terri, Terrie
Theresia (tur-REES-ee-yuh,
  tair-RESS-ee-yuh)
Tierra (tee-YAIR-ruh)
  Alternate spellings: Tiera

Valeria (val-ur-REE-yuh,
  val-AIR-ee-yuh [IT])
Valerie (VAL-ur-ree, vaw-lair-REE [FR])
  Alternate spellings: Valarie, Valorie
Vera (VEER-ruh, VAIR-ruh [IT/SP],
  BAIR-ruh [SP])
Verda (VUR-duh, VAIR-duh, VEER-duh)
Verla (VUR-luh, VAIR-luh, VEER-duh)
Verona (vur-ROH-nuh, vair-ROH-nuh
  [IT/SP], bair-ROH-nuh [SP])
Veronica (vur-RAW-nik-uh,
  vair-ROH-nee-kuh or
  bair-ROH-nee-kuh [SP])

■ AR ■

PARTNER POINTER:
Check the short O and OW lists,
too.

Amara (uh-MAR-ruh)
Amari (uh-MAR-ree)
Amaris (AM-ur-riss, uh-MAIR-riss)
Amparo (awm-PAR-roh [SP])
Ara (AR-uh, AIR-ruh)
    Alternate spellings: Era*
Arabella (air-ruh-BELL-uh)
Araceli (air-ruh-SELL-ee, ar-raw-SELL-ee
    or ar-raw-THEL-ee [SP])
    Alternate spellings: Aracely
Ardell (ar-DELL)
Ardella (ar-DELL-uh)
Ardis (AR-diss)
Ardith (AR-dith)
Arely (AIR-ruh-lee, AR-ruh-lee,
    uh-RELL-ee)
    Alternate spellings: Areli
Aria (AR-ree-yuh [IT])
Ariana (ar-ree-YAW-nuh [HEB/IT])
    Alternate spellings: Aryana
Arianna (ar-ree-YAN-uh)
    Alternate spellings: Aryanna
Ariel (AIR-ree-yell, AR-ree-yell,
    ar-ree-YELL [HEB/FR])
Ariella (ar-ree-YELL-uh [HEB])
    Alternate spellings: Ariela
Arielle (air-ree-YELL, ar-ree-YELL [FR])
Arlene (ar-LEEN [CG])
    Alternate spellings: Arleen, Arline
Arlie (AR-lee)
    Alternate spellings: Arly
Armani (ar-MAW-nee [AA/IT])
Armida (ar-MEE-duh [SP])
Arrie (AR-ree)
Artie (ART-ee)
    Alternate spellings: Aarti [EI]
Arvilla (ar-VILL-uh)
Aurore (ar-ROR, ar-ROR-ree,
    ow-RORRR [FR])

Barb (BARB)
Barbara (BAR-bur-ruh, BAR-bar-aw [IT/SP],
    VAR-var-raw [SP]; see also Barbra)
Barbra (BAR-bruh; see also Barbara)

Carina (kar-EE-nuh [IT/SP], kuh-RIN-uh [SCAN])
    Alternate spellings: Karina
Carla (KAR-luh, KARRR-law [IT/SP])

Alternate spellings: Karla [GER]
Carlene (kar-LEEN)
    Alternate spellings: Carleen, Karlene
Carlotta (kar-LAW-tuh, karrr-LOH-taw
    [IT/SP])
Carly (KAR-lee)
    Alternate spellings: Carley, Carlie,
    Karli, Carlee, Karlee, Karlie, Karly,
    Carli, Karley
Carma (KAR-muh [HEB])
    Alternate spellings: Karma
Carmel (kar-MELL [HEB])
    Alternate spellings: Karmel
Carmela (kar-MELL-uh [HEB],
    karrr-MELL-aw [IT/SP])
    Alternate spellings: Carmella, Karmela
Carmelita (kar-mell-LEE-tuh [IT/SP])
Carmen (KAR-men [SP])
Carolina (kair-oh-LY-nuh,
    kar-oh-LEE-nuh [GER/IT/SP])
Caroline (KAIR-oh-lin, kair-oh-LYN,
    kar-oh-LEEN [FR])
    Alternate spellings: Carolyn, Karolyn,
    Carolynn
Carson (KAR-sen)
Carys (KAR-ris [WL], KAIR-ris)
Charla (SHAR-luh)
    Alternate spellings: Sharla
Charlene (shar-LEEN [FR])
    Alternate spellings: Sharlene,
    Charleen, Charline [FR]
Charles (CHARLZ, SHARL [FR])
Charlie (CHAR-lee)
Charlotte (SHAR-lutt; see also
    Charolette)
Charmaine (shar-MAYN [FR])
Charolette (SHAR-oh-lett; see also
    Charlotte)
Ciara (see-YAR-ruh, kee-YAR-ruh [IT],
    KEER-ruh [IR])
    Alternate spellings: Kiara*, Chiara [IT],
    Kira, Kiera, Keira
Clara (KLAIR-ruh, KLAR-ruh [IT/SP])
Clarabelle (KLAIR-ruh-bell,
    klar-ruh-BELL [FR])
    Alternate spellings: Claribel
Clarice (klair-REES, klar-REES [FR])
Clarine (klair-REEN, klar-REEN [FR])

Dagmar (DAG-mar [SCAN])
Damaris (DAM-ur-riss, duh-MAIR-ris,
    duh-MAR-ris)
Dara (DAR-ruh, DAW-rah with
    pronounced H at end [AR])

Darby (DAR-bee)
Darcy (DAR-see [IR], dar-SEE [FR])
    Alternate spellings: Darci, Darcie
Darla (DAR-luh)
Darlene (dar-LEEN [BR/FR])
    Alternate spellings: Darleen, Darline

Farrah (FAIR-ruh, FAR-rah or far-RAH
    with pronounced H at end [AR])
    Alternate spellings: Farah

Garnett (GAR-net)
    Alternate spellings: Garnet

Harlene (har-LEEN)
Harley (HAR-lee)
Harmony (HAR-mun-ee)

Isamar (ee-SAW-mar/ee-THAW-mar or
    EES-mar/EETH-mar [SP])

Kara (KAIR-ruh [IR], KAR-ruh)
    Alternate spellings: Cara [IT]
Kari (KAR-ree, KAIR-ree)
    Alternate spellings: Carrie*, Cari,
    Karie, Carie, Cary, Carri
Karina (kar-REE-nuh)
Katarina (kat-uh-REE-nuh,
    kaw-tar-REE-nuh [GER])
    Alternate spellings: Katerina, Katharina*
Kiara (kee-YAR-ruh [IT], KEER-ruh [IR])
    Alternate spellings: Ciara, Chiara [IT],
    Kira, Kiera, Keira

Lara (LAW-ruh [IT/SP], LAIR-ruh)
    Alternate spellings: Lera

Mara (MAR-raw [HEB/IT], MAIR-ruh)
    Alternate spellings: Maira, Marah
Marcelina (mar-sell-EE-nuh or
    mar-thell-EE-nuh [SP], mar-che-LEE-nuh
    [IT])
Marceline (mar-sell-EEN with sustained N
    [FR])
Marcella (mar-SELL-uh or mar-THELL-uh
    [SP], mar-CHELL-uh [IT])
    Alternate spellings: Marcela [SP]
Marcelle (mar-SELL [FR])
Marci (MAR-see)
    Alternate spellings: Marcie, Marcy
Margaret (MAR-gret, MAR-gur-ret)
    Alternate spellings: Margret,
    Margarett, Margarette, Margarete
Margaretta (mar-gar-RET-uh)

Margarita (mar-gar-REE-taw [SP])
Marge (MARJ)
Margie (MAR-jee, MAR-gee)
    Alternate spellings: Margy
Margit (MAR-git, mar-GEET [HUN/SCAN])
Margo (MAR-goh, mar-GOH [FR])
    Alternate spellings: Margot
Marguerite (mar-gur-REET [FR])
    Alternate spellings: Margarete
Mari (MAR-ree [SP], MAIR-ree)
    Alternate spellings: Mary*, Maree
Maria (mar-REE-yuh [IT/SP], mar-RY-yuh)
    Alternate spellings: Mariah*, Moriah*
Mariah (mar-RY-yuh, muh-RY-yuh)
    Alternate spellings: Maria*, Moriah*
Mariam (MAIR-ree-yum, MAR-ree-yum
    [AR])
    Alternate spellings: Maryam
Mariana (mar-ee-YAWN-nuh [IT/SP])
    Alternate spellings: Marianna
Maricela (mar-ree-SELL-luh or
    mar-ree-THELL-luh [SP])
    Alternate spellings: Marisela
Marie (mar-REE, mair-RHEE [FR])
    Alternate spellings: Maree
Mariel (MAIR-ree-yell, MAR-ree-yell [GER],
    mair-ree-YELL [FR])
    Alternate spellings: Marielle [FR]
Mariella (mair-ree-YELL-uh,
    mar-ree-YELL-uh [SP])
    Alternate spellings: Mariela
Marietta (mair-ree-YET-uh,
    mar-ree-YET-uh [IT])
Marilena (mar-ree-LEN-uh [IT]; see also
    Marlena)
Marina (mar-REE-naw [IT/GER/GRK/RUSS/SP])
Marisa (mar-REE-suh, mar-RISS-uh,
    mar-REE-zuh [IT])
    Alternate spellings: Marissa*
Marisol (mar-ree-SOHL or
    mar-ree-THOHL [SP])
Marissa (mar-RISS-uh, mar-REE-saw or
    mar-REE-thaw [SP])
    Alternate spellings: Marisa*
Marita (mar-REE-taw [SP])
Maritza (mar-REET-zaw)
Marjorie (MAR-jur-ree)
    Alternate spellings: Margery, Marjory
Marla (MAR-luh)
Marlena (mar-LAY-nuh, mar-LEN-uh;
    see also Marilena)
Marlene (mar-LEEN, mar-LEEN-uh [GER])
Marley (MAR-lee)
    Alternate spellings: Marlee

Marlo (MAR-loh)
Marlyn (MAR-lin)
　Alternate spellings: Marlen
Marlys (MAR-liss [GER])
　Alternate spellings: Marlis
Marna (MAR-nuh)
Marnie (MAR-nee)
Marsha (MARSH-uh)
　Alternate spellings: Marcia
Marta (MART-uh [IT/SP])
Martha (MARTH-uh)
Martina (mar-TEE-nuh [IT/SP])
Marva (MAR-vuh)
Marvel (MAR-vul, mar-VELL [FR])

Parker (PAR-kur)
Parvati (PAR-vaw-tee [EI])
　Alternate spellings: Parvathi
Pilar (pee-LAR [SP])

Rosario (rrroh-SAR-ree-yoh [IT/SP],
　rrroh-THAR-ree-yoh)

Samara (suh-MAR-ruh, suh-MAIR-ruh,
　suh-MARRR-ruh with pronounced H
　at end [AR])
　Alternate spellings: Samarrah
Sarah (SAIR-ruh, SAR-ruh [HEB],
　SARRR-rah with pronounced H at
　end [AR])
　Alternate spellings: Sara
Scarlett (SKAR-let)
　Alternate spellings: Scarlet
Shara (SHAR-ruh, SHAIR-ruh)
Sharon (SHAIR-ren, shar-ROHN [HEB])
　Alternate spellings: Sharron, Sharyn,
　Sharen, Sheron, Sherron

Tamara (TAM-uh-ruh, tuh-MAR-ruh [AR/EI],
　tuh-MAIR-ruh [AA], tuh-MAR [HEB],
　TAW-mar-ruh [RUS])
　Alternate spellings: Tamera, Tamar
　[HEB], Tamarah [AR]
Tara (TAR-ruh [IR], TAIR-ruh,
　TARRR-raw [EI])
　Alternate spellings: Terra, Tera, Tarah
Tarsha (TAR-shuh)
Tiara (tee-YAR-ruh)

Xiomara (see-yoh-MAR-aw or
　shee-yoh-MAR-raw [SP])

Yarden (YAR-den [HEB])
　Alternate spellings: Jordan*

Yareli (yar-RELL-ee [SP])
Yaritza (yar-REET-zuh [SP])

Zara (ZAR-ruh [HEB]; see also Sarah)
　Alternate spellings: Zarah
Zaria (zuh-RY-yuh, ZAR-ree-yuh)

■ LONG E (EE) ■

PARTNER POINTER:
Check the OI list, too.

Aaliyah (uh-LEE-yuh [AA], AW-lee-yuh
　[HEB/AR])
　Alternate spellings: Aliyah, Aliya,
　Aleah*, Alia
Abigail (AB-big-ayl, aw-vee-GYL [HEB])
　Alternate spellings: Abbigail, Abigayle,
　Abigale, Abagail, Avigayil [HEB]
Abby (AB-bee)
　Alternate spellings: Abbey, Abbie
Abrianna (ab-ree-YAWN-uh)
Abril (AB-rill, AY-brill, aw-BREEL [AR/SP],
　awv-REEL [SP])
Addie (ADD-ee)
Adelaide (ADD-uh-layd [GER], add-eh-LED
　or uh-dell-uh-YEED [FR])
Adelia (uh-DEE-lee-yuh,
　aw-DELL-ee-yuh [IT])
Adelina (ad-uh-LEE-nuh,
　aw-dell-LEE-nuh [IT/SP])
Adeline (AD-uh-lin, ADD-uh-lyn,
　ad-dell-LEEN with sustained N [FR])
　Alternate spellings: Adaline
Adella (uh-DELL-uh [GER], aw-DELL-uh
　[IT/SP], aw-DEE-luh or AW-dill-uh [AR])
　Alternate spellings: Adela
Adrian (AY-dree-yen)
　Alternate spellings: Adriane
Adriana (ay-dree-YAWN-uh,
　aw-dree-YAWN-uh [SP])
Adrianna (ay-dree-YAN-uh)
Adrienne (ay-dree-YAN, ay-dree-YEN
　with sustained N [FR])
　Alternate spellings: Adriane
Agostina (ag-oh-STEEN-uh [IT])
Agustina (ag-uh-STEE-nuh,
　aw-goos-TEEN-uh or
　aw-gooth-TEEN-uh [SP])
Aida (eye-YEE-duh [AR], aw-YEE-duh,
　EYE-duh, AY-duh)
　Alternate spellings: Ada*, Adah, Eda*
Aileen (AY-leen [IR], eye-LEEN)

Alternate spellings: Eileen*, Ilene, Aline*, Allene, Alene

Ainsley (AYNZ-lee)

Aisha (eye-YEE-shuh or EYE-yee-shuh [AR], aw-YEE-shuh, EYE-shuh)
Alternate spellings: Iesha

Aisling (ASH-leeng [IR])

Akiko (AW-kee-koh [JAP])

Akira (uh-KEER-uh [AA/SCOT])

Alani (uh-LAW-nee, uh-LAN-nee, uh-LAY-nee)

Albertine (al-bur-TEEN, awl-bair-TEEN with sustained N [FR])

Albina (al-BEE-nuh [IT])

Aleah (uh-LAY-yuh, uh-LEE-yuh, AW-lee-yuh [AR/HEB])
Alternate spellings: Aaliyah*, Aliyah, Aliya, Alia

Alejandra (aw-lee-HAWN-druh [SP])

Alessandra (aw-lee-SAWN-druh [IT])

Aleta (uh-LEE-duh)
Alternate spellings: Alida

Alexandria (al-ek-ZAN-dree-yuh)
Alternate spellings: Alexandrea

Alexandrie (al-ek-sawn-DREE with short N [FR]

Alexia (uh-LEK-see-yuh, al-LEK-see-uh [IT])

Ali (aw-LEE, AL-ee)
Alternate spellings: Allie*, Ally

Alice (AL-liss, al-LEES [FR])
Alternate spellings: Alyce

Alicia (uh-LEE-shuh, aw-LEE-see-yuh or aw-LEE-thee-yuh [SP])
Alternate spellings: Elisha, Alysha, Alycia, Alecia, Alesha, Alysia, Alisha

Alina (uh-LEE-nuh)
Alternate spellings: Alena

Aline (ay-LEEN, aw-LEN [FR])
Alternate spellings: Allene, Alline, Alene

Alisa (uh-LEE-suh, aw-LEE-suh [HEB/SP], aw-LEE-thuh [SP])
Alternate spellings: Elisa*, Alysa

Alize (uh-LEEZ, aw-LEEZ [FR], al-LEE-zay)

Allie (AL-lee)
Alternate spellings: Ally, Ali

Allison (AL-liss-sun, al-lee-SAW with short N [FR])
Alternate spellings: Alison, Allyson, Alyson

Almeda (al-MAY-duh, al-MEE-duh)
Alternate spellings: Almeta

Altagracia (awl-tuh-GRAW-see-yuh or awl-tuh-GRAW-thee-yuh [SP])

Althea (al-THEE-yuh)

Alvera (al-VEER-ruh, al-VAIR-ruh)

Alvina (al-VEE-nuh)
Alternate spellings: Alvena

Amalia (uh-MAW-lee-yuh [HEB])
Alternate spellings: Amalya, Amaliah

Amani (uh-MAW-nee; see also Imani)

Amari (uh-MAR-ree)

Amelia (uh-MEE-lee-yuh, aw-MELL-ee-yuh [IT])
Alternate spellings: Emilia, Emelia

Amelie (aw-may-LEE [FR]; see also Emilie)

America (uh-MAIR-rik-uh, aw-MAIR-ree-kuh [IT])

Amie (em-MAY or aw-MEE [FR], AW-mee [HEB], AY-mee)
Alternate spellings: Amy*, Aimee, Ami [HEB]

Amina (AW-min-uh or aw-MEE-nuh [HEB] with pronounced H at end [AR])

Amira (AW-mur-ruh or aw-MEER-ruh [HEB] with pronounced H at end [AR], aw-meer-RAW [HEB])

Amiya (AW-mee-yuh, uh-MY-yuh)
Alternate spellings: Amiyah, Amaya*, Amya [HEB]

Amy (AY-mee)
Alternate spellings: Aimee, Ami*, Amie*

Anahi (ann-AW-hee [SP])

Anaïs (aw-naw-YEES [FR], ann-NY-yiss)

Anastasia (aw-naw-STAW-zee-yuh or aw-naw-STAW-zhuh [RUS], ann-uh-STAY-shuh, aw-naw-STAW-see-yuh [IT], aw-naw-staw-SEE-yuh [GRK])
Alternate spellings: Anastacia

Anastasie (ann-aw-staw-ZEE [FR])

Andrea (ANN-dree-yuh, ann-DRAY-yuh [IT], awn-DRAY-yuh [SP])
Alternate spellings: Andria

Angeles (ANN-jell-ess, ANN-jell-eez, AWN-hell-ess or awn-HELL-eth [SP])

Angelia (ann-JELL-ee-yuh, awn-JELL-ee-yuh [IT])

Angelica (ann-JELL-ik-uh, awn-jell-EEK-uh, awn-HELL-ee-kuh [SP])
Alternate spellings: Anjelica

Angelina (ann-jell-EE-nuh, awn-jell-EE-nuh [IT], awn-hell-LEE-nuh [SP])

Angeline (ann-jell-EEN, ann-zhe-LEEN with sustained N [FR])

Angelique (ann-jell-LEEK, an-zhe-LEEK
    [FR])
Angelita (ann-jell-LEE-tuh,
    awn-hell-LEE-tuh [SP])
Angie (ANN-jee)
Anissa (uh-NISS-uh, aw-NEES-suh [AR])
Anita (uh-NEE-tuh, aw-NEE-tuh [IT/SP])
Anitra (uh-NEET-ruh)
Aniya (aw-NY-yuh, uh-NEE-yuh,
    AW-nee-yuh [HEB])
    Alternate spellings: Aniyah, Anaya*,
    Anya*, Analla
Anjali (AWN-jaw-lee, awn-JAW-lee,
    awn-jaw-LEE)
Annalise (ann-uh-LEES [GER/FR])
    Alternate spellings: Analise, Annelise
Annamarie (ann-uh-muh-REE,
    aw-nuh-maw-REE [FR])
Annie (ANN-ee)
Annika (AW-nik-uh or ANN-ik-uh [SCAN],
    aw-NEE-kuh [AA], aw-NEE-kuh with
    pronounced H at end [AR])
    Alternate spellings: Anika
Annis (ANN-iss, aw-NEES)
Annmarie (ann-muh-REE)
Ansley (ANZ-lee)
Antonia (ann-TOH-nee-yuh,
    awn-TOH-nee-yuh [IT/SP])
Antonietta (an-toh-nee-YETT-uh [IT])
Antonina (an-toh-NEE-nuh [IT])
Araceli (air-ruh-SELL-ee, ar-raw-SELL-ee
    or ar-raw-THEL-ee [SP])
    Alternate spellings: Aracely
Arely (AIR-ruh-lee, AR-ruh-lee,
    uh-RELL-ee)
    Alternate spellings: Areli
Aria (AR-ree-yuh [IT])
Ariana (ar-ree-YAW-nuh [HEB/IT])
    Alternate spellings: Aryana
Arianna (ar-ree-YAN-uh)
    Alternate spellings: Aryanna
Ariel (AIR-ree-yell, AR-ree-yell,
    ar-ree-YELL [HEB/FR])
Ariella (ar-ree-YELL-uh [HEB])
    Alternate spellings: Ariela
Arielle (air-ree-YELL, ar-ree-YELL [FR])
Arlene (ar-LEEN [CG])
    Alternate spellings: Arleen, Arline
Arlie (AR-lee)
    Alternate spellings: Arly
Armani (ar-MAW-nee [AA/IT])
Armida (ar-MEE-duh [SP])
Arrie (AR-ree)
Artie (ART-ee)
    Alternate spellings: Aarti [EI]

Ashanti (uh-SHAWN-tee)
Ashley (ASH-lee)
    Alternate spellings: Ashleigh, Ashlee,
    Ashly, Ashely , Ashli, Ashlie, Ashely
Asia (AY-zhuh [AA], AW-see-yuh with
    pronounced H at end [AR])
    Alternate spellings: Aja, Eja
Athena (uh-THEE-nuh)
Aubrey (AWB-ree)
    Alternate spellings: Aubree, Aubrie
Audie (AW-dee)
Audrey (AWD-ree)
    Alternate spellings: Audry
Augustine (aw-guss-TEEN, ag-oo-STEEN
    with sustained N [FR])
Aurea (OR-ree-yuh, or-RAY-yuh,
    ow-REE-yuh or ow-RAY-yuh [SP])
Aurelia (or-RELL-ee-yuh,
    ow-RELL-ee-yuh [IT])
Aurore (or-ROR, or-ROR-ree,
    ow-RORRR [FR])
Avery (AY-vur-ree)

Bailey (BAY-lee)
    Alternate spellings: Baylee, Bailee
Bambi (BAM-bee)
Beatrice (BEE-yuh-triss, bay-yuh-TREES
    [FR/SP], vay-yuh-TRITH [SP])
    Alternate spellings: Beatriz [SP]
Beatrix (BEE-yuh-triks [GER/SCAN],
    bay-yuh-TREEKS [IT])
Becky (BEK-ee)
Bellamy (BELL-uh-mee)
Benita (ben-NEE-tuh or
    ven-NEE-tuh [SP])
Bennie (BEN-ee)
Berenice (bur-NEES)
    Alternate spellings: Bernice,
    Berniece, Burnice, Berneice,
Bernardine (bur-nuh-DEEN,
    bair-nar-DEEN [FR])
    Alternate spellings: Bernadine
Bernita (bair-NEE-tuh or vair-NEE-tuh [SP],
    bur-NEE-tuh)
Bertie (BUR-tee)
Bessie (BESS-ee)
Bethany (BETH-in-nee)
Betsy (BET-see)
Bettina (bet-TEE-nuh [GER], bet-TEEN with
    sustained N [FR])
Betty (BET-ee, BED-dee)
    Alternate spellings: Bettye, Bettie
Beulah (BYOO-luh, bee-YOO-luh)
    Alternate spellings: Bulah, Beaulah,
    Beula

Beverly (BEV-ur-lee)
Alternate spellings: Beverley, Beverlee
Bianca (bee-YAWN-kuh [IT/SP],
vee-YAWN-kuh [SP])
Billie (BILL-ee)
Alternate spellings: Billye, Billy
Birdie (BUR-dee)
Bobbie (BAW-bee)
Alternate spellings: Bobbi, Bobby,
Bobbye
Bonita (boh-NEE-tuh or voh-NEE-tuh [SP])
Bonnie (BAW-nee [CG])
Alternate spellings: Bonny
Brandy (BRAN-dee)
Alternate spellings: Brandie, Brandi,
Brandee [SCAN]
Bree (BREE [CG])
Bria (BREE-yuh)
Alternate spellings: Brea
Brianna (bree-YAN-nuh or bree-YAWN-uh
[IR])
Alternate spellings: Briana, Breanna,
Bryanna, Breana, Bryana, Breonna,
Brionna
Brianne (bree-YAN, bree-YAWN [FR])
Alternate spellings: Breanne, Breann,
Briann
Brielle (bree-YELL [FR])
Brigitte (brih-GIT-uh, bree-ZHEET [FR])
Brisa (BREE-suh)
Britney (BRIT-nee)
Alternate spellings: Brittney, Brittni,
Britni, Brittny
Brittany (BRIT-uh-nee)
Alternate spellings: Britany, Brittanie
Buffy (BUFF-ee)

Callie (KAL-ee)
Alternate spellings: Cali, Kali, Kallie,
Caleigh
Camilla (kam-MILL-luh, kaw-MEE-luh [IT/SP])
Alternate spellings: Camila
Camille (kam-MEEL [FR])
Camry (KAM-ree)
Cándida (KAWN-did-uh [SP], kan-DEE-duh)
Candy (KAN-dee)
Alternate spellings: Candi, Kandi,
Kandy
Carina (kar-REE-nuh [IT/SP], kuh-RIN-uh
[SCAN])
Alternate spellings: Karina
Carlene (kar-LEEN)
Alternate spellings: Carleen, Karlene
Carly (KAR-lee)
Alternate spellings: Carley, Carlie,

Karli, Carlee, Karlee, Karlie, Karly,
Carli, Karley
Carmelita (kar-mell-LEE-tuh [IT/SP])
Carolee (KAIR-oh-lee)
Carolina (kair-oh-LY-nuh,
kar-oh-LEE-nuh [GER/IT/SP])
Caroline (KAIR-oh-lin, kair-oh-LYN,
kar-oh-LEEN [FR])
Alternate spellings: Carolyn, Karolyn,
Carolynn
Carrie (KAIR-ree)
Alternate spellings: Kerri, Kerry, Kari*,
Cari, Carey, Karrie, Karie, Carie, Cary,
Carri, Kerrie
Casey (KAY-see)
Alternate spellings: Kasey, Kacie,
Kaci, Casie, Kacy
Cassidy (KASS-sid-ee [IR])
Alternate spellings: Kassidy
Cassie (KASS-ee)
Alternate spellings: Kassie
Catalina (kat-uh-LEE-nuh,
kaw-taw-LEE-nuh [SP])
Catherine (KATH-ur-rin, kat-REEN [FR];
see also Kathrine)
Alternate spellings: Katheryn,
Katharine, Catharine
Catina (kat-EE-nuh)
Cecil (SESS-ill, SEE-sill)
Cecile (sess-SEEL, say-SEEL [FR])
Alternate spellings: Cecile [FR]
Cecilia (se-SEE-lee-yuh [IT/SP],
che-CHEE-lee-uh [IT],
the-THEE-lee-yuh [SP])
Alternate spellings: Cecelia [CG]
Cecily (SESS-ill-ee [CG])
Cedar (SEE-dur)
Ceil (SEEL)
Celestina (sell-ess-TEE-nuh,
chell-ess-TEE-nuh [IT])
Celestine (sell-ess-TEEN,
say-less-TEEN [FR])
Alternate spellings: Célestine [FR]
Celia (SEE-lee-yuh or THEE-lee-yuh [SP])
Alternate spellings: Selia [CG]
Celina (che-LEE-nuh [IT], sell-LEE-nuh)
Alternate spellings: Selena*, Selina,
Salina
Celine (sell-EEN, say-LEEN [FR])
Alternate spellings: Céline [FR]
Ceres (SEER-reez, sair-REES [FR])
Alternate spellings: Cerise [FR]
Charisse (shuh-REES, shair-RRREEZ [FR])
Alternate spellings: Cherise
Charity (CHAIR-rit-ee)

Charlene (shar-LEEN [FR])
  Alternate spellings: Sharlene,
  Charleen, Charline [FR]
Charlie (CHAR-lee)
Chasity (CHAS-sit-ee)
Chastity (CHAS-tit-ee)
Chelsea (CHEL-see, SHELL-zee)
  Alternate spellings: Chelsey, Chelsi
Cherie (shair-REE [FR], SHAIR-ree,
  shuh-REE, CHAIR-ree)
  Alternate spellings: Cheri, Sheree*,
  Sherrie, Sherie Cherry*, Sherry*)
Cherry (CHAIR-ree, SHAIR-ree)
  Alternate spellings: Cherie*, Cheri,
  Sherry*, Sherrie, Sherie
Chiquita (chee-KEE-tuh [SP])
Chloë (KLOH-wee [GRK], kloh-WAY [FR])
  Alternate spellings: Chloé
Chrissy (KRIS-see)
  Alternate spellings: Crissy
Christen (KRISS-sen, KRISS-ten,
  krees-TA with short N [FR])
  Alternate spellings: Kristen*
Christian (KRISS-chen, kree-stee-YAN [FR])
  Alternate spellings: Kristian,
  Christiane [FR]
Christiana (kris-tee-YAWN-uh,
  krees-tee-YAWN-aw [IT])
  Alternate spellings: Cristiana
Christina (kris-TEE-nuh, kree-STEE-nuh
  [IT/SP], kreeth-TEE-nuh [SP])
  Alternate spellings: Kristina, Cristina
  [IT/SP], Krystina
Christine (kris-TEEN, kree-STEEN [FR])
  Alternate spellings: Kristine,
  Christene, Christeen
Christy (KRIS-tee)
  Alternate spellings: Kristy, Kristie,
  Cristy, Christie, Christi
Ciara (see-YAR-ruh, kee-YAR-ruh [IT],
  KEER-ruh [IR])
  Alternate spellings: Kiara*, Chiara [IT],
  Kira, Kiera, Keira
Cindy (SIN-dee)
  Alternate spellings: Cindi, Cyndi
Citlali (sit-LAW-lee)
Clarice (klair-REES, klar-REES [FR])
Clarine (klair-REEN, klar-REEN [FR])
Claudia (KLAW-dee-yuh, KLOW-dee-yuh
  [IT/SP])
Claudie (KLAW-dee, kloh-DEE [FR])
Claudine (klaw-DEEN, kloh-DEEN with
  sustained N [FR])
Clementina (klem-en-TEE-nuh [IT/SP])

Clementine (KLEM-en-tyn, klem-en-
  TEEN with sustained N [FR])
Clemmie (KLEM-mee, klem-MEE [FR])
Cleo (KLEE-yoh, KLAY-oh [FR])
  Alternate spellings: Cléo
Cleora (klee-YOR-ruh)
Cleta (KLEE-tuh)
Clotilde (kloh-TIL-dee or kloh-TIL-duh [GER],
  kloh-TEELD [FR], kloh-TEEL-deh [IT])
  Alternate spellings: Clothilde [FR]
Cody (KOH-dee)
Colleen (kaw-LEEN [IR], koh-LEEN)
  Alternate spellings: Coleen
Concepcion (kohn-sep-see-YOHN or
  kohn-thep-thee-YOHN [SP])
Connie (KAW-nee)
Cordelia (kor-DEE-lee-yuh [SP])
Cordia (KOR-dee-yuh)
Cordie (KOR-dee)
Corina (kor-REE-nuh [SP])
  Alternate spellings: Corinna
Corinne (kor-REEN [GRK/FR], kor-RIN)
  Alternate spellings: Corrine, Corine,
  Corene, Coreen
Cornelia (kor-NEE-lee-yuh)
Courtney (KORT-nee)
  Alternate spellings: Kourtney,
  Kortney, Cortney
Creola (kree-YOH-luh [NA])
Crystal (KRIS-tell, krees-TAWL or
  krees-TELL [FR])
  Alternate spellings: Krystal, Cristal,
  Kristal, Krystle, Chrystal, Christal,
  Christel, Christelle [FR]
Cybelle (see-BELL [FR]; see also Sybil)
  Alternate spellings: Cybele [SCAN]
Cynthia (SIN-thee-yuh)

Dagny (DAG-nee)
Daisy (DAY-zee)
Dalia (DAW-lee-yuh [HEB], DAL-lee-yuh [SCAN])
  Alternate spellings: Dahlia, Daliah,
  Daliya or Dalya [HEB]
Dania (DAN-ee-yuh, DAY-nee-yuh,
  duh-NEE-yuh or duh-NY-yuh [AA],
  DAWN-yuh or DAW-nee-yuh [HEB])
  Alternate spellings: Daniya, Danya
Danita (duh-NEE-tuh, daw-NEE-tuh)
  Alternate spellings: Donita
Darby (DAR-bee)
Darcy (DAR-see [IR], dar-SEE [FR])
  Alternate spellings: Darci, Darcie
Darian (DAIR-ree-yen)
Darlene (dar-LEEN [BR/FR])

Alternate spellings: Darleen, Darline

Dasia (DAY-zhuh [AA], DAY-shuh [GRK/RUS], DAY-see-yuh)

Davina (duh-VEE-nuh, daw-VEE-nuh [HEB/IT])

Dean (DEEN)

Deann (dee-YAN, dee-YAWN [FR])
Alternate spellings: Deanne, Dionne*

Deanna (dee-YAN-uh, dee-YAWN-uh)
Alternate spellings: Deana

Deasia (dee-YAY-zhuh, dee-YAY-see-yuh)

Debbie (DEB-ee)
Alternate spellings: Debbi, Debby, Debi

Dee (DEE)

Deedee (DEE-dee)

Deepa (DEE-puh [EI])

Deidre (DEED-ruh [CG], DEED-ree)
Alternate spellings: Deidra, Dedra

Deirdre (DEER-druh or DAIR-druh [IR], DEER-dree)

Delaney (del-AY-nee)

Delia (DEE-lee-yuh, DEL-ee-yah [IT/SP])

Delisa (del-EE-suh)

Delfina (del-FEE-nuh [IT/SP])

Delphia (del-FEE-yuh)

Delphine (del-FEEN [FR])

Demetria (dem-MEET-ree-yuh)

Demi (dem-MEE [FR])

Deneen (duh-NEEN [AA/IR])
Alternate spellings: Denene

Denise (den-NEES, den-NEEZ [FR])
Alternate spellings: Denisse, Denice

Desiree (DEZ-ih-ray, dez-ee-RAY [FR])
Alternate spellings: Desirae

Dessie (DES-see)

Destiny (DESS-tin-ee)
Alternate spellings: Destinee, Destiney, Destini

Diana (dy-YAN-uh, dee-YAWN-uh [IT/SP])
Alternate spellings: Dayana*, Dianna

Diane (dy-YAN, dee-YAN [FR])
Alternate spellings: Diann, Dianne, Dian, Deann*, Deanne, Dionne*

Dina (DEE-nuh [IT], DY-nuh, dee-NAW [HEB])
Alternate spellings: Dena, Deena, Deana, Dinah

Dionne (DEE-yawn [AA], dee-YAW with short N [FR/GRK])
Alternate spellings: Diane*, Diann, Dianne, Dian, Deann*, Deanne

Dixie (DIK-see)

Dolly (DAW-lee)
Alternate spellings: Dollie

Dominga (doh-MEEN-guh [SP])

Dominique (daw-min-EEK, doh-mee-NEEK [FR])
Alternate spellings: Dominque, Domonique

Donnie (DAW-nee)

Doreen (dor-REEN)
Alternate spellings: Dorene, Dorine

Dori (DOR-ree [GRK/HEB])

Dorothea (dor-roh-THEE-yuh)

Dorothy (DOR-roh-thee)
Alternate spellings: Dorathy

Dorthy (DOR-thee)

Dottie (DAW-tee)

Dovie (DUV-ee)

Earlene (ur-LEEN [CG])
Alternate spellings: Earline, Erlene

Easter (EES-tur)

Ebony (EBB-uh-nee [AA])
Alternate spellings: Eboni

Eda (ED-duh, EE-duh, AY-duh)
Alternate spellings: Ada*

Eddie (ED-ee)

Eden (EE-den [HEB])

Edie (EED-ee)

Edith (EE-dith)
Alternate spellings: Edythe

Edrie (ED-ree, EED-ree)

Edwina (ed-WEE-nuh)

Effie (EFF-ee)

Eileen (eye-LEEN [CG])
Alternate spellings: Aileen*, Ilene

Elaine (ee-LAYN)
Alternate spellings: Elayne

Elana (ee-law-NAW [HEB], ell-LAW-nuh; see also Elena)
Alternate spellings: Ilana*, Alana*, Alanna*

Eleanora (el-len-NOR-ruh, el-lee-yuh-NOR-ruh, eh-lay-oh-NOR-uh [IT/SP])
Alternate spellings: Elenora, Eleonora [IT/SP] (see also Elnora)

Electa (el-LEK-tuh or ee-LEK-tuh)

Elena (uh-LAY-nuh, ee-LAY-nuh, ell-LAY-nuh [SP], ELL-en-uh [IT])
Alternate spellings: Alaina, Alayna, Elaina, Alena, Alayna, Alaina (see Helena)

Elfrieda (el-FREE-duh)

Eliana (el-lee-YAW-nuh [IT/SP], ELL-ee-yaw-nuh [HEB]; see also Iliana)

Elida (el-LEE-duh or el-LY-duh)

Elisa (ee-LEE-suh, el-LEE-suh or

el-LEETH-uh [SP], uh-LEE-suh)
Alternate spellings: Alisa, Alysa
Elise (ee-LEES, el-LEES [GER], ay-LEEZ [FR])
Alternate spellings: Elyse, Elease,
Elise [FR]
Eliza (uh-LY-zuh, ee-LY-zuh, el-LEE-zuh [IT])
Alternate spellings: Aliza, Alizah,
Aleeza [HEB]
Elizabeth (el-LIZ-uh-beth, el-lee-SHEE-vuh
[HEB], el-lee-zuh-BET [FR])
Alternate spellings: Elisabeth [FR],
Elisheva or Elisheba [HEB]
Ellie (EL-lee)
Elmira (el-MY-ruh, el-MEER-ruh)
Elois (el-OH-wiss, EE-loh-wiss,
EL-oh-weez)
Alternate spellings: Eloise*, Elouise
Eloisa (el-oh-WEE-suh)
Eloise (EL-oh-weez, el-oh-WEEZ,
ay-loh-WEEZ [FR])
Alternate spellings: Elouise, Elois*,
Éloisé [FR]
Elsie (EL-see [GER])
Elvera (el-VEER-ruh [IT], el-VAIR-ruh)
Elvia (EL-vee-yuh, el-VEE-yuh)
Emelina (em-uh-LEEN-uh [GER/SP/RUS])
Emeline (em-uh-LEEN with sustained N
[FR], em-uh-LYN, EM-uh-lin)
Alternate spellings: Emmeline,
Emmaline, Emelyn, Emaleen
Emiko (EM-ee-koh [JAP])
Emilia (eh-MEE-lee-yuh [IT],
uh-MEE-lee-yuh)
Alternate spellings: Emelia, Amelia*
Emilie (em-el-LEE [FR], EM-ill-ee; see also
Amelie)
Alternate spellings: Emily*, Emilee,
Emely, Emmalee
Emily (EM-ill-ee)
Alternate spellings: Emilee, Emely,
Emilie*, Emmalee
Emmie (EM-mee)
Alternate spellings: Emmy, Eme, Emi
[JAP]
Ena (EE-nuh)
Enid (EE-nid)
Enola (ee-NOH-luh)
Enriqueta (en-ree-KET-tuh [SP])
Era (EER-ruh, AIR-ruh)
Alternate spellings: Ara*
Erica (AIR-rik-uh [SCAN], AIR-ree-kuh [IT])
Alternate spellings: Erika, Ericka
Erlinda (ur-LIN-duh, air-LEEN-duh [SP])
Ermina (ur-MEE-nuh, air-MEE-nuh [SP];

see also Hermina)
Ernestina (ur-ness-TEE-nuh,
air-ness-TEE-nuh [IT])
Ernestine (UR-ness-teen)
Alternate spellings: Earnestine
Essie (ESS-ee [HEB])
Estefania (es-tef-FAWN-ee-yuh or
eth-tef-FAWN-ee-yuh [SP])
Estefany (es-TEF-en-ee, es-tef-FAWN-ee)
Alternate spellings: Estefani
Ethelene (eth-ell-LEEN)
Étienne (ay-tee-YEN [FR])
Ettie (ET-ee, ED-ee)
Eugenia (yoo-JEE-nee-yuh,
yoo-JAY-nee-yuh, oo-JEN-ee-yuh [IT],
ay-yoo-HAY-nee-yuh [SP])
Eugenie (yoo-JEE-nee, yoo-JAY-nee,
ay-yoo-HAY-nee [SP], oo-zhay-NEE [FR])
Alternate spellings: Eugénie [FR]
Eulalia (yoo-LAY-lee-yuh,
ay-yoo-LAW-lee-yuh [SP])
Eulalie (yoo-LAY-lee, oo-law-LEE [FR])
Eva (EE-vuh, EV-uh [IT], AY-vuh [SP])
Alternate spellings: Ava*, Iva*
Evangelina (ev-van-jell-LEE-nuh [IT],
ay-vawn-hell-LEE-nuh [SP])
Evangeline (ev-an-jell-LEEN)
Eve (EEV, EV, CHAW-vuh with
guttural CH [HEB])
Alternate spellings: Chava [HEB]
Evelyne (ee-vuh-LEEN, ev-uh-LEEN)
Alternate spellings: Eveline [FR]
Evie (EE-vee)
Exie (EK-see)

Fabiola (fab-ee-YOH-luh)
Fairy (FAIR-ree)
Fannie (FAN-ee)
Alternate spellings: Fanny
Fatima (FAW-tim-uh or FAWT-muh [AR],
fat-EE-muh [IT])
Felicia (fell-LEE-shuh, fell-LEE-see-yuh
or fell-LEE-thee-yuh [SP])
Alternate spellings: Felecia, Felisha
Felicitá (fel-ee-chee-TAW [IT])
Felicity (fell-LISS-sit-ee)
Felipa (fell-LEE-puh [SP]
Filomena (fee-loh-MEN-uh [IT/SP],
fill-oh-MEE-nuh)
Alternate spellings: Philomena*
Fiona (fee-YOH-nuh [IR])
Fleta (FLEE-tuh)
Florine (flor-REEN)
Alternate spellings: Florene

Florrie (FLOR-ree)
Flossie (FLAW-see)
Francine (fran-SEEN, frawn-SEEN with sustained N [FR])
Francisca (fran-SIS-kuh, fran-SEES-kuh or fran-THEETH-kuh [SP])
Frankie (FRAYN-kee)
Freddie (FRED-ee)
Frida (FREE-duh [GER/HEB])
Alternate spellings: Freda, Freida, Frieda, Freeda

Gabriel (GAY-bree-yell, gaw-bree-ELL or gaw-vree-ELL [HEB], gab-brrree-YELL [FR/SP/IT])
Alternate spellings: Gavriel [HEB]
Gabriela (gaw-bree-YELL-uh [SP], gab-ree-YELL-uh, gaw-vree-ELL-uh [HEB])
Alternate spellings: Gabriella*, Gavriela [HEB]
Gabriella (gab-ree-YELL-uh [IT], gaw-vree-ELL-uh [HEB])
Alternate spellings: Gabriela*, Gavriela [HEB]
Gabrielle (gab-ree-YELL [FR], gaw-bree-YELL)
Galilea (gal-ee-LAY-yuh, gal-ee-LEE-yuh)
Genevieve (JEN-uh-veev [CG], zhen-uh-vee-YEV or zhawn-vee-YEV [FR])
Alternate spellings: Geneviève
Genoveva (jen-oh-VEE-vuh, jen-oh-VAY-vuh)
Georgene (jor-JEEN, zhor-ZHEEN with sustained N [FR])
Alternate spellings: Georgine
Georgiana (jor-jee-YAN-nuh)
Alternate spellings: Georgianna
Georgianne (jor-jee-YAN, zhor-zhee-YAW with short N [FR])
Alternate spellings: Georgiane
Georgie (JOR-jee)
Georgina (jor-JEE-nuh)
Alternate spellings: Giorgina
Geraldine (jair-rull-DEEN)
Alternate spellings: Jeraldine
Gertie (GUR-dee)
Gia (JEE-yuh)
Giada (JAW-duh [IT], jee-YAW-duh, JAY-duh)
Alternate spellings: Jada*, Jayda, Jaida

Gianna (jee-YAWN-uh or JAW-nuh [IT])
Alternate spellings: Giana, Jana*, Janna, Johnna, Jonna
Gigi (JEE-jee [IT], zhee-ZHEE [FR])
Gillian (GIL-ee-yen [CG], JIL-ee-yen)
Alternate spellings: Jillian*
Gina (JEE-nuh [IT])
Alternate spellings: Jena, Jeanna, Jeana, Gena
Ginny (JIN-ee; see also Jenny)
Giovanna (joh-VAW-nuh [IT], jee-yoh-VAW-nuh)
Giselle (jiz-ELL, zhee-ZELL [FR])
Alternate spellings: Gisselle, Jizelle
Glennie (GLEN-ee)
Gloria (GLOR-ree-yuh [IT/SP])
Goldia (GOHL-dee-yuh)
Goldie (GOHL-dee)
Gracie (GRAY-see)
Graciela (graw-see-YELL-uh or graw-thee-YELL-uh [SP])
Gregoria (gre-GOR-ree-yuh [IT])
Griselda (griz-ELL-duh [GER], gree-SELL-duh or gree-THELL-duh [SP])
Alternate spellings: Grizelda
Guillermina (yair-MEE-nuh [SP])
Guinevere (GWIN-uh-veer [WL])
Gussie (GUS-see)

Hadley (HAD-lee)
Hailey (HAY-lee)
Alternate spellings: Haley, Hayley, Haylee, Hailee, Haleigh, Hailie, Haylie, Halie, Hali, Hayleigh
Hallie (HAL-ee)
Alternate spellings: Halle [SCAN], Haleigh, Halie, Hali
Harlene (har-LEEN)
Harley (HAR-lee)
Harmony (HAR-mun-ee)
Harriet (HAIR-ree-yet [GER])
Alternate spellings: Harriett, Harriette
Hassie (HAS-see)
Hattie (HAD-ee)
Haydee (HAY-dee)
Heidi (HY-dee [GER])
Helene (hel-LEEN, ay-LEN with sustained N [FR])
Alternate spellings: Hélène
Henrietta (hen-ree-YET-uh [GER])
Henriette (hen-ree-YET [GER], aw-ree-YET with short N [FR])
Hermina (hur-MEE-nuh, air-MEE-nuh [SP]; see also Ermina)

Hermine (hur-MEEN)
Herminia (air-MEE-nee-yuh [SP],
    hur-MIN-ee-yuh, hur-MEE-nee-yuh)
Hermione (hur-MY-yoh-nee [BR])
Hettie (HED-ee)
Hilde (HIL-dee [SCAN])
Hillary (HIL-ur-ree)
    Alternate spellings: Hilary
Hiroko (HEE-roh-koh [JAP])
Holly (HAW-lee)
    Alternate spellings: Hollie, Holli
Honey (HUN-ee)
Hortencia (hor-TEN-see-yuh,
    or-TEN-see-yuh or
    or-TEN-thee-yuh [SP])
    Alternate spellings: Hortensia

Icie (EYE-see, ISS-ee)
Ida (EYE-duh [GER], EE-duh [IR])
    Alternate spellings: Ide
Ilana (ill-LAW-nuh, uh-LAW-nuh,
    ee-law-NAW [HEB])
    Alternate spellings: Alana*, Alanna*,
    Elana*
Iliana (ill-ee-YAW-nuh [SP]; see also Eliana)
    Alternate spellings: Ileana
Ilona (ee-LOH-nuh [HUN])
Ima (EYE-muh, EE-muh)
Imani (im-AW-nee [AA], ee-MEN-ee [AR];
    see also Amani)
Imelda (ee-MEL-duh [SP])
Imogene (IM-oh-jeen or IM-oh-jen [BR])
    Alternate spellings: Emogene, Imogen,
Ina (EYE-nuh, EE-nuh)
India (IN-dee-yuh)
Inez (ee-NEZ, eye-NESS or eye-NETH
    [SP], ee-NESS [FR])
    Alternate spellings: Inès [FR]
Inga (EEN-guh [SCAN])
    Alternate spellings: Inge
Ingeborg (EEN-guh-borg [SCAN])
Ingrid (EEN-grid [SCAN])
Ione (eye-YOH-nee, eye-YOHN [FR])
Irene (eye-REEN, ee-RAY-nuh [HUN],
    ee-REN or ee-ray-NAY [FR])
    Alternate spellings: Irène or Iréné
Irma (UR-muh [GER], YEER-muh [IT],
    EER-muh [SP])
    Alternate spellings: Erma
Isabel (IZ-uh-bell, ee-zaw-BELL [FR],
    EE-saw-bell or ee-saw-BELL or ee-
    thuh-VELL [SP])
    Alternate spellings: Isabelle [FR],
    Isabell, Isobel

Isabela (iz-uh-BELL-uh, ee-saw-BELL-uh
    or ee-thaw-VELL-uh [SP],
    ee-zuh-BELL-uh [IT])
    Alternate spellings: Isabella [IT], Izabela
Isadora (iz-uh-DOR-ruh, ee-saw-DOR-ruh
    [IT/SP], ee-thaw-DOR-ruh [SP])
Isadore (IZ-uh-dor, ee-see-DOR [FR])
    Alternate spellings: Isidore [FR]
Isamar (ee-SAW-mar/ee-THAW-mar or
    EES-mar/EETH-mar [SP])
Itzel (IT-sell, eet-ZELL [NA])
Iva (EYE-vuh, EE-vuh)
    Alternate spellings: Ivah, Eva*
Ivelisse (ee-vuh-LEES, eye-vuh-LEES)
Ivory (EYE-vor-ree)
Ivy (EYE-vee)

Jacey (JAY-see)
    Alternate spellings: Jaycee
Jackie (JAK-ee)
    Alternate spellings: Jacque*
Jacque (ZHAWK [FR], JAK-ee)
    Alternate spellings: Jackie*
Jacqueline (JAK-uh-lin, JAK-well-lin,
    jak-LEEN, zhawk-uh-LEEN with
    sustained N [FR])
    Alternate spellings: Jaqueline,
    Jaquelyn, Jackeline, Jaquelin,
    Jacquline, Jacalyn
Jalisa (juh-LEE-suh [AA], JAL-iss-uh [AR];
    see also Julissa)
Jaliyah (juh-LEE-yuh [AA])
Jamie (JAY-mee)
    Alternate spellings: Jaime, Jami,
    Jaimie, Jayme, Jammie
Jamila (juh-MEEL-uh with pronounced H
    at end [AR])
Janice (JAN-iss, juh-NEES [AA])
    Alternate spellings: Janis
Janie (JAY-nee)
Janine (jan-NEEN)
Janiya (jan-NY-yuh, jan-NEE-yuh [AR])
    Alternate spellings: Janiyah
Jannie (JAN-nee)
Jasmine (JAZ-min, jass-MEEN,
    (JAS-oo-meen [JAP]), yaz-MEEN [AR],
    yass-MEEN [HEB/PER])
    Alternate spellings: Jasmin, Jazmin,
    Jazmine, Jazmyn, Jasmyn, Jazmyne,
    Yasmin*, Yazmin, Yasmine*, Yasmeen
Jaylene (jay-LEEN)
Jean (JEEN [CG], ZHAN [FR])
    Alternate spellings: Jeanne [FR], Gene,
    Jeane

Jeanine (jen-NEEN [CG], zhan-NEEN [FR])
Alternate spellings: Janeen
Jeannie (JEE-nee)
Alternate spellings: Jeanie, Genie
Jennifer (JEN-nif-ur [WL], zheh-nee-FAIR [FR])
Alternate spellings: Jenifer, Genifer
Jenny (JEN-ee; see also Ginny)
Alternate spellings: Jennie, Geni
Jeri (JAIR-ree)
Alternate spellings: Jerri, Geri, Gerri, Jerry, Gerry, Jerrie
Jerline (jur-LEEN [AA])
Jessenia (jes-SAY-nee-yuh, jes-SEN-ee-yuh, yes-SEE-nuh [AR], hes-SAY-nee-yuh or he-THAY-nee-yuh [SP])
Alternate spellings: Yessenia*
Jessie (JESS-ee)
Alternate spellings: Jesse, Jessi
Jettie (JET-ee)
Jillian (JIL-ee-yen)
Alternate spellings: Gillian*
Jimmie (JIM-ee)
Jocelyn (JAW-sell-lin, JAWS-lin, zhoh-sell-LEEN [FR], yoh-SELL-een [SP])
Alternate spellings: Joselyn, Joceline [FR], Joycelyn*, Yoselin*
Jodie (JOH-dee)
Alternate spellings: Jodi, Jody
Joey (JOH-wee)
Johnnie (JAW-nee)
Alternate spellings: Jonnie, Johnie
Jolene (joh-LEEN)
Jolie (JOH-lee, joh-LEE, zho-LEE [FR])
Joni (JOH-nee)
Alternate spellings: Joanne
Josefina (joh-sef-FEE-nuh, ho-sef-FEE-nuh or ho-thef-FEE-nuh [SP])
Alternate spellings: Josephina
Josephine (joh-sef-FEEN, zho-zay-FEEN with sustained N [FR])
Alternate spellings: Joséphine
Josie (JOH-see, zho-SAY [FR])
Alternate spellings: Josée [FR]
Jothi (JOH-tee [EI])
Journey (JUR-nee)
Jovita (joh-VEE-tuh [AA], ho-VEE-tuh or ho-BEE-tuh [SP])
Judith (JOO-dith, zhoo-DEET [FR], YOO-dit or yuh-HOO-dit [HEB])
Alternate spellings: Yudit or Yehudit* [HEB]

Judy (JOO-dee)
Alternate spellings: Judi, Judie
Julia (JOO-lee-yuh, HOO-lee-yuh [SP])
Alternate spellings: Giulia [IT]
Juliana (joo-lee-YAWN-uh [IT], joo-lee-YAN-uh, hoo-lee-YAWN-uh [SP], yoo-lee-YAWN-nuh [SP/RUS])
Alternate spellings: Julianna, Giuliana [IT], Yuliana* [RUS]
Julianne (joo-lee-YAN, zhoo-lee-YEN [FR])
Alternate spellings: Juliann, Julienne [FR]
Julie (JOO-lee, zhoo-LEE [FR])
Alternate spellings: Juli
Juliet (JOO-lee-yet, zhoo-lee-YET [FR])
Alternate spellings: Juliet, Juliette
Justina (jus-TEE-nuh)
Justine (juh-STEEN, zhoo-STEEN with sustained N [FR])

Kaliyah (KAW-lee-yuh or kuh-LEE-yuh [AA], kaw-LEE-yuh [HW])
Alternate spellings: Kalia [HW]
Kami (KAM-ee)
Kaori (KOW-ree [JAP])
Kari (KAR-ree, KAIR-ree)
Alternate spellings: Carrie*, Cari, Karie, Carie, Cary, Carri
Karina (kar-REE-nuh)
Karyme (kuh-REE-muh [AR], kaw-REEM)
Katarina (kat-uh-REE-nuh, kaw-tar-REE-nuh [GER])
Alternate spellings: Katerina, Katharina*
Kathaleen (kath-uh-LEEN)
Katharina (kath-ur-REE-nuh, kat-uh-REE-nuh)
Alternate spellings: Katarina*, Katerina
Kathleen (kath-LEEN [CG])
Alternate spellings: Cathleen
Kathrine (KATH-rin, kath-REEN; see also Catherine)
Alternate spellings: Cathryn, Cathrine, Kathryn [CG], Kathryne
Kathy (KATH-ee [CG])
Alternate spellings: Cathy, Kathi, Kathie, Cathie, Cathey, Cathi
Katie (KAY-tee, kaw-TEE [FR])
Alternate spellings: Katy, Kati
Katrina (kat-REE-nuh or kaw-TREE-nuh [GER])
Alternate spellings: Catrina
Kattie (KAT-ee)

Kaylee (KAY-lee)
Alternate spellings: Kailey, Kayleigh, Kaylie, Kaleigh, Kaley, Kailee, Kayley, Kayli, Kali, Caleigh, Keli [HW]
Kecia (KEE-see-yuh or KEE-shee-yuh or KEE-shuh [AA])
Alternate spellings: Keisha*, Keshia*, Kisha, Keesha
Keely (KEE-lee [CG])
Alternate spellings: Keeley, Kiele*
Keiki (KAY-kee or kay-YEE-kee [HW])
Keisha (KEE-shuh [AA])
Alternate spellings: Kisha, Keesha, Kecia*, Keshia*
Keishla (KEESH-luh)
Kelly (KEL-lee)
Alternate spellings: Kelley, Kelli, Kellie
Kelsey (KEL-see)
Alternate spellings: Kelsie, Kelsea, Kelsi, Kelcie
Kennedy (KEN-uh-dee)
Alternate spellings: Kennedi
Kenzie (KEN-zee; see also Kinsey)
Keshia (KEE-shee-yuh or KEE-shuh [AA])
Alternate spellings: Kisha, Keesha, Kecia*, Keisha*
Khadijah (kud-DEE-zhuh or kud-DEED-juh [AA], chu-DEE-juh with guttural CH at beginning and pronounced H at end [AR])
Kiana (kee-YAW-naw)
Alternate spellings: Kianna, Quiana
Kiara (kee-YAR-ruh [IT], KEER-ruh [IR])
Alternate spellings: Ciara, Chiara [IT], Kira, Kiera, Keira
Kiele (kee-YAY-lay [HW], KEE-lee)
Alternate spellings: Keely*, Keeley
Kierra (kee-YAIR-ruh)
Kimberly (KIM-bur-lee)
Alternate spellings: Kimberlee, Kimberley, Kimberli
Kinsey (KIN-zee; see also Kenzie)
Kirsten (KEER-sten [SCAN], KURS-ten)
Alternate spellings: Kirstin, Kiersten, Kierstin
Kirstie (KEER-stee, KURS-tee)
Kitty (KIT-tee)
Alternate spellings: Kittie
Kizzy (KIZ-ee)
Kori (KOR-ree)
Alternate spellings: Corey, Cori, Cory, Corrie,
Kya (KEE-yuh, KY-yuh)

Alternate spellings: Kiya, Kia, Kaya*, Kaia, Kaiya [JAP]
Kyla (KY-luh or KEE-luh [IR])
Alternate spellings: Kayla*, Kaila, Cayla, Keyla, Kaylah, Kaela, Keila
Kylie (KY-lee [CG])
Alternate spellings: Kylee, Kiley, Kyleigh

Lacey (LAY-see)
Alternate spellings: Lacy, Lacie, Laci
Laisha (ly-YEE-shuh [AA])
Lakeisha (luh-KEE-shuh [AA])
Alternate spellings: Lakisha, Lakesha
Lakeshia (luh-KEE-shee-yuh [AA])
Laney (LAY-nee)
Laquita (luh-KWEE-tuh or luh-KEE-tuh)
Latrice (luh-TREES [AA])
Lavera (luh-VEER-ruh)
Lavina (luh-VEE-nuh [AA])
Lavinia (luh-VIN-ee-yuh; see also Luvenia)
Lea (LEE-yuh, LAY-yuh [HEB])
Alternate spellings: Leah, Lia, Leia
Leandra (lee-YAN-druh, lee-YAWN-druh)
Leanna (lee-YAN-nuh, lee-YAW-nuh [IT])
Alternate spellings: Liana [IT]
Leanne (lee-YAN, lay-YAW with short N [FR])
Alternate spellings: Leeann, Leann
Leatrice (LEE-yuh-triss, LAY-yuh-triss, lee-yuh-TREES, lay-uh-TREES)
Leena (LEE-nuh [RUS])
Leigh (LEE)
Alternate spellings: Lee
Leila (LEE-luh, LAY-luh [AR/HEB/PER])
Alternate spellings: Laila, Leila, Layla*, Lela, Lelah, Lyla
Leilani (lay-LAWN-ee [HW])
Lelia (LEE-lee-yuh, LAY-lee-yuh, LEL-ee-yuh [IT])
Lempi (LEM-pee [SCAN])
Lena (LEE-nuh, LEN-uh [IT])
Alternate spellings: Lina*, Lenna
Lennie (LEN-nee)
Leola (lee-YOH-luh, lay-YOH-luh)
Leona (lee-YOH-nuh, lay-YOH-nuh)
Leone (lee-YOH-nee [GER], lay-yoh-NEE [FR])
Alternate spellings: Léonie [FR]
Leonor (LEE-yoh-nor, len-NOR)
Alternate spellings: Leonore, Lenore*
Leonora (lee-yoh-NOR-ruh, lay-oh-NOR-uh [IT/SP])

Alternate spellings: Eleonora [IT/SP],
   Lenora*
Leora (lee-YOR-ruh [HEB])
   Alternate spellings: Liora
Leota (lee-YOH-tuh)
Lesia (LEE-shuh [AA], LEE-see-yuh)
   Alternate spellings: Lisha
Leslie (LES-lee)
   Alternate spellings: Lesly, Lesley, Lesli
Lessie (LES-see)
Leta (LEE-duh)
   Alternate spellings: Lida [RUS]
Letha (LEETH-uh)
   Alternate spellings: Leatha
Leticia (luh-TEE-shuh, let-EE-see-yuh or
   let-EE-thee-yuh [SP])
   Alternate spellings: Latisha, Letitia
Letizia (let-TEET-zee-yuh [IT])
Lettie (LET-tee)
Lexi (LEK-see)
   Alternate spellings: Lexie
Libby (LIB-bee)
   Alternate spellings: Libbie
Liberty (LIB-ur-tee)
Liesel (LEE-zull [GER])
Lila (LY-luh [AR], LEE-luh)
   Alternate spellings: Layla*, Laila,
   Leila*, Leyla, Lela, Lelah, Lyla, Lilah
Lilia (LIL-ee-yuh)
Liliana (lil-ee-YAWN-uh,
   lee-lee-YAWN-uh [IT/SP])
   Alternate spellings: Lilliana
Lilike (LIL-ik-uh, LEE-lee-kuh [HUN])
Lilla (LIL-luh, LEE-luh [IT])
Lilliam (LIL-ee-yem)
Lillian (LIL-ee-yen)
   Alternate spellings: Lilian, Lilyan
Lilo (LEE-loh [HW])
Lily (LIL-ee)
   Alternate spellings: Lilly, Lillie
Lina (LEE-nuh [IT])
   Alternate spellings: Lena*
Linda (LIN-duh, LEEN-duh [IT/SP])
   Alternate spellings: Lynda
Lindsey (LIN-zee)
   Alternate spellings: Lindsay, Lyndsey,
   Lyndsay, Linsey
Lindy (LIN-dee)
Ling (LEENG [CH])
Linnea (lin-NAY-yuh [SCAN], lin-NEE-yuh)
Linnie (LIN-nee)
Lisa (LEE-suh)
   Alternate spellings: Lesa, Leisa,

Leesa, Lise*, Lissa*, Lysa
Lise (LEE-zuh [GER], LEEZ [FR], LEE-suh)
   Alternate spellings: Lisa*, Lesa, Leisa,
   Leesa, Lissa*, Lysa
Lissa (LISS-uh, LEE-suh)
   Alternate spellings: Lesa, Leisa ,
   Leesa, Lise*, Lisa*
Lissette (liz-ZET, lee-SET, lee-ZET [FR])
   Alternate spellings: Lisette, Lizette,
   Lizeth*
Litzy (LIT-zee)
Livia (LIV-ee-yuh)
Liza (LY-zuh, LEE-zuh [IT])
Lizzie (LIZ-ee)
Lolita (loh-LEE-taw [SP])
Lonnie (LAW-nee)
   Alternate spellings: Lonie
Lorelei (LOR-rell-lee, LOR-rell-ly [GER])
Lorena (lor-RAY-nuh, lor-REE-nuh,
   lor-REN-uh [IT/SP])
Lorene (lor-REEN, LOR-ren, lor-RAYN [FR])
   Alternate spellings: Laureen, Loreen,
   Lorine, Laurine, Lauren*, Lauryn,
   Loren, Lorraine*
Lori (LOR-ree)
   Alternate spellings: Laurie, Lauri,
   Lorie, Lorrie, Lorri
Loriann (lor-ree-YAN)
Lottie (LAW-tee)
Lou (LOO)
   Alternate spellings: Lu, Lue
Louella (loo-WELL-uh)
   Alternate spellings: Luella
Louie (LOO-wee)
Louise (loo-WEEZ [FR])
Lovie (LUV-ee)
Lucia (LOO-shuh, loo-CHEE-yuh [IT/SCAN],
   loo-SEE-yuh or loo-THEE-yuh [SP])
Luciena (loo-see-YEN-uh)
Lucienne (loo-see-YAN, loo-see-YEN
   with sustained N [FR])
Lucila (loo-SEE-luh)
Lucille (loo-SEEL [FR])
   Alternate spellings: Lucile
Lucrecia (loo-KREE-shuh,
   loo-KREE-see-yuh, loo-KRESS-ee-
   yuh or loo-KRETH-ee-yuh [SP],
   loo-KRET-zee-yuh [IT])
   Alternate spellings: Lucretia, Lucrezia
   [IT]
Lucy (LOO-see, loo-SEE [FR])
   Alternate spellings: Lucie [FR]
Ludie (LOO-dee)

Luisa (loo-WEEZ-uh [IT], loo-WEES-uh
    [GER/SP], loo-WEETH-uh)
    Alternate spellings: Louisa
Lupita (loo-PEE-tuh [SP])
Lurline (lur-LEEN)
Luvenia (loo-VEN-nee-yuh,
    loo-VAY-nee-yuh; see also Lavinia)
    Alternate spellings: Louvenia
Lyda (LY-duh, LEE-duh)
    Alternate spellings: Lida
Lydia (LID-ee-yuh, LEE-dee-yuh [IT],
    lee-DEE [FR])
    Alternate spellings: Lidia [IT], Lidie [FR]
Lyric (LEER-rik [AA])

Mackenzie (muh-KEN-zee, mik-KEN-zee,
    mak-KEN-zee)
    Alternate spellings: Mckenzie, Makenzie
Macy (MAY-see)
    Alternate spellings: Macie, Macey, Maci
Madie (MAY-dee, MAD-ee)
    Alternate spellings: Maddie, Maddy,
    Mattie
Magdalene (mag-duh-LEEN,
    MAG-duh-len)
    Alternate spellings: Magdalen*
Maggie (MAG-ee [CG])
Magnolia (mag-NOH-lee-yuh)
Maleah (maw-LAY-yuh [HW], muh-LEE-yuh)
Malia (maw-LEE-yuh [HW/AA], muh-LEE-
    haw [AR], MAW-lee-yuh)
    Alternate spellings: Maleah*, Maliyah
Malika (MEL-ik-uh or mal-EE-kuh [AR],
    MAW-lee-kuh [EI/HUN], muh-LY-kuh [AA])
    Alternate spellings: Mallika [EI],
    Malikah, Milika, Mylika, Malaika*
Mallory (MAL-or-ree, MAL-ur-ree)
Malvina (mal-VEE-nuh [SP])
Mamie (MAY-mee)
    Alternate spellings: Maymie
Mammie (MAM-ee)
Mandy (MAN-dee)
Marcelina (mar-sell-EE-nuh or
    mar-thell-EE-nuh [SP],
    mar-che-LEE-nuh [IT])
Marceline (mar-sell-EEN with sustained
    N [FR])
Marci (MAR-see)
    Alternate spellings: Marcie, Marcy
Margarita (mar-gar-REE-taw [SP])
Margie (MAR-jee, MAR-gee)
    Alternate spellings: Margy
Margit (MAR-git, mar-GEET [HUN/SCAN])
Marguerite (mar-gur-REET [FR])

Alternate spellings: Margarete
Mari (MAR-ree [SP], MAIR-ree)
    Alternate spellings: Mary*, Maree
Maria (mar-REE-yuh [IT/SP], mar-RY-yuh)
    Alternate spellings: Mariah*, Moriah*
Mariam (MAIR-ree-yum, MAR-ree-yum
    [AR])
    Alternate spellings: Maryam
Marian (MAIR-ree-yen)
    Alternate spellings: Marion
Mariana (mar-ee-YAWN-nuh [IT/SP])
    Alternate spellings: Marianna
Marianne (mair-ree-YAN)
    Alternate spellings: Maryann,
    Maryanne, Mariann
Maribel (MAIR-rib-bell, mair-ee-BELL [FR])
    Alternate spellings: Marybelle
Maricela (mar-ree-SELL-luh or
    mar-ree-THELL-luh [SP])
    Alternate spellings: Marisela
Marie (mar-REE, mair-RHEE [FR])
    Alternate spellings: Maree
Mariel (MAIR-ree-yell, MAR-ree-yell [GER],
    mair-ree-YELL [FR])
    Alternate spellings: Marielle [FR]
Mariella (mair-ree-YELL-uh,
    mar-ree-YELL-uh [SP])
    Alternate spellings: Mariela
Marietta (mair-ree-YET-uh,
    mar-ree-YET-uh [IT])
Marilee (MAIR-ril-lee)
Marilena (mar-ree-LEN-uh [IT]; see also
    Marlena)
Marina (mar-REE-nuh [IT/GER/GRK/RUSS/SP])
Marisa (mar-REE-suh, mar-RISS-uh,
    mar-REE-zuh [IT])
    Alternate spellings: Marissa*
Marisol (mar-ree-SOHL or
    mar-ree-THOHL [SP])
Marissa (mar-RISS-uh, mar-REE-suh or
    mar-REE-thuh [SP])
    Alternate spellings: Marisa*
Marita (mar-REE-tuh [SP])
Maritza (mar-REET-zuh)
Marjorie (MAR-jur-ree)
    Alternate spellings: Margery, Marjory
Marlene (mar-LEEN, mar-LEEN-uh [GER])
Marley (MAR-lee)
    Alternate spellings: Marlee
Marnie (MAR-nee)
Martina (mar-TEE-nuh [IT/SP])
Mary (MAIR-ree)
    Alternate spellings: Mari*, Merry
Marybeth (mair-ree-BETH)

Alternate spellings: Maribeth
Maryellen (mair-ree-YELL-en)
Maryjane (mair-ree-JAYN)
Maryjo (mair-ree-JOH)
Marylou (mair-ree-LOO)
Alternate spellings: Marilou
Matilda (muh-TIL-duh [GER], mat-TEEL-deh [IT])
Alternate spellings: Matilde*, Mathilda
Matilde (muh-TIL-dee, mat-TEELD [FR],
mat-TEEL-day [SP], mat-TIL-duh [GER])
Alternate spellings: Matilda*,
Mathilda, Mathilde [FR]
Maudie (MAW-dee)
Maureen (mor-REEN)
Alternate spellings: Maurine
Maxie (MAK-see)
Maxine (mak-SEEN [FR])
Mazie (MAY-zee)
Megan (MAY-gen [IR], MEG-en, MEE-gen)
Alternate spellings: Meghan, Meagan,
Maegan, Meaghan, Meghann
Melanie (MEL-en-ee, may-lan-NEE [FR])
Alternate spellings: Melany, Melonie,
Mélanie
Melina (mel-LEE-nuh)
Melinda (mel-LIN-duh, muh-LIN-duh)
Alternate spellings: Malinda
Melisa (mel-LEE-suh, muh-LISS-uh)
Melissa (muh-LISS-uh, mel-LISS-uh,
may-lee-SAW [FR])
Alternate spellings: Melisa*, Mellissa,
Malissa, Mellisa, Melissa
Mellie (MEL-ee)
Melody (MEL-oh-dee)
Alternate spellings: Melodie
Melvina (mel-VEE-nuh [CG])
Mercedes (mair-SED-ess or
mair-THED-eth [SP], mur-SAY-deez)
Merlene (mur-LEEN)
Mertie (MUR-tee)
Alternate spellings: Myrtie
Meta (MEE-tuh, MAY-tuh)
Alternate spellings: Meda
Mia (MEE-yuh [IT])
Alternate spellings: Miah, Miya, Mya,
Myah
Micah (MY-kuh, MEE-chaw with guttural
CH [HEB])
Alternate spellings: Micha [HEB]
Michael (MY-kell, mee-chy-ELL with
guttural CH [HEB])
Michaela (mik-ELL-uh or mik-y-YELL-uh
[IT], muh-KAY-luh, mee-chy-ELL-uh

with guttural CH [HEB])
Alternate spellings: Makayla*,
Mikayla, Mckayla, Mikaela, Micaela,
Makaila, Mikala
Michelina (mee-shell-EE-nuh [IT],
mik-ell-LEE-nuh [SP])
Michelle (muh-SHELL, mish-ELL,
mee-SHELL [FR], MEE-shell)
Alternate spellings: Michele, Michell,
Mechelle, Machelle, Michèle [FR]
Michiko (MEE-chee-koh [JAP])
Mickey (MIK-ee)
Alternate spellings: Mickie
Migdalia (mig-DAW-lee-yuh)
Milagros (mee-LAW-grohs [SP])
Millie (MILL-ee)
Mimi (MEE-mee, MEE-MEE [FR])
Mina (MEE-nuh [JAP/IT/SP])
Alternate spellings: Meena [EI]
Mindy (MIN-dee)
Alternate spellings: Mindi
Ming (MEENG [CH])
Minna (MIN-nuh or MEE-nuh [GER])
Minnie (MIN-nee [CG])
Mirabelle (MEER-ruh-bell,
mee-rab-BELL [FR])
Miracle (MEER-ruh-kull)
Miranda (mur-RAN-duh,
meer-RAWN-duh [SP])
Alternate spellings: Meranda,
Myranda, Maranda
Mireya (meer-RAY-yuh [SP])
Miriam (MEER-ee-yum, MAR-ree-yum
[AR], meer-YAWM [HEB])
Alternate spellings: Myriam
Missouri (miz-ZUR-ree)
Missy (MISS-ee)
Misty (MISS-tee)
Alternate spellings: Misti
Mittie (MITT-ee)
Mitzi (MIT-see)
Molly (MAW-lee)
Alternate spellings: Mollie
Monique (moh-NEEK [FR])
Moriah (mor-RY-yuh, moh-ree-YAW [HEB],
muh-RY-yuh)
Alternate spellings: Moriya [HEB],
Moria, Mariah*, Maria*
Mossie (MAW-see)
Muriel (MUR-ee-yell [CG/HEB])
Myrtice (mur-TEES, meer-TEES)

Nadia (NAW-dee-yuh, NAW-dee-yah
with pronounced H at end [AR],

NAD-ee-yuh [IT])
Alternate spellings: Nadje [GER],
Nadya [RUS]
Nadine (nay-DEEN, nad-EEN with
sustained N [FR])
Naheed (NAW-heed [PER])
Nakia (nuh-KEE-yuh [AA])
Nancy (NAN-see)
Alternate spellings: Nanci, Nancie
Nannie (NAN-ee)
Naomi (nay-YOH-mee or NOH-mee [HEB],
ny-YOH-mee, NAW-oh-mee [JAP])
Natalia (nat-TAW-lee-yuh,
nat-taw-LEE-yuh [IT])
Alternate spellings: Natalya, Nathalia
Natalie (NAD-uh-lee, naw-taw-LEE [HEB],
nat-tal-LEE [FR])
Alternate spellings: Nataly, Nathalie
[FR], Natalee
Natividad (naw-tee-vee-DAWD [SP])
Natsumi (NAT-soo-mee [JAP])
Nayeli (ny-YELL-ee, naw-YELL-ee [SP],
NY-yell-ee, NAY-yell-ee)
Alternate spellings: Nayely, Nayelli
Nélida (NELL-ee-duh [SP], nell-LEE-duh)
Nellie (NELL-ee)
Alternate spellings: Nelly
Neta (NEE-tuh, NETT-uh [HEB]; see also
Nita)
Alternate spellings: Netta
Nettie (NET-ee)
Neva (NEE-vuh, NAY-vuh, NEV-uh)
Neyla (NY-luh [AR], NAY-luh, NEE-luh [IR])
Alternate spellings: Nila, Nyla*, Neala
or Neila [IR]
Nia (NEE-yuh [CG])
Nicola (NIK-oh-luh, nee-KOH-luh [IT])
Nicole (nik-KOHL, nee-KOHL [FR])
Alternate spellings: Nichole, Nikole,
Nichol, Nicolle
Nicolette (nik-oh-LET, nee-koh-LET [FR])
Nikita (nik-EE-tuh [GER])
Nikki (NIK-ee)
Alternate spellings: Niki
Nina (NEE-nuh [AR/FR/HEB/IT/RUS/SP], NY-nuh)
Alternate spellings: Neena
Nita (NEE-tuh [HEB/SP])
Alternate spellings: Neta
Nixie (NIK-see [GER])
Noelia (noh-WELL-ee-yuh)
Noemi (no-WEM-ee, noh-WAY-mee [IT/SP],
noh-way-MEE [FR])
Alternate spellings: Noémie

Noreen (nor-REEN [AR/IR])
Alternate spellings: Norene, Norine
Nyah (NEE-yuh or NY-yuh [AA])
Alternate spellings: Nya, Nia [WL]
Nyasia (ny-YAY-zhuh, ny-YAY-see-yuh,
nee-YAY-zhuh)
Nydia (NID-ee-yuh, NEE-dee-yuh [SP])
Nyla (NY-luh, NEE-luh)
Alternate spellings: Nila, Neyla*

Octavia (awk-TAY-vee-yaw,
awk-TAW-vee-yaw or
ohk-TAW-bee-yaw [SP])
Odalys (oh-DAW-lees [SP], oh-daw-LEES)
Alternate spellings: Odalis
Odie (OH-dee)
Olene (oh-LEEN [AA])
Oleta (oh-LEE-tuh or oh-LET-uh [AA])
Oliana (oh-lee-YAWN-uh [HW])
Olina (oh-LEE-nuh [HW])
Olivia (oh-LIV-ee-yuh, oh-LEE-vee-yaw
[IT/SP], oh-LEE-bee-yaw [SP],
uh-LIV-ee-yuh)
Alternate spellings: Alivia
Olivie (oh-lee-VEE [FR])
Ollie (AW-lee)
Onie (OH-nee, WUN-ee)
Ophelia (oh-FEE-lee-yuh,
oh-FELL-ee-yuh [IT/SP])
Alternate spellings: Ofelia [IT/SP]
Oralia (or-RAL-lee-yuh [SP])
Otilia (oh-TILL-ee-yuh [SP])
Alternate spellings: Otylia [GER]
Ottilie (aw-TILL-ee [SCAN])
Ouida (WEE-duh [FR])

Pansy (PAN-zee)
Paris (PAIR-riss, pair-RRREE [FR])
Parisa (puh-REE-suh, pair-ree-SUH [PER])
Parvati (PAR-vaw-tee [EI])
Alternate spellings: Parvathi
Patrica (pat-TREE-suh)
Patrice (pat-REES [FR])
Patricia (pat-RISH-uh, pat-REES-ee-yuh
[FR/SP], pat-REE-thee-yuh [SP])
Patrizia (pat-REET-zee-yuh [IT])
Patsy (PAT-see)
Patty (PAT-ee)
Alternate spellings: Patti, Pattie
Paulina (paw-LEE-nuh)
Pauline (paw-LEEN, poh-LEEN [FR])
Pearlie (PUR-lee)
Pearline (pur-LEEN)

Peggy (PEG-ee [CG])
 Alternate spellings: Peggie
Penelope (pen-NELL-oh-pee,
 pay-nay-LOHP)
 Alternate spellings: Pénélope
Penny (PEN-ee)
 Alternate spellings: Pennie, Penni
Philomena (fill-oh-MEE-nuh)
 Alternate spellings: Filomena*
Phoebe (FEE-bee [FR/GRK])
Phoenix (FEE-niks [AA/GRK])
Pilar (pee-LAR [SP])
Ping (PEENG [CH])
Pinkie (PEENG-kee)
Polly (PAW-lee)
Poppy (PAW-pee)
Presley (PRESS-lee)
Priscila (pris-SIL-uh, pree-SEE-luh or
 pree-THEE-luh [SP])
 Alternate spellings: Priscilla
Providenci (praw-vid-DEN-see)

Queen (KWEEN)
Queenie (KWEE-nee)

Rafaela (raff-ay-YELL-uh, raff-eye-ELL-uh
 [IT], raw-fuh-ELL-uh [HEB/SP])
Ramonita (ray-moh-NEE-tuh)
Randi (RAN-dee)
 Alternate spellings: Randy
Ranee (RRRAW-nee [EI], ren-NAY)
 Alternate spellings: Renae, Rene,
 Rena*, Renea*, Renee*
Reagan (RAY-gen, REE-gen [IR])
 Alternate spellings: Raegan, Regan
Reba (REE-buh)
Reese (REES)
Regina (rej-EE-nuh [IT])
Rena (REE-nuh [HEB], ren-NAY)
 Alternate spellings: Renae, Rene,
 Renee*, Renea*, Ranee*
Renita (ray-NEE-tuh [SP])
Ressie (RES-see)
Retha (REE-thuh, REE-tuh)
 Alternate spellings: Rita*
Reva (REE-vuh [HEB])
Rhea (REE-yuh [GRK], RAY-yuh)
 Alternate spellings: Reia, Reya [SP]
Rhiannon (ree-YAN-nun [WL], REE-yen-en)
Rianna (ree-YAN-uh)
 Alternate spellings: Reanna
Rikki (RIK-ee)
 Alternate spellings: Ricki

Riley (RY-lee)
 Alternate spellings: Rylee, Rylie,
 Ryleigh, Reilly
Rita (REE-tuh [IT/SP])
 Alternate spellings: Reta, Retha*, Rheta
Robbie (RAW-bee)
Rocio (rrroh-SEE-yoh or rrroh-THEE-yoh
 [SP])
Ronnie (RAW-nee)
 Alternate spellings: Roni
Rory (ROR-ree)
Rosalia (roh-ZAL-ee-yuh,
 rrroh-saw-LEE-yuh or
 rrroh-thaw-LEE-yuh [SP])
Rosalie (ROH-zuh-lee)
 Alternate spellings: Rosalee
Rosalina (rrroh-saw-LEE-nuh or
 rrroh-thaw-LEE-nuh [SP])
Rosalinda (rrroh-saw-LEEN-duh or
 rrroh-thaw-LEEN-duh [SP])
Rosaline (roh-suh-LEEN, RAW-zuh-lin)
 Alternate spellings: Roselyn*,
 Rosalyn*, Rosalind*
Rosario (rrroh-SAR-ree-yoh [IT/SP],
 rrroh-THAR-ree-yoh)
Rosemarie (rohz-mair-REE [FR])
Rosemary (ROHZ-mair-ree)
Rosia (ROH-zee-yuh)
Rosina (roh-ZEE-nuh [CG/IT])
Rosita (rrroh-SEE-tuh or
 rrroh-THEE-tuh [SP])
Rossie (RAW-see)
Rowena (roh-WEE-nuh [CG/IR])
Roxie (RAWK-see)
Ruby (ROO-bee)
 Alternate spellings: Rubye, Rubie
Ruthie (ROO-thee, ROO-tee [HEB])
 Alternate spellings: Ruthe, Ruti [HEB]

Sabina (sab-BEE-nuh)
Sabine (sab-BEEN with sustained N [FR])
Sabrina (sab-BREE-nuh [IT])
Sadie (SAY-dee)
 Alternate spellings: Sadye
Sally (SAL-ee)
 Alternate spellings: Sallie
Salome (sal-LOH-mee, SAW-loh-may,
 suh-LOHM, SAL-loh-may [BR],
 saw-loh-MAY [FR], shaw-LOHM [HEB])
 Alternate spellings: Salomé [FR],
 Shalom [HEB]
Samira (suh-MEER-uh with pronounced
 H at end [AR])

Sammie (SAM-ee)
Sandy (SAN-dee)
  Alternate spellings: Sandi
Saniya (suh-NY-yuh or suh-NEE-yuh [AA],
  san-NY-yuh [AR], SAWN-yuh)
  Alternate spellings: Saniyya [AR],
  Sanya*, Sonia*, Sonya
Santina (san-TEE-nuh [IT])
Santos (SAWN-tohs or THAWN-tohs [SP])
Sarahi (suh-RAW-hee [AA])
Selena (sell-LEEN-uh, sell-LEN-uh or
  thell-LEN-uh [SP])
  Alternate spellings: Celina*, Selina,
  Salina
Serena (sur-REEN-uh, suh-REN-uh [IT/SP],
  thu-REN-uh [SP])
  Alternate spellings: Sarina
Serenity (sur-REN-it-ee)
Shakira (shuh-KEER-ruh [AA],
  SHAW-keer-ruh or SHAK-eer-ruh [AR])
Shameka (shuh-MEE-kuh [AA])
  Alternate spellings: Shamika
Shamira (shuh-MEER-ruh [HEB])
Shandi (SHAWN-dee [AA]; see also
  Shanthi)
Shani (SHAW-nee [AA])
Shania (shuh-NY-yuh, shuh-NEE-yuh)
  Alternate spellings: Shaniya
Shanice (shuh-NEES [AA])
Shanika (shuh-NEE-kuh [AA])
Shaniqua (shuh-NEEK-wuh [AA])
Shanita (shuh-NEE-tuh [AA])
Shanthi (SHAWN-tee [EI];
  see also Shandi)
Shaylee (SHAY-lee [AA/CG])
Sheba (SHEE-buh [AR])
Sheena (SHEE-nuh [IR])
  Alternate spellings: Sheenagh
Sheila (SHEE-luh [CG], SHAY-hell-uh [PER],
  SHAY-luh, SHY-luh)
  Alternate spellings: Shiela, Shaila [EI]
Shelby (SHEL-bee)
  Alternate spellings: Shelbie, Shelbi
Shelia (SHEE-lee-yuh, shu-LEE-yuh [AA])
Shelly (SHEL-lee)
  Alternate spellings: Shelley, Shellie,
  Shelli
Sheree (shuh-REE)
  Alternate spellings: Cherie*, Cheri,
  Sherrie, Sherie
Sherita (shuh-REE-tuh [AA])
Sherry (SHAIR-ree)
  Alternate spellings: Cherie*, Cheri,
  Sheree*, Sherrie, Cherry*, Sherri,

Shari*, Sherie
Shirlene (shur-LEEN)
Shirley (SHUR-lee)
  Alternate spellings: Shirlee
Sidonie (sid-OH-nee, SID-oh-nee,
  see-doh-NEE [FR])
Sienna (see-YEN-uh, shee-YAY-nuh [JAP])
Sierra (see-YAIR-ruh)
  Alternate spellings: Cierra, Ciera
Signe (ZEEN-yaw [SCAN], SEEN-yeh [FR])
  Alternate spellings: Cigne
Sigrid (SIG-rid [SCAN], see-GREED [FR])
Simone (sim-OHN, see-MOHN with
  sustained N [FR])
Sonia (SOHN-yaw [IT/HEB/RUS/SP],
  soh-NEE-yaw or thoh-NEE-yaw [SP],
  SOH-nee-yuh with pronounced H at
  end [AR], SAWN-yuh [RUS])
  Alternate spellings: Sonya [RUS], Sonja
  [SCAN]
Soomie (SOO-mee [KOR])
Sophia (soh-FEE-yuh [GRK/IT/SP],
  thoh-FEE-yuh [SP])
  Alternate spellings: Sofia [IT/SP]
Sophie (SOH-fee [GRK], soh-FEE [FR])
Spring (SPREENG)
Stacia (STAY-shuh, STAY-see-yuh,
  STAW-zee-yuh [RUS])
  Alternate spellings: Stasia [RUS]
Stacy (STAY-see)
  Alternate spellings: Stacey, Stacie,
  Staci
Stephania (stef-FAW-nee-yuh)
  Alternate spellings: Stefania [IT]
Stephanie (STEF-uh-nee [GRK],
  stay-faw-NEE [FR])
  Alternate spellings: Stephany, Stefani,
  Stephani, Stefanie, Stephenie,
  Stephanie [FR]
Stevie (STEE-vee)
Stormy (STOR-mee)
Sudie (SOO-dee)
Sunny (SUN-ee)
Susie (SOO-zee)
  Alternate spellings: Suzy
Sybil (SIB-bull, see-BEEL [FR];
  see also Cybelle)
  Alternate spellings: Syble, Sibyl,
  Sybille [FR]
Sydney (SID-nee)
  Alternate spellings: Sidney, Sydnee,
  Sydni, Sydnie
Sylvia (SIL-vee-yuh or THIL-vee-yuh [SP],
  SEEL-vee-yuh [IT])

Alternate spellings: Silvia
Sylvie (SILL-vee, seel-VEE [FR])

Talia (TAW-lee-yuh [HEB], tuh-LEE-yuh [AA])
Alternate spellings: Thalia, Taliyah,
Talya
Tami (TAM-ee)
Alternate spellings: Tammie, Tamie,
Tammi
Tamia (TAM-ee-yuh, TAWM-yuh)
Alternate spellings: Tamya
Tamika (tam-EE-kuh [AA])
Alternate spellings: Tameka,
Tomeka*, Tomika
Tamiko (TAM-ee-koh [JAP])
Tania (TAWN-yuh, TAN-yuh [IT],
tuh-NEE-yuh [AA])
Alternate spellings: Tanya, Taniya,
Tawnya, Tonya*, Tonja, Tonia
Tanisha (tuh-NEESH-uh [AA])
Alternate spellings: Tanesha, Tenisha
Tatiana (taw-tee-YAWN-uh,
tat-ee-YAWN-uh)
Alternate spellings: Tatyana
Tawny (TAW-nee)
Teagan (TEE-gen [IR], TAY-gen)
Tennie (TEN-ee)
Tennille (ten-NEEL)
Teresa (tur-REE-suh, tair-REZ-uh [IT],
tair-RESS-suh or tair-RETH-uh [SP])
Alternate spellings: Theresa, Teressa
(see also Tressa)
Teresita (tair-ress-SEE-taw or
tair-ress-THEE-taw [SP])
Teri (TAIR-ree)
Alternate spellings: Terry, Terri, Terrie
Tessie (TES-see
Thea (THEE-yuh, TAY-yuh)
Alternate spellings: Taya*, Tea
Theo (THEE-yoh, TAY-yoh [FR])
Alternate spellings: Théo [FR]
Theodora (thee-yuh-DOR-ruh,
tay-oh-DOR-ruh [IT])
Alternate spellings: Teodora [IT]
Theola (thee-YOH-luh)
Therese (tur-REES, tay-REZ [FR])
Alternate spellings: Terese, Thérèse
Theresia (tur-REES-ee-yuh,
tair-RESS-ee-yuh)
Tiana (tee-YAWN-uh, tee-YAN-nuh)
Alternate spellings: Tianna
Tiara (tee-YAR-ruh)
Tierra (tee-YAIR-ruh)
Alternate spellings: Tiera

Tiffany (TIF-uh-nee)
Alternate spellings: Tiffani, Tiffanie
Tillie (TILL-ee [GER])
Tina (TEE-nuh)
Alternate spellings: Tena, Teena
Tisha (TEESH-uh or TISH-uh [AA])
Toby (TOH-bee, TOH-vee [HEB])
Tomeka (toh-MEE-kuh or tuh-MEE-kuh [AA])
Alternate spellings: Tomika, Tamika*,
Tameka
Tommie (TAW-mee)
Toni (TOH-nee)
Tori (TOR-ree)
Tracy (TRAY-see)
Alternate spellings: Traci, Tracey Tracie
Tressie (TRESS-ee)
Trena (TREN-nuh [SP], TREE-nuh)
Alternate spellings: Trina*
Treva (TREE-vuh, TRAY-vuh)
Trina (TREE-nuh)
Alternate spellings: Trena*
Trinidad (TRIN-id-add, tree-nee-DAD [SP])
Trinity (TRIN-it-ee)
Tristan (TRIS-ten [WL], trees-TAW with
short N [FR], trees-TAWN or
treeth-TAWN [SP])
Alternate spellings: Tristen
Trudy (TROO-dee [GER])
Alternate spellings: Trudie, Trude
Tyesha (ty-YEESH-uh [AA])

Unique (yoo-NEEK)

Valencia (val-LEN-see-yuh,
vuh-LEN-chuh [IT], vaw-LEN-see-yaw
or baw-LEN-thee-yaw [SP])
Valentina (val-en-TEEN-uh [IT/SP])
Valentine (VAL-en-tyn, val-en-TEEN with
sustained N [FR])
Valeria (val-ur-REE-yuh, val-AIR-ee-yuh
[IT])
Valerie (VAL-ur-ree, vaw-lair-REE [FR])
Alternate spellings: Valarie, Valorie
Vallie (VAL-ee)
Veda (VEE-duh, VAY-duh)
Alternate spellings: Vada*, Vida*
Vena (VEE-nuh, VEN-uh [IT])
Venita (ven-NEE-tuh)
Venus (VEE-niss)
Vera (VEER-ruh, VAIR-ruh [IT/SP], BAIR-ruh
[SP])
Verda (VUR-duh, VAIR-duh, VEER-duh)
Verla (VUR-luh, VAIR-luh, VEER-duh)
Verlie (VUR-lee)

Verna (VUR-nuh, VEER-nuh)
Vernice (vur-NEES)
Veronica (vur-RAW-nik-uh,
    vair-ROH-nee-kuh or
    bair-ROH-nee-kuh [SP])
Versie (VUR-see)
Vicenta (vee-SEN-tuh or bee-THEN-tuh
    [SP])
Vicky (VIK-ee)
    Alternate spellings: Vicki, Vikki,
    Vickey, Vickie
Victoria (vik-TOR-ree-yuh,
    veek-TOR-ree-yaw or
    beek-TOR-ree-yaw [SP])
Vida (VY-duh, VEE-duh)
    Alternate spellings: Veda*, Vita*
Vilma (VILL-muh, VEEL-muh or
    BEEL-muh [SP])
Vina (VEE-nuh)
Vincenza (veen-CHEN-zuh [IT])
Vinnie (VIN-ee)
Viola (vy-YOH-luh, vee-YOH-law [IT/SP],
    bee-YOH-law [SP])
Violetta (vee-yoh-LET-uh [IT])
Violette (vee-yoh-LETT [FR])
Virgie (VUR-gee, VUR-jee)
    Alternate spellings: Vergie
Virginia (vur-JIN-yuh, veer-JEE-nee-yuh
    [IT], veer-HEE-nee-yuh or
    beer-HEE-nee-yuh [SP])
Virginie (veer-zhee-NEE [FR])
Vita (VEE-tuh [IT], VY-duh)
    Alternate spellings: Vida*, Veda*
Viva (VEE-vuh [IT/SP])
Vivia (VIV-ee-yuh)
Vivian (VIV-ee-yen)
    Alternate spellings: Vivien
Viviana (viv-ee-YAWN-uh)
Vivienne (viv-ee-YAN, vee-vee-YENN [FR])
    Alternate spellings: Vivien
Vonnie (VAW-nee)

Waneta (wah-NET-uh, wah-NEE-tuh)
    Alternate spellings: Wanita, Juanita*
Wendy (WEN-dee)
    Alternate spellings: Wendi, Windy*
Whitley (WIT-lee)
Whitney (WIT-nee)
Wilhelmina (vill-hel-MEE-nuh [GER])
Wilhelmine (vill-hel-MEEN [GER])
Willamina (will-uh-MEE-nuh)
Willene (will-LEEN)
Willia (WILL-ee-yuh)
Willie (WILL-ee)

Windy (WIN-dee, WEN-dee)
    Alternate spellings: Wendy*, Wendi
Winnie (WIN-ee)
Wylie (WY-lee)

Xena (ZEE-nuh [GRK])
    Alternate spellings: Zena, Zina*
Xia (hee-YAW [CH])
Ximena (hee-MEN-uh [SP])
    Alternate spellings: Jimena
Xiomara (see-yoh-MAR-ruh or
    shee-yoh-MAR-ruh [SP])
Xiu (HEE-yoo [CH])

Yadira (yad-DEER-ruh [HEB/SP])
Yanira (yan-NEER-ruh [AA/GRK/HEB/SP])
Yareli (yar-RELL-ee [SP])
Yaritza (yar-REET-zuh [SP])
Yasmin (YAZ-min, yass-MEEN [HEB/PER])
    Alternate spellings: Yazmin,
    Yasmine*, Yasmeen, Jasmine*,
    Jasmin, Jazmin, Jazmine, Jazmyn,
    Jasmyn, Jazmyne
Yasmine (yaz-MEEN [AR], yass-MEEN [HEB])
    Alternate spellings: Yazmin, Yasmin*,
    Yasmeen, Jasmine*, Jasmin, Jazmin,
    Jazmine, Jazmyn, Jasmyn, Jazmyne
Yesenia (yess-SAY-nee-yuh,
    yee-SEN-ee-yuh or ye-THEN-ee-yuh
    [SP], yes-SEE-nuh [AR])
    Alternate spellings: Yessenia,
    Jessenia*
Yoselin (YAW-sell-in, YAWZ-lin,
    yoh-SEL-een or yoh-THEL-een [SP])
    Alternate spellings: Joselyn*
Yoshiko (YOH-shee-koh [JAP])
Yuliana (yoo-lee-YAWN-uh [SP/RUS]
    Alternate spellings: Juliana*
Yvette (ee-VETT [FR], iv-ETT)
    Alternate spellings: Ivette, Evette
Yvonne (iv-AWN, ee-VOHN [FR])
    Alternate spellings: Ivonne*, Evonne

Zaida (ZAY-duh, zy-YEE-duh, zaw-HED-
    uh with pronounced H at end [AR])
Zaria (zuh-RY-yuh, ZAR-ree-yuh)
Zina (ZY-nuh, ZEE-nuh [AR])
    Alternate spellings: Zena, Xena*
Zita (ZEE-tuh)
Zoë (ZOH-wee [GRK/HEB], zoh-WAY [FR])
    Alternate spellings: Zoey, Zoie, Zoé [FR]

■ SHORT E (EH OR E) ■

PARTNER POINTER:
Short E, I, and U often sound similar.

Adelaide (ADD-uh-layd [GER], add-eh-LED
or uh-dell-uh-YEED [FR])
Adele (uh-DELL [GER], ad-DEL)
Alternate spellings: Adell, Adelle
Adelia (uh-DEE-lee-yuh,
aw-DELL-ee-yuh [IT])
Adelina (ad-uh-LEE-nuh, aw-dell-LEE-nuh
[IT/SP])
Adeline (AD-uh-lin, ADD-uh-lyn,
ad-dell-LEEN with sustained N [FR])
Alternate spellings: Adaline
Adella (uh-DELL-uh [GER], aw-DELL-uh
[IT/SP], aw-DEE-luh or AW-dill-uh [AR])
Alternate spellings: Adela
Adrian (AY-dree-yen)
Alternate spellings: Adriane
Adrienne (ay-dree-YAN, ay-dree-YEN
with sustained N [FR])
Alternate spellings: Adriane
Agnes (AG-ness, an-YES [FR])
Agnese (an-YEZ-eh or an-YEZ [FR])
Alejandra (aw-leh-HAWN-druh [SP])
Alessandra (aw-leh-SAWN-druh [IT])
Alex (AL-eks)
Alexa (uh-LEK-suh, aw-LEK-suh or
aw-LEK-thuh [SP])
Alexandra (al-ek-ZAN-druh,
al-ek-ZAWN-druh)
Alexandria (al-ek-ZAN-dree-yuh)
Alternate spellings: Alexandrea
Alexandrie (al-ek-sawn-DREE with short
N [FR]
Alexia (uh-LEK-see-yuh, al-LEK-see-uh [IT])
Alexis (uh-LEK-siss)
Alternate spellings: Alexys, Alexus
Alfreda (al-FRAY-duh, al-FRED-uh [IT])
Aline (ay-LEEN, aw-LEN [FR])
Alternate spellings: Allene, Alline,
Alene
Angel (AYN-jell, AWN-hell [SP])
Angela (ANN-jell-uh, AWN-jell-uh [IT],
AWN-hell-uh or awn-HELL-uh [SP])
Angeles (ANN-jell-ess, ANN-jell-eez,
AWN-hell-ess or awn-HELL-eth [SP])
Angelia (ann-JELL-ee-yuh,
awn-JELL-ee-yuh [IT])
Angelica (ann-JELL-ik-uh, awn-jell-EEK-
uh, awn-HELL-ee-kuh [SP])
Alternate spellings: Anjelica

Angelina (ann-jell-EE-nuh,
awn-jell-EE-nuh [IT], awn-hell-LEE-nuh
[SP])
Angeline (ann-jell-EEN, ann-zhe-LEEN
with sustained N [FR])
Angelique (ann-jell-LEEK, an-zhe-LEEK
[FR])
Angelita (ann-jell-LEE-tuh,
awn-hell-LEE-tuh [SP])
Anjanette (ann-juh-NET)
Annabella (ann-uh-BELL-uh)
Alternate spellings: Anabela [IT]
Annabelle (ANN-uh-bell, an-uh-BELL [FR])
Alternate spellings: Annabel, Anabel,
Annabell
Annetta (ann-NET-uh)
Annette (ann-NET)
Antoinette (ann-twah-NET [FR])
Antonetta (ann-toh-NET-uh)
Antonette (ann-toh-NET)
Antonietta (an-toh-nee-YETT-uh [IT])
Arabella (air-ruh-BELL-uh)
Araceli (air-ruh-SELL-ee, ar-raw-SELL-ee
or ar-raw-THEL-ee [SP])
Alternate spellings: Aracely
Ardell (ar-DELL)
Ardella (ar-DELL-uh)
Ariel (AIR-ree-yell, AR-ree-yell,
ar-ree-YELL [HEB/FR])
Ariella (ar-ree-YELL-uh [HEB])
Alternate spellings: Ariela
Arielle (air-ree-YELL, ar-ree-YELL [FR])
Ashton (ASH-ten)
Alternate spellings: Ashtyn
Aspen (ASS-pen)
Aurelia (or-RELL-ee-yuh,
ow-RELL-ee-yuh [IT])

Babette (bab-BET [FR])
Becky (BEK-ee)
Belen (bell-LEN [SP])
Belinda (bell-IN-duh)
Bella (BELL-uh [IT])
Bellamy (BELL-uh-mee)
Belle (BELL with sustained L [FR])
Alternate spellings: Bell
Belva (BELL-vuh)
Benita (ben-NEE-tuh or ven-NEE-tuh [SP])
Bennie (BEN-ee)
Bernadette (bur-nuh-DET, bair-nuh-DET
[FR])
Bess (BESS)
Bessie (BESS-ee)
Beth (BETH)

Bethany (BETH-in-nee)
Bethel (BETH-ell)
Betsy (BET-see)
Bette (BET)
Bettina (bet-TEE-nuh [GER], bet-TEEN with
    sustained N [FR])
Betty (BET-ee, BED-dee)
    Alternate spellings: Bettye, Bettie
Beverly (BEV-ur-lee)
    Alternate spellings: Beverley, Beverlee
Brenda (BREN-duh [SCAN])
Brenna (BREN-nuh)
Brielle (bree-YELL [FR])

Cadence (KAY-dens)
    Alternate spellings: Kadence, Kaydence
Campbell (KAM-bell)
Candace (KAN-dess)
    Alternate spellings: Candice, Kandice,
    Kandace, Candis
Carmel (kar-MELL [HEB])
    Alternate spellings: Karmel
Carmela (kar-MELL-uh [HEB],
    karrr-MELL-uh [IT/SP])
    Alternate spellings: Carmella, Karmela
Carmelita (kar-mell-LEE-tuh [IT/SP])
Carmen (KAR-men [SP])
Cecil (SESS-ill, SEE-sill)
Cecile (sess-SEEL, say-SEEL [FR])
    Alternate spellings: Cécile [FR]
Cecilia (se-SEE-lee-yuh [IT/SP],
    che-CHEE-lee-uh [IT],
    the-THEE-lee-yuh [SP])
    Alternate spellings: Cecelia [CG]
Cecily (SESS-ill-ee [CG])
Celeste (sell-EST, chell-ESS-teh [IT],
    say-LEST [FR])
    Alternate spellings: Céleste [FR]
Celestina (sell-ess-TEE-nuh,
    chell-ess-TEE-nuh [IT])
Celestine (sell-ess-TEEN, say-less-TEEN
    [FR])
    Alternate spellings: Célestine [FR]
Celina (che-LEE-nuh [IT], sell-LEE-nuh)
    Alternate spellings: Selena*, Selina,
    Salina
Celine (sell-EEN, say-LEEN [FR])
    Alternate spellings: Céline [FR]
Chanel (shan-NELL [FR])
    Alternate spellings: Chanelle
Chantel (shawn-TELL, shan-TELL [AA/FR])
    Alternate spellings: Shantel,
    Chantelle , Shantell
Charolette (SHAR-roh-let; see also

Charlotte)
Chelsea (CHEL-see, SHELL-zee)
    Alternate spellings: Chelsey, Chelsi
Christen (KRISS-sen, KRISS-ten,
    krees-TA with short N [FR])
    Alternate spellings: Kristen*
Christian (KRISS-chen, kree-stee-YAN [FR])
    Alternate spellings: Kristian,
    Christiane [FR]
Claudette (klaw-DET, kloh-DET [FR])
Clementina (klem-en-TEE-nuh [IT/SP])
Clementine (KLEM-en-tyn,
    klem-en-TEEN with sustained N [FR])
Clemmie (KLEM-mee, klem-MEE [FR])
Colette (koh-LET [FR])
    Alternate spellings: Collette
Concepcion (kohn-sep-see-YOHN or
    kohn-thep-thee-YOHN [SP])
Concetta (kohn-CHET-tuh [IT])
Cybelle (see-BELL [FR]; see also Sybil)
    Alternate spellings: Cybele [SCAN]

Danelle (dan-NELL [FR], daw-NELL [HEB])
Danette (dan-NETT [FR])
Daniela (dan-YELL-uh [IT], dawn-YELL-uh
    [HEB/SP])
    Alternate spellings: Daniella
Danielle (dan-YELL [FR], dawn-YELL [HEB])
    Alternate spellings: Danyelle
Debbie (DEB-ee)
    Alternate spellings: Debbi, Debby, Debi
Deborah (DEB-ur-uh, dev-OR-uh [HEB])
    Alternate spellings: Debra, Debora,
    Debrah, Debbra, Devora or Devorah
    [HEB]
Delaney (del-AY-nee)
Delfina (del-FEE-nuh [IT/SP])
Delia (DEE-lee-yuh, DEL-ee-yah [IT/SP])
Delilah (del-LY-luh [HEB])
    Alternate spellings: Delila
Delisa (del-EE-suh)
Dell (DEL)
Della (DEL-uh)
Delma (DEL-muh [SP])
Delois (del-OH-wiss [AA])
Delpha (DEL-fuh)
Delphia (del-FEE-yuh)
Delphine (del-FEEN [FR])
Delta (DEL-tuh)
Demetria (dem-MEET-ree-yuh)
Demi (dem-MEE [FR])
Denise (den-NEES, den-NEEZ [FR])
    Alternate spellings: Denisse, Denice
Desiree (DEZ-ih-ray, dez-ee-RAY [FR])

Alternate spellings: Desirae
Dessie (DES-see)
Destiny (DESS-tin-ee)
Alternate spellings: Destinee,
Destiney, Destini
Devin (DEV-en)
Alternate spellings: Devon, Devan,
Devyn
Dexter (DEK-stur)
Dolores (doh-LOR-ess [SP])
Alternate spellings: Delores, Deloris,
Doloris

Ebba (EBB-uh)
Ebony (EBB-uh-nee [AA])
Alternate spellings: Eboni
Eda (ED-duh, EE-duh, AY-duh)
Alternate spellings: Ada*
Eddie (ED-ee)
Edna (ED-nuh [HEB/SP])
Edrie (ED-ree, EED-ree)
Edwina (ed-WEE-nuh)
Effie (EFF-ee)
Elana (ee-law-NAW [HEB], ell-LAW-nuh;
see also Elena)
Alternate spellings: Ilana*, Alana*,
Alanna*
Elba (EL-buh)
Elda (EL-duh)
Eldora (ell-DOR-ruh [SP])
Eleanor (EL-len-nor, el-lay-yoh-NOR
[FR])
Alternate spellings: Eleanore, Elinor,
Elinore, Elenor, Eléonore [FR]
Eleanora (el-len-NOR-ruh,
el-lee-yuh-NOR-ruh,
eh-lay-yoh-NOR-uh [IT/SP])
Alternate spellings: Elenora, Eleonora
[IT/SP] (see also Elnora)
Electa (el-LEK-tuh or ee-LEK-tuh)
Elena (uh-LAY-nuh, ee-LAY-nuh,
ell-LAY-nuh [SP], ELL-en-uh [IT])
Alternate spellings: Alaina, Alayna,
Elaina, Alena, Alayna, Alaina (see
Helena)
Elfrieda (el-FREE-duh)
Eliana (el-lee-YAW-nuh [IT/SP],
ELL-ee-yaw-nuh [HEB]; see also Iliana)
Elida (el-LEE-duh or el-LY-duh)
Elisa (ee-LEE-suh, el-LEE-suh or
el-LEETH-uh [SP], uh-LEE-suh)
Alternate spellings: Alisa, Alysa
Elise (ee-LEES, el-LEES [GER], ay-LEEZ [FR])
Alternate spellings: Elyse, Elease,

Élise [FR]
Elissa (el-LISS-suh)
Alternate spellings: Elyssa
Eliza (uh-LY-zuh, ee-LY-zuh, el-LEE-zuh [IT])
Alternate spellings: Aliza, Alizah,
Aleeza [HEB]
Elizabeth (el-LIZ-uh-beth, el-lee-SHEE-vuh
[HEB], el-lee-zuh-BET [FR])
Alternate spellings: Elisabeth [FR],
Elisheva or Elisheba [HEB]
Ella (EL-luh)
Ellamae (EL-luh-may)
Elle (ELL [FR])
Ellen (EL-lin)
Alternate spellings: Elin [SCAN]
Ellie (EL-lee)
Elma (EL-muh)
Elmira (el-MY-ruh, el-MEER-ruh)
Elna (EL-nuh)
Elnora (el-NOR-ruh)
Elois (el-OH-wiss, EE-loh-wiss,
EL-oh-weez)
Alternate spellings: Eloise*, Élouise
Eloisa (el-oh-WEE-suh)
Eloise (EL-oh-weez, el-oh-WEEZ,
ay-loh-WEEZ [FR])
Alternate spellings: Elouise, Elois*,
Éloise [FR]
Elsa (EL-suh [GER/SP], EL-zuh [SCAN])
Alternate spellings: Else [FR], Elza
Elsie (EL-see [GER])
Elta (EL-tuh)
Elva (EL-vuh)
Elvera (el-VEER-ruh [IT], el-VAIR-ruh)
Elvia (EL-vee-yuh, el-VEE-yuh)
Elvira (el-VY-ruh)
Emelina (em-uh-LEEN-uh [GER/SP/RUS])
Emeline (em-uh-LEEN with sustained N
[FR], em-uh-LYN, EM-uh-lin)
Alternate spellings: Emmeline,
Emmaline, Emelyn, Emaleen
Emerald (EM-ur-ruld)
Emerson (EM-ur-sun)
Emiko (EM-ee-koh [JAP])
Emilia (eh-MEE-lee-yuh [IT],
uh-MEE-lee-yuh)
Alternate spellings: Emelia, Amelia*
Emilie (em-el-LEE [FR], EM-ill-ee; see also
Amelie)
Alternate spellings: Emily*, Emilee,
Emely, Emmalee
Emily (EM-ill-ee)
Alternate spellings: Emilee, Emely,
Emilie*, Emmalee

Emma (EM-muh [SP])

Emmanuela (em-man-WELL-uh [IT]; see also Manuela)

Emmie (EM-mee)
Alternate spellings: Emmy, Eme, Emi [JAP]

Enriqueta (en-ree-KET-tuh [SP])

Ernestina (ur-ness-TEE-nuh, air-ness-TEE-nuh [IT])

Ernestine (UR-ness-teen)
Alternate spellings: Earnestine

Esmeralda (ez-mur-RAWL-duh, ess-mair-RAL-duh or eth-mair-RAL-duh [SP])

Esmerelda (ez-mur-RELL-duh, ess-mair-RAL-duh or eth-mair-RAL-duh [SP])

Esperanza (ess-pair-AWN-suh or eth-pair-AWN-suh [SP]; see also Speranza)

Essence (ESS-sens [AA])

Essie (ESS-ee [HEB])

Esta (ESS-tuh)

Estefania (es-tef-FAWN-ee-yuh or eth-tef-FAWN-ee-yuh [SP])

Estefany (es-TEF-en-ee, es-tef-FAWN-ee)
Alternate spellings: Estefani

Estella (ess-TELL-uh or eth-TELL-uh)
Alternate spellings: Estela [SP]

Estelle (es-TELL [FR])

Esther (ESS-tur, ess-TAIR [FR/HEB])
Alternate spellings: Ester

Estrella (ess-TRAY-yuh or eth-TRAY-yuh [SP])

Etha (EE-thuh, ET-tuh)
Alternate spellings: Etta*

Ethel (ETH-ell)

Ethelene (eth-ell-LEEN)

Ethelyn (ETH-ell-lin)

Étienne (ay-tee-YEN [FR])

Etta (ET-tuh)
Alternate spellings: Etha*

Ettie (ET-ee, ED-ee)

Eugenia (yoo-JEE-nee-yuh, yoo-JAY-nee-yuh, oo-JEN-ee-yuh [IT], ay-yoo-HAY-nee-yuh [SP])

Eva (EE-vuh, EV-uh [IT], AY-vuh [SP])
Alternate spellings: Ava*, Iva*

Evangelina (ev-van-jell-LEE-nuh [IT], ay-vawn-hell-LEE-nuh [SP])

Evangeline (ev-an-jell-LEEN)

Eve (EEV, EV [FR], CHAW-vuh with guttural CH [HEB])
Alternate spellings: Chava [HEB]

Evelyn (EV-uh-lin)

Alternate spellings: Evelin, Evalyn

Evelyne (ee-vuh-LEEN, ev-uh-LEEN)
Alternate spellings: Eveline [FR]

Evon (EV-en)

Exie (EK-see)

Felicia (fell-LEE-shuh, fell-LEE-see-yuh or fell-LEE-thee-yuh [SP])
Alternate spellings: Felecia, Felisha

Felicitá (fel-ee-chee-TAW [IT])

Felicity (fell-LISS-sit-ee)

Felipa (fell-LEE-puh [SP])

Filomena (fee-loh-MEN-uh [IT/SP], fill-oh-MEE-nuh)
Alternate spellings: Philomena*

Florence (FLOR-rens, flor-RAWS with short N [FR])

Frances (FRAN-sess)
Alternate spellings: Francis

Francesca (fran-CHESS-kuh [IT], fran-SESS-kuh)
Alternate spellings: Franchesca, Francheska

Freddie (FRED-ee)

Gabriel (GAY-bree-yell, gaw-bree-ELL or gaw-vree-ELL [HEB], gab-brrree-YELL [FR/SP/IT])
Alternate spellings: Gavriel [HEB]

Gabriela (gaw-bree-YELL-uh [SP], gab-ree-YELL-uh, gaw-vree-ELL-uh [HEB])
Alternate spellings: Gabriella*, Gavriela [HEB]

Gabriella (gab-ree-YELL-uh [IT], gaw-vree-ELL-uh [HEB])
Alternate spellings: Gabriela*, Gavriela [HEB]

Gabrielle (gab-ree-YELL [FR], gaw-bree-YELL)

Garnett (GAR-net)
Alternate spellings: Garnet

Gaynell (gay-NELL [AA])

Gemma (JEM-uh)

Genesis (JEN-uh-sis)

Geneva (jen-EE-vuh)

Genevieve (JEN-uh-veev [CG], zhen-uh-vee-YEV or zhawn-vee-YEV [FR])
Alternate spellings: Geneviève

Genoveva (jen-oh-VEE-vuh, jen-oh-VAY-vuh)

Georgette (jor-JET, zhor-ZHET [FR])

Gisela (jiz-ZELL-uh)
Alternate spellings: Gisella, Jizella

Giselle (jiz-ELL, zhee-ZELL [FR])
  Alternate spellings: Gisselle, Jizelle
Glenda (GLEN-duh [WL])
Glenn (GLEN)
  Alternate spellings: Glen, Glynn, Glin
Glenna (GLEN-nuh [IR/WL])
Glennie (GLEN-ee)
Golden (GOHL-den)
Graciela (graw-see-YELL-uh or graw-
  thee-YELL-uh [SP])
Gregoria (gre-GOR-ree-yuh [IT])
Greta (GRED-uh)
Gretchen (GRECH-en)
Gretel (GRED-ull [GER/SCAN])
Griselda (griz-ELL-duh [GER], gree-SELL-
  duh or gree-THELL-duh [SP])
  Alternate spellings: Grizelda
Gwen (GWEN [WL])
Gwendolyn (GWEN-doh-lin [WL])

Haven (HAY-ven)
Hayden (HAY-den)
Hazel (HAY-zull [CG], HAW-zell)
  Alternate spellings: Hazle
Heather (HETH-ur)
Heaven (HEV-en)
Hedwig (HED-wig, HAYT-vik [GER])
Helen (HEL-len)
  Alternate spellings: Hellen
Helena (hel-AY-nuh, HEL-en-uh; see also
  Elena)
Helene (hel-LEEN, ay-LEN with
  sustained N [FR])
  Alternate spellings: Hélène
Helga (HEL-guh [SCAN], ELL-gah [SP])
Henrietta (hen-ree-YET-uh [GER])
Henriette (hen-ree-YET [GER], aw-ree-YET
  with short N [FR])
Hester (HES-tur)
Hettie (HED-ee)
Hildred (HIL-dred [SCAN])
Hortencia (hor-TEN-see-yuh, or-TEN-
  see-yuh or or-TEN-thee-yuh [SP])
  Alternate spellings: Hortensia
Hortense (HOR-tens)

Idell (eye-DELL)
Idella (eye-DELL-uh)
Imani (im-AW-nee [AA], ee-MEN-ee [AR];
  see also Amani)
Imelda (ee-MEL-duh [SP], im-MEL-duh)
Imogene (IM-oh-jeen or IM-oh-jen [BR])
  Alternate spellings: Emogene, Imogen,
Inez (ee-NEZ, eye-NESS or eye-NETH

[SP], ee-NESS [FR])
  Alternate spellings: Inès [FR]
Isabel (IZ-uh-bell, ee-zaw-BELL [FR],
  EE-saw-bell or ee-saw-BELL or ee-
  thuh-VELL [SP])
  Alternate spellings: Isabelle [FR],
  Isabell, Isobel
Isabela (iz-uh-BELL-uh, ee-saw-BELL-uh
  or ee-thaw-VELL-uh [SP], ee-zuh-
  BELL-uh [IT])
  Alternate spellings: Isabella [IT],
  Izabella
Itzel (IT-sell, eet-ZELL [NA])
Izetta (eye-ZET-tuh)

Jacqueline (JAK-uh-lin, JAK-well-lin,
  jak-LEEN, zhawk-uh-LEEN with
  sustained N [FR])
  Alternate spellings: Jaqueline,
  Jaquelyn, Jackeline, Jaquelin,
  Jacquline, Jacalyn
Jaden (JAY-den)
  Alternate spellings: Jayden, Jaiden,
  Jaidyn
Jaelyn (JAY-len)
  Alternate spellings: Jaylin, Jalyn,
  Jaylynn, Jailyn, Jalynn, Jaylyn
Janelle (jan-NELL)
  Alternate spellings: Janell, Janel,
  Jenelle
Janessa (jan-NESS-uh [AA])
Janet (JAN-net)
Jeanette (jen-NET [CG], zhan-NET [FR])
  Alternate spellings: Janette, Jannette
Jen (JEN [WL])
  Alternate spellings: Zhen [CH]
Jenna (JEN-nuh)
  Alternate spellings: Jena, Jeanna,
  Jeana, Gena
Jennifer (JEN-nif-ur [WL], zheh-nee-FAIR
  [FR])
  Alternate spellings: Jenifer, Genifer
Jenny (JEN-ee; see also Ginny)
  Alternate spellings: Jennie, Geni
Jessenia (jes-SAY-nee-yuh,
  jes-SEN-ee-yuh, yes-SEE-nuh [AR],
  hes-SAY-nee-yuh or
  he-THAY-nee-yuh [SP])
  Alternate spellings: Yessenia*
Jessica (JES-sik-uh)
  Alternate spellings: Jessika, Jesica
Jessie (JESS-ee)
  Alternate spellings: Jesse, Jessi
Jetta (JET-tuh, JED-uh)

Jettie (JED-ee)
Jocelyn (JAW-sell-lin, JAWS-lin,
   zhoh-sell-LEEN [FR], yoh-SELL-een [SP])
   Alternate spellings: Joselyn, Joceline
   [FR], Joycelyn*, Yoselin*
Joelle (joh-WELL, zho-WELL [FR])
Joellen (joh-WELL-en)
Joetta (joh-WET-uh [AA])
Jordan (JOR-den, YAR-den [HEB])
   Alternate spellings: Jordyn, Yarden*
Joretta (joh-RET-tuh)
Josefa (joh-SEF-uh, ho-SEF-uh or
   ho-THEF-uh [SP], YOH-sif-faw or
   yoh-sif-FAW [HEB])
   Alternate spellings: Josepha, Yosifa [HEB]
Josefina (joh-sef-FEE-nuh,
   ho-sef-FEE-nuh or ho-thef-FEE-nuh
   [SP])
   Alternate spellings: Josephina
Josephine (joh-sef-FEEN, zho-zay-FEEN
   with sustained N [FR])
   Alternate spellings: Joséphine
Josette (joh-ZET or zho-ZET [FR])
Juliet (JOO-lee-yet, zhoo-lee-YET [FR])
   Alternate spellings: Juliet, Juliette

Karen (KAIR-ren)
   Alternate spellings: Karin, Caryn,
   Caren, Karyn, Karon, Karan, Caron,
   Karren
Kayden (KAY-den)
Kelly (KEL-lee)
   Alternate spellings: Kelley, Kelli, Kellie
Kelsey (KEL-see)
   Alternate spellings: Kelsie, Kelsea,
   Kelsi, Kelcie
Kendall (KEN-dell)
   Alternate spellings: Kendal
Kendra (KEN-druh)
Kenna (KEN-nuh)
Kennedy (KEN-uh-dee)
   Alternate spellings: Kennedi
Kenneth (KEN-neth)
Kenya (KEN-yuh [AA])
   Alternate spellings: Kenia
Kenyatta (ken-YAW-tuh [AA])
Kenzie (KEN-zee; see also Kinsey)
Keshia (KEE-shee-yuh or KEE-shuh [AA])
   Alternate spellings: Kisha, Keesha,
   Kecia*, Keisha*
Kristen (KRIS-ten [CG])
   Alternate spellings: Kristin, Christin,
   Christen*, Kristyn, Kristan, Cristin

Lanette (lan-NET; see also Lynette)
Laurel (LOR-rel)
Lauren (LOR-ren)
   Alternate spellings: Lauryn, Loren,
   Lorene*
Lauretta (lor-RET-uh, low-RET-uh [IT])
   Alternate spellings: Loretta*
Laurette (lor-RETT [FR])
Lelia (LEE-lee-yuh, LAY-lee-yuh,
   LEL-ee-yuh [IT])
Lempi (LEM-pee [SCAN])
Lena (LEE-nuh, LEN-uh [IT])
   Alternate spellings: Lina*, Lenna
Lennie (LEN-nee)
Lenora (len-OR-ruh [SP])
   Alternate spellings: Leonora*
Lenore (len-NOR)
   Alternate spellings: Leonor*, Leonore
Leonor (LEE-yoh-nor, len-NOR)
   Alternate spellings: Leonore, Lenore*
Leslie (LES-lee)
   Alternate spellings: Lesly, Lesley, Lesli
Lessie (LES-see)
Leticia (luh-TEE-shu, let-EE-see-yuh or
   let-EE-thee-yuh [SP])
   Alternate spellings: Latisha, Letitia
Letizia (let-TEET-zee-yuh [IT])
Lettie (LET-ee, LED-ee)
Lexi (LEK-see)
   Alternate spellings: Lexie
Lexus (LEK-sis)
Lilliam (LIL-ee-yem)
Lillian (LIL-ee-yen)
   Alternate spellings: Lilian, Lilyan
Lisbet (LIZ-bet or liz-BET)
Lissette (liz-ZET, lee-SET, lee-ZET [FR])
   Alternate spellings: Lisette, Lizette,
   Lizeth*
Lizabeth (LY-zuh-beth, LIZ-uh-beth)
Lizbeth (LIZ-beth, liz-BETH; see also
   Lisbet)
   Alternate spellings: Lisbeth
Lizeth (LY-zeth, liz-ZET)
   Alternate spellings: Lissette, Lisette,
   Lizette
London (LUN-den)
Lorelei (LOR-rell-lee, LOR-rell-ly [GER])
Lorena (lor-RAY-nuh, lor-REE-nuh,
   lor-REN-uh [IT/SP])
Lorene (lor-REEN, LOR-ren, lor-RAYN [FR])
   Alternate spellings: Laureen, Loreen,
   Lorine, Laurine, Lauren*, Lauryn,
   Loren, Lorraine*

Lorenza (lor-REN-zuh [IT])
Loretta (lor-RET-uh [IT])
  Alternate spellings: Lauretta*
Lorraine (lor-RAYN, lor-REN [FR])
  Alternate spellings: Loraine, Laraine,
  Lorene*
Louella (loo-WELL-uh)
  Alternate spellings: Luella
Lourdes (LOR-dess or LOR-deth [SP],
  LOORD [FR])
Luciena (loo-see-YEN-uh)
Lucienne (loo-see-YAN, loo-see-YEN
  with sustained N [FR])
Luetta (loo-WET-uh)
Luvenia (loo-VEN-nee-yuh,
  loo-VAY-nee-yuh; see also Lavinia)
  Alternate spellings: Louvenia
Lynette (lin-NETT [FR]; see also Lanette)
  Alternate spellings: Lynnette, Linette,
  Lanette

Mackenzie (muh-KEN-zee, mik-KEN-zee,
  mak-KEN-zee)
  Alternate spellings: Mckenzie,
  Makenzie
Madelena (mad-uh-LEN-uh [IT])
Magdalen (MAG-duh-len)
  Alternate spellings: Magdalene*
Mairwen (MY-yur-wen or MYR-wen [WL],
  MAIR-wen)
Manuela (man-WELL-uh [SP]; see also
  Emmanuela)
Marcelina (mar-sell-EE-nuh or
  mar-thell-EE-nuh [SP],
  mar-che-LEE-nuh [IT])
Marceline (mar-sell-EEN with sustained
  N [FR])
Marcella (mar-SELL-uh or mar-THELL-uh
  [SP], mar-CHELL-uh [IT])
  Alternate spellings: Marcela [SP]
Marcelle (mar-SELL [FR])
Margaret (MAR-gret, MAR-gur-ret)
  Alternate spellings: Margret,
  Margarett, Margarette, Margarete
Margaretta (mar-gar-RET-uh)
Marian (MAIR-ree-yen)
  Alternate spellings: Marion
Maribel (MAIR-rib-bell, mair-ee-BELL [FR])
  Alternate spellings: Marybelle
Maricela (mar-ree-SELL-luh or
  mar-ree-THELL-luh [SP])
  Alternate spellings: Marisela
Mariel (MAIR-ree-yell, MAR-ree-yell [GER],
  mair-ree-YELL [FR])

  Alternate spellings: Marielle [FR]
Mariella (mair-ree-YELL-uh,
  mar-ree-YELL-uh [SP])
  Alternate spellings: Mariela
Marietta (mair-ree-YET-uh,
  mar-ree-YET-uh [IT])
Marilena (mar-ree-LEN-uh [IT]; see also
  Marlena)
Marlena (mar-LAY-nuh, mar-LEN-uh;
  see also Marilena)
Marvel (MAR-vul, mar-VELL [FR])
Marybeth (mair-ree-BETH)
  Alternate spellings: Maribeth
Maryellen (mair-ree-YELL-en)
Maybelle (may-BELL)
  Alternate spellings: Maybell
McKenna (mik-KEN-uh, muh-KEN-uh)
  Alternate spellings: Makenna,
  Makena,
Meadow (MED-oh)
Meg (MEG [CG])
Megan (MAY-gen [IR], MEG-en, MEE-gen)
  Alternate spellings: Meghan, Meagan,
  Maegan, Meaghan, Meghann
Melanie (MEL-en-ee, may-lan-NEE [FR])
  Alternate spellings: Melany, Melonie,
  Mélanie
Melba (MEL-buh)
Melina (mel-LEE-nuh)
Melinda (mel-LIN-duh, muh-LIN-duh)
  Alternate spellings: Malinda
Melisa (mel-LEE-suh, muh-LISS-uh)
Meliss (mel-LISS)
Melissa (muh-LISS-uh, mel-LISS-uh,
  may-lee-SAW [FR])
  Alternate spellings: Melisa*, Mellissa,
  Malissa, Mellisa, Melissa
Mellie (MEL-ee)
Melody (MEL-oh-dee)
  Alternate spellings: Melodie
Melva (MEL-vuh [CG])
Melvina (mel-VEE-nuh [CG])
Michael (MY-kell, mee-chy-ELL with
  guttural CH [HEB])
Michaela (mik-ELL-uh or mik-y-YELL-uh
  [IT], muh-KAY-luh, mee-chy-ELL-uh
  with guttural CH [HEB])
  Alternate spellings: Makayla*,
  Mikayla, Mckayla, Mikaela, Micaela,
  Makaila, Mikala
Michelina (mee-shell-EE-nuh [IT],
  mik-ell-LEE-nuh [SP])
Michelle (muh-SHELL, mish-ELL,
  mee-SHELL [FR], MEE-shell)

Alternate spellings: Michele, Michell, Mechelle, Machelle, Michèle [FR]

Millicent (MILL-iss-ent)

Morgan (MOR-gen)

Mozella (moh-ZELL-uh)

Mozelle (moh-ZELL)
Alternate spellings: Mozell

Muriel (MUR-ee-yell [CG/HEB])

Nanette (nan-NET [FR])
Alternate spellings: Nannette

Nayeli (ny-YELL-ee, naw-YELL-ee [SP], NY-yell-ee, NAY-yell-ee)
Alternate spellings: Nayely, Nayelli

Nedra (NED-ruh, NAY-druh)

Nelda (NELL-duh)

Nélida (NELL-ee-duh [SP], nell-LEE-duh)

Nell (NELL)
Alternate spellings: Nelle

Nella (NELL-uh [IT])

Nellie (NELL-ee)
Alternate spellings: Nelly

Neta (NEE-tuh, NETT-uh [HEB], NED-uh; see also Nita)
Alternate spellings: Netta

Nettie (NET-ee, NED-ee)

Neva (NEE-vuh, NAY-vuh, NEV-uh)

Nevaeh (nev-AY-yuh, nev-VY-yuh)

Nicolette (nik-oh-LET, nee-koh-LET [FR])

Noelia (noh-WELL-ee-yuh)

Noelle (noh-WELL [FR])
Alternate spellings: Noel

Noemi (no-WEM-ee, noh-WAY-mee [IT/SP], noh-way-MEE [FR])
Alternate spellings: Noémie

Novella (noh-VEL-uh [IT])

Odell (oh-DELL [AA/IR])

Odessa (oh-DESS-uh)

Odetta (oh-DETT-uh)

Odette (oh-DET [FR])

Ofelia (oh-FELL-ee-yuh [IT/SP], oh-FEE-lee-yuh)
Alternate spellings: Ophelia*

Oleta (oh-LEE-tuh or oh-LET-uh [AA])

Ozella (oh-ZELL-uh)

Pamela (PAM-el-uh)
Alternate spellings: Pamala

Pamella (pam-ELL-uh [IT])

Paoletta (pow-LET-uh [IT])

Patience (PAY-shens)

Pauletta (paw-LET-uh)

Paulette (paw-LET, poh-LET [FR])

Payton (PAY-ten)
Alternate spellings: Peyton

Peggy (PEG-ee [CG])
Alternate spellings: Peggie

Penelope (pen-NELL-oh-pee, pay-nay-LOHP)
Alternate spellings: Pénélope

Penny (PEN-ee)
Alternate spellings: Pennie, Penni

Petra (PAY-truh [GRK/HUN], PET-ruh)

Petranella (pay-truh-NELL-uh)

Precious (PRESH-iss)

Presley (PRESS-lee)

Princess (PRIN-sess)

Prudence (PROO-dens)

Rachel (RAY-chell, ruh-CHELL with guttural CH [HEB], raw-SHELL [FR])
Alternate spellings: Rachael, Racheal

Rachelle (raw-SHELL [FR])
Alternate spellings: Richelle, Rochelle*

Rafaela (raf-fay-YELL-uh, raf-fy-YELL-uh [IT], raw-fuh-ELL-uh [HEB/SP])

Raquel (rrrak-ELL [FR/SP], raw-KEL)
Alternate spellings: Racquel

Raven (RAY-ven [AA])

Rebecca (reb-EK-uh, RIV-kuh [HEB], rrreb-AY-kuh [SP])
Alternate spellings: Rebekah, Rebeca, Rivka* or Rivke [HEB]

Regina (rej-EE-nuh [IT])

Rena (REE-nuh [HEB], ren-NAY)
Alternate spellings: Renae, Rene, Renee*, Renea*, Ranee*

Renata (ren-AW-tuh [IT])

Renea (ren-NAY-yuh, ren-NAY)
Alternate spellings: Renee*

Renee (ren-NAY, rrren-NAY [FR])
Alternate spellings: Renée [FR], Renae, Rene, Rena*, Renea*, Ranee*

Ressie (RES-see)

Retta (RET-tuh)

Rezsin (REZH-in [HUN])

Rhiannon (ree-YAN-nun [WL], REE-yen-en)

Rochelle (roh-SHELL or ruh-SHELL [FR])
Alternate spellings: Rachelle*, Richelle

Rosella (roh-ZELL-uh)
Alternate spellings: Rozella

Rosetta (roh-ZET-tuh [IT])

Ryan (RY-yen)
Alternate spellings: Ryann [CG]

Scarlett (SKAR-let)
  Alternate spellings: Scarlet
Selena (sell-LEEN-uh, sell-LEN-uh or
  thell-LEN-uh [SP])
  Alternate spellings: Celina*, Selina,
  Salina
Selma (SEL-muh [GER/SCAN/SP])
  Sequoia (seh-KOI-yuh [NA])
  Alternate spellings: Sequoya
Serena (sur-REEN-uh, suh-REN-uh [IT/SP],
  thu-REN-uh [SP])
  Alternate spellings: Sarina
Serenity (sur-REN-it-ee)
Shannon (SHAN-en [IR])
  Alternate spellings: Shannan, Shanon
Sharon (SHAIR-ren, shar-ROHN [HEB])
  Alternate spellings: Sharron, Sharyn,
  Sharen, Sheron, Sherron
Sienna (see-YEN-uh, shee-YAY-nuh [JAP])
Signe (ZEEN-yaw [SCAN], SEEN-yeh [FR])
  Alternate spellings: Cigne
Stella (STEL-luh [IT])
Stephania (stef-FAW-nee-yuh)
  Alternate spellings: Stefania [IT]
Stephanie (STEF-uh-nee [GRK],
  stay-faw-NEE [FR])
  Alternate spellings: Stephany, Stefani,
  Stephani, Stefanie, Stephenie,
  Stephanie [FR]
Suellen (soo-WELL-en)
Suzette (soo-ZETT [FR])

Tamela (TAM-el-uh or tam-ELL-uh [AA])
  Alternate spellings: Tamala
Tangela (TAN-jell-uh)
Tatum (TAY-tem)
Tennie (TEN-ee)
Tennille (ten-NEEL)
Tess (TES)
Tessa (TES-suh)
Tessie (TES-see)
Thelma (THEL-muh)
Tressa (TRESS-uh; see also Teressa)
  Alternate spellings: Tresa
Tressie (TRESS-ee)
Trena (TREN-nuh [SP], TREE-nuh)
  Alternate spellings: Trina*
Tristan (TRIS-ten [WL], trees-TAW with
  short N [FR], trees-TAWN or
  treeth-TAWN [SP])
  Alternate spellings: Tristen

Valencia (val-LEN-see-yuh,
  vuh-LEN-chuh [IT], vaw-LEN-see-yaw

or baw-LEN-thee-yaw [SP])
Valentina (val-en-TEEN-uh [IT/SP])
Valentine (VAL-en-tyn, val-en-TEEN with
  sustained N [FR])
Valeria (val-ur-REE-yuh, val-AIR-ee-yuh [IT])
Vanessa (van-NESS-suh)
  Alternate spellings: Vanesa, Venessa
Velda (VEL-duh)
Vella (VEL-luh)
Velma (VEL-muh)
Velva (VEL-vuh)
Vena (VEE-nuh, VEN-uh [IT])
Venita (ven-NEE-tuh)
Vernell (vur-NELL)
Vesta (VESS-tuh)
Vicenta (vee-SEN-tuh or bee-THEN-tuh
  [SP])
Vincenza (veen-CHEN-zuh [IT])
Violet (VY-yoh-let)
Violetta (vee-yoh-LET-uh [IT])
Violette (vee-yoh-LETT [FR])
Vivienne (viv-ee-YAN, vee-vee-YEN with
  sustained N [FR])
  Alternate spellings: Vivien

Waleska (vaw-LESS-kuh or wall-LESS-kuh)
  Alternate spellings: Valeska
Waneta (wah-NET-uh, wah-NEE-tuh)
  Alternate spellings: Wanita, Juanita*
Wilhelmina (vill-hel-MEE-nuh [GER])
Wilhelmine (vill-hel-MEEN [GER])
Winifred (WIN-uh-fred [CG])
  Alternate spellings: Winnifred

Ximena (hee-MEN-uh [SP])
  Alternate spellings: Jimena

Yarden (YAR-den [HEB])
  Alternate spellings: Jordan*
Yareli (yar-RELL-ee [SP])
Yesenia (yess-SAY-nee-yuh,
  yee-SEN-ee-yuh or ye-THEN-ee-yuh
  [SP], yes-SEE-nuh [AR])
  Alternate spellings: Yessenia,
  Jessenia*
Yetta (YET-uh)
Yvette (ee-VETT [FR], iv-ETT)
  Alternate spellings: Ivette, Evette

Zelda (ZELL-duh [GER])
Zella (ZEL-luh)
Zelma (ZEL-muh; see also Selma)
Zenda (ZEN-duh [PER])
Zetta (ZET-tuh, ZED-duh)

■ LONG I (EYE OR Y) ■

Abigail (AB-big-ayl, aw-vee-GYL [HEB])
  Alternate spellings: Abbigail, Abigayle,
  Abigale, Abagail, Avigayil [HEB]
Adeline (AD-uh-lin, ADD-uh-lyn,
  ad-dell-LEEN with sustained N [FR])
  Alternate spellings: Adaline
Aida (eye-YEE-duh [AR], aw-YEE-duh,
  EYE-duh, AY-duh)
  Alternate spellings: Ada*, Adah, Eda*
Aiko (EYE-koh [JAP])
Aileen (AY-leen [IR], eye-LEEN)
  Alternate spellings: Eileen*, Ilene,
  Aline*, Allene, Alene
Aisha (eye-YEE-shuh or EYE-yee-shuh
  [AR], aw-YEE-shuh, EYE-shuh)
  Alternate spellings: Iesha
Amiya (AW-mee-yuh, uh-MY-yuh)
  Alternate spellings: Amiyah, Amaya*,
  Amya [HEB]
Anaïs (aw-naw-EES [FR], ann-NY-yiss)
Aniya (aw-NY-yuh, uh-NEE-yuh,
  AW-nee-yuh [HEB])
  Alternate spellings: Aniyah, Anaya*,
  Anya*, Analla
Anya (AWN-yuh [RUS], uh-NY-yuh)
  Alternate spellings: Aniya*, Aniyah,
  Analla
Ayana (ay-YAWN-uh, eye-YAWN-uh)
  Alternate spellings: Ayana, Aiyana,
  Iyana
Ayanna (ay-YAN-uh, eye-YAN-uh)
  Alternate spellings: Iyanna
Ayla (AY-luh, EYE-luh)
Aylin (AY-lin, EYE-lin)

Carolina (kair-oh-LY-nuh, kar-oh-LEE-nuh
  [GER/IT/SP])
Caroline (KAIR-oh-lin, kair-oh-LYN,
  kar-oh-LEEN [FR])
  Alternate spellings: Carolyn, Karolyn,
  Carolynn
Chaya (SHY-yuh, CHY-yuh [HEB/EI])
Cheyenne (shy-ANN)
  Alternate spellings: Cheyanne,
  Shyanne, Shyann
China (CHY-nuh)
Clementine (KLEM-en-tyn,
  klem-en-TEEN with sustained N [FR])
Cypress (SY-priss)

Dayana (DAY-yaw-nuh [AA], dy-YAN-nuh)
  Alternate spellings: Diana*, Dianna

Delilah (del-LY-luh [HEB])
  Alternate spellings: Delila
Diamond (DY-mund)
Diana (dy-YAN-uh, dee-YAWN-uh [IT/SP])
  Alternate spellings: Dayana*, Dianna
Diane (dy-YAN, dee-YAN [FR])
  Alternate spellings: Diann, Dianne,
  Dian, Deann*, Deanne, Dionne*
Dina (DEE-nuh [IT], DY-nuh, dee-NAW [HEB])
  Alternate spellings: Dena, Deena,
  Deana, Dinah

Eileen (eye-LEEN [CG])
  Alternate spellings: Aileen*, Ilene
Elida (el-LEE-duh or el-LY-duh)
Elmira (el-MY-ruh, el-MEER-ruh)
Elvira (el-VY-ruh)
Emeline (em-uh-LEEN with sustained N
  [FR], em-uh-LYN, EM-uh-lin)
  Alternate spellings: Emmeline,
  Emmaline, Emelyn, Emaleen

Freya (FRAY-yuh or FRY-yuh [SCAN])
  Alternate spellings: Freja

Heidi (HY-dee [GER])
Hermione (hur-MY-yoh-nee [BR])

Icie (EYE-see, ISS-ee)
Ida (EYE-duh [GER], EE-duh [IR])
  Alternate spellings: Ide
Idell (eye-DELL)
Idella (eye-DELL-uh)
Ila (EYE-luh)
Ima (EYE-muh, EE-muh)
Ina (EYE-nuh, EE-nuh)
Inez (ee-NEZ, eye-NESS or eye-NETH
  [SP], ee-NESS)
  Alternate spellings: Inès [FR]
Iola (eye-YOH-luh)
Iona (eye-YOH-nuh [IR])
Ione (eye-YOH-nee, eye-YOHN [FR])
Ira (EYE-ruh)
Ireland (EYER-lend)
Irene (eye-REEN, ee-RAY-nuh [HUN],
  ee-REN or ee-ray-NAY [FR])
  Alternate spellings: Irène or Iréné
Iris (EYE-riss)
Isis (EYE-sis)
Iva (EYE-vuh, EE-vuh)
  Alternate spellings: Ivah, Eva*
Ivelisse (ee-vuh-LEES, eye-vuh-LEES)
Ivory (EYE-vor-ree)
Ivy (EYE-vee)

Izetta (eye-ZET-tuh)
Izora (eye-ZOR-ruh)

Jamya (juh-MY-yuh [AA])
Janiya (jan-NY-yuh [AA], jan-NEE-yuh [AA/AR])
  Alternate spellings: Janiyah
Jemima (jem-MY-muh, yuh-MY-muh [HEB])
  Alternate spellings: Yemima* [HEB]

Kaya (KY-yuh [NA/SCAN/JAP], KAY-yuh)
  Alternate spellings: Kaia [SCAN], Kaiya
  [JAP], Kya*, Kiya, Kia
Kayla (KAY-luh or KY-luh [IR])
  Alternate spellings: Kaila, Cayla [HEB],
  Keyla, Kaylah, Kaela, Keila, Kala,
  Kyla*, Keilah [HEB], Khayla*
Kya (KEE-yuh, KY-yuh)
  Alternate spellings: Kiya, Kia, Kaya*,
  Kaia, Kaiya [JAP]
Kyla (KY-luh or KEE-luh [IR])
  Alternate spellings: Kayla*, Kaila,
  Cayla, Keyla, Kaylah, Kaela, Keila
Kyle (KYL)
Kylie (KY-lee [CG])
  Alternate spellings: Kylee, Kiley,
  Kyleigh

Laisha (ly-YEE-shuh [AA])
Layla (LAY-luh, LY-luh [HEB], LY-luh with
  pronounced H at end [AR])
  Alternate spellings: Laila, Leila*,
  Leyla, Lela, Lelah, Lila*, Lyla, Lilah
Lila (LY-luh [AR], LEE-luh)
  Alternate spellings: Layla*, Laila,
  Leila*, Leyla, Lela, Lelah, Lyla, Lilah
Liza (LY-zuh, LEE-zuh [IT])
Lizabeth (LY-zuh-beth, LIZ-uh-beth)
Lizeth (LY-zeth, liz-ZET)
  Alternate spellings: Lissette, Lisette,
  Lizette
Lorelei (LOR-rell-lee, LOR-rell-ly [GER])
Lyda (LY-duh, LEE-duh)
  Alternate spellings: Lida

Mai (MY [JAP/VI], MAY)
Mairwen (MY-yur-wen or MYR-wen [WL],
  MAIR-wen)
Malaika (muh-LY-kuh [AA])
  Alternate spellings: Malika*, Malikah
Maria (mar-REE-yuh [IT/SP], mar-RY-yuh)
  Alternate spellings: Mariah*, Moriah*
Mariah (mar-RY-yuh, muh-RY-yuh)
  Alternate spellings: Maria*, Moriah*
Maya (MY-yuh [EI/GRK/NA])

  Alternate spellings: Mya, Maia [HEB],
  Myah
Mayra (MAY-ruh, MY-ruh)
  Alternate spellings: Maira, Myra*, Mira
Micah (MY-kuh, MEE-chaw with guttural
  CH [HEB])
  Alternate spellings: Micha [HEB]
Michael (MY-kell, mee-chy-ELL with
  guttural CH [HEB])
Michaela (mik-ELL-uh or mik-y-YELL-uh
  [IT], muh-KAY-luh, mee-chy-ELL-uh
  with guttural CH [HEB])
  Alternate spellings: Makayla*,
  Mikayla, Mckayla, Mikaela, Micaela,
  Makaila, Mikala
Moriah (mor-RY-yuh, moh-ree-YAW [HEB],
  muh-RY-yuh)
  Alternate spellings: Moriya [HEB],
  Moria, Mariah*, Maria*
Myra (MY-ruh)
  Alternate spellings: Mayra*, Maira

Nayeli (ny-YELL-ee, naw-YELL-ee [SP],
  NY-yell-ee, NAY-yell-ee)
  Alternate spellings: Nayely, Nayelli
Nevaeh (nev-AY-yuh, nev-VY-yuh)
Neyla (NY-luh [AR], NAY-luh, NEE-luh [IR])
  Alternate spellings: Nila, Nyla*, Neala
  or Neila [IR]
Nina (NEE-nuh [AR/FR/HEB/IT/RUS/SP], NY-nuh)
  Alternate spellings: Neena
Nyah (NEE-yuh or NY-yuh [AA])
  Alternate spellings: Nya, Nia [WL]
Nyasia (ny-YAY-zhuh, ny-YAY-see-yuh,
  nee-YAY-zhuh)
Nydia (NID-ee-yuh, NEE-dee-yuh [SP])
Nyla (NY-luh, NEE-luh)
  Alternate spellings: Nila, Neyla*

Piper (PY-pur)

Rafaela (raf-fay-YELL-uh, raf-fy-YELL-uh
  [IT], raw-fuh-ELL-uh [HEB/SP])
Riley (RY-lee)
  Alternate spellings: Rylee, Rylie,
  Ryleigh, Reilly
Ryan (RY-yen)
  Alternate spellings: Ryann [CG]

Sanaa (SAW-naw or suh-NY [AR])
Saniya (suh-NY-yuh or suh-NEE-yuh [AA],
  san-NY-yuh [AR], SAWN-yuh)
  Alternate spellings: Saniyya [AR],
  Sanya*, Sonia*, Sonya

Sarai (suh-RY [HEB])
Sariah (suh-RY-yuh)
Shania (shuh-NY-yuh, shuh-NEE-yuh)
   Alternate spellings: Shaniya
Skye (SKY)
   Alternate spellings: Sky
Skyla (SKY-luh [CG])
Skylar (SKY-lur)
   Alternate spellings: Skyler

Taya (TAY-yuh, TY-yuh)
   Alternate spellings: Tea, Thea*
Thyra (THY-ruh, TY-ruh)
   Alternate spellings: Tyra*, Tira
Twila (TWY-luh)
   Alternate spellings: Twyla
Tyesha (ty-YEESH-uh [AA])
Tyler (TY-lur)
Tyra (TY-ruh [SCAN/AA])
   Alternate spellings: Thyra*, Tira

Vida (VY-duh, VEE-duh)
   Alternate spellings: Veda*, Vita*
Viola (vy-YOH-luh, vee-YOH-law [IT/SP],
   bee-YOH-law [SP])
Violet (VY-yoh-let)
Vita (VEE-tuh [IT], VY-duh)
   Alternate spellings: Vida*, Veda*

Winona (win-OH-nuh [NA], wy-NOH-nuh [BR])
   Alternate spellings: Wynona, Wenona
Wyatt (WY-yet)
Wylie (WY-lee)

Yahaira (juh-HY-ruh or yaw-HY-ruh [SP])
   Alternate spellings: Yajaira
Yemima (yuh-MY-muh [HEB])
   Alternate spellings: Jemima*

Zaida (ZAY-duh, zy-YEE-duh,
   zaw-HED-uh with pronounced H at
   end [AR])
Zaria (zuh-RY-yuh, ZAR-ree-yuh)
Zina (ZY-nuh, ZEE-nuh [AR])
   Alternate spellings: Zena, Xena*
Zoraida (zoh-RAY-duh with pronounced
   H at end [AR], zor-RY-duh [SP])

■ **SHORT I (I)** ■

PARTNER POINTER:
Short E, I, and U often sound similar.

Abigail (AB-big-ayl, aw-vee-GYL [HEB])
   Alternate spellings: Abbigail,
   Abigayle, Abigale, Abagail, Avigayil
   [HEB]
Abril (AB-rill, AY-brill, aw-BREEL [AR/SP],
   awv-REEL [SP])
Addison (ADD-iss-un)
Adeline (AD-uh-lin, ADD-uh-lyn,
   ad-dell-LEEN with sustained N [FR])
   Alternate spellings: Adaline
Alanis (uh-LAW-niss, uh-LAN-niss)
Alexis (uh-LEK-siss)
   Alternate spellings: Alexys, Alexus
Alice (AL-liss, al-LEES [FR])
   Alternate spellings: Alyce
Alissa (uh-LISS-uh)
   Alternate spellings: Elissa, Alyssa,
   Elyssa, Allyssa
Allison (AL-liss-sun, al-lee-SAW with
   short N [FR])
   Alternate spellings: Alison, Allyson,
   Alyson
Amaris (AM-ur-riss, uh-MAIR-riss,
   uh-MAR-riss)
Amaryllis (am-uh-RILL-iss)
America (uh-MAIR-rik-uh,
   aw-MAIR-ree-kuh [IT])
Amina (AW-min-uh or aw-MEE-nuh [HEB]
   with pronounced H at end [AR])
Anissa (uh-NISS-uh, aw-NEES-suh [AR])
Annika (AW-nik-uh or ANN-ik-uh [SCAN],
   aw-NEE-kuh [AA], aw-NEE-kuh with
   pronounced H at end [AR])
   Alternate spellings: Anika
Annis (ANN-iss, aw-NEES)
Ardis (AR-diss)
Ardith (AR-dith)
Arvilla (ar-VILL-uh)
Ashlyn (ASH-lin)
   Alternate spellings: Ashlynn
Astrid (AST-rid [BR/SCAN])
Avis (AY-viss)
Avlyn (AV-lin)
Awilda (uh-WILL-duh)
Aylin (AY-lin, EYE-lin)

Beatrice (BEE-yuh-triss, bay-yuh-TREES
   [FR/SP], vay-yuh-TRITH [SP])
   Alternate spellings: Beatriz [SP]

Beatrix (BEE-yuh-triks [GER/SCAN], bay-yuh-TREEKS [IT])
Belinda (bell-IN-duh)
Beryl (BAIR-rill)
Bethany (BETH-in-nee)
Billie (BILL-ee)
  Alternate spellings: Billye, Billy
Bridget (BRID-jid or BRID-jet [IR])
  Alternate spellings: Bridgett, Bridgette, Brigit [SCAN]Bridie (BRY-dee [CG])
Brigitte (brih-GIT-uh, bree-ZHEET [FR])
Britney (BRIT-nee)
  Alternate spellings: Brittney, Brittni, Britni, Brittny
Brittany (BRIT-uh-nee)
  Alternate spellings: Britany, Brittanie
Brooklyn (BROOK-lin)
  Alternate spellings: Brooklynn
Brunilda (broo-NIL-duh)
Brynn (BRIN [WL])

Calista (kuh-LISS-tuh)
Camilla (kam-MILL-luh, kaw-MEE-luh [IT/SP])
  Alternate spellings: Camila
Cándida (KAWN-did-uh [SP], kan-DEE-duh)
Carina (kar-REE-nuh [IT/SP], kuh-RIN-uh [SCAN])
Carissa (kuh-RISS-uh)
  Alternate spellings: Karissa, Carisa, Charissa*
Carys (KAR-ris [WL], KAIR-ris)
Cassidy (KASS-sid-ee [IR])
  Alternate spellings: Kassidy
Cecil (SESS-ill, SEE-sill)
Cecily (SESS-ill-ee [CG])
Charissa (shuh-RISS-uh, kuh-RISS-uh)
  Alternate spellings: Carissa*
Charity (CHAIR-rit-ee)
Chasity (CHAS-sit-ee)
Chastity (CHAS-tit-ee)
Cherish (CHAIR-rish)
Cheryl (SHAIR-rill)
  Alternate spellings: Sheryl, Cheryle, Sherrill, Sherryl
Chris (KRIS)
  Alternate spellings: Kris
Chrissy (KRIS-see)
  Alternate spellings: Crissy
Christen (KRISS-sen, KRISS-ten, krees-TA with short N [FR])
  Alternate spellings: Kristen*
Christian (KRISS-chen, kree-stee-YAN [FR])
  Alternate spellings: Kristian,

Christiane [FR]
Christiana (kris-tee-YAWN-uh, krees-tee-YAWN-aw [IT])
  Alternate spellings: Cristiana
Christina (kris-TEE-nuh, kree-STEE-nuh [IT/SP], kreeth-TEE-nuh [SP])
  Alternate spellings: Kristina, Cristina [IT/SP], Krystina
Christine (kris-TEEN, kree-STEEN [FR])
  Alternate spellings: Kristine, Christene, Christeen
Christopher (KRIS-toh-fur)
Christy (KRIS-tee)
  Alternate spellings: Kristy, Kristie, Cristy, Christie, Christi
Cinda (SIN-duh)
Cindy (SIN-dee)
  Alternate spellings: Cindi, Cyndi
Citlali (sit-LAW-lee)
Clarissa (klair-RISS-uh)
Clotilde (kloh-TIL-dee or kloh-TIL-duh [GER], kloh-TEELD [FR], kloh-TEEL-deh [IT])
  Alternate spellings: Clothilde [FR]
Corinne (kor-REEN [GRK/FR], kor-RIN)
  Alternate spellings: Corrine, Corine, Corene, Coreen
Corliss (KOR-liss)
Crystal (KRIS-tell, krees-TAWL or krees-TELL [FR])
  Alternate spellings: Krystal, Cristal, Kristal, Krystle, Chrystal, Christal, Christel, Christelle [FR]
Cynthia (SIN-thee-yuh)
Cypress (SY-priss)

Dallas (DAL-liss)
Damaris (DAM-ur-riss, duh-MAIR-ris, duh-MAR-ris)
Danica (DAN-ik-uh)
Daryl (DAIR-rill)
Davin (DAV-in [IR])
Desiree (DEZ-ih-ray, dez-ee-RAY [FR])
  Alternate spellings: Desirae
Dimple (DIM-pull)
Dixie (DIK-see)
Dominique (daw-min-EEK, doh-mee-NEEK [FR])
  Alternate spellings: Dominque, Domonique
Dorinda (dor-RIN-duh)
Doris (DOR-riss)
  Alternate spellings: Dorris
Dorit (DOR-rit [GER/HEB])
Drucilla (droo-SILL-uh)

Dylan (DILL-en)

Ellen (EL-lin)
Alternate spellings: Elin [SCAN]
Elois (el-OH-wiss, EE-loh-wiss,
EL-oh-weez)
Alternate spellings: Eloise*, Elouise
Emeline (em-uh-LEEN with sustained N
[FR], em-uh-LYN, EM-uh-lin)
Alternate spellings: Emmeline,
Emmaline, Emelyn, Emaleen
Emily (EM-ill-ee)
Alternate spellings: Emilee, Emely,
Emilie*, Emmalee
Enid (EE-nid)
Erica (AIR-rik-uh [SCAN], AIR-ree-kuh [IT])
Alternate spellings: Erika, Ericka
Erin (AIR-rin [CG])
Eris (AIR-riss)
Erlinda (ur-LIN-duh, air-LEEN-duh [SP])
Ethelyn (ETH-ell-lin)
Evelyn (EV-uh-lin)
Alternate spellings: Evelin, Evalyn

Fatima (FAW-tim-uh or FAWT-muh [AR],
fat-EE-muh [IT])
Felicity (fell-LISS-sit-ee)
Francisca (fran-SIS-kuh, fran-SEES-kuh
or fran-THEETH-kuh [SP])

Genesis (JEN-uh-sis)
Geralyn (JAIR-rull-lin)
Alternate spellings: Jerilyn
Gilda (GIL-duh, JIL-duh [IT])
Gillian (GIL-ee-yen [CG], JIL-ee-yen)
Alternate spellings: Jillian*
Ginger (JIN-jur)
Ginny (JIN-ee; see also Jenny)
Gisela (jiz-ZELL-uh)
Alternate spellings: Gisella, Jizella
Giselle (jiz-ELL, zhee-ZELL [FR])
Alternate spellings: Gisselle, Jizelle
Gladys (GLAD-iss)
Alternate spellings: Gladyce [WL]
Glynis (GLIN-iss [WL])
Griselda (griz-ELL-duh [GER], gree-SELL-duh
or gree-THELL-duh [SP])
Alternate spellings: Grizelda
Gwendolyn (GWEN-doh-lin [WL])
Gwyneth (GWIN-eth [WL])

Hedwig (HED-wig, HAYT-vik [GER])
Hilda (HIL-duh [HEB/SCAN])
Hilde (HIL-dee [SCAN])

Hildegarde (HIL-duh-gard [SCAN])
Alternate spellings: Hildegard
Hildred (HIL-dred [SCAN])
Hildur (HIL-dur [SCAN])
Hillary (HIL-ur-ree)
Alternate spellings: Hilary
Hilma (HIL-muh)

Icie (EYE-see, ISS-ee)
Ilana (il-LAW-nuh, uh-LAW-nuh,
ee-law-NAW [HEB])
Alternate spellings: Alana*, Alanna*,
Elana*
Iliana (il-ee-YAW-nuh [SP]; see also Eliana)
Alternate spellings: Ileana
Ilsa (IL-suh [SCAN])
Alternate spellings: Ilse [GER]
Imani (im-AW-nee [AA], ee-MEN-ee [AR];
see also Amani)
Imelda (ee-MEL-duh [SP], im-MEL-duh)
Imogene (IM-oh-jeen or IM-oh-jen [BR])
Alternate spellings: Emogene,
Imogen, India (IN-dee-yuh)
Ingrid (EEN-grid [SCAN])
Iris (EYE-riss)
Isabel (IZ-uh-bell, ee-zaw-BELL [FR],
EE-saw-bell or ee-saw-BELL
or ee-thuh-VELL [SP])
Alternate spellings: Isabelle [FR],
Isabell, Isobel
Isabela (iz-uh-BELL-uh, ee-saw-BELL-uh
or ee-thaw-VELL-uh [SP],
ee-zuh-BELL-uh [IT])
Alternate spellings: Isabella [IT], Izabella
Isadora (iz-uh-DOR-ruh, ee-saw-DOR-ruh
[IT/SP], ee-thaw-DOR-ruh [SP])
Isadore (IZ-uh-dor, ee-see-DOR [FR])
Alternate spellings: Isidore [FR]
Isis (EYE-sis)
Itzel (IT-sell, eet-ZELL [NA])

Jaclyn (JAK-lin)
Alternate spellings: Jacklyn
Jacqueline (JAK-uh-lin, JAK-well-lin,
jak-LEEN, zhawk-uh-LEEN with
sustained N [FR])
Alternate spellings: Jaqueline,
Jaquelyn, Jackeline, Jaquelin,
Jacquline, Jacalyn
Janice (JAN-iss, juh-NEES [AA])
Alternate spellings: Janis
Jasmine (JAZ-min, jass-MEEN,
(JAS-oo-meen [JAP]), yaz-MEEN [AR],
yass-MEEN [HEB/PER])

Alternate spellings: Jasmin, Jazmin, Jazmine, Jazmyn, Jasmyn, Jazmyne, Yasmin*, Yazmin, Yasmine*, Yasmeen

Jazlyn (JAZZ-lin)

Jennifer (JEN-nif-ur [WL], zheh-nee-FAIR [FR])
Alternate spellings: Jenifer, Genifer

Jerrica (JAIR-rik-uh)

Jessica (JES-sik-uh)
Alternate spellings: Jessika, Jesica

Jill (JIL)

Jillian (JIL-ee-yen)
Alternate spellings: Gillian*

Jimmie (JIM-ee)

Jocelyn (JAW-sell-lin, JAWS-lin, zhoh-sell-LEEN [FR], yoh-SELL-een [SP])
Alternate spellings: Joselyn, Joceline [FR], Joycelyn*, Yoselin*

Josefa (joh-SEF-uh, ho-SEF-uh or ho-THEF-uh [SP], YOH-sif-faw or yoh-sif-FAW [HEB])
Alternate spellings: Josepha, Yosifa [HEB]

Joslyn (JAWZ-lin)

Joycelyn (JOI-suh-lin or JAW-suh-lin)
Alternate spellings: Jocelyn*, Joselyn

Judith (JOO-dith, zhoo-DEET [FR], YOO-dit or yuh-HOO-dit [HEB])
Alternate spellings: Yudit or Yehudit* [HEB]

Julissa (joo-LIS-suh or juh-LIS-uh [AA]; see also Jalisa)

Justice (JUS-tiss)

Kaitlyn (KAYT-lin [IR])
Alternate spellings: Katelyn, Caitlin, Caitlyn, Kaitlin, Katelynn, Kaitlynn, Katelin, Katlin*, Katlyn , Katlynn

Kalyn (KAL-in, KAY-lin)
Alternate spellings: Kaylin*

Kathlyn (KATH-lin)

Kathrine (KATH-rin, kath-REEN; see also Catherine)
Alternate spellings: Cathryn, Cathrine, Kathryn [CG], Kathryne

Katlin (KAT-lin, KAYT-lin)
Alternate spellings: Katlyn , Katlynn, Kaitlyn*

Kaylin (KAY-lin [IR])
Alternate spellings: Kaylyn, Kaelyn, Kailyn, Kaylynn, Kalyn*, Kaylen

Kim (KIM)

Kimberly (KIM-bur-lee)
Alternate spellings: Kimberlee, Kimberley, Kimberli

Kinsey (KIN-zee; see also Kenzie)

Kitty (KIT-tee)
Alternate spellings: Kittie

Kizzy (KIZ-ee)

Krista (KRIS-tuh [SCAN])
Alternate spellings: Christa, Krysta

Kristen (KRIS-ten [CG])
Alternate spellings: Kristin, Christin, Christen*, Kristyn, Kristan, Cristin

Larissa (luh-RISS-uh)

Lavinia (luh-VIN-ee-yuh; see also Luvenia)

Lexus (LEK-sis)

Libby (LIB-bee)
Alternate spellings: Libbie

Liberty (LIB-ur-tee)

Lilia (LIL-ee-yuh)

Liliana (lil-ee-YAWN-uh, lee-lee-YAWN-uh [IT/SP])
Alternate spellings: Lilliana

Lilike (LIL-ik-uh, LEE-lee-kuh [HUN])

Lilla (LIL-luh, LEE-luh [IT])

Lilliam (LIL-ee-yem)

Lillian (LIL-ee-yen)
Alternate spellings: Lilian, Lilyan

Lillith (LIL-ith, LIL-it [HEB])
Alternate spellings: Lilith, Lilit [HEB]

Lily (LIL-ee)
Alternate spellings: Lilly, Lillie

Linda (LIN-duh, LEEN-duh [IT/SP])
Alternate spellings: Lynda

Lindsey (LIN-zee)
Alternate spellings: Lindsay, Lyndsey, Lyndsay, Linsey

Lindy (LIN-dee)

Linnea (lin-NAY-yuh [SCAN], lin-NEE-yuh)

Linnie (LIN-nee)

Lisbet (LIZ-bet or liz-BET)

Lissa (LISS-uh, LEE-suh)
Alternate spellings: Lesa, Leisa , Leesa, Lise*, Lisa*

Lissette (liz-ZET, lee-SET, lee-ZET [FR])
Alternate spellings: Lisette, Lizette, Lizeth*

Litzy (LIT-zee)

Liv (LIV)

Livia (LIV-ee-yuh)

Liz (LIZ)

Lizabeth (LY-zuh-beth, LIZ-uh-beth)

Lizbeth (LIZ-beth, liz-BETH; see also Lisbet)
Alternate spellings: Lisbeth

Lizeth (LY-zeth, liz-ZET)

Alternate spellings: Lissette, Lisette, Lizette

Lizzie (LIZ-ee)

Lois (LOH-wiss [GRK])

Lucinda (loo-SIN-duh)

Lydia (LID-ee-yuh, LEE-dee-yuh [IT], lee-DEE [FR])
Alternate spellings: Lidia [IT], Lidie [FR]

Lynette (lin-NETT [FR]; see also Lanette)
Alternate spellings: Lynnette, Linette, Lanette

Lynn (LIN)
Alternate spellings: Lyn, Lynne

Madeline (MAD-uh-lin, MAD-uh-lyn, MAD-lin, mad-dell-LYN or mad-dell-LEN with sustained N [FR])
Alternate spellings: Madelyn, Madeleine, Madalyn, Madelynn, Madilyn, Madalynn, Madaline

Madison (MAD-iss-un)
Alternate spellings: Madisyn, Madyson, Maddison, Madisen

Malika (MEL-ik-uh or mal-EE-kuh [AR], MAW-lee-kuh [EI/HUN], muh-LY-kuh [AA])
Alternate spellings: Mallika [EI], Malikah, Milika, Mylika, Malaika*

Margit (MAR-git, mar-GEET [HUN/SCAN])

Maribel (MAIR-rib-bell, mair-ee-BELL [FR])
Alternate spellings: Marybelle

Marilee (MAIR-ril-lee)

Marilyn (MAIR-ril-lin)
Alternate spellings: Marilynn, Marylin, Marylyn, Merilyn

Marissa (mar-RISS-uh, mar-REE-suh or mar-REE-thuh [SP])
Alternate spellings: Marisa*

Marlyn (MAR-lin)
Alternate spellings: Marlen

Marlys (MAR-liss [GER])
Alternate spellings: Marlis

Matilda (muh-TIL-duh [GER], mat-TEEL-deh [IT])
Alternate spellings: Matilde*, Mathilda

Matilde (muh-TIL-dee, mat-TEELD [FR], mat-TEEL-day [SP], mat-TIL-duh [GER])
Alternate spellings: Matilda*, Mathilda, Mathilde [FR]

Mavis (MAY-viss)

McCoy (mik-KOI [CG])

McKenna (mik-KEN-uh, muh-KEN-uh)
Alternate spellings: Makenna, Makena,

Melisa (mel-LEE-suh, muh-LISS-uh)

Meliss (mel-LISS)

Melissa (muh-LISS-uh, mel-LISS-uh, may-lee-SAW [FR])
Alternate spellings: Melisa*, Mellissa, Malissa, Mellisa, Melissa

Meredith (MAIR-ruh-dith)

Meryl (MAIR-rill)

Michaela (mik-ELL-uh or mik-y-YELL-uh [IT], muh-KAY-luh, mee-chy-ELL-uh with guttural CH [HEB])
Alternate spellings: Makayla*, Mikayla, Mckayla, Mikaela, Micaela, Makaila, Mikala

Michelina (mee-shell-EE-nuh [IT], mik-ell-LEE-nuh [SP])

Michelle (muh-SHELL, mish-ELL, mee-SHELL [FR], MEE-shell)
Alternate spellings: Michele, Michell, Mechelle, Machelle, Michèle [FR]

Mickey (MIK-ee)
Alternate spellings: Mickie

Migdalia (mig-DAW-lee-yuh)

Mildred (MILL-drid)

Millicent (MILL-iss-ent)

Millie (MILL-ee)

Mindy (MIN-dee)
Alternate spellings: Mindi

Minerva (MIN-ur-vuh)

Minna (MIN-nuh or MEE-nuh [GER])

Minnie (MIN-nee [CG])

Missouri (miz-ZUR-ree)

Missy (MISS-ee)

Misty (MISS-tee)
Alternate spellings: Misti

Mittie (MITT-ee)

Mitzi (MIT-see)

Monica (MAW-nik-uh)
Alternate spellings: Monika

Myrtis (MUR-tiss)

Nicola (NIK-oh-luh, nee-KOH-luh [IT])

Nicole (nik-KOHL, nee-KOHL [FR])
Alternate spellings: Nichole, Nikole, Nichol, Nicolle

Nicolette (nik-oh-LET, nee-koh-LET [FR])

Nikita (nik-EE-tuh [GER])

Nikki (NIK-ee)
Alternate spellings: Niki

Nilda (NILL-duh)

Nilsa (NILL-suh)

Nina (NEE-nuh [AR/FR/HEB/IT/RUS/SP], NY-nuh)
Alternate spellings: Neena

Nita (NEE-tuh [HEB/SP])
Alternate spellings: Neta

Nixie (NIK-see [GER])
Nydia (NID-ee-yuh, NEE-dee-yuh [SP])

Olive (AW-liv)
Olivia (oh-LIV-ee-yuh, oh-LEE-vee-yaw
 [IT/SP], oh-LEE-bee-yaw [SP],
 uh-LIV-ee-yuh)
 Alternate spellings: Alivia
Otilia (oh-TILL-ee-yuh [SP])
 Alternate spellings: Otylia [GER]
Ottilie (aw-TILL-ee [SCAN])

Paris (PAIR-riss, pair-RRREE [FR])
Patricia (pat-RISH-uh, pat-REES-ee-yuh
 [FR/SP], pat-REE-thee-yuh [SP])
Precious (PRESH-iss)
Priscila (pris-SIL-uh, pree-SEE-luh or
 pree-THEE-luh [SP])
 Alternate spellings: Priscilla
Providenci (praw-vid-DEN-see)

Quinn (KWIN)

Rezsin (REZH-in [HUN])
Rilla (RILL-uh [GER/SCAN])
Rivka (RIV-kuh [HEB])
 Alternate spellings: Rivke
Robyn (RAW-bin)
 Alternate spellings: Robin, Robbin
Roselyn (ROHZ-lin, RAW-zuh-lin)
 Alternate spellings: Rosalyn*,
 Rosaline*, Rosalind*
Roslyn (RAWZ-lin; see also Rosalyn)

Sidonie (sid-OH-nee, SID-oh-nee,
 see-doh-NEE [FR])
Sigrid (SIG-rid [SCAN], see-GREED [FR])
Simone (sim-OHN, see-MOHN with
 sustained N [FR])
Siobhan (shiv-AWN [IR])
 Alternate spellings: Shevaun, Shavon,
 Chevonne
Sister (SIS-tur)
Sybil (SIB-bull, see-BEEL [FR]; see also
 Cybelle)
 Alternate spellings: Syble, Sibyl,
 Sybille [FR]
Sydney (SID-nee)
 Alternate spellings: Sidney, Sydnee,
 Sydni, Sydnie
Sylvia (SEEL-vee-yuh [IT], SIL-vee-yuh or
 THIL-vee-yuh [SP])
 Alternate spellings: Silvia
Sylvie (SILL-vee, SEEL-vee [FR])

Tabitha (TAB-ith-uh)
 Alternate spellings: Tabatha
Taryn (TAIR-rin [CG])
Tiffany (TIF-uh-nee)
 Alternate spellings: Tiffani, Tiffanie
Tillie (TILL-ee [GER])
Tisha (TEESH-uh or TISH-uh [AA])
Trinidad (TRIN-id-add, tree-nee-DAD [SP])
Trinity (TRIN-it-ee)
Trisha (TRISH-uh)
 Alternate spellings: Tricia
Trista (TRIS-tuh [CG])
Tristan (TRIS-ten [WL], trees-TAW with
 short N [FR], trees-TAWN or
 treeth-TAWN [SP])
 Alternate spellings: Tristen

Vicky (VIK-ee)
 Alternate spellings: Vicki, Vikki,
 Vickey, Vickie
Victoria (vik-TOR-ree-yuh,
 veek-TOR-ree-yaw or
 beek-TOR-ree-yaw [SP])
Vinnie (VIN-ee)
Virginia (vur-JIN-yuh, veer-JEE-nee-yuh
 [IT], veer-HEE-nee-yuh or
 beer-HEE-nee-yuh [SP])
Viv (VIV)
Vivia (VIV-ee-yuh)
Vivian (VIV-ee-yen)
 Alternate spellings: Vivien
Viviana (viv-ee-YAWN-uh)
Vivienne (viv-ee-YAN, vee-vee-YEN with
 sustained N [FR])
 Alternate spellings: Vivien

Whitley (WIT-lee)
Whitney (WIT-nee)
Wilda (WILL-duh, VILL-duh [GER])
Wilhelmina (vill-hel-MEE-nuh [GER])
Wilhelmine (vill-hel-MEEN [GER])
Willa (WILL-uh)
Willamina (will-uh-MEE-nuh)
Willene (will-LEEN)
Willia (WILL-ee-yuh)
Willie (WILL-ee)
Willow (WILL-oh)
Wilma (WILL-muh, VILL-muh [GER])
 Alternate spellings: Vilma*
Windy (WIN-dee, WEN-dee)
 Alternate spellings: Wendy*, Wendi
Winifred (WIN-uh-fred [CG])
 Alternate spellings: Winnifred
Winnie (WIN-ee)

Winona (win-OH-nuh [NA], wy-NOH-nuh [BR])
Alternate spellings: Wynona, Wenona

Yasmin (YAZ-min, yass-MEEN [HEB/PER])
Alternate spellings: Yazmin, Yasmine*,
Yasmeen, Jasmine*, Jasmin, Jazmin,
Jazmine, Jazmyn, Jasmyn, Jazmyne
Yehudit (yuh-HOO-dit or YOO-dit [HEB])
Alternate spellings: Yudit, Judith*
Yoselin (YAW-sell-in, YAWZ-lin,
yoh-SEL-een or yoh-THEL-een [SP])
Alternate spellings: Joselyn*
Yvette (ee-VETT [FR], iv-ETT)
Alternate spellings: Ivette, Evette
Yvonne (iv-AWN, ee-VOHN [FR])
Alternate spellings: Ivonne*, Evonne

■ LONG O (OH) ■

PARTNER POINTER:
Check the OI and OR lists, too.

Agostina (ag-oh-STEEN-uh [IT])
Aiko (EYE-koh [JAP])
Akiko (AW-kee-koh [JAP])
Alondra (uh-LAWN-druh, aw-LOHN-druh
[SP])
Amparo (awm-PAR-roh [SP])
Antonetta (ann-toh-NET-uh)
Antonette (ann-toh-NET)
Antonia (ann-TOH-nee-yuh,
awn-TOH-nee-yuh [IT/SP])
Antonietta (an-toh-nee-ETT-uh [IT])
Antonina (an-toh-NEE-nuh [IT])

Bonita (boh-NEE-tuh or voh-NEE-tuh [SP])

Carolee (KAIR-oh-lee)
Carolina (kair-oh-LY-nuh, kar-oh-LEE-nuh
[GER/IT/SP])
Caroline (KAIR-oh-lin, kair-oh-LYN,
kar-oh-LEEN [FR])
Alternate spellings: Carolyn, Karolyn,
Carolynn
Charolette (SHAR-oh-lett; see also
Charlotte)
Chloë (KLOH-wee [GRK], kloh-WAY [FR])
Alternate spellings: Chloé
Christopher (KRIS-toh-fur)
Claudette (klaw-DET, kloh-DET [FR])
Claudia (KLAW-dee-yuh, KLOW-dee-yuh
[IT/SP])
Claudie (KLAW-dee, kloh-DEE [FR])

Claudine (klaw-DEEN, kloh-DEEN with
sustained N [FR])
Cleo (KLEE-yoh, KLAY-oh [FR])
Alternate spellings: Cléo
Clotilde (kloh-TIL-dee or kloh-TIL-duh [GER],
kloh-TEELD [FR], kloh-TEEL-deh [IT])
Alternate spellings: Clothilde [FR]
Coco (KOH-koh)
Cody (KOH-dee)
Colette (koh-LET [FR])
Alternate spellings: Collette
Colleen (kaw-LEEN [IR], koh-LEEN)
Alternate spellings: Coleen
Concepcion (kohn-sep-see-YOHN or
kohn-thep-thee-YOHN [SP])
Concetta (kohn-CHET-tuh [IT])
Consuelo (kohn-SWAY-loh or
kohn-THWAY-loh [SP])
Creola (kree-YOH-luh [NA])

Dakota (duh-KOH-tuh)
Delois (del-OH-wiss [AA])
Dolores (doh-LOR-ess [SP])
Alternate spellings: Delores, Deloris,
Doloris
Dominga (doh-MEEN-guh [SP])
Dominique (daw-min-EEK,
doh-mee-NEEK [FR])
Alternate spellings: Dominque,
Domonique
Dorothea (dor-roh-THEE-yuh)
Dorothy (DOR-roh-thee)
Alternate spellings: Dorathy

Eleanor (EL-len-nor, el-lay-yoh-NOR [FR])
Alternate spellings: Eleanore, Elinor,
Elinore, Elenor, Eleonore [FR]
Eleanora (el-len-NOR-ruh,
el-lee-yuh-NOR-ruh,
eh-lay-yoh-NOR-uh [IT/SP])
Alternate spellings: Elenora, Eleonora
[IT/SP] (see also Elnora)
Elois (el-OH-wiss, EE-loh-wiss,
EL-oh-weez)
Alternate spellings: Eloise*, Elouise
Eloisa (el-oh-WEE-suh)
Eloise (EL-oh-weez, el-oh-WEEZ,
ay-loh-WEEZ [FR])
Alternate spellings: Elouise, Elois*,
Éloïse [FR]
Emiko (EM-ee-koh [JAP])
Enola (ee-NOH-luh)

Fabiola (fab-ee-YOH-luh)

Filomena (fee-loh-MEN-uh [IT/SP], fill-oh-MEE-nuh)
  Alternate spellings: Philomena*
Fiona (fee-YOH-nuh [IR])
Flo (FLOH)

Genoveva (jen-oh-VEE-vuh, jen-oh-VAY-vuh)
Giovanna (joh-VAW-nuh [IT], jee-yoh-VAW-nuh)
Golda (GOHL-duh)
Golden (GOHL-den)
Goldia (GOHL-dee-yuh)
Goldie (GOHL-dee)
Gwendolyn (GWEN-doh-lin [WL])

Hermione (hur-MY-yoh-nee [BR])
Hiroko (HEE-roh-koh [JAP])
Hope (HOHP)

Ilona (ee-LOH-nuh [HUN])
Imogene (IM-oh-jeen or IM-oh-jen [BR])
  Alternate spellings: Emogene, Imogen, Iola (eye-YOH-luh)
Iona (eye-YOH-nuh [IR])
Ione (eye-YOH-nee, eye-YOHN [FR])

Jo (JOH)
  Alternate spellings: Joe
Joan (JOHN)
Joanna (joh-WAN-uh, joh-WAH-nuh)
  Alternate spellings: Joana, Johana
Jocelyn (JAW-sell-lin, JAWS-lin, zhoh-sell-LEEN [FR], yoh-SELL-een [SP])
  Alternate spellings: Joslyn, Joceline [FR], Joycelyn*, Yoselin*
Jodie (JOH-dee)
  Alternate spellings: Jodi, Jody
Joelle (joh-WELL, zho-WELL [FR])
Joellen (joh-WELL-en)
Joetta (joh-WET-uh [AA])
Joey (JOH-wee)
Johanna (joh-HAN-uh, joh-HAW-nuh, joh-WAN-uh, yo-HAW-nuh [GER], yoh-CHAW-nuh with guttural CH [HEB])
  Alternate spellings: Johana, Yochana [HEB]
Jolene (joh-LEEN)
Jolie (JOH-lee, joh-LEE, zho-LEE [FR])
Joni (JOH-nee)
  Alternate spellings: Joanie
Joretta (joh-RET-tuh)
Josefa (joh-SEF-uh, ho-SEF-uh or ho-THEF-uh [SP], YOH-sif-faw or yoh-sif-FAW [HEB])
  Alternate spellings: Josepha, Yosifa [HEB]
Josefina (joh-sef-FEE-nuh, ho-sef-FEE-nuh or ho-thef-FEE-nuh [SP])
  Alternate spellings: Josephina
Josephine (joh-sef-FEEN, zho-zay-FEEN with sustained N [FR])
  Alternate spellings: Joséphine
Josette (joh-ZET or zho-ZET [FR])
Josie (JOH-see, zho-SAY [FR])
  Alternate spellings: Josée [FR]
Jothi (JOH-tee [EI])
Jovita (joh-VEE-tuh [AA], ho-VEE-tuh or ho-BEE-tuh [SP])

Keiko (KAY-koh [JAP])

Latonya (luh-TOHN-yuh or luh-TAWN-yuh[AA])
  Alternate spellings: Latanya*
Leola (lee-YOH-luh, lay-YOH-luh)
Leona (lee-YOH-nuh, lay-YOH-nuh)
Leone (lee-YOH-nee [GER], lay-yoh-NEE [FR])
  Alternate spellings: Léonie [FR]
Leonor (LEE-yoh-nor, len-NOR)
  Alternate spellings: Leonore, Lenore*
Leonora (lee-yoh-NOR-ruh, lay-oh-NOR-uh [IT/SP])
  Alternate spellings: Eleonora [IT/SP], Lenora*
Leota (lee-YOH-tuh)
Lilo (LEE-loh [HW])
Logan (LOH-gen)
Lois (LOH-wiss [GRK])
Lola (LOH-luh, LOH-law [SP])
Lolita (loh-LEE-taw [SP])
Loma (LOH-muh)
Lona (LOH-nuh, LAW-nuh)
  Alternate spellings: Lana*
Lucero (loo-SAIR-roh or loo-THAIR-roh [SP])

Madonna (muh-DAWN-uh, mad-OH-nuh [IT])
Magnolia (mag-NOH-lee-yuh)
Margo (MAR-goh, mar-GOH [FR])
  Alternate spellings: Margot
Marisol (mar-ree-SOHL or mar-ree-THOHL [SP])
Marlo (MAR-loh)
Maryjo (mair-ree-JOH)
Masako (MAW-sak-oh [JAP])
Meadow (MED-oh)

Melody (MEL-oh-dee)
 Alternate spellings: Melodie
Michiko (MEE-chee-koh [JAP])
Milagros (mee-LAW-grohs [SP])
Modesta (moh-DESS-tuh or
 moh-DETH-tuh [SP])
Moe (MOH, MOH-way [JAP])
Mona (MOH-nuh [IR])
Monique (moh-NEEK [FR])
Monserrat (mohn-sair-RRRAWT [FR])
 Alternate spellings: Monserrate
Moriah (mor-RY-yuh, moh-ree-YAW [HEB],
 muh-RY-yuh)
 Alternate spellings: Moriya [HEB],
 Moria, Mariah*, Maria*
Mozella (moh-ZELL-uh)
Mozelle (moh-ZELL)
 Alternate spellings: Mozell

Naoma (nay-YOH-muh)
 Alternate spellings: Neoma*
Naomi (nay-YOH-mee or NOH-mee [HEB],
 ny-YOH-mee, NAW-oh-mee [JAP])
Neoma (nee-YOH-muh, nay-YOH-muh)
 Alternate spellings: Naoma*
Nicola (NIK-oh-luh, nee-KOH-luh [IT])
Nicole (nik-KOHL, nee-KOHL [FR])
 Alternate spellings: Nichole, Nikole,
 Nichol, Nicolle
Nicolette (nik-oh-LET, nee-koh-LET [FR])
Noelia (noh-WELL-ee-yuh)
Noelle (noh-WELL [FR])
 Alternate spellings: Noel
Noemi (no-WEM-ee, noh-WAY-mee [IT/SP],
 noh-way-MEE [FR])
 Alternate spellings: Noémie
Nola (NOH-luh [IR])
Nona (NOH-nuh)
Nova (NOH-vuh)
Novella (noh-VEL-uh [IT])

Octavia (awk-TAY-vee-yaw,
 awk-TAW-vee-yaw or
 ohk-TAW-bee-yaw [SP])
Odalys (oh-DAW-lees [SP], oh-daw-LEES)
 Alternate spellings: Odalis
Odell (oh-DELL [AA/IR])
Odessa (oh-DESS-uh)
Odetta (oh-DETT-uh)
Odette (oh-DET [FR])
Odie (OH-dee)
Ofelia (oh-FELL-ee-yuh [IT/SP],
 oh-FEE-lee-yuh)
 Alternate spellings: Ophelia*

Ola (OH-luh [HEB/SCAN])
 Alternate spellings: Olah
Olene (oh-LEEN [AA])
Oleta (oh-LEE-tuh or oh-LET-uh [AA])
Olga (OHL-gaw [GER/SP])
Oliana (oh-lee-YAWN-uh [HW])
Olina (oh-LEE-nuh [HW])
Olivia (oh-LIV-ee-yuh, oh-LEE-vee-yaw
 [IT/SP], oh-LEE-bee-yaw [SP],
 uh-LIV-ee-yuh)
 Alternate spellings: Alivia
Olivie (oh-lee-VEE [FR])
Oma (OH-muh [AR])
Omayra (oh-MY-ruh, oh-MAY-ruh)
Ona (OH-nuh)
Onie (OH-nee, WUN-ee)
Opal (OH-pull)
Ophelia (oh-FEE-lee-yuh)
 Alternate spellings: Ofelia*
Otilia (oh-TILL-ee-yuh [SP])
 Alternate spellings: Otylia [GER]
Ouida (WEE-duh [FR])
Ova (OH-vuh)
Ozella (oh-ZELL-uh)

Paloma (pal-OH-muh [IT],
 paw-LOH-maw [SP])
Paola (POW-luh [IT], paw-OH-law [SP])
Penelope (pen-NELL-oh-pee,
 pay-nay-LOHP)
 Alternate spellings: Pénélope
Philomena (fill-oh-MEE-nuh)
 Alternate spellings: Filomena*
Pomona (puh-MOH-nuh)

Ramona (ram-OH-nuh,
 rrraw-MOH-naw [SP])
 Alternate spellings: Romona
Ramonita (ray-moh-NEE-tuh)
Rhoda (ROH-duh)
Roberta (rub-BUR-tuh, roh-BAIR-tuh)
Rochelle (roh-SHELL or ruh-SHELL [FR])
 Alternate spellings: Rachelle*, Richelle
Rocio (rrroh-SEE-yoh or rrroh-THEE-yoh
 [SP])
Rolanda (roh-LAWN-duh, roh-LAN-duh
 [IT])
Roma (ROH-muh [HEB/IT])
Romaine (roh-MAYN, rrroh-MEN [FR])
Romana (rrroh-MAW-nuh [SP])
Rona (ROH-nuh [CG/HEB])
Rosa (ROH-zuh, RRROH-suh [IT/SP],
 RRROH-thuh [SP])
Rosalia (roh-ZAL-ee-yuh,

rrroh-saw-LEE-yuh or
rrroh-thaw-LEE-yuh [SP])
Rosalie (ROH-zuh-lee)
Alternate spellings: Rosalee
Rosalina (rrroh-saw-LEE-nuh or
rrroh-thaw-LEE-nuh [SP])
Rosalinda (rrroh-saw-LEEN-duh or
rrroh-thaw-LEEN-duh [SP])
Rosaline (roh-suh-LEEN, RAW-zuh-lin)
Alternate spellings: Roselyn*,
Rosalyn*, Rosalind*
Rosamond (ROH-zuh-mund)
Alternate spellings: Rosamund
Rosanna (roh-ZAN-uh, roh-SAW-nuh [IT])
Alternate spellings: Roseanna,
Rossanna, Rossana
Rosario (rrroh-SAR-ree-yoh [IT/SP],
rrroh-THAR-ree-yoh)
Rosaura (roh-ZOR-ruh)
Rose (ROHZ)
Roseann (roh-ZAN)
Alternate spellings: Rosanne,
Roseanne, Rosann
Rosella (roh-ZELL-uh)
Alternate spellings: Rozella
Roselyn (ROHZ-lin, RAW-zuh-lin)
Alternate spellings: Rosalyn*,
Rosaline*, Rosalind*
Rosemarie (rohz-mair-REE [FR])
Rosemary (ROHZ-mair-ree)
Rosetta (roh-ZET-tuh [IT])
Rosia (ROH-zee-yuh)
Rosina (roh-ZEE-nuh [CG/IT])
Rosita (rrroh-SEE-tuh or rrroh-THEE-tuh
[SP], roh-ZEE-tuh)
Roxana (rawk-SAW-nuh, rawk-SAN-nuh,
rrrohk-SAW-nuh or rrrohk-THAW-nuh
[SP], rrruk-SAW-nuh with pronounced H
at end [AR])
Alternate spellings: Roxanna
Roxanne (rawk-SAN, rohk-SAW with
short N [FR])
Alternate spellings: Roxann, Roxane
Rowan (ROH-wen [IR])
Rowena (roh-WEE-nuh [CG/IR])

Salome (sal-LOH-mee, SAW-loh-may,
suh-LOHM, SAL-loh-may [BR],
saw-loh-MAY [FR], shaw-LOHM [HEB])
Alternate spellings: Salomé [FR],
Shalom [HEB]
Santos (SAWN-tohs or THAWN-tohs [SP])
Sharon (SHAIR-ren, shar-ROHN [HEB])
Alternate spellings: Sharron, Sharyn,

Sharen, Sheron, Sherron
Shoshana (shoh-SHAW-naw [HEB];
see also Susana, Suzanne)
Sidonie (sid-OH-nee, SID-oh-nee,
see-doh-NEE [FR])
Simone (sim-OHN, see-MOHN with
sustained N [FR])
Socorro (soh-KOR-rroh or
thoh-KOR-rroh [SP])
Soheila (soh-HAY-luh [PER])
Soledad (soh-leh-DAWD or
thoh-leh-DAWD [SP])
Sondra (SOHN-draw or THOHN-draw [SP],
SAWN-druh)
Alternate spellings: Sandra*, Saundra
Sonia (SOHN-yaw [IT/HEB/RUS/SP],
soh-NEE-yaw or thoh-NEE-yaw [SP],
SOH-nee-yuh with pronounced H at
end [AR], SAWN-yuh [RUS])
Alternate spellings: Sonya [RUS], Sonja
[SCAN]
Sophia (soh-FEE-yuh [GRK/IT/SP],
thoh-FEE-yuh [SP])
Alternate spellings: Sofia [IT/SP]
Sophie (SOH-fee [GRK], soh-FEE [FR])

Tamiko (TAM-ee-koh [JAP])
Theo (THEE-yoh, TAY-yoh [FR])
Alternate spellings: Théo [FR]
Theodora (thee-yuh-DOR-ruh,
tay-oh-DOR-ruh [IT])
Alternate spellings: Teodora [IT]
Theola (thee-YOH-luh)
Toby (TOH-bee, TOH-vee [HEB])
Tomasa (toh-MAW-suh [IT/SP], toh-
MAWTH-uh [SP])
Alternate spellings: Tomassa
Tomeka (toh-MEE-kuh or tuh-MEE-kuh [AA])
Alternate spellings: Tomika, Tamika*,
Tameka
Tomoko (TOH-moh-koh [JAP])
Toni (TOH-nee)
Tonya (TOHN-yuh [IT], TAWN-yuh)
Alternate spellings: Tonja, Tonia,
Tania*, Tanya, Taniya, Tawnya

Verona (vur-ROH-nuh, vair-ROH-nuh
[IT/SP], bair-ROH-nuh [SP])
Veronica (vur-RAW-nik-uh,
vair-ROH-nee-kuh or
bair-ROH-nee-kuh [SP])
Viola (vy-YOH-luh, vee-YOH-law [IT/SP],
bee-YOH-law [SP])
Violet (VY-yoh-let)

Violetta (vee-yoh-LET-uh [IT])
Violette (vee-yoh-LETT [FR])

Willow (WILL-oh)
Winona (win-OH-nuh [NA], wy-NOH-nuh [BR])
    Alternate spellings: Wynona, Wenona

Xiomara (see-yoh-MAR-ruh or
    shee-yoh-MAR-ruh [SP])

Yoko (YOH-koh [JAP])
Yolanda (yoh-LAWN-daw [SP],
    yoh-LAN-duh [IT])
    Alternate spellings: Yolonda, Iolanda [IT]
Yoselin (YAW-sell-in, YAWZ-lin,
    yoh-SEL-een or yoh-THEL-een [SP])
    Alternate spellings: Joselyn*
Yoshiko (YOH-shee-koh [JAP])

Zoë (ZOH-wee [GRK/HEB], zoh-WAY [FR])
    Alternate spellings: Zoey, Zoie, Zoé [FR]
Zola (ZOH-luh)
Zona (ZOH-nuh [HEB])

■ SHORT O (AW OR AH) ■

PARTNER POINTER:
Check out the AR and OW lists, too.

Aaliyah (uh-LEE-yuh [AA], AW-lee-yuh
    [HEB/AR])
    Alternate spellings: Aliyah, Aliya,
    Aleah*, Alia
Abigail (AB-big-ayl, aw-vee-GYL [HEB])
    Alternate spellings: Abbigail, Abigayle,
    Abigale, Abagail, Avigayil [HEB]
Abrianna (ab-ree-YAWN-uh)
Abril (AB-rill, AY-brill, aw-BREEL [AR/SP],
    awv-REEL [SP])
Adelia (uh-DEE-lee-yuh,
    aw-DELL-ee-yuh [IT])
Adelina (ad-uh-LEE-nuh,
    aw-dell-LEE-nuh [IT/SP])
Adella (uh-DELL-uh [GER], aw-DELL-uh
    [IT/SP], aw-DEE-luh or AW-dill-uh [AR])
    Alternate spellings: Adela
Adriana (ay-dree-YAWN-uh,
    aw-dree-YAWN-uh [SP])
Agatha (AG-uh-thuh, AW-guh-tuh [IT],
    ag-GAT [FR])
    Alternate spellings: Agathe [FR]
Agustina (ag-uh-STEE-nuh,
    aw-goos-TEEN-uh or

aw-gooth-TEEN-uh [SP])
Aida (eye-YEE-duh [AR], aw-YEE-duh,
    EYE-duh, AY-duh)
    Alternate spellings: Ada*, Adah, Eda*
Aisha (eye-YEE-shuh or EYE-yee-shuh
    [AR], aw-YEE-shuh, EYE-shuh)
    Alternate spellings: Iesha
Akiko (AW-kee-koh [JAP])
Alana (uh-LAW-nuh)
    Alternate spellings: Alanna*, Elana*,
    Ilana*
Alani (uh-LAW-nee, uh-LAN-nee,
    uh-LAY-nee)
Alanis (uh-LAW-niss, uh-LAN-niss)
Alanna (uh-LAN-nuh, uh-LAW-nuh)
    Alternate spellings: Alana*, Elana*,
    Ilana*
Alba (AL-buh, AWL-baw [IT/SP], AWL-vaw
    [SP])
Albertine (al-bur-TEEN, awl-bair-TEEN
    with sustained N [FR])
Alda (AL-duh, AWL-duh)
Aleah (uh-LAY-yuh, uh-LEE-yuh, AW-
    lee-yuh [AR/HEB])
    Alternate spellings: Aaliyah*, Aliyah,
    Aliya, Alia
Alejandra (aw-leh-HAWN-druh [SP])
Alessandra (aw-leh-SAWN-druh [IT])
Alexa (uh-LEK-suh, aw-LEK-suh or
    aw-LEK-thuh [SP])
Alexandra (al-eks-ZAN-druh,
    al-eks-ZAWN-druh)
Alexandrie (al-ek-sawn-DREE with short
    N [FR])
Ali (aw-LEE, AL-ee)
    Alternate spellings: Allie*, Ally
Alicia (uh-LEE-shuh, aw-LEE-see-yuh or
    aw-LEE-thee-yuh [SP])
    Alternate spellings: Elisha, Alysha,
    Alycia, Alecia, Alesha, Alysia,
    Alisha
Aline (ay-LEEN, aw-LEN [FR])
    Alternate spellings: Allene, Alline,
    Alene
Alisa (uh-LEE-suh, aw-LEE-suh [HEB/SP],
    aw-LEE-thuh [SP])
    Alternate spellings: Elisa*, Alysa
Alize (uh-LEEZ, aw-LEEZ [FR],
    al-LEE-zay)
Allison (AL-liss-sun, al-lee-SAW with
    short N [FR])
    Alternate spellings: Alison, Allyson,
    Alyson
Alma (AWL-maw [SP])

Alondra (uh-LAWN-druh, aw-LOHN-druh [SP])

Alta (AWL-tuh [IT])

Altagracia (awl-tuh-GRAW-see-yuh or awl-tuh-GRAW-thee-yuh [SP])

Alva (AL-vuh, AWL-vaw)

Amalia (uh-MAW-lee-yuh [HEB])
Alternate spellings: Amalya, Amaliah

Amanda (uh-MAN-duh, aw-MAWN-duh [SP])

Amani (uh-MAW-nee; see also Imani)

Amaya (uh-MY-yuh, aw-MY-yuh [SP])
Alternate spellings: Amya [HEB], Amiya*, Amiyah

Amber (AM-bur, AWM-bur [AR])

Amelia (uh-MEE-lee-yuh, aw-MELL-ee-yuh [IT])
Alternate spellings: Emilia, Emelia

Amelie (aw-may-LEE [FR]; see also Emilie)

Amie (em-MAY or aw-MEE [FR], AW-mee [HEB], AY-mee)
Alternate spellings: Amy*, Aimee, Ami [HEB]

Amina (AW-min-uh or aw-MEE-nuh [HEB] with pronounced H at end [AR])

Amira (AW-mur-ruh or aw-MEER-ruh [HEB] with pronounced H at end [AR], aw-meer-RAW [HEB])

Amiya (AW-mee-yuh, uh-MY-yuh)
Alternate spellings: Amiyah, Amaya*, Amya [HEB]

Amparo (awm-PAR-roh [SP])

Anahi (ann-AW-hee [SP])

Anaís (aw-naw-YEES [FR], ann-NY-yiss)

Anastasia (aw-naw-STAW-zee-yuh or aw-naw-STAW-zhuh [RUS], ann-uh-STAY-shuh, aw-naw-STAW-see-yuh [IT], aw-naw-staw-SEE-yuh [GRK])
Alternate spellings: Anastacia

Anastasie (ann-aw-staw-ZEE [FR])

Andrea (ANN-dree-yuh, ann-DRAY-yuh [IT], awn-DRAY-yuh [SP])
Alternate spellings: Andria

Angel (AYN-jell, AWN-hell [SP])

Angela (ANN-jell-uh, AWN-jell-uh [IT], AWN-hell-uh or awn-HELL-uh [SP])

Angeles (ANN-jell-ess, ANN-jell-eez, AWN-hell-ess or awn-HELL-eth [SP])

Angelia (ann-JELL-ee-yuh, awn-JELL-ee-yuh [IT])

Angelica (ann-JELL-ik-uh, awn-jell-EEK-uh, awn-HELL-ee-kuh [SP])
Alternate spellings: Anjelica

Angelina (ann-jell-EE-nuh, awn-jell-EE-nuh [IT], awn-hell-LEE-nuh [SP])

Angelita (ann-jell-LEE-tuh, awn-hell-LEE-tuh [SP])

Anissa (uh-NISS-uh, aw-NEES-suh [AR])

Anita (uh-NEE-tuh, aw-NEE-tuh [IT/SP])

Aniya (aw-NY-yuh, uh-NEE-yuh, AW-nee-yuh [HEB])
Alternate spellings: Aniyah, Anaya*, Anya*, Analla

Anjali (AWN-jaw-lee, awn-JAW-lee, awn-jaw-LEE)

Anna (ANN-uh, AW-nuh)
Alternate spellings: Ana [SP]

Annamarie (ann-uh-muh-REE, aw-nuh-maw-REE [FR])

Annika (AW-nik-uh or ANN-ik-uh [SCAN], aw-NEE-kuh [AA] with pronounced H at end [AR])
Alternate spellings: Anika

Annis (ANN-iss, aw-NEES)

Antoinette (ann-twah-NET [FR])

Antonia (ann-TOH-nee-yuh, awn-TOH-nee-yuh [IT/SP])

Anya (AWN-yuh [RUS], uh-NY-yuh)
Alternate spellings: Aniya*, Aniyah, Analla

Araceli (air-ruh-SELL-ee, ar-raw-SELL-ee or ar-raw-THEL-ee [SP])
Alternate spellings: Aracely

Ariana (ar-ree-YAW-nuh [HEB/IT])
Alternate spellings: Aryana

Armani (ar-MAW-nee [AA/IT])

Asia (AY-zhuh [AA], AW-see-yuh with pronounced H at end [AR])
Alternate spellings: Aja, Eja

Asha (AW-shuh [AA/EI/AR], ASH-uh)

Ashanti (uh-SHAWN-tee)

Assunta (aw-SOON-tuh [IT/SP], aw-THOON-tuh [SP])

Aubrey (AWB-ree)
Alternate spellings: Aubree, Aubrie

Audie (AW-dee)

Audra (AWD-ruh)

Audrey (AWD-ree)
Alternate spellings: Audry

Augusta (aw-GUSS-tuh, ow-GOOS-tuh [IT], aw-GOOS-taw or aw-GOOTH-taw [SP])

Augustine (aw-guss-TEEN, ag-oo-STEEN with sustained N [FR])

Autumn (AW-tum)

Ava (AY-vuh, AW-vuh)
Alternate spellings: Eva*

Ayana (ay-YAWN-uh, eye-YAWN-uh)
    Alternate spellings: Ayana, Aiyana,
    Iyana

Bianca (bee-YAWN-kuh [IT/SP],
    vee-YAWN-kuh [SP])
Blanca (BLAWN-kuh or VLAWN-kuh [SP])
Blanche (BLANCH, BLAWNSH [FR])
    Alternate spellings: Blanch
Blossom (BLAWS-sum)
Bobbie (BAW-bee)
    Alternate spellings: Bobbi, Bobby,
    Bobbye
Bonnie (BAW-nee [CG])
    Alternate spellings: Bonny
Brianne (bree-YAN, bree-YAWN [FR])
    Alternate spellings: Breanne, Breann,
    Briann
Brianna (bree-YAN-nuh or
    bree-YAWN-uh [IR])
    Alternate spellings: Briana, Breanna,
    Bryanna, Breana, Bryana, Breonna,
    Brionna

Camila (kaw-MEE-luh [IT/SP])
Cándida (KAWN-did-uh [SP],
    kan-DEE-duh)
Cassandra (kuh-SAN-druh [GRK],
    kaw-SAWN-draw or
    kaw-THAWN-draw [SP])
    Alternate spellings: Kassandra,
    Casandra, Kasandra
Catalina (kat-uh-LEE-nuh,
    kaw-taw-LEE-nuh [SP])
Chana (CHAW-naw with guttural CH [HEB],
    SHAW-nuh, SHAY-nuh, SHAN-nuh)
    Alternate spellings: Hannah*, Hanna,
    Hana, Hanaa, Shawna*, Shauna,
    Shonna, Shayna*, Shana, Shanna
Chanda (CHAWN-duh [EI], SHAN-duh,
    SHAWN-duh)
    Alternate spellings: Shanda*
Chandra (CHUN-drrruh [EI],
    CHAWN-druh, SHAWN-druh)
Chantal (shawn-TAWL, shaw-TAL with
    short N [FR])
Chantel (shawn-TELL, shan-TELL [FR])
    Alternate spellings: Shantel,
    Chantelle , Shantell
Christiana (kris-tee-YAWN-uh,
    krees-tee-YAWN-aw [IT])
    Alternate spellings: Cristiana
Citlali (sit-LAW-lee)
Claudette (klaw-DET, kloh-DET [FR])

Claudia (KLAW-dee-yuh, KLOW-dee-yuh
    [IT/SP])
Claudie (KLAW-dee, kloh-DEE [FR])
Claudine (klaw-DEEN, kloh-DEEN with
    sustained N [FR])
Connie (KAW-nee)
Constance (KAWN-stens, kaw-STAWS
    with short Ns [FR])
Crystal (KRIS-tell, krees-TAWL or
    krees-TELL [FR])
    Alternate spellings: Krystal, Cristal,
    Kristal, Krystle, Chrystal, Christal,
    Christel, Christelle [FR]

Dalia (DAW-lee-yuh [HEB], DAL-lee-yuh
    [SCAN])
    Alternate spellings: Dahlia, Daliah,
    Daliya or Dalya [HEB]
Dana (DAY-nuh, DAWN-uh [HEB])
    Alternate spellings: Dayna, Dena,
    Danna*
Danelle (dan-NELL [FR], daw-NELL [HEB])
Dania (DAN-ee-yuh, DAY-nee-yuh,
    duh-NEE-yuh or duh-NY-yuh [AA],
    DAWN-yuh or DAW-nee-yuh [HEB])
    Alternate spellings: Daniya, Danya
Daniela (dan-YELL-uh [IT], dawn-YELL-uh
    [HEB/SP])
    Alternate spellings: Daniella
Danielle (dan-YELL [FR], dawn-YELL [HEB])
    Alternate spellings: Danyelle
Danita (duh-NEE-tuh, daw-NEE-tuh)
    Alternate spellings: Donita
Danna (DAN-nuh, DAW-nuh [HEB])
    Alternate spellings: Dayna, Dena,
    Dana*Daphne (DAF-nee)
Dara (DAR-ruh, DAR-rah with
    pronounced H at end [AR])
Dawn (DAWN)
Dayana (DAY-yaw-nuh [AA], dy-YAN-nuh)
    Alternate spellings: Diana*, Dianna
Deann (dee-YAN, dee-YAWN)
    Alternate spellings: Deanne, Dionne*
Deanna (dee-YAN-uh, dee-YAWN-uh)
    Alternate spellings: Deana
Deja (DAY-zhaw [FR])
Diana (dy-YAN-uh, dee-YAWN-uh [IT/SP])
    Alternate spellings: Dayana*, Dianna
Dina (DEE-nuh [IT], DY-nuh, dee-NAW [HEB])
    Alternate spellings: Dena, Deena,
    Deana, Dinah
Dionne (DEE-yawn [AA], dee-YAW with
    short N [FR/GRK])
    Alternate spellings: Diane*, Diann,

Dianne, Dian, Deann*, Deanne
Dolly (DAW-lee)
  Alternate spellings: Dollie
Dominique (daw-min-EEK,
  doh-mee-NEEK [FR])
  Alternate spellings: Dominque,
  Domonique
Donna (DAW-nuh)
  Alternate spellings: Dona , Dawna
Donnie (DAW-nee)
Dottie (DAW-tee, DAW-dee)

Elana (ee-law-NAW [HEB], ell-LAW-nuh;
  see also Elena)
  Alternate spellings: Ilana*, Alana*,
  Alanna*
Eliana (el-lee-YAW-nuh [IT/SP],
  ELL-ee-yaw-nuh [HEB]; see also Iliana)
Esmeralda (ez-mur-RAWL-duh,
  ess-mair-RAL-duh or
  eth-mair-RAL-duh [SP])
Esperanza (ess-pair-AWN-suh or eth-
  pair-AWN-suh [SP]; see also Speranza)
Estefania (es-tef-FAWN-ee-yuh or
  eth-tef-FAWN-ee-yuh [SP])
Estefany (es-TEF-en-ee, es-tef-FAWN-ee)
  Alternate spellings: Estefani
Eulalia (yoo-LAY-lee-yuh,
  ay-yoo-LAW-lee-yuh [SP])
Eulalie (yoo-LAY-lee, oo-law-LEE [FR])
Evangelina (ev-van-jell-LEE-nuh [IT],
  ay-vawn-hell-LEE-nuh [SP])
Eve (EEV, EV [FR], CHAW-vuh [HEB])
  Alternate spellings: Chava [HEB]

Farrah (FAIR-ruh, FAR-rah or far-RAH
  with pronounced H at end [AR])
  Alternate spellings: Farah
Fatima (FAW-tim-uh or FAWT-muh [AR],
  fat-EE-muh [IT])
Felicita (fel-ee-chee-TAW [IT])
Feng (FAWNG [CH])
Fernanda (fur-NAN-duh [IT],
  fair-NAWN-duh [SP])
Florence (FLOR-rens, flor-RAWS with
  short N [FR])
Flossie (FLAW-see)
Fonda (FAWN-duh)
Francine (fran-SEEN, frawn-SEEN with
  sustained N [FR])

Gabriel (GAY-bree-ell, gaw-bree-ELL or
  gaw-vree-ELL [HEB], gab-brrree-YELL
  [FR/SP/IT])

Alternate spellings: Gavriel [HEB]
Gabriela (gaw-bree-YELL-uh [SP],
  gab-ree-YELL-uh,
  gaw-vree-ELL-uh [HEB])
  Alternate spellings: Gabriella*,
  Gavriela [HEB]
Gabriella (gab-ree-YELL-uh [IT],
  gaw-vree-ELL-uh [HEB])
  Alternate spellings: Gabriela*,
  Gavriela [HEB]
Gabrielle (gab-ree-YELL [FR],
  gaw-bree-YELL)
Genevieve (JEN-uh-veev [CG],
  zhen-uh-vee-YEV or
  zhawn-vee-YEV [FR])
  Alternate spellings: Geneviève
Georgianne (jor-jee-YAN,
  zhor-zhee-YAW with short N [FR])
  Alternate spellings: Georgiane
Giada (JAW-duh [IT], jee-YAW-duh,
  JAY-duh)
  Alternate spellings: Jada*, Jayda,
  Jaida
Gianna (jee-YAWN-uh or JAW-nuh [IT])
  Alternate spellings: Giana, Jana*,
  Janna, Johnna, Jonna
Giovanna (joh-VAW-nuh [IT],
  jee-yoh-VAW-nuh)
Graciela (graw-see-YELL-uh or
  graw-thee-YELL-uh [SP])
Guadalupe (gwah-duh-LOO-pay or
  gwah-THAW-loo-pay [SP])

Hannah (HAN-nuh, HAW-nuh,
  CHAW-naw with guttural CH [HEB],
  hen-NUH with pronounced H at end
  [AR])
  Alternate spellings: Hanna, Hana [JAP],
  Hanaa, Chana [HEB]
Hazel (HAY-zull [CG], HAW-zell)
  Alternate spellings: Hazle
Holly (HAW-lee)
  Alternate spellings: Hollie, Holli
Hua (huh-WAH [CH])

Ilana (ill-LAW-nuh, uh-LAW-nuh,
  ee-law-NAW [HEB])
  Alternate spellings: Alana*, Alanna*,
  Elana*
Iliana (ill-ee-YAW-nuh [SP]; see also Eliana)
  Alternate spellings: Ileana
Imani (im-AW-nee [AA], ee-MEN-ee [AR];
  see also Amani)
Isabel (IZ-uh-bell, ee-zaw-BELL [FR],

EE-saw-bell or ee-saw-BELL or
ee-thuh-VELL [SP])
Alternate spellings: Isabelle [FR],
Isabell, Isobel

Isabela (iz-uh-BELL-uh, ee-saw-BELL-uh
or ee-thaw-VELL-uh [SP],
ee-zuh-BELL-uh [IT])
Alternate spellings: Isabella [IT],
Izabella

Isadora (iz-uh-DOR-ruh, ee-saw-DOR-ruh
[IT/SP], ee-thaw-DOR-ruh [SP])

Isamar (ee-SAW-mar/ee-THAW-mar or
EES-mar/EETH-mar [SP])

Jacque (ZHAWK [FR], JAK-ee)
Alternate spellings: Jackie*

Jacqueline (JAK-uh-lin, JAK-well-lin,
jak-LEEN, zhawk-uh-LEEN with
sustained N [FR])
Alternate spellings: Jaqueline,
Jaquelyn, Jackeline, Jaquelin,
Jacquline, Jacalyn

Jada (JAY-duh [AA], YAY-duh or YAW-duh
[HEB])
Alternate spellings: Jayda, Jaida,
Giada*, Yada [HEB]

Jana (JAY-nuh, JAN-uh, JAW-nuh)
Alternate spellings: Janna, Gianna*,
Giana, Johnna, Jonna

Joanna (joh-WAN-uh, joh-WAH-nuh)
Alternate spellings: Joana, Johana

Jocelyn (JAW-sell-lin, JAWS-lin,
zhoh-sell-LEEN [FR], yoh-SELL-een [SP])
Alternate spellings: Joselyn, Joceline
[FR], Joycelyn*, Yoselin*

Johanna (joh-HAN-uh, joh-HAW-nuh,
joh-WAN-uh, yo-HAW-nuh [GER],
yoh-CHAW-nuh with guttural CH [HEB])
Alternate spellings: Johana, Yochana
[HEB]

Johnnie (JAW-nee)
Alternate spellings: Jonnie, Johnie

Josefa (joh-SEF-uh, ho-SEF-uh or
ho-THEF-uh [SP], YOH-sif-faw or yoh-
sif-FAW [HEB])
Alternate spellings: Josepha, Yosifa [HEB]

Joslyn (JAWZ-lin)

Joycelyn (JOY-suh-lin or JAW-suh-lin)
Alternate spellings: Jocelyn*, Joselyn

Juana (joo-WAH-naw, WAH-naw [SP])

Juanita (wah-NEE-tuh [SP])
Alternate spellings: Waneta*, Wanita

Juliana (joo-lee-YAWN-uh [IT],
joo-lee-YAN-uh, hoo-lee-YAWN-uh
[SP], yoo-lee-YAWN-nuh [SP/RUS])
Alternate spellings: Julianna, Giuliana
[IT], Yuliana* [RUS]

Kaliyah (KAW-lee-yuh or kuh-LEE-yuh [AA],
kaw-LEE-yuh [HW])
Alternate spellings: Kalia [HW]

Karyme (kuh-REE-muh [AR], kaw-REEM)

Katarina (kat-uh-REE-nuh,
kaw-tar-REE-nuh [GER])
Alternate spellings: Katerina,
Katharina*

Katie (KAY-tee, kaw-TEE [FR])
Alternate spellings: Katy, Kati

Kenyatta (ken-YAW-tuh [AA])

Ladonna (luh-DAWN-uh)

Lana (LAW-nuh or LAN-uh [CG])
Alternate spellings: Lona*, Lonna

Lashanda (luh-SHAWN-duh or
luh-SHAN-duh [AA])
Alternate spellings: Lashonda

Lashawn (luh-SHAWN [AA])

Latanya (luh-TAWN-yuh or luh-TAN-yuh
[AA])
Alternate spellings: Latonya*

Latasha (luh-TAW-shuh or luh-TASH-uh
[AA])
Alternate spellings: Latosha

Latonya (luh-TOHN-yuh or
luh-TAWN-yuh [AA])
Alternate spellings: Latanya*

Laura (LOR-ruh, LOW-ruh [IT],
LOR-ray [FR], law-OO-raw [SP])
Alternate spellings: Lora

Lavonne (luh-VAWN [AA])
Alternate spellings: Lavon

Lawanda (luh-WAND-uh [AA])

Leandra (lee-YAN-druh, lee-YAWN-druh)

Leanna (lee-YAN-nuh, lee-YAW-nuh [IT])
Alternate spellings: Liana [IT]

Leanne (lee-YAN, lay-YAW with short N
[FR])
Alternate spellings: Leeann, Leann

Leilani (lay-LAWN-ee [HW])

Liliana (lil-ee-YAWN-uh, lee-lee-YAWN-uh
[IT/SP])
Alternate spellings: Lilliana

Lonnie (LAW-nee)
Alternate spellings: Lonie

Lottie (LAW-tee, LAW-dee)

Luana (loo-WAH-nuh [GER/HW], loo-WAN-uh [IT])
Alternate spellings: Louanna

Madonna (muh-DAWN-uh, mad-OH-nuh [IT])
Mafalda (maf-FAWL-duh [IT])
Maleah (maw-LAY-yuh [HW], muh-LEE-yuh)
Malia (maw-LEE-yuh [HW/AA], muh-LEE-haw [AR], MAW-lee-yuh)
Alternate spellings: Maleah*, Maliyah
Malika (MEL-ik-uh or mal-EE-kuh [AR], MAW-lee-kuh [EI/HUN], muh-LY-kuh [AA])
Alternate spellings: Mallika [EI], Malikah, Milika, Mylika, Malaika*
Masako (MAW-sak-oh [JAP])
Maude (MAWD)
Maudie (MAW-dee)
Micah (MY-kuh, MEE-chaw with guttural CH [HEB])
Alternate spellings: Micha [HEB]
Migdalia (mig-DAW-lee-yuh)
Milagros (mee-LAW-grohs [SP])
Miranda (mur-RAN-duh, meer-RAWN-duh [SP])
Alternate spellings: Meranda, Myranda, Maranda
Molly (MAW-lee)
Alternate spellings: Mollie
Monica (MAW-nik-uh)
Alternate spellings: Monika
Monserrat (mohn-sair-RRRAWT [FR])
Alternate spellings: Monserrate
Montana (mawn-TAN-uh)
Moriah (mor-RY-yuh, moh-ree-YAW [HEB], muh-RY-yuh)
Alternate spellings: Moriya [HEB], Moria, Mariah*, Maria*
Mossie (MAW-see)

Nadia (NAW-dee-yuh, NAW-dee-yah with pronounced H at end [AR], NAD-ee-yuh [IT])
Alternate spellings: Nadje [GER], Nadya [RUS]
Naheed (NAW-heed [PER])
Naomi (nay-YOH-mee or NOH-mee [HEB], ny-YOH-mee, NAW-oh-mee [JAP])
Natalia (nat-TAW-lee-yuh, nat-taw-LEE-yuh [IT])
Alternate spellings: Natalya, Nathalia
Natalie (NAD-uh-lee, naw-taw-LEE [HEB], nat-tal-LEE [FR])

Alternate spellings: Nataly, Nathalie [FR], Natalee
Natasha (nat-TAW-shuh)
Alternate spellings: Natosha
Natividad (naw-tee-vee-DAWD [SP])
Nayeli (ny-YELL-ee, naw-YELL-ee [SP], NY-yell-ee, NAY-yell-ee)
Alternate spellings: Nayely, Nayelli

Octavia (awk-TAY-vee-yaw, awk-TAW-vee-yaw or ohk-TAW-bee-yaw [SP])
Odalys (oh-DAW-lees [SP], oh-daw-LEES)
Alternate spellings: Odalis
Olga (OHL-gaw [GER/SP])
Olive (AW-liv)
Ollie (AW-lee)
Ora (OR-raw [HEB])
Alternate spellings: Orah
Ottilie (aw-TILL-ee [SCAN])

Palma (PAWL-muh)
Paloma (pal-OH-muh [IT], paw-LOH-maw [SP])
Paola (POW-luh [IT], paw-OH-law [SP])
Paula (PAW-luh)
Pauletta (paw-LET-uh)
Paulette (paw-LET, poh-LET [FR])
Paulina (paw-LEE-nuh)
Pauline (paw-LEEN, poh-LEEN [FR])
Polly (PAW-lee)
Poppy (PAW-pee)
Providenci (praw-vid-DEN-see)

Rachel (RAY-chell, ruh-CHELL with guttural CH [HEB], raw-SHELL [FR])
Alternate spellings: Rachael, Racheal
Rachelle (raw-SHELL [FR])
Alternate spellings: Richelle, Rochelle*
Rafaela (raff-ay-YELL-uh, raff-eye-ELL-uh [IT], raw-fuh-ELL-uh [HEB/SP])
Ramona (ram-OH-nuh, rrraw-MOH-naw [SP])
Alternate spellings: Romona
Ranee (RRRAW-nee [EI], ren-NAY)
Alternate spellings: Renae, Rene, Rena*, Renea*, Renee*
Raquel (rrrak-ELL [FR/SP], raw-KEL)
Alternate spellings: Racquel
Rayna (RAW-haw-naw [AR], RAY-nuh)
Alternate spellings: Raina, Reina, Reyna*
Renata (ren-AW-tuh [IT])

Rhonda (RAWN-duh [WL])
  Alternate spellings: Ronda
Robbie (RAW-bee)
Robyn (RAW-bin)
  Alternate spellings: Robin, Robbin
Rolanda (roh-LAWN-duh, roh-LAN-duh [IT])
Romana (rrroh-MAW-nuh [SP])
Ronna (RAW-nuh)
Ronnie (RAW-nee)
  Alternate spellings: Roni
Rosalia (roh-ZAL-ee-yuh, rrroh-saw-LEE-yuh or rrroh-thaw-LEE-yuh [SP])
Rosalina (rrroh-saw-LEE-nuh or rrroh-thaw-LEE-nuh [SP])
Rosalind (RAW-zuh-lind, RAW-zuh-lin)
  Alternate spellings: Rosalyn*, Roselyn, Rosaline
Rosalinda (rrroh-saw-LEEN-duh or rrroh-thaw-LEEN-duh [SP])
Rosaline (roh-suh-LEEN, RAW-zuh-lin)
  Alternate spellings: Roselyn*, Rosalyn*, Rosalind*
Rosalyn (RAW-zuh-lin)
  Alternate spellings: Roselyn*, Rosaline*, Rosalind*
Rosanna (roh-ZAN-uh, roh-SAW-nuh [IT])
  Alternate spellings: Roseanna, Rossanna, Rossana
Roselyn (ROHZ-lin, RAW-zuh-lin)
  Alternate spellings: Rosalyn*, Rosaline*, Rosalind*
Roslyn (RAWZ-lin; see also Rosalyn)
Rossie (RAW-see)
Roxana (rawk-SAW-nuh, rawk-SAN-nuh, rrrohk-SAW-nuh or rrrohk-THAW-nuh [SP], rrruk-SAW-nuh with pronounced H at end [AR])
  Alternate spellings: Roxanna
Roxanne (rawk-SAN, rohk-SAW with short N [FR])
  Alternate spellings: Roxann, Roxane
Roxie (RAWK-see)

Sade (shaw-DAY [AA])
Salma (SAL-muh, SAWL-muh [HEB/SP], THAWL-muh [SP], SUL-muh with pronounced H at end [AR])
Salome (sal-LOH-mee, SAW-loh-may, suh-LOHM, SAL-loh-may [BR], saw-loh-MAY [FR], shaw-LOHM [HEB])
  Alternate spellings: Salomé [FR], Shalom [HEB]

Sanaa (SAW-naw or suh-NY [AR])
Sandra (SAND-ruh [IT], SAWN-draw or THAWN-draw [SP])
  Alternate spellings: Sondra*, Saundra
Santa (SAWN-tuh or THAWN-tuh [SP])
Santana (sawn-TAW-nuh or thawn-TAW-nuh [SP], san-TAN-nuh)
Santos (SAWN-tohs or THAWN-tohs [SP])
Sanya (SAWN-yuh)
  Alternate spellings: Saniya*, Sonia*, Sonya
Sarahi (suh-RAW-hee [AA])
Sasha (SAW-shuh [GER/RUS], SASH-uh)
  Alternate spellings: Sacha, Sascha
Shakira (shuh-KEER-ruh [AA], SHAW-keer-ruh or SHAK-eer-ruh [AR])
Shalonda (shuh-LAWN-duh [AA])
Shana (SHAWN-nuh, SHAN-nuh [AA])
  Alternate spellings: Shawna*, Shanna, Shauna, Chana*, Shonna
Shanda (SHAN-duh or SHAWN-duh [AA])
  Alternate spellings: Chanda*
Shandi (SHAWN-dee [AA]; see also Shanthi)
Shani (SHAW-nee [AA])
Shanta (SHAWN-tuh [EI], SHAN-tuh, shawn-TAY [AA])
  Alternate spellings: Shante*, Shantay
Shante (shawn-TAY [AA], shaw-TAY with short N [FR])
  Alternate spellings: Shanta*, Shantay, Chanté [FR]
Shanthi (SHAWN-tee [EI]; see also Shandi)
Shawn (SHAWN [IR])
  Alternate spellings: Sian [WL], Shan [CH]
Shawna (SHAW-nuh [IR])
  Alternate spellings: Shauna, Chana*, Shonna, Shana
Shawanda (shuh-WAND-uh [AA])
Shelva (SHELL-vuh, shawl-VAW [HEB])
Shonda (SHAWN-duh [AA])
Shoshana (shoh-SHAW-naw [HEB]; see also Susana, Suzanne)
Siobhan (shiv-AWN [IR])
  Alternate spellings: Shevaun, Shavon, Chevonne
Sondra (SOHN-draw or THOHN-draw [SP], SAWN-druh)
  Alternate spellings: Sandra*, Saundra
Sonia (SOHN-yaw [IT/HEB/RUS/SP], soh-NEE-yaw or thoh-NEE-yaw [SP], SOH-nee-yuh with pronounced H at end [AR], SAWN-yuh [RUS])
  Alternate spellings: Sonya [RUS], Sonja [SCAN]

Speranza (spair-RAWN-zuh [IT]; see also
    Esperanza)
Stacia (STAY-shuh, STAY-see-yuh,
    STAW-zee-yuh [RUS])
    Alternate spellings: Stasia [RUS]
Stephania (stef-FAW-nee-yuh)
    Alternate spellings: Stefania [IT]
Stephanie (STEF-uh-nee [GRK],
    stay-faw-NEE [FR])
    Alternate spellings: Stephany, Stefani,
    Stephani, Stefanie, Stephenie,
    Stéphanie [FR]
Susana (soo-ZAN-uh, soo-ZAW-nuh [IT],
    soo-SAW-nuh or thoo-THAW-nuh [SP])
    Alternate spellings: Susanna,
    Suzanna (see also Shoshana)

Talia (TAW-lee-yuh [HEB], tuh-LEE-yuh [AA])
    Alternate spellings: Thalia, Taliyah,
    Talya
Tamia (TAM-ee-yuh, TAWM-yuh)
    Alternate spellings: Tamya
Tania (TAWN-yuh, TAN-yuh [IT],
    tuh-NEE-yuh [AA])
    Alternate spellings: Tanya, Taniya,
    Tawnya, Tonya*, Tonja, Tonia
Tasha (TAW-shuh, TASH-uh)
    Alternate spellings: Tosha
Tatiana (taw-tee-YAWN-uh,
    tat-ee-YAWN-uh)
    Alternate spellings: Tatyana
Tawana (tuh-WAH-nuh [AA])
    Alternate spellings: Tawanna
Tawanda (tuh-WAND-uh [AA])
Tawny (TAW-nee)
Tiana (tee-YAWN-uh, tee-YAN-nuh)
    Alternate spellings: Tianna
Tomasa (toh-MAW-suh [IT/SP],
    toh-MAWTH-uh [SP])
    Alternate spellings: Tomassa
Tommie (TAW-mee)
Tristan (TRIS-ten [WL], trees-TAW with
    short N [FR], trees-TAWN or
    treeth-TAWN [SP])
    Alternate spellings: Tristen

Valencia (val-LEN-see-yuh,
    vuh-LEN-chuh [IT], vaw-LEN-see-yaw
    or baw-LEN-thee-yaw [SP])
Veronica (vur-RAW-nik-uh,
    vair-ROH-nee-kuh or
    bair-ROH-nee-kuh [SP])
Viviana (viv-ee-YAWN-uh)
Von (VAWN)

Alternate spellings: Vawn, Vaughn
Vonda (VAWN-duh)
Vonnie (VAW-nee)

Waleska (vaw-LESS-kuh or
    wall-LESS-kuh)
    Alternate spellings: Valeska
Wanda (WAND-uh)
Waneta (wah-NET-uh, wah-NEE-tuh)
    Alternate spellings: Wanita, Juanita*

Xia (hee-YAW [CH])

Yahaira (juh-HY-ruh or yaw-HY-ruh [SP])
    Alternate spellings: Yajaira
Yolanda (yoh-LAWN-daw [SP],
    yoh-LAN-duh [IT])
    Alternate spellings: Yolonda, Iolanda [IT]
Yoselin (YAW-sell-in, YAWZ-lin,
    yoh-SEL-een or yoh-THEL-een [SP])
    Alternate spellings: Joselyn*
Yuliana (yoo-lee-YAWN-uh [SP/RUS])
    Alternate spellings: Juliana*
Yumuna (YAW-moo-nuh [EI])
Yvonne (iv-AWN, ee-VOHN [FR])
    Alternate spellings: Ivonne*, Evonne

Zaida (ZAY-duh, zy-YEE-duh,
    zaw-HED-uh with pronounced H at
    end [AR])
Zsa-zsa (ZHAW-ZHAW [HUN], ZAW-zaw)
    Alternate spellings: Zaza [HEB]
Zulma (ZULL-muh [AR])

■ OI ■

PARTNER POINTER:
Check the long E, long O, and OR
lists, too.

Floy (FLOI)

Joy (JOI)
Joyce (JOIS)
Joycelyn (JOI-suh-lin or JAW-suh-lin)
    Alternate spellings: Jocelyn*, Joselyn

Latoya (luh-TOI-yuh [AA])
Loyce (LOIS)

McCoy (mik-KOI [CG])
Moira (MOI-ruh [IR])

Sequoia (seh-KOI-yuh [NA])
Alternate spellings: Sequoya

Toya (TOI-yuh [AA/JAP/SCAN])
Alternate spellings: Toyah

Zoila (ZOI-luh, SOI-luh or soh-LAW [SP])

■ OR ■

PARTNER POINTER:
Check the long O and OI lists, too.

Aurea (OR-ree-yuh, or-RAY-yuh,
    ow-REE-yuh or ow-RAY-yuh [SP])
Aurelia (or-RELL-ee-yuh,
    ow-RELL-ee-yuh [IT])
Aurora (or-ROR-ruh, ow-ROR-ruh [IT])
Aurore (or-ROR, or-ROR-ree,
    ow-RORRR [FR])

Cleora (klee-YOR-ruh)
Cora (KOR-ruh)
Coral (KOR-rull)
Cordelia (kor-DEE-lee-yuh [SP])
Cordia (KOR-dee-yuh)
Cordie (KOR-dee)
Corina (kor-REE-nuh [SP])
Alternate spellings: Corinna
Corinne (kor-REEN [GRK/FR], kor-RIN)
Alternate spellings: Corrine, Corine,
    Corene, Coreen
Corliss (KOR-liss)
Cornelia (kor-NEE-lee-yuh)
Courtney (KORT-nee)
Alternate spellings: Kourtney,
    Kortney, Cortney

Deborah (DEB-ur-ruh, dev-OR-ruh [HEB])
Alternate spellings: Debra, Debora,
    Debrah, Debbra, Devora or Devorah
    [HEB]
Dolores (doh-LOR-ess [SP])
Alternate spellings: Delores, Deloris,
    Doloris
Dora (DOR-ruh [SP])
Dorcas (DOR-kuss)
Doreen (dor-REEN)
Alternate spellings: Dorene, Dorine
Dori (DOR-ree [GRK/HEB])
Dorinda (dor-RIN-duh)
Doris (DOR-riss)
Alternate spellings: Dorris

Dorit (DOR-rit [GER/HEB])
Dorotha (DOR-rith-uh)
Alternate spellings: Doretha
Dorothea (dor-roh-THEE-yuh)
Dorothy (DOR-roh-thee)
Alternate spellings: Dorathy
Dortha (DOR-thuh)
Dorthy (DOR-thee)

Eldora (ell-DOR-ruh [SP])
Eleanor (EL-len-nor, el-lay-yoh-NOR [FR])
Alternate spellings: Eleanore, Elinor,
    Elinore, Elenor, Eleonore [FR]
Eleanora (el-len-NOR-ruh,
    el-lee-yuh-NOR-ruh,
    eh-lay-oh-NOR-uh [IT/SP])
Alternate spellings: Elenora, Eleonora
    [IT/SP] (see also Elnora)
Elnora (el-NOR-ruh)
Eudora (yoo-DOR-ruh)

Flora (FLOR-ruh [IT/SP])
Florence (FLOR-rens, flor-RAWS with
    short N [FR])
Florida (FLOR-rid-uh, flor-REE-duh [SP])
Florine (flor-REEN)
Alternate spellings: Florene
Florrie (FLOR-ree)

George (JORJ, ZHORZH [FR])
Alternate spellings: Georges [FR]
Georgene (jor-JEEN, zhor-ZHEEN with
    sustained N [FR])
Alternate spellings: Georgine
Georgette (jor-JET, zhor-ZHET [FR])
Georgia (JOR-juh)
Alternate spellings: Giorgia
Georgiana (jor-jee-YAN-nuh)
Alternate spellings: Georgianna
Georgianne (jor-jee-YAN, zhor-zhee-
    YAW with short N [FR])
Alternate spellings: Georgiane
Georgie (JOR-jee)
Georgina (jor-JEE-nuh)
Alternate spellings: Giorgina
Gloria (GLOR-ree-yuh [IT/SP])
Gregoria (gre-GOR-ree-yuh [IT])

Hortencia (hor-TEN-see-yuh, or-TEN-
    see-yuh or or-TEN-thee-yuh [SP])
Alternate spellings: Hortensia
Hortense (HOR-tens)

Ingeborg (EEN-guh-borg [SCAN])

Isadora (iz-uh-DOR-ruh, ee-saw-DOR-ruh [IT/SP], ee-thaw-DOR-ruh [SP])
Isadore (IZ-uh-dor, ee-see-DOR [FR])
Alternate spellings: Isidore [FR]
Ivory (EYE-vor-ree)
Izora (eye-ZOR-ruh)

Jordan (JOR-den, YAR-den [HEB])
Alternate spellings: Jordyn, Yarden*

Kori (KOR-ree)
Alternate spellings: Corey, Cori, Cory, Corrie,

Laura (LOR-ruh, LOW-ruh [IT], LOR-ray [FR], law-OO-raw [SP])
Alternate spellings: Lora
Laurel (LOR-rel)
Lauren (LOR-ren)
Alternate spellings: Lauryn, Loren, Lorene*
Lauretta (lor-RET-uh, low-RET-uh [IT])
Alternate spellings: Loretta*
Laurette (lor-RETT [FR])
Lenora (len-OR-ruh [SP])
Alternate spellings: Leonora*
Lenore (len-NOR)
Alternate spellings: Leonor*, Leonore
Leonor (LEE-yoh-nor, len-NOR)
Alternate spellings: Leonore, Lenore*
Leonora (lee-yoh-NOR-ruh, lay-oh-NOR-uh [IT/SP])
Alternate spellings: Eleonora [IT/SP], Lenora*
Leora (lee-YOR-ruh [HEB])
Alternate spellings: Liora
Lorelei (LOR-rell-lee, LOR-rell-ly [GER])
Lorena (lor-RAY-nuh, lor-REE-nuh, lor-REN-uh [IT/SP])
Lorene (lor-REEN, LOR-ren, lor-RAYN [FR])
Alternate spellings: Laureen, Loreen, Lorine, Laurine, Lauren*, Lauryn, Loren, Lorraine*
Lorenza (lor-REN-zuh [IT])
Loretta (lor-RET-uh [IT])
Alternate spellings: Lauretta*
Lori (LOR-ree)
Alternate spellings: Laurie, Lauri, Lorie, Lorrie, Lorri
Loriann (lor-ree-YAN)
Lorna (LOR-nuh)
Lorraine (lor-RAYN, lor-REN [FR])
Alternate spellings: Loraine, Laraine, Lorene*

Lourdes (LOR-dess or LOR-deth [SP], LOORD [FR])

Mallory (MAL-or-ree, MAL-ur-ree)
Maura (MOR-ruh, MOW-ruh [IT])
Maureen (mor-REEN)
Alternate spellings: Maurine
Morgan (MOR-gen)
Moriah (mor-RY-yuh, moh-ree-YAW [HEB], muh-RY-yuh)
Alternate spellings: Moriya [HEB], Moria, Mariah*, Maria*

Nora (NOR-ruh [AR/GR/HEB/IR])
Alternate spellings: Norah
Noreen (nor-REEN [AR/IR])
Alternate spellings: Norene, Norine
Norma (NOR-muh)

Ora (OR-raw [HEB])
Alternate spellings: Orah
Oralia (or-RAL-lee-yuh [SP])
Orla (OR-luh [IR])

Portia (POR-shuh)
Alternate spellings: Porsha, Porsche

Rory (ROR-ree)
Rosaura (roh-ZOR-ruh)

Socorro (soh-KOR-rrroh or thoh-KOR-rrroh [SP])
Stormy (STOR-mee)

Theodora (thee-yuh-DOR-ruh, tay-oh-DOR-ruh [IT])
Alternate spellings: Teodora [IT]
Thora (THOR-ruh)
Tori (TOR-ree)

Victoria (vik-TOR-ree-yuh, veek-TOR-ree-yaw or beek-TOR-ree-yaw [SP])

Zora (ZOR-ruh [HEB])
Zoraida (zoh-RAY-duh with pronounced H at end [AR], zor-RY-duh [SP])

■ OW ■

PARTNER POINTER:
Check the short O and AR lists, too.

Augusta (aw-GUSS-tuh, ow-GOOS-tuh [IT],
   aw-GOOS-taw or aw-GOOTH-taw [SP])
Aurea (OR-ree-yuh, or-RAY-yuh,
   ow-REE-yuh or ow-RAY-yuh [SP])
Aurelia (or-RELL-ee-yuh,
   ow-RELL-ee-yuh [IT])
Aurora (or-ROR-ruh, ow-ROR-ruh [IT])
Aurore (or-ROR, or-ROR-ree, ow-RORRR
   [FR])

Claudia (KLAW-dee-yuh, KLOW-dee-yuh
   [IT/SP])

Kaori (KOW-ree [JAP])

Laura (LOR-ruh, LOW-ruh [IT], LOR-ray [FR],
   law-OO-raw [SP])
   Alternate spellings: Lora
Lauretta (lor-RET-uh, low-RET-uh [IT])
   Alternate spellings: Loretta*

Maura (MOR-ruh, MOW-ruh [IT])

Paola (POW-luh [IT], paw-OH-law [SP])
Paoletta (pow-LET-uh [IT])
Paolina (pow-LEE-nuh [IT])

Scout (SKOWT)

■ OO ■

PARTNER POINTER:
Check the UR list, too.

Agustina (ag-uh-STEE-nuh, aw-goos-
   TEEN-uh or aw-gooth-TEEN-uh [SP])
Assunta (aw-SOON-tuh [IT/SP],
   aw-THOON-tuh [SP])
Augusta (aw-GUSS-tuh, ow-GOOS-tuh [IT],
   aw-GOOS-taw or aw-GOOTH-taw [SP])
Augustine (aw-guss-TEEN, ag-oo-STEEN
   with sustained N [FR])

Beulah (BYOO-luh, bee-YOO-luh)
   Alternate spellings: Bulah, Beaulah,
   Beula
Blue (BLOO)
   Alternate spellings: Blu

Brooke (BROOK)
   Alternate spellings: Brook
Brooklyn (BROOK-lin)
   Alternate spellings: Brooklynn
Brunilda (broo-NIL-duh)

Cruz (KROOS or KROOTH [SP])

Drew (DROO)
Drucilla (droo-SILL-uh)
Dulce (DOOL-say or DOOL-thay [SP])

Eudora (yoo-DOR-ruh)
Eugenia (yoo-JEE-nee-yuh,
   yoo-JAY-nee-yuh, oo-JEN-ee-yuh [IT],
   ay-yoo-HAY-nee-yuh [SP])
Eugenie (yoo-JEE-nee, yoo-JAY-nee, ay-
   yoo-HAY-nee [SP], oo-zhay-NEE [FR])
   Alternate spellings: Eugénie [FR]
Eula (YOO-luh)
   Alternate spellings: Eulah
Eulalia (yoo-LAY-lee-yuh,
   ay-yoo-LAW-lee-yuh [SP])
Eulalie (yoo-LAY-lee, oo-law-LEE [FR])
Eunice (YOO-niss)
Eura (YOO-ruh)

Gertrude (GUR-trood [GER])
Guadalupe (gwah-duh-LOO-pay or
   gwah-THAW-loo-pay [SP])
Gudrun (GOO-drun [SCAN])

Hulda (HOOL-duh, CHOOL-duh with
   guttural CH [HEB])
   Alternate spellings: Chulda [HEB]

Jasmine (JAZ-min, jass-MEEN,
   JAS-oo-meen [JAP], yaz-MEEN [AR],
   yass-MEEN [HEB/PER])
   Alternate spellings: Jasmin, Jazmin,
   Jazmine, Jazmyn, Jasmyn, Jazmyne,
   Yasmin*, Yazmin, Yasmine*, Yasmeen
Jesusa (hay-SOO-suh)
Jetta (JET-uh)
Jettie (JET-ee)
Jewel (JOO-well)
   Alternate spellings: Jewell
Juana (joo-WAH-naw, WAH-naw [SP])
Juanita (wah-NEE-tuh [SP])
   Alternate spellings: Waneta*, Wanita
Judith (JOO-dith, zhoo-DEET [FR],
   YOO-dit or yuh-HOO-dit [HEB])
   Alternate spellings: Yudit or Yehudit*
   [HEB]

Judy (JOO-dee)
Alternate spellings: Judi, Judie
Julia (JOO-lee-yuh, HOO-lee-yuh [SP])
Alternate spellings: Giulia [IT]
Juliana (joo-lee-YAWN-uh [IT],
joo-lee-YAN-uh, hoo-lee-YAWN-uh [SP],
yoo-lee-YAWN-nuh [SP/RUS])
Alternate spellings: Julianna, Giuliana
[IT], Yuliana* [RUS]
Julianne (joo-lee-YAN, zhoo-lee-YEN [FR])
Alternate spellings: Juliann, Julienne [FR]
Julie (JOO-lee, zhoo-LEE [FR])
Alternate spellings: Juli
Juliet (JOO-lee-yet, zhoo-lee-YET [FR])
Alternate spellings: Juliet, Juliette
Julissa (joo-LIS-suh or juh-LIS-suh [AA];
see also Jalisa)
June (JOON)
Justine (juh-STEEN, zhoo-STEEN with
sustained N [FR])

LaRue (luh-ROO)
Laura (LOR-ruh, LOW-ruh [IT], LOR-ray [FR],
law-OO-raw [SP])
Alternate spellings: Lora
Lou (LOO)
Alternate spellings: Lu, Lue
Louella (loo-WELL-uh)
Alternate spellings: Luella
Louie (LOO-wee)
Louise (loo-WEEZ [FR])
Lourdes (LOR-dess or LOR-deth [SP],
LOORD [FR])
Luana (loo-WAH-nuh [GER/HW],
loo-WAN-uh [IT])
Alternate spellings: Louanna
Luann (loo-WAN)
Alternate spellings: Luanne, Louann
Lucero (loo-SAIR-roh or loo-THAIR-roh
[SP])
Lucia (LOO-shuh, loo-CHEE-yuh [IT/SCAN],
loo-SEE-yuh or loo-THEE-yuh [SP])
Luciena (loo-see-YEN-uh)
Lucienne (loo-see-YAN, loo-see-YEN
with sustained N [FR])
Lucila (loo-SEE-luh)
Lucille (loo-SEEL [FR])
Alternate spellings: Lucile
Lucinda (loo-SIN-duh)
Lucrecia (loo-KREE-shuh,
loo-KREE-see-yuh,
loo-KRESS-ee-yuh or
loo-KRETH-ee-yuh [SP],
loo-KRET-zee-yuh [IT])

Alternate spellings: Lucretia, Lucrezia
[IT]
Lucy (LOO-see, loo-SEE [FR])
Alternate spellings: Lucie [FR]
Ludie (LOO-dee)
Luetta (loo-WET-uh)
Luisa (loo-WEEZ-uh [IT], loo-WEES-uh
[GER/SP], loo-WEETH-uh)
Alternate spellings: Louisa
Lula (LOO-luh [AR])
Lulu (LOO-loo, LOO-LOO [AR/FR])
Luna (LOO-nuh [SP])
Lupe (LOO-pay [SP])
Lupita (loo-PEE-tuh [SP])
Luvenia (loo-VEN-nee-yuh,
loo-VAY-nee-yuh; see also Lavinia)
Alternate spellings: Louvenia
Luz (LOOS or LOOTH [SP])

Marylou (mair-ree-LOO)
Alternate spellings: Marilou

Natsumi (NAT-soo-mee [JAP])

Prudence (PROO-dens)
Pura (PYOO-ruh)

Ruby (ROO-bee)
Alternate spellings: Rubye, Rubie
Rumer (ROO-mur [BR])
Ruth (ROOTH, ROOT [HEB])
Alternate spellings: Ruthe, Rut [HEB]
Ruthann (roo-THAN)
Ruthie (ROO-thee, ROO-tee [HEB])
Alternate spellings: Ruthe, Ruti [HEB]

Soomie (SOO-mee [KOR])
Sudie (SOO-dee)
Sue (SOO)
Suellen (soo-WELL-en)
Sugine (SOO-jin [KOR])
Alternate spellings: Sujin
Susan (SOO-zen)
Alternate spellings: Suzan
Susana (soo-ZAN-uh, soo-ZAW-nuh [IT],
soo-SAW-nuh or thoo-THAW-nuh [SP])
Alternate spellings: Susanna,
Suzanna (see also Shoshana)
Susie (SOO-zee)
Alternate spellings: Suzy
Suzanne (soo-ZAN [FR])
Alternate spellings: Susanne, Suzann,
Susann (see also Shoshana)
Suzette (soo-ZETT [FR])

Tallulah (tuh-LOO-luh [NA])
   Alternate spellings: Tallula [IR]
Trudy (TROO-dee [GER])
   Alternate spellings: Trudie, Trude
Tuk Yoon (took YOON [KOR])
Tvuna (tuh-VOO-nuh [HEB])

Uma (OO-muh [EI])
Una (OO-nuh [IR/IT], YOO-nuh)
   Alternate spellings: Euna, Oona or
   Oonagh [IR]
Unique (yoo-NEEK)
Ursula (UR-soo-luh [SCAN])

Xiu (HEE-yoo [CH])

Yehudit (yuh-HOO-dit or YOO-dit [HEB])
   Alternate spellings: Yudit, Judith*
Yuliana (yoo-lee-YAWN-uh [SP/RUS])
   Alternate spellings: Juliana*
Yuka (YOO-kuh [JAP])
Yumuna (YAW-moo-nuh [EI])

Zula (ZOO-luh)
Zulma (ZUL-muh or ZOOL-muh [AR])

■ SHORT U (UH OR U) ■

PARTNER POINTER:
**Short E, I, and U often sound
similar. Please note that we are not
including names that only end in
"uh" on this list, because there are
too many.**

Aaliyah (uh-LEE-yuh [AA], AW-lee-yuh
   [HEB/AR])
   Alternate spellings: Aliyah, Aliya,
   Aleah*, Alia
Acacia (uh-KAY-shuh)
Adelaida (add-uh-LAY-duh)
Adelaide (ADD-uh-layd [GER],
   add-eh-LED or uh-dell-uh-YEED [FR])
Adele (uh-DELL [GER], ad-DEL)
   Alternate spellings: Adell, Adelle
Adelia (uh-DEE-lee-yuh,
   aw-DELL-ee-yuh [IT])
Adelina (ad-uh-LEE-nuh,
   aw-dell-LEE-nuh [IT/SP])
Adeline (AD-uh-lin, ADD-uh-lyn,
   ad-dell-LEEN with sustained N [FR])
   Alternate spellings: Adaline
Adella (uh-DELL-uh [GER], aw-DELL-uh

[IT/SP], aw-DEE-luh or AW-dill-uh [AR])
   Alternate spellings: Adela
Afton (AF-tun [IR])
Agatha (AG-uh-thuh, AW-guh-tuh [IT],
   ag-GAT [FR])
   Alternate spellings: Agathe [FR]
Agustina (ag-uh-STEE-nuh,
   aw-goos-TEEN-uh or
   aw-gooth-TEEN-uh [SP])
Akira (uh-KEER-uh [AA/SCOT])
Alana (uh-LAW-nuh)
   Alternate spellings: Alanna*, Elana*,
   Ilana*
Alani (uh-LAW-nee, uh-LAN-nee,
   uh-LAY-nee)
Alanis (uh-LAW-niss, uh-LAN-niss)
Alanna (uh-LAN-nuh, uh-LAW-nuh)
   Alternate spellings: Alana*, Elana*,
   Ilana*
Aleah (uh-LAY-yuh, uh-LEE-yuh,
   AW-lee-yuh [AR/HEB])
   Alternate spellings: Aaliyah*, Aliyah,
   Aliya, Alia
Aleta (uh-LEE-duh)
   Alternate spellings: Alida
Alexa (uh-LEK-suh, aw-LEK-suh or
   aw-LEK-thuh [SP])
Alexia (uh-LEK-see-yuh, al-LEK-see-uh [IT])
Alexis (uh-LEK-siss)
   Alternate spellings: Alexys, Alexus
Alicia (uh-LEE-shuh, aw-LEE-see-yuh or
   aw-LEE-thee-yuh [SP])
   Alternate spellings: Elisha, Alysha,
   Alycia, Alecia, Alesha, Alysia, Alisha
Alina (uh-LEE-nuh)
   Alternate spellings: Alena
Alisa (uh-LEE-suh, aw-LEE-suh [HEB/SP],
   aw-LEE-thuh [SP])
   Alternate spellings: Elisa*, Alysa
Alissa (uh-LISS-uh)
   Alternate spellings: Elissa, Alyssa,
   Elyssa, Allyssa
Alize (uh-LEEZ, aw-LEEZ [FR], al-LEE-zay)
Alondra (uh-LAWN-druh, aw-LOHN-druh
   [SP])
Amalia (uh-MAW-lee-yuh [HEB])
   Alternate spellings: Amalya, Amaliah
Amanda (uh-MAN-duh, aw-MAWN-duh
   [SP])
Amani (uh-MAW-nee; see also Imani)
Amara (uh-MAR-ruh)
Amari (uh-MAR-ree)
Amaris (AM-ur-riss, uh-MAIR-riss,
   uh-MAR-riss)

Amaryllis (am-uh-RILL-iss)
Amaya (uh-MY-yuh, aw-MY-yuh [SP])
 Alternate spellings: Amya [HEB],
 Amiya*, Amiyah
Amelia (uh-MEE-lee-yuh,
 aw-MELL-ee-yuh [IT])
 Alternate spellings: Emilia, Emelia
America (uh-MAIR-ik-uh,
 aw-MAIR-ee-kuh [IT])
Anissa (uh-NISS-uh, aw-NEES-suh [AR])
Anita (uh-NEE-tuh, aw-NEE-tuh [IT/SP])
Anitra (uh-NEET-ruh)
Aniya (aw-NY-yuh, uh-NEE-yuh,
 AW-nee-yuh [HEB])
 Alternate spellings: Aniyah, Anaya*,
 Anya*, Analla
Anjanette (ann-juh-NET)
Annabella (ann-uh-BELL-uh)
 Alternate spellings: Anabela [IT]
Annabelle (ANN-uh-bell, an-uh-BELL [FR])
 Alternate spellings: Annabel, Anabel,
 Annabell
Annalise (ann-uh-LEES [GER/FR])
 Alternate spellings: Analise, Annelise
Annamae (ANN-uh-may)
Annamarie (ann-uh-muh-REE,
 aw-nuh-maw-REE [FR])
Anne (ANN)
 Alternate spellings: Ann
Annmarie (ann-muh-REE)
Arabella (air-uh-BELL-uh)
Araceli (air-ruh-SELL-ee, ar-raw-SELL-ee
 or ar-raw-THEL-ee [SP])
 Alternate spellings: Aracely
Arely (AIR-ruh-lee, AR-ruh-lee,
 uh-RELL-ee)
 Alternate spellings: Areli
Athena (uh-THEE-nuh)
Augusta (aw-GUSS-tuh, ow-GOOS-tuh
 [IT], aw-GOOS-taw or aw-GOOTH-taw
 [SP])
Augustine (aw-guss-TEEN, ag-oo-STEEN
 with sustained N [FR])
Awilda (uh-WILL-duh)

Beatrice (BEE-yuh-triss, bay-yuh-TREES
 [FR/SP], vay-yuh-TRITH [SP])
 Alternate spellings: Beatriz [SP]
Beatrix (BEE-yuh-triks [GER/SCAN],
 bay-yuh-TREEKS [IT])
Bernadette (bur-nuh-DET, bair-nuh-DET
 [FR])
Bernardine (bur-nuh-DEEN,
 bair-nar-DEEN [FR])

 Alternate spellings: Bernadine
Brittany (BRIT-uh-nee)
 Alternate spellings: Britany, Brittanie

Calista (kuh-LISS-tuh)
Carina (kar-EE-nuh [IT/SP], kuh-RIN-uh [SCAN])
 Alternate spellings: Karina
Carissa (kuh-RISS-uh)
 Alternate spellings: Karissa, Carisa,
 Charissa*
Cassandra (kuh-SAN-druh [GRK],
 kaw-SAWN-draw or
 kaw-THAWN-draw [SP])
 Alternate spellings: Kassandra,
 Casandra, Kasandra
Catalina (kat-uh-LEE-nuh,
 kaw-taw-LEE-nuh [SP])
Chandra (CHUN-drrruh [EI],
 CHAWN-druh, SHAWN-druh)
Charissa (shuh-RISS-uh, kuh-RISS-uh)
 Alternate spellings: Carissa*
Charisse (shuh-REES, shair-RRREEZ [FR])
 Alternate spellings: Cherise
Cherie (shair-REE [FR], SHAIR-ree,
 shuh-REE, CHAIR-ree)
 Alternate spellings: Cheri, Sheree*,
 Sherrie, Sherie Cherry*, Sherry*)
Coral (KOR-rull)

Dakota (duh-KOH-tuh)
Damaris (DAM-ur-riss, duh-MAIR-ris,
 duh-MAR-ris)
Danita (duh-NEE-tuh, daw-NEE-tuh)
 Alternate spellings: Donita
Deneen (duh-NEEN [AA/IR])
 Alternate spellings: Denene
Dovie (DUV-ee)

Eliza (uh-LY-zuh, ee-LY-zuh, el-LEE-zuh
 [IT])
 Alternate spellings: Aliza, Alizah,
 Aleeza [HEB]
Emelina (em-uh-LEEN-uh [GER/SP/RUS])
Emeline (em-uh-LEEN with sustained N
 [FR], em-uh-LYN, EM-uh-lin)
 Alternate spellings: Emmeline,
 Emmaline, Emelyn, Emaleen
Evelyn (EV-uh-lin)
 Alternate spellings: Evelin, Evalyn
Evelyne (ee-vuh-LEEN, ev-uh-LEEN)
 Alternate spellings: Eveline [FR]

Genesis (JEN-uh-sis)
Genevieve (JEN-uh-veev [CG],

zhen-uh-vee-YEV or zhawn-vee-YEV
[FR])
Alternate spellings: Geneviève

Honey (HUN-ee)
Hong (HUNG [CH])
Hunter (HUN-tur)

Isabel (IZ-uh-bell, ee-zaw-BELL [FR],
EE-saw-bell or ee-saw-BELL or
ee-thuh-VELL [SP])
Alternate spellings: Isabelle [FR],
Isabell, Isobel
Isabela (iz-uh-BELL-uh, ee-saw-BELL-uh
or ee-thaw-VELL-uh [SP],
ee-zuh-BELL-uh [IT])
Alternate spellings: Isabella [IT],
Izabella
Isadora (iz-uh-DOR-ruh,
ee-saw-DOR-ruh [IT/SP],
ee-thaw-DOR-ruh [SP])
Isadore (IZ-uh-dor, ee-see-DOR [FR])
Alternate spellings: Isidore [FR]

Jacqueline (JAK-uh-lin, JAK-well-lin,
jak-LEEN, zhawk-uh-LEEN with
sustained N [FR])
Alternate spellings: Jaqueline,
Jaquelyn, Jackeline, Jaquelin,
Jacquline, Jacalyn
Jakayla (juh-KAY-luh [AA])
Jalisa (juh-LEE-suh [AA], JAL-iss-uh [AR];
see also Julissa)
Jaliyah (juh-LEE-yuh [AA])
Jamila (juh-MEEL-uh with pronounced H
at end [AR])
Jamya (juh-MY-yuh [AA])
Judith (JOO-dith, zhoo-DEET [FR],
YOO-dit or yuh-HOO-dit [HEB])
Alternate spellings: Yudit or Yehudit*
[HEB]
Justice (JUS-tis [AA])
Justina (jus-TEE-nuh)
Justine (juh-STEEN, zhoo-STEEN with
sustained N [FR])

Kaliyah (KAW-lee-yuh or kuh-LEE-yuh [AA])
Alternate spellings: Kalia [HW]
Karyme (kuh-REE-muh [AR], kaw-REEM)
Katarina (kat-uh-REE-nuh,
kaw-tar-REE-nuh [GER])
Alternate spellings: Katerina,
Katharina*
Kathaleen (kath-uh-LEEN)

Katharina (kath-ur-REE-nuh,
kat-uh-REE-nuh)
Alternate spellings: Katarina*,
Katerina
Kennedy (KEN-uh-dee)
Alternate spellings: Kennedi
Khadijah (kud-DEE-zhuh or kud-DEED-juh
[AA], chu-DEE-juh with guttural CH at
beginning and pronounced H at end
[AR])

Ladonna (luh-DAWN-uh)
Lakeisha (luh-KEE-shuh [AA])
Alternate spellings: Lakisha, Lakesha
Lakeshia (luh-KEE-shee-yuh [AA])
Laquita (luh-KWEE-tuh or luh-KEE-tuh)
Larissa (luh-RISS-uh)
LaRue (luh-ROO)
Lashanda (luh-SHAWN-duh or
luh-SHAN-duh [AA])
Alternate spellings: Lashonda
Lashawn (luh-SHAWN [AA])
Latanya (luh-TAWN-yuh or luh-TAN-yuh
[AA])
Alternate spellings: Latonya*
Latasha (luh-TAW-shuh or luh-TASH-uh
[AA])
Alternate spellings: Latosha
Latonya (luh-TOHN-yuh or
luh-TAWN-yuh[AA])
Alternate spellings: Latanya*
Latoya (luh-TOI-yuh [AA])
Latrice (luh-TREES [AA])
Lavadà (luh-VAY-duh)
Lavera (luh-VEER-ruh)
Laverna (luh-VUR-nuh)
Laverne (luh-VURN)
Alternate spellings: Lavern
Lavina (luh-VEE-nuh [AA])
Lavinia (luh-VIN-ee-yuh; see also Luvenia)
Lavonne (luh-VAWN [AA])
Alternate spellings: Lavon
Lawanda (luh-WAND-uh [AA])
Leatrice (LEE-yuh-triss, LAY-yuh-triss,
lee-yuh-TREES, lay-uh-TREES)
Leticia (luh-TEE-shuh, let-EE-see-yuh or
let-EE-thee-yuh [SP])
Alternate spellings: Latisha, Letitia
Lizabeth (LY-zuh-beth, LIZ-uh-beth)
London (LUN-den)
Lovie (LUV-ee)

Maddalena (mad-duh-LAY-nuh [IT])
Madelena (mad-uh-LEN-uh [IT])

Madeline (MAD-uh-lin, MAD-uh-lyn,
MAD-lin, mad-dell-LYN or
mad-dell-LEN with sustained N [FR])
Alternate spellings: Madelyn,
Madeleine, Madalyn, Madelynn,
Madilyn, Madalynn, Madaline
Madonna (muh-DAWN-uh, mad-OH-nuh
[IT])
Magdalen (MAG-duh-len)
Alternate spellings: Magdalene*
Magdalena (mag-duh-LAY-nuh [SP])
Magdalene (mag-duh-LEEN,
MAG-duh-len)
Alternate spellings: Magdalen*
Makayla (muh-KAY-luh or mak-KAY-luh
[CG/SP])
Alternate spellings: Mikayla,
Michaela*, McKayla, Mikaela, Micaela,
Makaila, Mikala
Malaika (muh-LY-kuh [AA])
Alternate spellings: Malika*, Malikah
Maleah (maw-LAY-yuh [HW], muh-LEE-yuh)
Malia (maw-LEE-yuh [HW/AA], muh-LEE-
haw [AR], MAW-lee-yuh)
Alternate spellings: Maleah*, Maliyah
Matilda (muh-TIL-duh [GER], mat-TEEL-deh
[IT])
Alternate spellings: Matilde*, Mathilda
Matilde (muh-TIL-dee, mat-TEELD [FR],
mat-TEEL-day [SP], mat-TIL-duh [GER])
Alternate spellings: Matilda*,
Mathilda, Mathilde [FR]
Melinda (mel-LIN-duh, muh-LIN-duh)
Alternate spellings: Malinda
Melisa (mel-LEE-suh, muh-LISS-uh)
Meliss (mel-LISS)
Melissa (muh-LISS-uh, mel-LISS-uh,
may-lee-SAW [FR])
Alternate spellings: Melisa*, Mellissa,
Malissa, Mellisa, Mélissa
Michelle (muh-SHELL, mish-ELL,
mee-SHELL [FR], MEE-shell)
Alternate spellings: Michele, Michell,
Mechelle, Machelle, Michèle [FR]

Nakia (nuh-KEE-yuh [AA])

Olivia (oh-LIV-ee-yuh, oh-LEE-vee-yaw
[IT/SP], oh-LEE-bee-yaw [SP], uh-LIV-ee-
yuh)
Alternate spellings: Alivia
Onie (OH-nee, WUN-ee)
Opal (OH-pull)

Parisa (puh-REE-suh, pair-ree-SUH [PER])

Rafaela (raf-fay-YELL-uh, raf-fy-YELL-uh
[IT], raw-fuh-ELL-uh [HEB/SP])
Ramona (ram-OH-nuh, rrraw-MOH-naw
[SP])
Alternate spellings: Romona
Roberta (rub-BUR-tuh, roh-BAIR-tuh)

Salma (SAL-muh, SAWL-muh [HEB/SP],
THAWL-muh [SP], SUL-muh with
pronounced H at end [AR])
Salome (sal-LOH-mee, SAW-loh-may,
suh-LOHM, SAL-loh-may [BR],
saw-loh-MAY [FR], shaw-LOHM [HEB])
Alternate spellings: Salomé [FR],
Shalom [HEB]
Samara (suh-MAR-ruh, suh-MAIR-ruh,
suh-MARRR-ruh with pronounced H
at end [AR])
Alternate spellings: Samarrah
Samira (suh-MEER-uh with pronounced
H at end [AR])
Saniya (suh-NY-yuh or suh-NEE-yuh [AA],
san-NY-yuh [AR], SAWN-yuh)
Alternate spellings: Saniyya [AR],
Sanya*, Sonia*, Sonya
Sarahi (suh-RAW-hee [AA])
Sarai (suh-RY [HEB])
Sariah (suh-RY-yuh)
Savannah (suh-VAN-uh)
Alternate spellings: Savanna,
Savanah, Savana
Shakira (shuh-KEER-ruh [AA],
SHAW-keer-ruh or SHAK-eer-ruh [AR])
Shalonda (shuh-LAWN-duh [AA])
Shameka (shuh-MEE-kuh [AA])
Alternate spellings: Shamika
Shamira (shuh-MEER-ruh [HEB])
Shania (shuh-NY-yuh, shuh-NEE-yuh)
Alternate spellings: Shaniya
Shanice (shuh-NEES [AA])
Shanika (shuh-NEE-kuh [AA])
Shaniqua (shuh-NEEK-wuh [AA])
Shanita (shuh-NEE-tuh [AA])
Sharonda (shuh-RAWN-duh [AA])
Sheree (shuh-REE)
Alternate spellings: Cherie*, Cheri,
Sherrie, Sherie
Sherita (shuh-REE-tuh [AA])
Summer (SUM-mur)
Sunny (SUN-ee)
Sunshine (SUN-shyn)

Tallulah (tuh-LOO-luh [NA])
  Alternate spellings: Tallula [IR]
Tamara (TAM-uh-ruh, tuh-MAR-ruh [AR/EI],
  tuh-MAIR-ruh [AA], tuh-MAR [HEB],
  TAW-mar-ruh [RUS])
  Alternate spellings: Tamera, Tamar
  [HEB], Tamarah [AR]
Tamatha (TAM-uth-uh)
  Alternate spellings: Tamitha
Tanisha (tuh-NEESH-uh [AA])
  Alternate spellings: Tanesha, Tenisha
Tawana (tuh-WAH-nuh [AA])
  Alternate spellings: Tawanna
Tawanda (tuh-WAND-uh [AA])
Tvuna (tuh-VOO-nuh [HEB])

Willamina (will-uh-MEE-nuh)
Winifred (WIN-uh-fred [CG])
  Alternate spellings: Winnifred

Yahaira (juh-HY-ruh or yaw-HY-ruh [SP])
  Alternate spellings: Yajaira
Yehudit (yuh-HOO-dit or YOO-dit [HEB])
  Alternate spellings: Yudit, Judith*
Yemima (yuh-MY-muh [HEB])
  Alternate spellings: Jemima*

Zaria (zuh-RY-yuh, ZAR-ree-yuh)
Zulma (ZUL-muh or ZOOL-muh [AR])

■ UR ■

PARTNER POINTER:
Check the OO list, too.

Alberta (al-BUR-tuh, al-BAIR-tuh [IT/SP],
  al-VAIR-tuh [SP])
Albertha (al-BURTH-uh)
Albertine (al-bur-TEEN, awl-bair-TEEN
  with sustained N [FR])
Alverta (al-VUR-tuh)
Amaris (AM-ur-riss, uh-MAIR-riss,
  uh-MAR-riss)
Amber (AM-bur, AWM-bur [AR])
Amira (AW-mur-ruh or aw-MEER-ruh
  [HEB] with pronounced H at end [AR],
  aw-meer-RAW [HEB])
Avery (AY-vur-ee)

Barbara (BAR-bur-ruh, BAR-bar-ruh [IT/SP],
  VAR-var-ruh [SP]; see also Barbra)
Berenice (bur-NEES)
  Alternate spellings: Bernice,

Berniece, Burnice, Berneice,
  Bernadette (bur-nuh-DET,
  bair-nuh-DET [FR])
Bernardine (bur-nuh-DEEN,
  bair-nar-DEEN [FR])
  Alternate spellings: Bernadine
Bernita (bair-NEE-tuh or vair-NEE-tuh [SP],
  bur-NEE-tuh)
Berta (BUR-tuh, BAIR-tuh [IT/SP],
  VAIR-tuh [SP])
Bertha (BURTH-uh, BUR-tuh [GER])
Bertie (BUR-tee)
Beverly (BEV-ur-lee)
  Alternate spellings: Beverley,
  Beverlee
Birdie (BUR-dee)

Cameron (KAM-ur-en)
  Alternate spellings: Camryn, Kamryn
Catherine (KATH-ur-rin, kat-REEN [FR];
  see also Kathrine)
  Alternate spellings: Katheryn,
  Katharine, Catharine
Cedar (SEE-dur)
Chandler (CHAND-lur)
Christopher (KRIS-toh-fur)

Damaris (DAM-ur-riss, duh-MAIR-ris,
  duh-MAR-ris)
Deborah (DEB-ur-uh, dev-OR-uh [HEB])
  Alternate spellings: Debra, Debora,
  Debrah, Debbra, Devora or Devorah
  [HEB]
Dexter (DEK-stur)

Earlene (ur-LEEN [CG])
  Alternate spellings: Earline, Erlene
Easter (EES-tur)
Emerald (EM-ur-ruld)
Emerson (EM-ur-sun)
Erlinda (ur-LIN-duh, air-LEEN-duh [SP])
Ermina (ur-MEE-nuh, air-MEE-nuh [SP];
  see also Hermina)
Erna (UR-nuh, AIR-nuh)
Ernestina (ur-ness-TEE-nuh,
  air-ness-TEE-nuh [IT])
Ernestine (UR-ness-teen)
  Alternate spellings: Earnestine
Esmeralda (ez-mur-RAWL-duh,
  ess-mair-RAL-duh or
  eth-mair-RAL-duh [SP])
Esmerelda (ez-mur-RELL-duh,
  ess-mair-RAL-duh or
  eth-mair-RAL-duh [SP])

Esther (ESS-tur, ess-TAIR [FR/HEB])
  Alternate spellings: Ester

Fern (FURN)
  Alternate spellings: Ferne
Fernanda (fur-NAN-duh [IT],
  fair-NAWN-duh [SP])

Gerda (GUR-duh [SCAN])
Germaine (jur-MAYN, zhair-MAYN with
  sustained N [FR])
Gertie (GUR-dee)
Gertrude (GUR-trood [GER])
Ginger (JIN-jur)

Heather (HETH-ur)
Hermina (hur-MEE-nuh, air-MEE-nuh [SP];
  see also Ermina)
Hermine (hur-MEEN)
Herminia (air-MEE-nee-yuh [SP],
  hur-MIN-ee-yuh, hur-MEE-nee-yuh)
Hermione (hur-MY-yoh-nee [BR])
Herta (HUR-tuh)
Hester (HES-tur)
Hildur (HIL-dur [SCAN])
Hillary (HIL-ur-ree)
  Alternate spellings: Hilary
Hunter (HUN-tur)

Irma (UR-muh [GER], YEER-muh [IT],
  EER-muh [SP])
  Alternate spellings: Erma

Jennifer (JEN-nif-ur [WL], zheh-nee-FAIR
  [FR])
  Alternate spellings: Jenifer, Genifer
Jerline (jur-LEEN [AA])
Journey (JUR-nee)

Katharina (kath-ur-REE-nuh,
  kat-uh-REE-nuh)
  Alternate spellings: Katarina*,
  Katerina
Kimberly (KIM-bur-lee)
  Alternate spellings: Kimberlee,
  Kimberley, Kimberli
Kirsten (KEER-sten [SCAN], KURS-ten)
  Alternate spellings: Kirstin, Kiersten,
  Kierstin
Kirstie (KEER-stee, KURS-tee)

Laverna (luh-VUR-nuh)
Laverne (luh-VURN)
  Alternate spellings: Lavern

Liberty (LIB-ur-tee)
Lura (LUR-ruh)
Lurline (lur-LEEN)

Mairwen (MY-yur-wen or MYR-wen [WL],
  MAIR-wen)
Mallory (MAL-or-ree, MAL-ur-ree)
Margaret (MAR-gret, MAR-gur-ret)
  Alternate spellings: Margret,
  Margarett, Margarette, Margarete
Marguerite (mar-gur-REET [FR])
  Alternate spellings: Margarete
Marjorie (MAR-jur-ree)
  Alternate spellings: Margery, Marjory
Mercedes (mair-SED-ess or
  mair-THED-eth [SP], mur-SAY-deez)
Merle (MURL)
  Alternate spellings: Myrle, Myrl
Merlene (mur-LEEN)
Mertie (MUR-tee)
  Alternate spellings: Myrtie
Minerva (MIN-ur-vuh)
Miranda (mur-RAN-duh,
  meer-RAWN-duh [SP])
  Alternate spellings: Meranda,
  Myranda, Maranda
Mirta (MUR-tuh)
Missouri (miz-ZUR-ree)
Muriel (MUR-ee-yell [CG/HEB])
Myrna (MUR-nuh [CG])
Myrtice (mur-TEES, meer-TEES)
Myrtis (MUR-tiss)
Myrtle (MUR-tull)

Parker (PAR-kur)
Pearl (PURL)
  Alternate spellings: Pearle
Pearlie (PUR-lee)
Pearline (pur-LEEN)
Perla (PUR-luh, PAIR-luh [IT/SP])
Piper (PY-pur)

Roberta (rub-BUR-tuh, roh-BAIR-tuh)
Rumer (ROO-mur [BR])

Sailor (SAY-lur)
Serena (sur-REEN-uh, suh-REN-uh [IT/SP],
  thu-REN-uh [SP])
  Alternate spellings: Sarina
Serenity (sur-REN-it-ee)
Shirlene (shur-LEEN)
Shirley (SHUR-lee)
  Alternate spellings: Shirlee
Sister (SIS-tur)

Skylar (SKY-lur)
Alternate spellings: Skyler
Summer (SUM-mur)

Taylor (TAY-lur)
Alternate spellings: Tayler
Teresa (tur-REE-suh, tair-REZ-uh [IT],
tair-RESS-suh or tair-RETH-uh [SP])
Alternate spellings: Theresa, Teressa
(see also Tressa)
Therese (tur-REES, tay-REZ [FR])
Alternate spellings: Terese, Thérèse
Theresia (tur-REES-ee-yuh,
tair-RESS-ee-yuh)
Tyler (TY-lur)

Ursula (UR-soo-luh [SCAN])

Valeria (val-ur-REE-yuh, val-AIR-ee-yuh
[IT])
Valerie (VAL-ur-ree, vaw-lair-REE [FR])
Alternate spellings: Valarie, Valorie

Verda (VUR-duh, VAIR-duh, VEER-duh)
Vernie (VUR-nee)
Verla (VUR-luh, VAIR-luh, VEER-duh)
Verlie (VUR-lee)
Verna (VUR-nuh, VEER-nuh)
Vernell (vur-NELL)
Vernice (vur-NEES)
Verona (vur-ROH-nuh, vair-ROH-nuh
[IT/SP], bair-ROH-nuh [SP])
Veronica (vur-RAW-nik-uh, vair-RAW-
nee-kuh [IT/SP], bair-RAW-nee-kuh [SP])
Versie (VUR-see)
Virgie (VUR-gee, VUR-jee)
Alternate spellings: Vergie
Virginia (vur-JIN-yuh, veer-JEE-nee-yuh
[IT], veer-HEE-nee-yuh or
beer-HEE-nee-yuh [SP])
Virginie (veer-zhee-NEE [FR])

Zhi (JUR [CH])

> **Long A** (AY); **Short A** (A); **AIR**; **AR**; **Long E** (EE); **Short E** (EH or E); **Long I** (EYE or Y); **Short I** (I); **Long O** (OH); **Short O** (AW); **OI**; **OR**; **OO**; **Short U** (UH or U); **UR**

■ LONG A (AY) ■

PARTNER POINTER:
Check out the AIR list, too.

Abe (AYB [HEB])
Abel (AY-bell, AW-vell [HEB], aw-BELL [SP])
  Alternate spellings: Able
Abraham (AYB-ri-ham, awv-ruh-HAWM [HEB])
  Alternate spellings: Avraham [HEB]
Abram (AY-brum, aw-VRAWM [HEB])
  Alternate spellings: Avram [HEB]
Adolph (AYD-awlf [GER], ad-DAWLF [FR])
  Alternate spellings: Adolphe [FR], Adolf
Adolphus (uh-DAWL-fus, ay-DAWL-fus)
Adrian (AY-dree-yen, , aw-DREE-yawn [SP], ad-ree-AW with short N [FR]))
  Alternate spellings: Adrien [FR]
Adriel (AY-dree-yell, aw-dree-YELL [HEB])
Aidan (AY-den [IR], ED-in [HEB])
  Alternate spellings: Aiden, Ayden, Adan, Aden
Alexandre (al-eks-ZAWN-dray, al-ek-SAW-druh with short N [FR])
Alfredo (awl-FRAY-doh [IT/SP])
Amos (AY-mohs, AW-mohs [HEB])
Andre (AWN-dray, awn-DRAY [FR])
  Alternate spellings: Andra, Andrée [FR]
Andrea (awn-DRAY-yuh [GRK/IT])
Andreas (awn-DRAY-yes [GRK])
Andres (awn-DRAYS [SP])
Angel (AYN-jell, AWN-hell [SP])
  Alternate spellings: Ángel
Angus (AYN-guss [IR])
Asa (AY-suh [HEB])
Avery (AY-vur-ree)

Bailey (BAY-lee)
Basil (BAY-zill, BAZ-ill [BR])
Blaine (BLAYN)
  Alternate spellings: Blane
Blaise (BLAYZ, BLEZ [FR])

Alternate spellings: Blaze
Blake (BLAYK)
Brady (BRAY-dee)
Brayden (BRAY-den [CG], BRAY-dawn [IR])
  Alternate spellings: Braden, Braeden, Braydon, Braiden, Braedon, Bradyn

Cade (KAYD)
  Alternate spellings: Kade
Caden (KAY-den)
  Alternate spellings: Kaden, Cayden, Kayden, Kaiden, Kadin, Caiden, Kaeden
Cael (KYL, KAYL [CG/HEB])
  Alternate spellings: Cale*, Kale*, Kael
Cale (KAYL [CG/HEB])
  Alternate spellings: Cael*, Kale*, Kael
Caleb (KAY-leb, KAY-luv [HEB])
  Alternate spellings: Kaleb, Kalev [HEB]
Casey (KAY-see)
  Alternate spellings: Kasey
Cason (KAY-sen)
Chaney (CHAY-nee)
  Alternate spellings: Cheney
Chase (CHAYS)
Clay (KLAY)
Clayton (KLAY-ten)
Clemence (klay-MAWS with short N [FR])
Clement (KLEM-ent, kluh-MENT, klay-MAW with short N [FR])
  Alternate spellings: Clément [FR]
Cleo (KLEE-yoh, KLAY-oh [FR])
  Alternate spellings: Cléo
Craig (KRAYG, KREG)
  Alternate spellings: Kraig

Dale (DAYL [GER])
Dana (DAY-nuh, DAW-nuh [SP])
Dandre (DAWN-dray)
Dane (DAYN [SCAN])
Dave (DAYV)
Davey (DAY-vee)
  Alternate spellings: Davy
David (DAY-vid, daw-VEED [HEB], dav-EED [FR])

Davion (DAY-vee-yohn or day-vee-YOHN [AA])
Davis (DAY-vis)
Davon (DAY-vun [AA], DAV-in [IR])
 Alternate spellings: Davin
Dayton (DAY-ten)
Deonte (dee-YAWN-tay [AA])
 Alternate spellings: Dionte
Devonte (duh-VAWN-tay [AA])
 Alternate spellings: Devante,
 Davonte, Devonta, Devontae
Dewayne (duh-WAYN or DWAYN [AA])
 Alternate spellings: Duwayne,
 Dwayne*, Duane, Dwain
Diego (dee-YAY-goh [SP])
Django (JAYN-goh)
Drake (DRAYK)
Draven (DRAY-ven [AA])
Dwayne (DWAYN [CG])
 Alternate spellings: Duane, Dwain,
 Dewayne*, Duwayne

Einar (AY-nar [SCAN])
Eino (AY-noh [SCAN])
Eliseo (el-LEE-see-yoh, el-lee-ZAY-yoh [IT],
 el-lee-SAY-yoh [IT/SP], el-lee-THAY-yoh
 [SP])
Emil (ay-MEEL [FR])
 Alternate spellings: Emile

Fabian (FAY-bee-yen, faw-bee-AWN [FR])
Felipe (fel-LEE-pay [SP])
Felix (FEEL-iks, fel-LEEKS [SP], fay-LEEKS
 [FR])
 Alternate spellings: Félix [SP]
Frank (FRAYNK, FRAWK with short N [FR])
Frankie (FRAYN-kee)
Franklin (FRAYN-klin)
 Alternate spellings: Franklyn
Frederick (FRED-ur-rik [GER],
 fray-day-REEK [FR])
 Alternate spellings: Frederic, Frédéric
 [FR]

Gabe (GAYB)
Gabriel (GAY-bree-ell, gaw-bree-ELL or
 gaw-vree-ELL [HEB], gab-brrree-YELL
 [FR/SP/IT])
 Alternate spellings: Gavriel [HEB]
Gage (GAYJ)
 Alternate spellings: Gaige
Gale (GAYL [CG])
 Alternate spellings: Gael, Gayle
Galen (GAY-lin [GRK])

Alternate spellings: Gaylon
Gaylord (GAY-lord)
Gerard (jur-RARD, zhay-RAR [FR])
 Alternate spellings: Gerard [FR]
Grady (GRAY-dee [CG])
Graham (GRAM, GRAY-yum or
 GRAY-hum [BR])
Grayson (GRAY-sen)
 Alternate spellings: Greyson

Hamish (HAY-mish [SCOT])
Hank (HAYNK [GER])
Hayden (HAY-den)
 Alternate spellings: Haden
Hayward (HAY-wurd)
Haywood (HAY-wood)
Heber (HAY-bur, HEE-bur [BIB],
 ay-BAIR [IR])
Hosea (ho-ZAY-yuh, ho-SHEE-yuh [HEB])
 Alternate spellings: Hosheia

Isaiah (eye-ZAY-yuh, is-shy-YAW or is-
 shy-YAW-hoo [HEB])
 Alternate spellings: Isiah, Izaiah,
 Yeshaya or Yeshayahu [HEB]
Isaias (eye-ZAY-yes)
Ishmael (ISH-mayl, eesh-my-ELL [HEB],
 iss-maw-EEL [AR])
 Alternate spellings: Yishmael [HEB]
Ismael (IZ-mayl, eess-MAW-yell or
 eeth-MAW-yell [SP])
Israel (IZ-ree-yell, IZ-ray-yell [HEB],
 iss-raw-EEL [AR], eess-RAY-yell or
 eeth-RAY-yell [SP])
 Alternate spellings: Yisrael [HEB]

Jace (JAYS)
 Alternate spellings: Jayce, Jase
Jacob (JAY-kub, YAW-kohv [HEB],
 yaw-KOOB [AR])
 Alternate spellings: Jakob, Yakov* or
 Yaakov [HEB], Yakoub* [AR]
Jacoby (juh-KOH-bee, JAY-kub-ee)
 Alternate spellings: Jakobe, Jacobi
Jade (JAYD)
Jaden (JAY-den [AA], yaw-DAWN or
 yaw-DEEN [HEB])
 Alternate spellings: Jayden, Jaiden,
 Jadon [HEB], Jaydon, Jaeden, Jadyn,
 Yadon or Jadin or Yadin [HEB]
Jaime (JAY-mee, HY-may [SP])
 Alternate spellings: Jayme
Jair (JAY-yur [BIB], JAIR, yaw-EER or
 YAW-eer [HEB])

Alternate spellings: Jere*, Yair [HEB], Yahir*

Jake (JAYK)

Jalen (JAY-len [AA])
Alternate spellings: Jaylen, Jaylin, Jaylan, Jaylon

James (JAYMZ)

Jameson (JAY-mis-sun)
Alternate spellings: Jamison

Jamie (JAY-mee)
Alternate spellings: Jamey

Jason (JAY-sen)
Alternate spellings: Jayson, Jasen

Jay (JAY)

Javion (JAY-vee-yawn or JAY-vee-yun [AA])

Javon (JAY-vun [AA])
Alternate spellings: Javen and Javan, Jevon

Javonte (juh-VAWN-tay [AA])

Jermaine (jur-MAYN [AA], zhur-MA [FR]), Germaine, Jermain

JJ (JAY-JAY, JAY-jay)

Jorge (HOR-hay [SP])

Jose (ho-ZAY, YO-see [HEB], ho-SAY or ho-THAY [SP])
Alternate spellings: José [SP]

Josué (ho-soo-WAY or ho-thoo-WAY [SP])

Kale (KAW-lay [HW], KAYL)
Alternate spellings: Cale*, Cael*, Kael

Kalen (KAY-len)

Kane (KAYN)

Lacy (LAY-see)

Lafayette (law-fee-YET, law-fy-YET, law-fay-YET)

Lane (LAYN)
Alternate spellings: Layne

Layton (LAY-ten [BR])
Alternate spellings: Leighton

Leif (LEEF or LAYF [SCAN])

Leon (LEE-yawn [GER], lay-YAW with short N [FR], lay-YOHN [SP])
Alternate spellings: Léon [FR], León [SP]

Leonard (LEN-urd [GER], lay-yoh-NAR [FR])
Alternate spellings: Lenard, Léonard [FR]

Leonardo (lee-yoh-NAR-doh, lay-yoh-NAR-doh [SP])

Léonel (lay-yoh-NELL [FR])

Léopold (LEE-yup-old [GER], lay-yoh-POHLD [FR])
Alternate spellings: Léopold [FR]

Leopoldo (lay-yoh-POHL-doh [IT/SP])

Lupe (LOO-pay [SP])

Mahlon (MAY-len, MAW-len)

Major (MAY-jur)

Mason (MAY-sen)

Mateo (muh-TAY-yoh [SP])
Alternate spellings: Matteo

Maynard (MAY-nurd, MAY-nard)

Meyer (MAY-ur or may-YEER [HEB], MY-ur)
Alternate spellings: Meir

Mikhail (mee-KYL or mee-KY-yell [RUS], MEE-ky-yell, mik-KAYL)

Nate (NAYT)

Nathan (NAY-thin, nuh-TAWN [HEB])
Alternate spellings: Nathen, Natan [HEB]

Pacey (PAY-see)

Pepe (PEP-pay, PAY-pay [SP])

Peyton (PAY-ten)
Alternate spellings: Payton

Phelan (FAY-len, FWAY-lawn [IR])
Alternate spellings: Faelan, Faolan

Pietro (pee-YET-roh [IT], pee-YAY-troh)

Radames (RAW-duh-mes [EGY], RAD-uh-mes or RAD-uh-may [SP])

Raekwon (ray-KWAN [AA])

Rafael (RAF-ee-yell, raf-ee-YELL, rrraf-uh-YELL [FR], raw-faw-ELL [HEB/SP], rrraw-FAY-yell [SP])
Alternate spellings: Raphael, Raphaël

Ray (RAY)
Alternate spellings: Rey

Rayburn (RAY-burn)

Rayford (RAY-furd)

Raymon (RAY-mun)
Alternate spellings: Ramón*

Raymond (RAY-mund [GER], rrray-MAW with short N [FR])
Alternate spellings: Raymonde [FR]

Raymundo (rrray-MOON-doh [SP])

Raynard (RAY-nurd, ray-NARD)

Rayshawn (ray-SHAWN or ruh-SHAWN [AA])
Alternate spellings: Rashawn*

Reagan (RAY-gen, REE-gen)

Regis (REE-gis, ray-ZHEES [FR])
Alternate spellings: Régis [FR]

Reino (RAY-noh [SCAN])

Rémy (REM-ee, ray-MEE [FR])
Alternate spellings: Rémi

René (ren-NAY [FR])

Reyés (RAY-yes, RRRAY-yes [SP])

Reynaldo (rrray-NAWL-doh [SP])

Alternate spellings: Reinaldo

Roger (RAW-jur [GER], rrroh-ZHAIR or rrroh-ZHAY [FR])
Alternate spellings: Rodger

Romeo (ROH-mee-yoh, rrroh-MAY-yoh [SP])

Ruben (ROO-ben, ROO-ven or roo-VAYN [HEB], roo-BEN or roo-VEN [SP])
Alternate spellings: Reuben, Rubin, Rueben, Reuven or Ruvane [HEB], Rubén [SP]

Salvatore (sal-vuh-TOR-ray [IT])

Savion (SAY-vee-yawn or say-vee-YAWN [AA])

Sebastian (sub-BAS-chen, sub-BAS-tee-yen, say-bas-tee-YAW with short N [FR], say-baws-TAWN or thay-vaws-TAWN [SP])
Alternate spellings: Sabastian, Sebastien, Sébastien [FR], Sebastián [SP]

Sergei (SUR-gay or SAIR-gay [RUS])
Alternate spellings: Serge

Shane (SHAYN)
Alternate spellings: Shayne

Stacy (STAY-see)
Alternate spellings: Stacey

Tate (TAYT)

Tavion (TAY-vee-yawn or TAY-vee-yun [AA])

Tavon (TAY-vun or TAY-vawn [AA])
Alternate spellings: Tevon*, Tavin

Taye (TAY [AA])

Taylor (TAY-lur)
Alternate spellings: Tayler

Tedros (TAY-drohs [AA])

Teodoro (tay-yoh-DOR-roh [IT/SP])

Theo (THEE-yoh, TAY-yoh [FR])
Alternate spellings: Théo [FR]

Theodore (THEE-yuh-dor, tay-yoh-DOR [FR])
Alternate spellings: Theadore, Theodor, Théodore [FR]

Timothy (TIM-ith-ee, tee-moh-TAY [FR])
Alternate spellings: Timmothy, Timothée [FR]

Trace (TRAYS)

Tracy (TRAY-see)
Alternate spellings: Tracey

Tremaine (truh-MAYN [AA/CG])
Alternate spellings: Tremayne, Tremain

Trevion (TRAY-vee-yun or TRAY-vee-yawn [AA])

Trevon (TRAY-vun [AA], TREV-in)
Alternate spellings: Travon, Trevin, Treven

Trey (TRAY [AA])
Alternate spellings: Tre, Trae

Treyton (TRAY-ten [AA])

Wade (WAYD)

Waino (VAY-noh [SCAN])

Waylon (WAY-lun [AA])
Alternate spellings: Wayland

Waymon (WAY-mun [AA])

Wayne (WAYN)

Xavier (ZAY-vee-yur, eks-ZAY-vee-yur, haw-vee-YAIR or haw-bee-YAIR [SP], zav-YAY [FR])
Alternate spellings: Javier*, Xzavier, Zavier

Zaid (ZAY-yid [AR], ZAYD, zy-YEED; see also Syed)

Zane (ZAYN [AR/HEB])
Alternate spellings: Zain, Zayne, Zayn

■ SHORT A (A) ■

PARTNER POINTER:
Check out the AIR list, too.

Abdiel (ab-DEEL [AA/AR], awv-DEEL [HEB])
Alternate spellings: Avdiel [HEB]

Abdul (ab-DULL or ab-DOOL or awb-DOOL [AR])

Abdullah (ab-DULL-uh [AR], ab-DOO-luh [AA])

Abner (AB-nur, AWV-nur [HEB])
Alternate spellings: Avner [HEB]

Abraham (AYB-ri-ham, awv-ruh-HAWM [HEB])
Alternate spellings: Avraham [HEB]

Adam (AD-dum, aw-DAWM [HEB])

Addison (ADD-is-sin)

Adelard (AD-uh-lard)

Adelbert (AD-dull-burt [GER], ad-dell-BAIR [FR])

Adolph (AYD-awlf [GER], ad-DAWLF [FR])
Alternate spellings: Adolphe [FR], Adolf

Akeem (ak-EEM [AA])

Al (AL)

Alan (AL-len [CG], al-LE with short N [FR])
Alternate spellings: Allen, Allan, Allyn, Alain [FR]

Alastair (AL-iss-tur [BR])
  Alternate spellings: Alistair, Allistair
Albert (AL-burt [GER], al-BAIR [FR])
Albin (AL-bin)
Alec (AL-ek)
Alex (AL-eks)
Alexander (al-eks-ZAN-dur)
  Alternate spellings: Alexzander
Alexandre (al-eks-ZAWN-dray,
  al-ek-SAW-druh with short N [FR])
Alexandro (al-eks-ZAN-droh,
  al-eks-ZAWN-droh)
Alexis (uh-LEK-sis, aw-LEK-see or
  al-ek-SEES [FR])
Alf (ALF)
Alfie (AL-fee)
Alfonso (al-FAWN-zoh [IT],
  awl-FAWN-soh [SP])
  Alternate spellings: Alphonso, Alfonzo
Alford (AL-ford)
Alfred (AL-fred, al-FRED)
Alfredo (awl-FRAY-doh [IT/SP], al-FRAY-doh)
Alois (al-LOH-wees [GER])
Aloysius (al-oh-WISH-us)
Alpha (AL-fuh)
Alphonse (al-FAWNS, al-FAWS with
  short N [FR])
Alton (AL-tun, AWL-tun)
Alvie (AL-vee)
Alvin (AL-vin [GER])
Alvis (AL-viss)
Amador (AM-uh-dor, aw-maw-DOR [SP])
Ambrose (AM-brohz)
Anderson (AN-dur-sen)
Andrew (AND-roo)
Andy (AND-ee)
Angelo (AN-jell-oh, AWN-jell-oh [IT],
  AWN-hell-oh [SP])
Anibal (ANN-nib-bull [GRK], aw-noo-BAWL
  [EI], AW-nee-bawl [IT], aw-NEE-bawl [SP])
Ansel (AN-sell)
Anthony (AN-thun-ee)
Antoine (an-TWAHN, awn-TWAHN [FR])
  Alternate spellings: Antwan, Antwon,
  Antione
Anton (AN-tun [AA], awn-TONE [FR])
  Alternate spellings: Antone
Antonio (an-TOH-nee-yoh,
  awn-TOH-nee-yoh [IT/SP])
Antony (AN-tun-ee)
Asher (ASH-ur, AW-shur [HEB])
Ashley (ASH-lee)
Ashton (ASH-tun)
Atticus (AT-ik-us)

Axel (AK-sell [GER])

Basil (BAY-zill, BAZ-ill [BR])
Bilal (bee-LAWL or bee-LAL [AR/EI])
Brad (BRAD)
Bradford (BRAD-furd)
Bradley (BRAD-lee)
  Alternate spellings: Bradly
Brandon (BRAN-din [CG])
  Alternate spellings: Branden,
  Brandyn, Brandan
Brandt (BRANT [GER])
  Alternate spellings: Brant
Brannon (BRAN-in)
Braxton (BRAK-stun)

Calloway (KAL-oh-way)
Calvin (KAL-vin)
  Alternate spellings: Kalvin
Camden (KAM-din [CG])
Cameron (KAM-ur-ren, KAM-ren)
  Alternate spellings: Kameron,
  Camron, Kamron, Camren
Campbell (KAM-bull)
Candelario (kan-dell-AR-ree-oh [SP])
Candido (KAWN-dee-doh or
  kan-DEE-doh [SP])
Cannon (KAN-nen)
Cash (KASH)
Casimir (KASH-meer or kash-MEER [SLAV],
  KAZ-im-eer)
  Alternate spellings: Casimer, Kazimir
Casper (KAS-pur [GER])
  Alternate spellings: Caspar, Kasper
Cassidy (KAS-sid-ee)
Chad (CHAD)
  Alternate spellings: Chadd
Chadrick (CHAD-rik)
Chadwick (CHAD-wik)
Chance (CHANS)
Chandler (CHAND-lur)
Chaz (CHAZ)
  Alternate spellings: Chas
Christien (kree-stee-YAN [IT])

Dallas (DAL-lis)
Dallin (DAL-lin)
Dan (DAN, DAWN [HEB])
Dangelo (DAN-jell-oh [AA])
Daniel (DAN-yell, dawn-ee-YELL [HEB],
  dan-YELL [FR])
  Alternate spellings: Danial
Danny (DAN-ee [CG])
  Alternate spellings: Dannie

David (DAY-vid, daw-VEED [HEB], dav-EED [FR])

Davon (DAY-vun [AA], DAV-in [IR])
   Alternate spellings: Davin

Dax (DAKS)

Deangelo (dee-YAN-jell-oh [AA/IT])

Emmanuel (ee-MAN-yoo-well [AA], ee-mawn-yoo-ELL [HEB], em-man-WELL [FR], ee-mawn-yoo-WELL or ee-man-WELL [SP])
   Alternate spellings: Emanuel, Immanuel

Fernando (fur-NAN-doh, fair-NAWN-doh [SP])

Francesco (fran-CHESS-koh [IT])

Francis (FRAN-sis)
   Alternate spellings: Frances

Francisco (fran-SEES-koh or fran-THEETH-koh [SP])

Galvin (GAL-vin [CG])

Gannon (GAN-in [CG])

Gaston (GASS-tun [CG], gas-TOHN or gas-TAW with short N [FR])

Gavin (GAV-in [WL])
   Alternate spellings: Gaven, Gavyn

German (JUR-men, her-MAWN [SP], zhair-MA with short N [FR])
   Alternate spellings: Germán [SP], Germain [FR]

Graham (GRAM, GRAY-yum or GRAY-hum [BR])

Grant (GRANT [CG])

Granville (GRAN-vill)

Hakeem (haw-KEEM or hak-EEM [AR])

Hal (HAL [CG])

Hallie (HAL-ee)

Hamilton (HAM-ill-ten)

Hansel (HAN-sell, HAWN-sell [GER/SCAN])

Haskell (HAS-kull)

Jack (JAK)

Jackie (JAK-ee)
   Alternate spellings: Jacky

Jackson (JAK-sen)
   Alternate spellings: Jaxon, Jaxson

Jagger (JAG-ur)

Jasper (JAS-pur [BR])

Jazz (JAZ)

Jermaine (jur-MAYN [AA], zhur-MA [FR])
   Germaine, Jermain

Kerouac (KAIR-roh-wak)

Laddie (LAD-ee)

Lambert (LAM-burt [GER], lam-BAIR [FR])

Lance (LANS)

Landon (LAN-den)
   Alternate spellings: Landen

Lanny (LAN-ee)
   Alternate spellings: Lannie

Laszlo (LAZ-loh [HUN])

Lazaro (LAZ-uh-roh or luh-ZAR-oh [AA], law-ZAR-roh [IT])

Lazarus (LAZ-ur-russ)

Leander (lee-YAN-dur)

Lucas (LOO-kuss [GER/SCAN/SP], loo-KA [FR])
   Alternate spellings: Lukas

Mack (MAK)
   Alternate spellings: Mac

MacKenzie (muh-KEN-zee, mak-KEN-zee)

Maddox (MAD-eks)
   Alternate spelling: Mattox

Madison (MAD-iss-un)

Magnus (MAG-nes)

Malachi (MAL-uh-ky [IR], maw-law-CHEE with guttural CH [HEB])
   Alternate spellings: Malakai, Malachai

Malachy (MAL-uh-kee [IR])

Malcolm (MAL-kum [CG])
   Alternate spellings: Malcom

Malik (mul-EEK [AA], mal-EEK or MAL-ik or MUL-ik [AR])

Manley (MAN-lee)

Manny (MAN-ee [HEB/SP])

Manuel (man-WELL [SP])

Martin (MAR-tin, mar-TA with short N [FR], mar-TEEN [SP])
   Alternate spellings: Martín [SP]

Masaaki (mas-SAW-aw-kee [JAP])

Matt (MAT)

Matthew (MATH-yoo [HEB])
   Alternate spellings: Mathew

Maverick (MAV-ur-rik)

Max (MAKS)

Maxie (MAK-see)

Maxim (MAK-sim, mak-SEEM [RUS])
   Alternate spellings: Maksim

Maximilian (mak-sim-MIL-yen [GER], mak-see-meel-YA with short N [FR])
   Alternate spellings: Maximillian, Maximilien [FR]

Maximino (mak-sim-MEE-noh [SP])

Maximo (mak-SEE-moh [SP])

Maximus (MAK-sim-us)

Maxwell (MAK-swell)
Mohamed (moh-hawm-MUD or
    mo-HAM-med [AR])
    Alternate spellings: Mohammad,
    Mohammed, Muhammad
Montana (mawn-TAN-nuh)

Najib (na-ZHEEB [AR])
Nash (NASH)
Nat (NAT)
Nathaniel (nuh-THAN-yell,
    naw-tawn-ELL [HEB])
    Alternate spellings: Nathanael,
    Nathanial, Netanel [HEB]

Orlando (or-LAN-doh [AA], or-LAWN-doh
    [SP])

Paddy (PAD-ee)
Pasquale (pass-KAL [FR], paw-skoo-WALL
    or pawth-KWALL [SP])
    Alternate spellings: Pascual [SP], Pasqual
Pat (PAT)
Patrick (PAT-rik, PAR-rick or PAWD-rig [IR])
    Alternate spellings: Pádraig [IR]
Patsy (PAT-see)
Pax (PAKS)
Paxton (PAK-stun)

Radames (RAW-duh-mes [EGY],
    RAD-uh-mes or RAD-uh-may [SP])
Rafael (RAF-ee-yell, raf-ee-YELL,
    rrraf-uh-YELL [FR], raw-faw-ELL [HEB/SP],
    rrraw-FAY-yell [SP])
    Alternate spellings: Raphael, Raphaël
Ralph (RALF)
Ramsey (RAM-zee)
Rand (RAND)
Randolph (RAN-dawlf)
Randy (RAN-dee)
Ransom (RAN-sum)
Rashad (ruh-SHAWD or ruh-SHAD [AA/AR])
Rohan (ROH-han, rrroh-HAWN [EI])
Rolando (roh-LAN-doh,
    rrroh-LAWN-doh [SP])

Sal (SAL)
Salvador (sal-vaw-DOR or
    thal-baw-DOR [SP])
Salvatore (sal-vuh-TOR-ray [IT])
Sam (SAM)
Sammy (SAM-ee)
    Alternate spellings: Sammie
Samson (SAM-sun, sheem-SHOHN [HEB])

Alternate spellings: Shimshon [HEB]
Samuel (SAM-yoo-well, SAM-yool,
    SHMOO-well [HEB], sam-WELL [IT/SP])
    Alternate spellings: Shmuel [HEB]
Sandy (SAN-dee)
Sanford (SAN-furd)
Santino (san-TEE-noh [IT])
Satchel (SACH-ell)
Sasha (SAW-shuh [GER/RUS], SASH-uh)
    Alternate spellings: Sacha, Sascha
Sebastian (sub-BAS-chen,
    sub-BAS-tee-yen, say-bas-tee-YAW
    with short N [FR], say-baws-TAWN or
    thay-vaws-TAWN [SP])
    Alternate spellings: Sabastian,
    Sebastien Sébastien, [FR], Sebastián [SP]
Shad (SHAD)
Shannon (SHAN-nen)
    Alternate spellings: Shanon
Shaquille (shak-KEEL [AA])
    Alternate spellings: Shakil [AR]
Stan (STAN [GER])
Stanford (STAN-furd)
Stanley (STAN-lee [GER])
Stanton (STAN-ten)

Tad (TAD)
    Alternate spellings: Thad*
Talmadge (TAL-mej)
Talon (TAL-in)
Tanner (TAN-ur)
Thad (THAD, TAD)
    Alternate spellings: Tad*
Thaddeus (THAD-ee-yuss [GRK])
Thatcher (THACH-ur)
Trinidad (TRIN-id-add, tree-nee-DAWD
    [SP])

Val (VAL)
Valentin (val-en-TEEN [SP])
Valentine (VAL-en-tyn, vaw-lawn-TEEN
    [FR])
Van (VAN)
Vance (VANS)

Xavier (ZAY-vee-yur, ek-ZAY-vee-yur,
    haw-vee-YAIR or haw-bee-YAIR [SP],
    zav-YAY [FR]) *Alternate spellings:*
    Javier*, Xzavier, Zavier

Zack (ZAK)
Zachariah (zak-kur-RY-yuh,
    zuh-CHAW-ree-yuh with guttural CH
    [HEB], zuk-uh-REE-yuh [AR])

Alternate spellings: Zecharya [HEB]
Zachary (ZAK-ur-ree)
    Alternate spellings: Zackary, Zachery,
    Zackery, Zakary
Zander (ZAN-dur)
    Alternate spellings: Xander

■ AIR ■

PARTNER POINTER:
Check out the long A and short A
lists, too.

Aaron (AIR-en, aw-haw-ROHN [HEB],
    aw-ROHN [SP])
    Alternate spellings: Aron, Arron, Erin
    [IR], Aharon [HEB]
Adalberto (aw-dell-BAIR-toh [SP])
Adelbert (AD-dull-burt [GER], ad-dell-BAIR
    [FR])
Albert (AL-burt [GER], al-BAIR [FR])
Alberto (awl-BAIR-toh [IT/SP])
Americo (aw-mair-EE-ko or
    aw-MAIR-ee-koh [IT/SP])
Ari (AR-ree or AIR-ree [HEB])
Ariel (AIR-ee-yell or aw-ree-YELL [HEB],
    aw-rrree-YELL [FR])

Baron (BAIR-ren [GER])
    Alternate spellings: Barron
Barrett (BAIR-ret)
Barry (BAIR-ree [CG])
    Alternate spellings: Berry
Bernard (bur-NARD, bair-NAR [FR])
    Alternate spellings: Bernhard
Bernardo (bur-NAR-doh, bair-NAR-doh
    or vair-NAR-doh [SP])
Bertrand (BURT-rend, bair-TRAW with
    short N [FR])
Beryl (BAIR-rill [GRK/HEB])
    Alternate spellings: Beril
Blair (BLAIR)

Clarence (KLAIR-rens)
    Alternate spellings: Clarance

Darian (DAIR-ree-yen)
    Alternate spellings: Darien, Darion,
    Darrion, Darrian, Darrien
Darius (DAR-ree-yuss [HEB/PER],
    DAIR-ree-yes)
    Alternate spellings: Darrius

Darold (DAIR-ruld)
Darrell (DAIR-rull)
    Alternate spellings: Darryl, Daryl,
    Derrell, Daryle
Darren (DAIR-rin [CG])
    Alternate spellings: Darin, Darrin,
    Daron, Daren, Darron, Deron
Derek (DAIR-rik [GER])
    Alternate spellings: Derrick, Derick,
    Derik, Darrick, Dereck, Deric

Eliezer (el-lee-YEZ-ur [HEB/AA], el-LEE-zur,
    el-LY-zur, el-lee-ZAIR or el-lee-THAIR
    [SP])
Eric (AIR-rik [SCAN], air-REEK [FR])
    Alternate spellings: Erik, Erick, Erich,
    Aric
Ernesto (air-NES-toh [IT/SP], air-NETH-toh
    [SP])
Errol (AIR-rull)

Faron (FAIR-ren or FAIR-rohn [BR])
Farrell (FAIR-rull)
Federico (fed-air-EE-ko [IT])
Ferdinand (FUR-din-and,
    FAIR-din-nawnd [GER],
    fair-dee-NAW with short ND [FR])
Fergus (FUR-gus, FAIR-ges [IR])
Fermin (fair-MEEN [SP])
Fernand (fair-NAW with short ND [FR])
Fernando (fur-NAN-doh, fair-NAWN-doh
    [SP])

Garrett (GAIR-ret [CG])
    Alternate spellings: Garret, Garett
Garrick (GAR-rik [BR], GAIR-rik)
Garrison (GAIR-ris-sen)
Gary (GAIR-ree [GER])
    Alternate spellings: Garry, Geary*
Gearld (GAIR-ruld)
    Alternate spellings: Gerald*, Garold,
    Gerold
Geary (GEER-ree, JAIR-ree, GAIR-ree)
    Alternate spellings: Jerry*, Gerry,
    Gary*, Garry
Gerald (JAIR-ruld [GER])
    Alternate spellings: Jerald, Jerrold,
    Garold, Gerold
Geraldo (hair-RAWL-doh [SP])
Gerardo (hair-RAR-doh [SP])
Gerhard (GAIR-hart [GER])
German (JUR-men, her-MAWN [SP],
    zhair-MAN [FR])

Alternate spellings: German [SP],
Germain [FR]
Gilbert (GIL-burt, zheel-BAIR [FR])
Gilberto (gil-BAIR-toh, hil-BAIR-toh or
heel-VAIR-toh [SP])
Guillermo (gee-YAIR-moh or YAIR-moh
[SP])

Harold (HAIR-ruld [SCAN])
Harris (HAIR-ris)
Harrison (HAIR-ris-sen)
Harry (HAIR-ree)
Heber (HAY-bur, HEE-bur [BIB], ay-BAIR [IR])
Herbert (HUR-burt [GER], air-BAIR [FR])
Heriberto (air-ree-BAIR-toh or
air-ree-VAIR-toh [SP])
Herminio (air-MEE-nee-oh [SP])
Hernan (air-NAWN [SP])
Hidero (hee-DAIR-roh [JAP])
Hubert (HYOO-burt [GER], oo-BAIR [FR])
Humberto (oom-BAIR-toh or
oom-VAIR-toh [SP])

Jacari (juh-KAIR-ree or juh-KAR-ree or
JAK-ur-ree)
Jair (JAY-yur [BIB], JAIR, yaw-EER or
YAW-eer [HEB])
Alternate spellings: Jere*, Yair [HEB],
Yahir*
Jared (JAIR-red, yar-RED [HEB])
Alternate spellings: Jarod, Jarred,
Jarrod, Jerrod, Jerod, Jerad, Jered,
Yared [HEB]
Jarom (JAIR-rum, yar-ROHM [HEB])
Alternate spellings: Yarom [HEB]
Jaron (JAIR-ren, yar-ROHN [HEB])
Alternate spellings: Jaren, Yaron [HEB]
Jarrett (JAIR-ret)
Alternate spellings: Jarret
Javier (haw-vee-YAIR or haw-bee-YAIR [SP])
Alternate spellings: Xavier*
Jere (JAIR)
Alternate spellings: Jair*
Jeremiah (jair-ruh-MY-yuh,
yeer-mee-YAW-hoo [HEB])
Alternate spellings: Yirmeyahu [HEB]
Jeremy (JAIR-ruh-mee)
Alternate spellings: Jeramy, Jeremie,
Jeromy, Jeremey, Jeramie
Jerrell (juh-RELL or JAIR-rell [AA])
Alternate spellings: Jarrell, Jerel
Jerry (JAIR-ree)
Alternate spellings: Gerry [GER], Geary*

Kerouac (KAIR-roh-wak)
Kerry (KAIR-ree)
Alternate spellings: Carey, Cary

Ladarius (luh-DAIR-ee-yuss [AA])
Lambert (LAM-burt [GER], lam-BAIR [FR])
Laron (LAIR-ren, luh-RAWN [AA])
Larry (LAIR-ree)

Marion (MAIR-ree-yen)
Merrill (MAIR-rill)
Merritt (MAIR-rit)
Monserrate (mohn-sair-RAWT [IT])
Alternate spellings: Montserrat

Norberto (nor-BAIR-toh [IT/SP],
nor-VAIR-toh [SP])

Paris (PAIR-riss, pair-RRREE [FR])
Parrish (PAIR-rish)
Pierre (pee-YAIR [FR])

Rigoberto (ree-goh-BAIR-toh [SP])
Robert (RAW-burt, rrroh-BAIR [FR])
Roberto (rrroh-BAIR-toh [SP])
Roger (RAW-jur [GER], rrroh-ZHAIR or
rrroh-ZHAY [FR])
Alternate spellings: Rodger

Serge (SURJ, SAIRZH [FR])
Sergei (SUR-gay or SAIR-gay [RUS])
Alternate spellings: Serge
Sergio (SUR-jee-yoh, SAIR-jee-yoh or
SAIR-joh [IT], SAIR-hee-yoh or
THAIR-hee-yoh [SP])
Sheridan (SHAIR-rid-en [CG])
Sherrill (SHAIR-rill)

Terrell (tuh-RELL [AA], TAIR-rill)
Alternate spellings: Terrill
Terrence (TAIR-rens)
Alternate spellings: Terrance, Terence
Terry (TAIR-ree)

Xavier (ZAY-vee-yur, eks-ZAY-vee-yur,
haw-vee-YAIR or haw-bee-YAIR [SP],
zav-YAY [FR])
Alternate spellings: Javier*, Xzavier,
Zavier

■ AR ■

PARTNER POINTER:
Check the short O and OW lists,
too.

Aaron (AIR-en, aw-har-ROHN [HEB],
　　ar-ROHN [SP])
　　Alternate spellings: Aron, Arron, Erin
　　[IR], Aharon [HEB]
Álvaro (AWL-var-roh or AWL-bar-roh [SP])
Amari (uh-MAR-ree [AA])
Arcadio (ar-CAW-dee-yoh)
Arch (ARCH [GER])
Archibald (AR-chee-bawld [GER])
Archie (AR-chee [GER])
Ari (AR-ree or AIR-ree [HEB])
Ariel (AIR-ree-yell, AR-ree-yell,
　　ar-ree-YELL [HEB/FR])
Arjun (AR-jun, ar-JOON) [EI]
Ardell (ar-DELL)
Arden (AR-din)
Arlen (AR-lin [CG])
　　Alternate spellings: Arlin, Arlan
Arlie (AR-lee)
　　Alternate spellings: Arley
Arlis (AR-lis)
Arlo (AR-loh)
Armand (ar-MAWND, ar-MAW with
　　short N [FR])
　　Alternate spellings: Armond
Armando (ar-MAWN-doh [IT/SP])
Armani (ar-MAWN-ee)
Armstrong (ARMS-trawng)
Arnaldo (ar-NAWL-doh [IT/SP])
　　Alternate spellings: Arnoldo*
Arnav (ar-NAWV [EI/HEB])
Arne (AR-nee or ARN [GER/SCAN])
Arno (AR-noh)
Arnold (AR-nuld [GER])
Arnoldo (ar-NOHL-doh [IT/SP],
　　ar-NAWL-doh)
　　Alternate spellings: Arnaldo*
Arnulfo (ar-NOOL-foh [SP])
Art (ART)
Arthur (AR-thur [CG])
　　Alternate spellings: Arther
Artie (ART-ee)
Artis (ART-iss)
Arturo (ar-TOO-roh [IT/SP])
Arvid (AR-vid)
Arvil (AR-vil)
　　Alternate spellings: Arvel
Arvin (AR-vin [GER])

Barney (BAR-nee [GER])
Bart (BART [HEB])
Bartholomew (bar-THAW-lum-yoo)
Barton (BAR-tun)
Bernard (bur-NARD, bair-NAR [FR])
　　Alternate spellings: Bernhard
Bernardo (bur-NAR-doh, bair-NAR-doh
　　or vair-NAR-doh [SP])

Candelario (kan-dell-AR-ree-oh [SP])
Carl (KARL [GER])
　　Alternate spellings: Karl
Carlo (KAR-loh [IT])
Carlos (KAR-lohs [SP])
Carlton (KARL-ten)
　　Alternate spellings: Carleton
Carlyle (KAR-lyl)
Carmelo (kar-MEL-oh [IT/SP])
Carmen (KAR-men [SP])
Carmine (KAR-myn [IT])
Carnell (kar-NELL [BR])
Carter (KAR-tur)
Carson (KAR-sen)
　　Alternate spellings: Karson
Cesar (SAY-sar/THAY-thar or
　　SESS-ar/THE-thar [SP], SEE-zur)
　　Alternate spellings: Caesar*
Charles (CHARLZ, CHAR-rulz, SHARL [FR])
Charlie (CHAR-lee)
　　Alternate spellings: Charley
Clark (KLARK)

Darby (DAR-bee)
Dario (DAR-ree-yoh, dar-REE-yoh [IT/SP])
Darius (DAR-ree-yuss [HEB/PER],
　　DAIR-ree-yes)
　　Alternate spellings: Darrius
Darnell (dar-NELL [AA])
Darwin (DAR-win)
Delmar (del-MAR, DEL-mur)
　　Alternate spellings: Delmer*
Demarco (duh-MAR-koh)
Demarcus (duh-MAR-kuss [AA])
Demario (duh-MAR-ree-yoh [AA])

Edgar (ED-gur, ed-GAR [FR])
Edgardo (ed-GAR-doh [IT/SP])
Eduardo (ed-WAR-doh [IT/SP])
　　Alternate spellings: Edwardo—

Gardner (GARD-nur)
Garfield (GAR-feeld)
Garland (GAR-lend)
Garnett (GAR-net)

Alternate spellings: Garnet
Garrick (GAR-rik [BR], GAIR-rik)
Garth (GARTH)
Genaro (jen-NAR-roh [IT], hen-NAR-roh [SP])
Alternate spellings: Gennaro

Harding (HARD-eeng)
Hardy (HAR-dee [GER])
Harlan (HAR-len)
Alternate spellings: Harland, Harlen
Harley (HAR-lee)
Harmon (HAR-men [GER])
Harvey (HAR-vee)
Hilario (ee-LAR-ree-yoh [SP])

Jabari (juh-BAR-ree [AA])
Jacari (juh-KAIR-ree or juh-KAR-ree or JAK-ur-ree)
Jamar (jum-MAR [AA])
Jamarcus (jum-MAR-kuss [AA])
Jamari (jum-MAR-ree [AA])
Jara (JAR-ruh)
Jared (JAIR-red, yar-RED [HEB])
Alternate spellings: Jarod, Jarred, Jarrod, Jerrod, Jerod, Jerad, Jered, Yared [HEB]
Jarom (JAIR-rum, yar-ROHM [HEB])
Alternate spellings: Yarom [HEB]
Jaron (JAIR-ren, yar-ROHN [HEB])
Alternate spellings: Jaren, Yaron [HEB]
Jarvis (JAR-viss [GER])
Jomar (joh-MAR [BIB], juh-MAR [AA], OH-mar)
Alternate spellings: Omar*
Jordan (JOR-den, YAR-den [HEB])
Alternate spellings: Jordon, Jorden, Yarden*

Kamari (kuh-MAR-ee [AA])

Lamar (luh-MAR [AA/GER])
Lars (LARZ [SCAN])
Lazaro (LAZ-uh-roh or luh-ZAR-oh [AA], law-ZAR-roh [IT])
Leonard (LEN-urd [GER], lay-yoh-NAR [FR])
Alternate spellings: Lenard, Léonard [FR]
Leonardo (lee-yoh-NAR-doh, lay-yoh-NAR-doh [SP])
Levar (luh-VAR [AA])

Marcel (mar-SELL [FR])
Marcelino (mar-say-LEE-noh or mar-thay-LEE-noh [SP], mar-chell-LEE-noh [IT])

Alternate spellings: Marcellino [IT]
Marcellus (mar-SELL-us)
Marcelo (mar-SAY-yoh or mar-THAY-oh [SP], mar-CHELL-oh [IT])
Alternate spellings: Marcello [IT]
Marco (MAR-koh [IT/SP])
Marcos (MAR-kohs [SP])
Marcus (MAR-kus)
Alternate spellings: Marquis*, Markus, Marques
Margarito (mar-gar-REE-toh [SP])
Mariano (mar-ree-YAWN-oh [IT])
Mario (MAR-ree-yoh [IT/SP])
Mark (MARK)
Alternate spellings: Marc [FR]
Marlon (MAR-len)
Alternate spellings: Marlin, Marlyn
Marquez (MAR-kez or mar-KEZ, MAR-kess [SP])
Alternate spellings: Marquez
Marquis (MAR-kwiss or mar-KEEZ or mar-KEES [AA], mar-KEE [FR], MAR-kus)
Alternate spellings: Marquise, Marques, Marcus*, Markus
Marshall (MAR-shull)
Alternate spellings: Marshal, Marcial
Martin (MAR-tin, mar-TA with short N [FR], mar-TEEN [SP])
Alternate spellings: Martin [SP]
Marty (MAR-tee)
Marvin (MAR-vin)
Maynard (MAY-nurd, MAY-nard)
McArthur (mik-AR-thur [CG])

Narciso (nar-SIS-oh, nar-SEE-soh or nar-THEE-thoh [SP], nar-CHEE-soh [IT])

Omar (OH-mar or UM-ar [AR])
Alternate spellings: Jomar*
Omari (oh-MAR-ree [AA])
Omarion (oh-MAR-ree-yawn or uh-MAR-ree-yawn [AA])
Alternate spellings: Amarion

Parker (PAR-kur)
Patrick (PAT-rik, PAR-rick or PAWD-rig [IR])
Alternate spellings: Padraig [IR]

Ricardo (rrrree-KAR-doh [SP])
Richard (RICH-urd, rrree-SHAR [FR])
Rosario (rrroh-SAR-ree-yoh or rrroh-THAR-ree-yoh [SP])

Tariq (tar-RIK or TAR-rik [AR])

Alternate spellings: Tareq, Tarek
Tavares (tuh-VAR-ress [AA/IT])

Waldemar (WALL-duh-mar,
    VAWL-duh-mar [GER/SCAN])
    Alternate spellings: Valdemar [SCAN]
Warner (WOR-nur, WAR-nur,
    VAR-nur [GER])

Yarden (YAR-den [HEB])
    Alternate spellings: Jordan*, Jordon,
    Jorden

Zachariah (zak-kur-RY-yuh,
    zuh-CHAR-ree-yuh with guttural CH
    [HEB], zuk-uh-REE-yuh [AR])
    Alternate spellings: Zecharya [HEB]
Zechariah (zek-kur-RY-uh,
    zuh-CHAR-ree-uh with guttural CH
    [HEB], zuk-uh-REE-yuh [AR])
    Alternate spellings: Zecharya [HEB]

■ LONG E (EE) ■

PARTNER POINTER:
Check the OI list, too.

Abdiel (ab-DEEL [AA/AR])>, awv-DEEL [HEB])
    Alternate spellings: Avdiel [HEB]
Adonis (uh-DAWN-iss, aw-DOH-nees [SP])
Adrian (AY-dree-yen, , aw-DREE-yawn
    [SP], ad-ree-AW with short N [FR]))
    Alternate spellings: Adrien [FR]
Adriel (AY-dree-yell, aw-dree-YELL [HEB])
Akeem (ak-EEM [AA])
Alfie (AL-fee)
Ali (AW-lee or aw-LEE [AA/AR])
    Alternate spellings: Aali
Alois (al-LOH-wees [GER])
Alvie (AL-vee)
Amari (uh-MAR-ree [AA])
Americo (aw-mair-EE-ko or
    aw-MAIR-ee-koh [IT/SP])
Amir (aw-MEER [AR/HEB])
Anastacio (aw-naw-STAW-see-oh [SP])
Andy (AND-ee)
Anibal (ANN-nib-bull [GRK], aw-noo-BAWL
    [EI], AW-nee-bawl [IT], aw-NEE-bawl [SP])
Antonio (an-TOH-nee-yoh,
    awn-TOH-nee-yoh [IT/SP])
Antony (AN-tun-ee)
Arcadio (ar-CAW-dee-yoh)
Archibald (AR-chee-bawld [GER])

Archie (AR-chee [GER])
Ari (AR-ree or AIR-ree [HEB])
Ariel (AIR-ree-yell, AR-ree-yell,
    ar-ree-YELL [HEB/FR])
Arlie (AR-lee)
    Alternate spellings: Arley
Armani (ar-MAWN-ee)
Arne (AR-nee or ARN [GER/SCAN])
Artie (ART-ee)
Ashley (ASH-lee)
Aubrey (AW-bree)
Audie (AW-dee)
Augustin (aw-GUS-tin, oh-goos-TEEN or
    ow-goh-STAW with short N [FR], aw-
    goo-STEEN or aw-gooth-TEEN [SP])
    Alternate spellings: Agustin, Augustin
    [SP] Augustine
Aurelio (or-REL-ee-yoh [SP])
Avery (AY-vur-ree)

Bailey (BAY-lee)
Barney (BAR-nee [GER])
Barry (BAIR-ree [CG])
    Alternate spellings: Berry
Benicio (ben-EE-see-yoh or
    ven-EE-thee-yoh [SP])
Benito (ben-EE-toh or ven-EE-toh [SP])
Benjamin (BEN-juh-min, bin-yaw-MEEN
    [HEB], ben-zhaw-ME with short N [FR],
    ben-haw-MEEN or ven-haw-MEEN
    [SP])
    Alternate spellings: Binyamin [HEB],
    Benjamín [SP]
Benny (BEN-ee)
    Alternate spellings: Bennie
Bernie (BUR-nee)
Bienvenido (bee-yen-ben-EE-doh or
    vee-yen-ven-EE-doh [SP])
Bilal (bee-LAWL or bee-LAL [AR/EI])
Billy (BILL-ee [GER])
    Alternate spellings: Billie
Bixby (BIKS-bee)
Bobby (BAW-bee)
    Alternate spellings: Bobbie
Bradley (BRAD-lee)
    Alternate spellings: Bradly
Brady (BRAY-dee)
Braulio (BROH-lee-yoh, BROW-lee-yoh
    or VROW-lee-yoh [SP])
Brian (BRY-yen [CG], BREE-yen [IR])
    Alternate spellings: Bryan, Brayan [SP],
    Bryon, Brien
Brody (BROH-dee [CG])
    Alternate spellings: Brodie

Buddy (BUD-ee)
 Alternate spellings: Buddie
Burley (BUR-lee)

Caesar (SEE-zur)
 Alternate spellings: Cesar*
Candelario (kan-dell-AR-ree-oh [SP])
Candido (KAWN-dee-doh or
 kan-DEE-doh [SP])
Casey (KAY-see)
 Alternate spellings: Kasey
Casimir (KASH-meer or kash-MEER [SLAV],
 KAZ-im-eer)
 Alternate spellings: Casimer, Kazimir
Cecil (SEE-sill, SESS-ill)
Cecilio (ses-SEE-lee-yoh or
 the-THEE-lee-yoh [SP],
 che-CHEE-lee-yoh [IT])
Cedar (SEE-dur)
Cedric (SED-rik, SEED-rik)
 Alternate spellings: Cedrick, Sedrick
Celestino (sell-less-TEEN-oh or
 thell-leth-TEEN-oh [SP])
Cesar (SAY-sar/THAY-thar or
 SESS-ar/THE-thar [SP], SEE-zur)
 Alternate spellings: Caesar*
Chaney (CHAY-nee)
 Alternate spellings: Cheney
Charlie (CHAR-lee)
 Alternate spellings: Charley
Chauncey (CHAWN-see)
Chesley (CHESS-lee or CHEZ-lee)
Christian (KRIS-chen, KREE-stee-yawn
 or KREETH-tee-yawn [IT/SP],
 kree-stee-YAW with short N [FR])
 Alternate spellings: Cristian, Kristian
Christien (kree-stee-YAN [IT])
Claudie (KLAW-dee, kloh-DEE [FR])
Claudio (KLAW-dee-yoh, KLOW-dee-yoh
 [IT/SP])
Cleo (KLEE-yoh, KLAY-oh [FR])
 Alternate spellings: Cléo
Cleon (KLEE-yawn [GRK])
Cletus (KLEE-tis)
Cleve (KLEEV)
Cleveland (KLEEV-lend)
Cody (KOH-dee)
 Alternate spellings: Kody, Coty,
 Codey, Codie
Colby (KOHL-bee)
 Alternate spellings: Kolby
Constantine (kawn-stan-TEEN [FR])
Corey (KOR-ree)
 Alternate spellings: Cory, Korey, Kory

Cornelius (kor-NEE-lee-yes
Courtney (KORT-nee)
 Alternate spellings: Cortney
Cristobal (kree-STOH-bawl or
 kreeth-TOH-vawl or kree-stoh-VAWL
 [SP])
Cyril (SEER-ril, see-REEL [FR])
 Alternate spellings: Cyrille [FR]
Cyrus (SY-russ, see-ROOS [PER])

Damian (DAY-mee-yen, daw-mee-YAW
 with short N [FR])
 Alternate spellings: Damien, Damion,
 Dameon
Daniel (DAN-yell, dawn-ee-YELL [HEB],
 dan-YELL [FR])
 Alternate spellings: Danial
Danny (DAN-ee [CG])
 Alternate spellings: Dannie
Darby (DAR-bee)
Darian (DAIR-ree-yen)
 Alternate spellings: Darien, Darion,
 Darrion, Darrian, Darrien
Dario (DAR-ree-yoh, dar-REE-yoh [IT/SP])
Darius (DAR-ree-yuss [HEB/PER],
 DAIR-ree-yes)
 Alternate spellings: Darrius
Davey (DAY-vee)
 Alternate spellings: Davy
David (DAY-vid, daw-VEED [HEB],
 dav-EED [FR])
Davion (DAY-vee-yohn or day-vee-YOHN
 [AA])
Dean (DEEN)
 Alternate spellings: Deane
Deandre (dee-YAWN-dray [AA])
 Alternate spellings: Deondre
Deangelo (dee-YAN-jell-oh [AA/IT])
Dee (DEE)
Deepak (dee-PAWK [EI])
Demario (duh-MAR-ree-yoh [AA])
Demetrios (duh-MEE-tree-yohs [GRK])
Demetris (duh-MEE-tris [AA/GRK])
Demetrius (duh-MEE-tree-yes [GRK])
Denis (den-NEE [FR], DEN-iss)
 Alternate spellings: Dennis*
Denny (DEN-ee)
 Alternate spellings: Dennie
Deon (dee-YAWN [AA])
 Alternate spellings: Dion, Deion
Deonte (dee-YAWN-tay [AA])
 Alternate spellings: Dionte
Dermot (DUR-met [CG], DEER-mid [IR])
Dewey (DOO-wee [WL])

Diego (dee-YAY-goh [SP])
Diezel (DEE-zull)
Dillion (DILL-ee-yun, DILL-yen)
Dimitri (dim-MEE-tree [RUS/FR])
    Alternate spellings: Dmitri
Dino (DEE-noh [IT])
Dionisio (dee-yoh-NEE-see-yoh or
    dee-yoh-NEE-thee-yoh [SP])
Domenico (doh-MEN-ee-koh [IT])
Domingo (doh-MEEN-goh [SP])
Dominic (DAW-min-ik, doh-mee-NEEK [FR])
    Alternate spellings: Dominick,
    Dominik, Domenic, Dominique,
    Domenick
Donnie (DAWN-ee [CG])
    Alternate spellings: Donny
Dorian (DOR-ree-yen)
Dorsey (DOR-see)
Dudley (DUD-lee)
Dusty (DUS-tee)

Early (URL-ee)
    Alternate spellings: Earlie
Easton (EES-ten)
Eddie (ED-ee)
    Alternate spellings: Eddy
Efrain (eff-raw-EEN or EEF-rawn [HEB],
    EFF-ren [AA], eff-RA with short N [FR],
    eff-raw-EEN [SP], EE-fren or ef-RYN;
    see also Ephraim)
    Alternate spellings: Efrain [SP], Efren,
    Efron [HEB], Ephron
Eladio (el-LAW-dee-yoh or
    ee-LAW-dee-yoh or EL-lawd-yoh [SP])
Eli (EE-ly or ELL-ee [HEB])
    Alternate spellings: Elly
Elian (EL-lee-yawn [SP], EE-lee-yawn)
Elias (EE-lee-yaws [HEB], el-LEE-yaws or
    eh-LEE-yes [SP], ee-LY-yes)
Eliezer (el-lee-YEZ-ur [HEB/AA], el-LEE-zur,
    el-LY-zur, el-lee-ZAIR or el-lee-THAIR
    [SP])
Elijah (el-LY-zhuh or uh-LY-juh [AA],
    el-lee-YAW-hoo [HEB])
    Alternate spellings: Alijah, Eliyahu [HEB]
Eliseo (el-LEE-see-yoh, el-lee-ZAY-yoh [IT],
    el-lee-SAY-yoh [IT/SP], el-lee-THAY-yoh
    [SP])
Elisha (uh-LISH-uh or el-LY-shuh [AA],
    el-LEE-shuh [HEB])
Ellery (ELL-ur-ree)
Elliot (ELL-ee-yet)
    Alternate spellings: Elliott, Eliot
Emery (EM-ur-ree [GER])

    Alternate spellings: Emory
Émil (ay-MEEL [FR])
    Alternate spellings: Emile
Emiliano (em-eel-YAW-noh [SP],
    em-ee-lee-YAW-noh)
Emilio (em-MEE-lee-yoh [SP])
Emmanuel (ee-MAN-yoo-well [AA],
    ee-mawn-yoo-ELL [HEB],
    em-man-WELL [FR], ee-mawn-yoo-WELL
    or ee-man-WELL [SP])
    Alternate spellings: Emanuel,
    Immanuel
Enoch (EE-nuk, EE-nawk, chaw-NOCH
    with guttural CH [HEB])
    Alternate spellings: Chanoch [HEB]
Enos (EE-naws [HEB])
Enrico (en-REE-koh [IT])
Enrique (en-REE-kay [SP])
Ephraim (eff-RYM or ef-ry-EEM [HEB],
    ef-ry-YEEM or EFF-rem [AA])
    Alternate spellings: Efrayim [HEB],
    Efraim, Efrem (see also Efrain)
Epifanio (epp-if-FAW-nee-yoh [SP])
Erasmo (eh-RAWS-moh or ee-RAWS-
    moh [SP])
Eric (AIR-rik [SCAN], air-REEK [FR])
    Alternate spellings: Erik, Erick, Erich,
    Aric
Erling (UR-leeng)
Ernie (UR-nee [GER])
Ethan (EE-thin, EE-tawn [HEB])
    Alternate spellings: Ethen, Eitan or
    Etan [HEB]
Eugene (yoo-JEEN, oo-ZHEN [FR])
Eusebio (ay-yoo-SEB-ee-yoh or
    ay-yoo-THEV-ee-yoh [SP])
Ezekiel (ee-ZEE-kee-yell [AA],
    yeh-CHEZ-kel with guttural CH [HEB],
    ess-ay-KYL/eth-ay-KYL or
    ess-sy-KEEL/eth-y-KEEL [SP])
    Alternate spellings: Ezequiel,
    Yechezkel [HEB]

Fabian (FAY-bee-yen, faw-bee-AWN [FR])
Faustino (fow-STEEN-oh or
    fowth-TEEN-oh [SP])
Federico (fed-air-EE-ko [IT])
Felipe (fel-LEE-pay [SP])
Felix (FEEL-iks, fel-LEEKS [SP], fay-LEEKS
    [FR])
    Alternate spellings: Félix [SP]
Ferdinand (FUR-din-and,
    FAIR-din-nawnd [GER], fair-dee-NAW
    with short ND [FR])

Fermin (fair-MEEN [SP])
Fidel (fee-DELL [SP])
Finian (FIN-ee-yen [IR])
 Alternate spellings: Finnian
Finley (FIN-lee [CG])
 Alternate spellings: Finlay, Findlay
Florencio (flor-REN-see-yoh or
 flor-REN-thee-yoh [SP])
Florentino (flor-ren-TEE-noh [IT])
Florian (flor-ree-YAWN [FR])
Francisco (fran-SEES-koh or
 fran-THEETH-koh [SP])
Frankie (FRAYN-kee)
Freddy (FRED-ee [GER])
 Alternate spellings: Freddie, Fredy
Frederick (FRED-ur-rik [GER],
 fray-day-REEK [FR])
 Alternate spellings: Frederic, Frédéric
 [FR]
Freeman (FREE-men)
Friedrich (FREED-rik [GER])

Gabriel (GAY-bree-ell, gaw-bree-ELL or
 gaw-vree-ELL [HEB], gab-brrree-YELL
 [FR/SP/IT])
 Alternate spellings: Gavriel [HEB]
Garfield (GAR-feeld)
Gary (GAIR-ree [GER])
 Alternate spellings: Garry, Geary*
Geary (GEER-ree, JAIR-ree, GAIR-ree)
 Alternate spellings: Jerry*, Gerry,
 Gary*, Garry
Gene (JEEN)
 Alternate spellings: Jean*
Geo (JEE-yoh)
Gianni (jee-YAW-nee or JAWN-nee [IT])
 Alternate spellings: Johnny*, Johnnie,
 Johnie, Jonnie
Gideon (GID-ee-yun, GEED-ohn or
 geed-OHN [HEB])
 Alternate spellings: Gidon [HEB]
Gilbert (GIL-burt, zheel-BAIR [FR])
Gilberto (gil-BAIR-toh, hil-BAIR-toh or
 heel-VAIR-toh [SP])
Giles (JYLZ, ZHEEL [FR])
 Alternate spellings: Gilles [FR]
Gino (JEE-noh [IT])
Giovanni (jee-yoh-VAW-nee or
 joh-VAW-nee [AA/IT])
 Alternate spellings: Giovanny, Giovani,
 Jovani, Jovany, Jovanny, Jovanni
Giuseppe (joo-SEP-pee [IT], joo-ZEP-pee)
Godfrey (GAWD-free [GER])
Grady (GRAY-dee [CG])

Green (GREEN)
Gregorio (greg-OR-ree-oh [SP])
Gregory (GREG-ur-ree)
 Alternate spellings: Greggory
Guido (GWEE-doh [IT])
Guy (GY, GEE [FR])

Hakeem (haw-KEEM or hak-EEM [AR])
Hallie (HAL-ee)
Harding (HARD-eeng)
Hardy (HAR-dee [GER])
Harley (HAR-lee)
Harry (HAIR-ree)
Harvey (HAR-vee)
Heath (HEETH)
Heber (HAY-bur, HEE-bur [BIB], ay-BAIR [IR])
Henry (HEN-ree [GER], aw-REE with short
 N [FR])
 Alternate spellings: Henri [FR]
Heriberto (air-ree-BAIR-toh or
 air-ree-VAIR-toh [SP])
Herminio (air-MEE-nee-oh [SP])
Hezekiah (hez-uh-KY-yuh,
 chiz-kee-YAW-hoo with guttural ch
 [HEB])
 Alternate spellings: Chizkiyahu [HEB]
Hidero (hee-DAIR-roh [JAP])
Hilario (ee-LAR-ree-yoh [SP])
Hipolito (ee-POH-lee-toh [SP])
Hosea (ho-ZAY-yuh, ho-SHEE-yuh [HEB])
 Alternate spellings: Hosheia
Huey (HYOO-wee [GER])
Humphrey (HUM-free [GER])
Hurley (HUR-lee)

Ian (EE-yen, EYE-yen [BR])
 Alternate spellings: Ean, Iain, Ion
Ibrahim (EEB-ruh-heem or EEB-ruh-him
 [AA], ee-braw-HEEM or ib-raw-HEEM
 [AR])
Ignacio (eeg-NAW-see-yoh or
 eeg-NAW-thee-yoh [SP])
Irving (URV-eeng)
Isaac (EYE-zek, EET-zawk [HEB], is-HAWK
 [AR])
 Alternate spellings: Issac, Isaak,
 Yitzchak [HEB]
Isai (EE-sy or ee-sy-YEE [BIB], ee-SHY [HEB])
 Alternate spellings: Yishai (see also
 Jesse)
Ishmael (ISH-mayl, eesh-my-ELL [HEB],
 iss-maw-EEL [AR])
 Alternate spellings: Yishmael [HEB]
Isidor (IZ-id-or [GRK], ee-see-DOR [FR])

Alternate spellings: Isidore, Isador, Isadore

Isidro (ee-SEE-droh or ee-THEE-droh [SP])

Ismael (IZ-mayl, ees-MAW-yell or eeth-MAW-yell [SP])

Israel (IZ-ree-yell, IZ-ray-yell [HEB], iss-raw-EEL [AR], eess-RAY-yell or eeth-RAY-yell [SP])

Alternate spellings: Yisrael [HEB]

Itai (EE-ty [HEB])

Alternate spellings: Ittai

Ivan (EYE-ven, ee-VAWN or ee-BAWN [SP])

Ivory (EYE-vor-ree)

Izzy (IZ-zee)

Jabari (juh-BAR-ree [AA])

Jabreel (zhub-RRRREEL [AR])

Jacari (juh-KAIR-ree or juh-KAR-ree or JAK-ur-ree)

Jacinto (haw-SEEN-toh or haw-THEEN-toh [SP])

Jackie (JAK-ee)

Alternate spellings: Jacky

Jacoby (juh-KOH-bee, JAY-kub-ee)

Alternate spellings: Jakobe, Jacobi

Jaden (JAY-den [AA], yaw-DAWN or yaw-DEEN [HEB])

Alternate spellings: Jayden, Jaiden, Jadon [HEB], Jaydon, Jaeden, Jadyn, Yadon or Jadin or Yadin [HEB]

Jaheim (juh-HEEM [AA/AR])

Alternate spellings: Jahiem, Jaheem

Jaime (JAY-mee, HY-may [SP])

Alternate spellings: Jayme

Jair (JAY-yur [BIB], JAIR, yaw-EER or YAW-eer [HEB])

Alternate spellings: Jere*, Yair [HEB], Yahir*

Jaleel (jull-EEL [AA], zhul-EEL [AR])

Jamari (jum-MAR-ree [AA])

Jamie (JAY-mee)

Alternate spellings: Jamey

Jamil (jum-EEL or jum-ELL [AA], zhum-EEL [AR])

Alternate spellings: Jamel

Jamir (jum-EER [AA])

Janis (jaw-NEES or YAW-nis [SCAN])

Javier (haw-vee-YAIR or haw-bee-YAIR [SP])

Alternate spellings: Xavier*

Javion (JAY-vee-yawn or JAY-vee-yun [AA])

Jedidiah (jed-did-DY-yuh, yed-DEED-yaw [HEB])

Alternate spellings: Jedediah,

Jedidia, Yedidya [HEB]

Jeffrey (JEF-ree)

Alternate spellings: Jeffery, Geoffrey, Jeffry, Jefferey

Jennings (JEN-eengz)

Jeremiah (jair-uh-MY-uh, yeer-mee-YAW-hoo [HEB])

Alternate spellings: Yirmeyahu [HEB]

Jeremy (JAIR-ruh-mee)

Alternate spellings: Jeramy, Jeremie, Jeromy, Jeremey, Jeramie

Jerry (JAIR-ree)

Alternate spellings: Gerry [GER], Geary*

Jesse (JES-see, ee-SHY [HEB])

Alternate spellings: Jessie, Jessy, Yishai or Isai* [HEB]

Jimmy (JIM-ee)

Alternate spellings: Jimmie

Joachim (wah-KEEM, JOH-wah-kim, zho-wah-SHE with short N [FR], yo-WAH-kim [GER], yuh-ho-wuh-KEEM or yow-wuh-KEEM [HEB])

Alternate spellings: Joakim, Jehoiakim or Yehoyakim [HEB]

Joaquin (wah-KEEN, ho-wah-KEEN [SP], yuh-ho-wuh-CHEEN or yow-wuh-CHEEN with guttural CH [HEB])

Alternate spellings: Joaquin [SP], Jehoiachin or Yehoyachin [HEB]

Jody (JOH-dee)

Alternate spellings: Jodie

Joey (JOH-wee)

Johnny (JAWN-ee)

Alternate spellings: Johnnie, Johnie, Jonnie, Gianni*

Jordy (JOR-dee)

Jose (ho-ZAY, YO-see [HEB], ho-SAY or ho-THAY [SP])

Alternate spellings: José [SP]

Josiah (joh-ZY-yuh, yoh-shee-YAW-hoo or yoh-SHEE-yuh [HEB])

Alternate spellings: Yoshiyahu or Yoshiya [HEB]

Julian (JOO-lee-yen, zhoo-lee-YAW with short N [FR])

Alternate spellings: Julien

Julio (HOO-lee-yoh [SP])

Julius (JOO-lee-yes)

Junior (JOON-yur, JOO-nee-yur)

Junius (JOON-yes, JOO-nee-yes)

Alternate spellings: Junious

Kadeem (kuh-DEEM [AA/AR])

Kamari (kuh-MAR-ee [AA])

Kareem (kuh-REEM [AA], kuh-RRREEM [AR])
Keanu (kee-YAWN-oo [HW])
Keaton (KEE-ten)
Keegan (KEE-gen)
  Alternate spellings: Keagan, Kegan
Keenan (KEE-nin [CG])
Keith (KEETH [CG])
Kelby (KEL-bee)
Kelly (KEL-lee)
  Alternate spellings: Kelley
Kelsey (KEL-see)
Kenji (KEN-jee [JAP])
Kennedy (KEN-uh-dee [IR])
Kenny (KEN-ee [CG])
  Alternate spellings: Kenney
Keon (KEE-yen [IR/PER], KEE-yawn [AA])
  Alternate spellings: Keyon, Kian [IR/PER]
Kerry (KAIR-ree)
  Alternate spellings: Carey, Cary
Keshawn (kee-SHAWN [AA])
  Alternate spellings: Keyshawn
Khalid (kaw-LEED [AA], CHAW-leed with
  guttural CH or HAW-lid [AR])
Khalil (kaw-LEEL [AA], CHAW-leel with
  guttural CH [HEB/AR], HAW-leel [AR])
  Alternate spellings: Chalil [HEB], Halil,
  Hallil
Kiefer (KEE-fur [CG])
  Alternate spellings: Keefer
Kiel (KEEL [GER])
Kieran (KEER-ren [CG], KEER-rawn [IR])
  Alternate spellings: Ciaran, Kyran [PER]
King (KEENG)
Kirby (KUR-bee)
Kobe (KOH-bee [AA/HEB])
  Alternate spellings: Coby, Koby
Kyree (ky-REE [AA])

Lacy (LAY-see)
Ladarius (luh-DAIR-ee-yuss [AA])
Laddie (LAD-ee)
Lafayette (law-fee-YET, law-fy-YET,
  law-fay-YET)
Lanny (LAN-ee)
  Alternate spellings: Lannie
Larry (LAIR-ree)
Leamon (LEE-men)
Leander (lee-YAN-dur)
Lee (LEE [IR])
  Alternate spellings: Leigh
Leif (LEEF or LAYF [SCAN])
Leland (LEE-lend)
Lenny (LEN-nee)
  Alternate spellings: Lennie

Leo (LEE-yoh)
Leon (LEE-yawn [GER], lay-YAW with short
  N [FR], lay-YOHN [SP])
  Alternate spellings: Léon [FR], León [SP]
Leonardo (lee-yoh-NAR-doh,
  lay-yoh-NAR-doh [SP])
Leopold (LEE-yup-old [GER],
  lay-yoh-POHLD [FR])
  Alternate spellings: Léopold [FR]
Leroy (LEE-roi [AA], leh-RWAH [FR])
  Alternate spellings: Leeroy
Leslie (LES-lee)
  Alternate spellings: Lesley
Levi (LEE-vy or LEV-ee or LEE-vee [HEB])
Liam (LEE-yem [IR])
Lincoln (LEENG-ken)
Lindsey (LIN-zee)
  Alternate spellings: Lindsay
Lionel (LY-null, lee-yoh-NELL [FR])
Lisandro (lee-SAWN-droh [SP])
Lonnie (LAW-nee)
  Alternate spellings: Lonny
Louie (LOO-wee)
Louis (LOO-wiss [GER], loo-WEE [FR],
  loo-WEES [SP])
  Alternate spellings: Lewis, Luis [SP]
Luciano (loo-CHAW-noh [IT],
  loo-see-YAWN-oh or
  loo-thee-YAWN-oh [SP])
Lucien (LOO-shen, loo-see-YEN [FR])
  Alternate spellings: Lucian
Luigi (loo-WEE-jee [IT])

MacKenzie (muh-KEN-zee, mak-KEN-
  zee)
Makaio (maw-kaw-YEE-yoh or
  maw-KY-yoh [HW])
Malachi (MAL-uh-ky [IR], maw-law-CHEE
  with guttural CH [HEB])
  Alternate spellings: Malakai, Malachai
Malachy (MAL-uh-kee [IR])
Malik (mul-EEK [AA], mal-EEK or MAL-ik
  or MUL-ik [AR])
Manley (MAN-lee)
Manny (MAN-ee [HEB/SP])
Marcelino (mar-say-LEE-noh or
  mar-thay-LEE-noh [SP],
  mar-chell-LEE-noh [IT])
  Alternate spellings: Marcellino [IT]
Margarito (mar-gar-REE-toh [SP])
Mariano (mar-ree-YAWN-oh [IT])
Mario (MAR-ree-yoh [IT/SP])
Marion (MAIR-ree-yen)
Marquis (MAR-kwiss or mar-KEEZ or

mar-KEES [AA], mar-KEE [FR], MAR-kus)
Alternate spellings: Marquise,
Marques, Marcus*, Markus
Martin (MAR-tin, mar-TA with short N
[FR], mar-TEEN [SP])
Alternate spellings: Martin [SP]
Marty (MAR-tee)
Masaaki (mas-SAW-aw-kee [JAP])
Mauricio (mor-REE-see-yoh,
mow-REE-see-yoh or
mow-REE-thee-yoh [SP],
mow-REET-zee-yoh)
Alternate spellings: Mauritzio [IT]
Maury (MOR-ree)
Alternate spellings: Morry
Maxie (MAK-see)
Maxim (MAK-sim, mak-SEEM [RUS])
Alternate spellings: Maksim
Maximilian (mak-sim-MIL-yen [GER],
mak-see-meel-YA with short N [FR])
Alternate spellings: Maximillian,
Maximilien [FR]
Maximino (mak-sim-MEE-noh [SP])
Maximo (mak-SEE-moh [SP])
McKinley (mik-KIN-lee [CG])
Meyer (MAY-ur or may-YEER [HEB], MY-ur)
Alternate spellings: Meir
Micah (MY-kuh, MEE-chaw with guttural
CH [HEB])
Alternate spellings: Micha [HEB]
Michael (MY-kel, mee-chy-ELL with
guttural CH [HEB], mee-SHELL [FR])
Alternate spellings: Micheal, Mikel,
Michel, Michale, Michel [FR]
Miguel (mee-GEL [SP], mee-GWELL [AA])
Mikhail (mee-KYL [RUS], MEE-ky-yell,
mik-KAY-yell)
Milan (mee-LAWN [IT/RUS])
Ming (MEENG [CH])
Misael (mee-SY-yell or mee-THY-yell [SP])
Monte (MAWN-tee)
Alternate spellings: Monty
Montgomery (mawnt-GUM-ur-ree)
Murphy (MUR-fee)
Murray (MUR-ree)
Alternate spellings: Murry

Najee (NAW-jee or naw-JEE [AA])
Alternate spellings: Naji or Nagi [AR]
Najib (na-ZHEEB [AR])
Nakia (nuh-KEE-yuh [AA])
Napoleon (nuh-POH-lee-yen)
Narciso (nar-SIS-oh, nar-SEE-soh or
nar-THEE-thoh [SP], nar-CHEE-soh [IT])

Nasir (NAW-seer or nuh-SEER or
NAW-sur [AR])
Neftali (nef-TAW-lee, NAWF-taw-lee [HEB])
Alternate spellings: Naftali [HEB]
Nehemiah (nee-yuh-MY-yuh,
neh-CHEM-ee-yuh with guttural CH
[HEB])
Alternate spellings: Nechemya or
Nechemia [HEB]
Neil (NEEL, NEE-yull [CG])
Alternate spellings: Neal
Nicholas (NIK-ul-us, nee-koh-LAW [FR])
Alternate spellings: Nicolas, Nickolas,
Nikolas
Nicky (NIK-ee)
Nico (NEE-koh [IT])
Alternate spellings: Niko
Nikhil (nik-KEEL [EI])
Noe (noh-WAY [FR], NOH-wee)
Nunzio (NOON-zee-yoh [IT])

Oakley (OHK-lee)
Obie (OH-bee [AA])
Alternate spellings: Obi
Octavio (awk-TAW-vee-yoh or
ohk-TAW-bee-yoh [SP])
Odie (OH-dee)
Okey (OH-kee)
Ollie (AW-lee)
Omari (oh-MAR-ree [AA])
Omarion (oh-MAR-ree-yawn or
uh-MAR-ree-yawn [AA])
Alternate spellings: Amarion
O'Neal (oh-NEEL)
Orie (OR-ree, or-REE [HEB])

Pacey (PAY-see)
Paddy (PAD-ee)
Paris (PAIR-riss, pair-RRREE [FR])
Patricio (paw-TREE-see-yoh or
paw-TREE-thee-yoh [SP])
Patrizio (paw-TREET-zee-yoh [IT])
Patsy (PAT-see)
Percy (PER-see [BR])
Perry (PAIR-ree)
Pershing (PUR-sheeng)
Pete (PEET)
Peter (PEE-tur)
Philias (FILL-ee-yes)
Phillip (FILL-ip, fee-LEEP [FR])
Alternate spellings: Philip, Philippe [FR]
Phineas (FIN-ee-yes)
Alternate spellings: Finneas,
Phinnehas

Phoenix (FEEN-iks)
Pierce (PEERS [IR])
  Alternate spellings: Pearce
Pierre (pee-YAIR [FR])
Pietro (pee-YET-roh [IT], pee-YAY-troh)
Ping (PEENG [CH])
Porfirio (por-FEER-ree-yoh [SP])
Primitivo (pree-MEE-tee-voh [SP])

Quincy (KWIN-see)

Rafael (RAF-ee-yell, raf-y-YELL,
  rrraf-uh-YELL [FR], raw-faw-ELL [HEB/SP],
  rrraw-FAY-yell [SP])
  Alternate spellings: Raphael, Raphaël
Raheem (ruh-HEEM or raw-HEEM [AA/AR])
Raleigh (RAW-lee)
  Alternate spellings: Rollie
Ramiro (rrraw-MEER-roh [SP])
Ramsey (RAM-zee)
Randy (RAN-dee)
Rasheed (ruh-SHEED or raw-SHEED [AA/AR])
Ravi (RRRAW-vee [EI], RAW-vee [HEB])
  Alternate spellings: Rafi [AR]
Reagan (RAY-gen, REE-gen)
Reese (REES [WL])
  Alternate spellings: Reece, Rhys [FR]
Reid (REED)
  Alternate spellings: Reed
Refugio (ref-FOO-hee-yoh [SP])
Reggie (REJ-ee)
Regis (REE-gis, ray-ZHEES [FR])
  Alternate spellings: Régis [FR]
Remington (REM-eeng-ten)
Rémy (REM-ee, ray-MEE [FR])
  Alternate spellings: Rémi
Reno (REE-noh)
Ricardo (rrrree-KAR-doh [SP])
Richie (RICH-ee)
Ricky (RIK-ee)
  Alternate spellings: Rickey, Rickie, Ricki
Rico (REE-koh [IT/SP])
Rigoberto (ree-goh-BAIR-toh [SP])
Ringo (REEN-goh [JAP])
Riley (RY-lee [IR])
  Alternate spellings: Reilly, Rylee, Ryley
Rio (REE-yoh [SP])
Riordan (REER-den, ROR-den,
  ree-YOR-den [IR])
Robbie (RAW-bee)
  Alternate spellings: Robby
Rocky (RAW-kee)
Rodney (RAWD-nee)
Rodrigo (rrroh-DREE-goh [IT/SP])

Rogelio (rrroh-HELL-ee-yoh [SP])
Romeo (ROH-mee-yoh, rrroh-MAY-yoh
  [SP])
Ronnie (RAW-nee)
  Alternate spellings: Ronny
Rory (ROR-ree)
Rosario (rrroh-SAR-ree-yoh or
  rrroh-THAR-ree-yoh [SP])
Ruby (ROO-bee)
Rudy (ROO-dee [GER])
Rusty (RUS-tee)

Samir (saw-MEER or suh-MEER [AR])
Sammy (SAM-ee)
  Alternate spellings: Sammie
Samson (SAM-sun, sheem-SHOHN [HEB])
  Alternate spellings: Shimshon [HEB]
Sandy (SAN-dee)
Santiago (sawn-tee-YAW-goh or
  thawn-tee-YAW-goh [SP])
Santino (san-TEE-noh [IT])
Savion (SAY-vee-yawn or say-vee-YAWN
  [AA])
Scottie (SKAW-tee)
Sebastian (sub-BAS-chen,
  sub-BAS-tee-yen, say-bas-tee-YAW
  with short N [FR], say-baws-TAWN or
  thay-vaws-TAWN [SP])
  Alternate spellings: Sabastian,
  Sebastien, Sebastien [FR], Sebastian [SP]
Selby (SELL-bee)
Sergio (SUR-jee-yoh, SAIR-jee-yoh or
  SAIR-joh [IT], SAIR-hee-yoh or
  THAIR-hee-yoh [SP])
Seymour (SEE-mor)
Shaquille (shak-KEEL [AA])
  Alternate spellings: Shakil [AR]
Shelby (SHELL-bee)
Shing (SHEENG [CH])
ShinIchi (shin-EE-chee [JAP])
Sidney (SID-nee)
  Alternate spellings: Sydney
Silvio (SIL-vee-yoh [IT/SP], THIL-bee-yoh [SP])
Simeon (SIM-ee-yun [HEB])
Simon (SY-mun [GRK], shee-MOHN [HEB],
  see-MAW with short N [FR])
  Alternate spellings: Shimon [HEB]
Sincere (SIN-seer)
Sixto (SEEKS-toh [SP])
Sonny (SUN-ee)
Stacy (STAY-see)
  Alternate spellings: Stacey
Sterling (STUR-leeng)
  Alternate spellings: Stirling

Steve (STEEV)
Steven (STEE-ven)
    Alternate spellings: Stephen,
    Stephan, Stephon, Stevan
Stevie (STEE-vee)
Stoney (STOH-nee)
Syed (sy-YEED or SAY-yed [AR/AA], SY-yed
    [EI]; see also Zaid)
    Alternate spellings: Saeed, Said

Taurean (TOR-ree-yun [AA])
Tavion (TAY-vee-yawn or TAY-vee-yun
    [AA])
Teddy (TED-ee)
Telly (TEL-ee)
Terry (TAIR-ree)
Thaddeus (THAD-ee-yuss [GRK])
Theo (THEE-yoh, TAY-yoh [FR])
    Alternate spellings: Théo [FR]
Theodore (THEE-yuh-dor, tay-yoh-DOR
    [FR])
    Alternate spellings: Theadore,
    Theodor, Théodore [FR]
Tiernan (TEER-nin [CG])
Tierney (TEER-nee [IR])
Timmy (TIM-ee)
    Alternate spellings: Timmie
Timothy (TIM-ith-ee, tee-moh-TAY [FR])
    Alternate spellings: Timmothy,
    Timothée [FR]
Tito (TEE-toh [AA/IT/SP])
Toby (TOH-bee, toh-VEE [HEB])
    Alternate spellings: Tovi [HEB]
Tommy (TAW-mee)
    Alternate spellings: Tommie
Tony (TOH-nee)
    Alternate spellings: Toney
Tory (TOR-ree)
    Alternate spellings: Torrey
Tracy (TRAY-see)
    Alternate spellings: Tracey
Trevion (TRAY-vee-yun or
    TRAY-vee-yawn [AA])
Trinidad (TRIN-id-add,
    tree-nee-DAWD [SP])
Trinity (TRIN-it-ee)
Tristan (TRIS-ten [WL], trees-TAW with
    short N [FR], trees-TAWN or
    treeth-TAWN [SP])
    Alternate spellings: Tristen, Triston,
    Tristin, Trystan, Tristán [SP]
Tristian (TRIS-chen, TRIS-tee-yen)
Tyree (ty-REE or TY-ree [AA])
Tyrese (ty-REES [AA])

Tyshawn (TY-shawn or tuh-SHAWN or
    TEE-shawn [AA])
    Alternate spellings: Tshawn

Ulises (yoo-LISS-seez, oo-LEE-says or
    oo-LEETH-ayth [SP])
    Alternate spellings: Ulysses
Uriel (YUR-ree-yell [HEB])

Valentin (val-en-TEEN [SP])
Valentine (VAL-en-tyn, vaw-lawn-TEEN
    [FR])
Vernie (VUR-nee)
Vicente (vee-SEN-tay or bee-THEN-tay
    [SP])
Victor (VIK-tur, veek-TOR [FR], VEEK-tor
    or BEEK-tor [SP])
    Alternate spellings: Víctor [SP], Viktor
Vidal (vee-DAWL or bee-DAWL [SP])
Vidor (VEE-dor [HUN])
Virgilio (veer-JEE-lee-yoh [IT],
    veer-HEE-lee-yoh or
    beer-HEE-lee-yoh [SP])
Vito (VEE-toh [IT/SP], BEE-doh [SP])

Washington (WASH-eeng-ten)
Wellington (WELL-eeng-ten)
Wesley (WES-lee)
    Alternate spellings: Westley
Whitney (WIT-nee)
Wiley (WY-lee)
    Alternate spellings: Wylie
Willie (WIL-ee)
Willy (WIL-ee)
Winfield (WIN-feeld, VIN-feeld [GER])
Woody (WOO-dee)

Xavier (ZAY-vee-yur, eks-ZAY-vee-yur,
    haw-vee-YAIR or haw-bee-YAIR [SP],
    zav-YAY [FR])
    Alternate spellings: Javier*, Xzavier,
    Zavier

Yadiel (yaw-dee-YELL [SP])
Yahir (yaw-EER or YAW-eer [HEB])
    Alternate spellings: Yair [HEB], Jair*
Ye (EE-yeh [CH])
Yuri (YUR-ree [RUS])
Yuuji (YOO-oo-jee [JAP])

Zachariah (zak-kur-RY-yuh,
    zuh-CHAR-ree-yuh with guttural CH
    [HEB], zuk-uh-REE-yuh [AR])
    Alternate spellings: Zecharya [HEB]

Zachary (ZAK-ur-ree)
Alternate spellings: Zackary, Zachery,
Zackery, Zakary
Zaid (ZAY-yid [AR], ZAYD, zy-YEED;
see also Syed)
Zaire (zy-YEER [AA])
Zechariah (zek-kur-RY-uh,
zuh-CHAR-ree-uh with guttural CH
[HEB], zuk-uh-REE-yuh [AR])
Alternate spellings: Zecharya [HEB]
Zeke (ZEEK)
Zion (ZY-yun [AA], tsee-YOHN [HEB])
Alternate spellings: Tziyon

■ SHORT E (EH OR E) ■

PARTNER POINTER:
Short E, I, and U often
sound similar.

Abel (AY-bell, AW-vell [HEB], aw-BELL [SP])
Alternate spellings: Able
Adalberto (aw-dell-BAIR-toh [SP])
Adelbert (AD-dull-burt [GER], ad-dell-BAIR
[FR])
Adriel (AY-dree-yell, aw-dree-YELL [HEB])
Ahmed (AWH-med with pronounced H
in middle [AR])
Aidan (AY-den [IR], ED-in [HEB])
Alternate spellings: Aiden, Ayden,
Adan, Aden
Alan (AL-len [CG], al-LE with short N [FR])
Alternate spellings: Allen, Allan,
Allyn, Alain [FR]
Alden (AWL-den)
Alec (AL-ek)
Alejandro (aw-leh-HAWN-droh [SP])
Alessandro (aw-leh-SAWN-droh [IT])
Alex (AL-eks)
Alexander (al-eks-ZAN-dur)
Alternate spellings: Alexzander
Alexandre (al-eks-ZAWN-dray,
al-ek-SAW-druh with short N [FR])
Alexandro (al-eks-ZAN-droh,
al-eks-ZAWN-droh)
Alexis (uh-LEK-sis, aw-LEK-see or
al-ek-SEES [FR])
Alfred (AL-fred, al-FRED)
Andreas (awn-DRAY-yes [GRK])
Angel (AYN-jell, AWN-hell [SP])
Alternate spellings: Ángel
Angelo (AN-jell-oh, AWN-jell-oh [IT],
AWN-hell-oh [SP])

Ansel (AN-sell)
Anselmo (awn-SELL-moh [IT/SP],
awn-THELL-moh [SP])
Ardell (ar-DELL)
Ariel (AIR-ree-yell, AR-ree-yell,
ar-ree-YELL [HEB/FR])
August (AW-gest [GER], oh-GOOST [FR])
Alternate spellings: Auguste [FR]
Aurelio (or-REL-ee-yoh [SP])
Axel (AK-sell [GER])

Baron (BAIR-ren [GER])
Alternate spellings: Barron
Barrett (BAIR-ret)
Ben (BEN [HEB])
Benedict (BEN-uh-dikt)
Benicio (ben-EE-see-yoh or
ven-EE-thee-yoh [SP])
Benito (ben-EE-toh or ven-EE-toh [SP])
Benjamin (BEN-juh-min, bin-yaw-MEEN
[HEB], ben-zhaw-ME with short N [FR]
ben-haw-MEEN or ven-haw-MEEN [SP])
Alternate spellings: Binyamin [HEB],
Benjamín [SP]
Bennett (BEN-net)
Benny (BEN-ee)
Alternate spellings: Bennie
Benton (BEN-tin)
Bertrand (BURT-rend, bair-TRAW with
short N [FR])
Bienvenido (bee-yen-ben-EE-doh or
vee-yen-ven-EE-doh [SP])
Blaise (BLAYZ, BLEZ [FR])
Alternate spellings: Blaze
Brayden (BRAY-den [CG], BRAY-dawn [IR])
Alternate spellings: Braden, Braeden,
Braydon, Braiden, Braedon, Bradyn
Brendan (BREN-din)
Alternate spellings: Brenden, Brendon
Brennan (BREN-en)
Alternate spellings: Brennen
Brent (BRENT)
Brenton (BREN-ten)
Brett (BRET)
Alternate spellings: Bret
Brian (BRY-yen [CG], BREE-yen [IR])
Alternate spellings: Bryan, Brayan [SP],
Bryon, Brien
Bryant (BRY-yent [CG])
Bryson (BRY-sen)
Alternate spellings: Brycen
Burdette (bur-DETT)
Burnell (bur-NELL)
Burton (BUR-ten)

Alternate spellings: Berton
Byron (BY-ren)

Caden (KAY-den)
Alternate spellings: Kaden, Cayden,
Kayden, Kaiden, Kadin, Caiden,
Kaeden
Caleb (KAY-leb, KAY-luv [HEB])
Alternate spellings: Kaleb, Kalev [HEB]
Cameron (KAM-ur-ren, KAM-ren)
Alternate spellings: Kameron,
Camron, Kamron, Camren
Candelario (kan-dell-AR-ree-oh [SP])
Cannon (KAN-nen)
Carlton (KARL-ten)
Alternate spellings: Carleton
Carmelo (kar-MEL-oh [IT/SP])
Carmen (KAR-men [SP])
Carnell (kar-NELL [BR])
Carson (KAR-sen)
Alternate spellings: Karson
Cason (KAY-sen)
Cecil (SEE-sill, SESS-ill)
Cecilio (ses-SEE-lee-yoh or
the-THEE-lee-yoh [SP],
che-CHEE-lee-yoh [IT])
Cedric (SED-rik, SEED-rik)
Alternate spellings: Cedrick, Sedrick
Celestino (sell-less-TEEN-oh or
thell-leth-TEEN-oh [SP])
Cesar (SAY-sar/THAY-thar or
SESS-ar/THE-thar [SP], SEE-zur)
Alternate spellings: Caesar*
Chesley (CHESS-lee or CHEZ-lee)
Chester (CHES-tur)
Chet (CHET)
Christian (KRIS-chen, KREE-stee-yawn
or KREETH-tee-yawn [IT/SP],
kree-stee-YAW with short N [FR])
Alternate spellings: Cristian, Kristian
Clayton (KLAY-ten)
Clem (KLEM)
Cleménce (klay-MAWS with short N [FR])
Clemens (KLEM-inz)
Clement (KLEM-ent, kluh-MENT,
klay-MAW with short N [FR])
Alternate spellings: Clément [FR]
Clifton (KLIF-ten)
Clinton (KLIN-ten)
Coleman (KOHL-men [IR])
Alternate spellings: Colman
Colton (KOHL-ten)
Alternate spellings: Colten, Kolton
Cordell (kor-DELL [FR])

Cornell (kor-NELL [CG])
Cortéz (kor-TEZ [SP])

Dalton (DAWL-ten)
Damian (DAY-mee-yen, daw-mee-YAW
with short N [FR])
Alternate spellings: Damien, Damion,
Dameon
Damon (DAY-men)
Dangelo (DAN-jell-oh [AA])
Daniel (DAN-yell, dawn-ee-YELL [HEB],
dan-YELL [FR])
Alternate spellings: Danial
Darian (DAIR-ree-yen)
Alternate spellings: Darien, Darion,
Darrion, Darrian, Darrien
Darius (DAR-ree-yuss [HEB/PER],
DAIR-ree-yes)
Alternate spellings: Darrius
Darnell (dar-NELL [AA])
Dashiell (DASH-ell)
Dawson (DAW-sen)
Dayton (DAY-ten)
Deangelo (dee-YAN-jell-oh [AA/IT])
Declan (DEK-len [IR])
Dedrick (DED-rik [AA])
Delano (DEL-en-oh [CG])
Delbert (DEL-burt)
Dell (DELL)
Alternate spellings: Del
Delmar (del-MAR, DEL-mur)
Alternate spellings: Delmer*
Delmas (DEL-muss)
Delmer (DEL-mur)
Alternate spellings: Delmar*
Delton (DEL-ten)
Delvin (DEL-vin)
Demetrius (duh-MEE-tree-yes [GRK])
Dempsey (DEMP-see)
Denis (den-NEE [FR], DEN-iss)
Alternate spellings: Dennis*
Dennis (DEN-iss)
Alternate spellings: Denis*
Denny (DEN-ee)
Alternate spellings: Dennie
Denton (DENT-in)
Denver (DEN-vur)
Denzel (den-ZELL or DEN-zell [AA])
Denzil (DEN-zill [AA])
Dermot (DUR-met [CG], DEER-mid [IR])
Desmond (DEZ-mund [IR])
Destin (DES-tin)
Devin (DEV-in)
Alternate spellings: Devon, Deven,

Devan, Devyn
Dexter (DEK-stur)
Dezso (DEZH-oh [HUN])
Domenico (doh-MEN-ee-koh [IT])
Donnell (DAW-nell, DOH-null [IR])
    Alternate spellings: Donal, Donell
Dorian (DOR-ree-yen)
Dorman (DOR-men)
Douglas (DUG-less [CG])
    Alternate spellings: Douglass
Draven (DRAY-ven [AA])
Dylan (DIL-len [IR])
    Alternate spellings: Dillon, Dillan, Dylon

Earnest (UR-nest [GER])
Easton (EES-ten)
Ed (ED)
    Alternate spellings: Edd
Eddie (ED-ee)
    Alternate spellings: Eddy
Edgar (ED-gur, ed-GAR [FR])
Edgardo (ed-GAR-doh [IT/SP])
Edison (ED-is-sun)
Edmund (ED-mund)
    Alternate spellings: Edmond
Edsel (ED-sell)
Eduardo (ed-WAR-doh [IT/SP])
    Alternate spellings: Edwardo—
Edward (ED-wurd)
Edwin (ED-win)
Efrain (eff-raw-EEN or EEF-rawn [HEB],
    EFF-ren [AA], eff-RA with short N [FR],
    eff-raw-EEN [SP], EE-fren or ef-RYN;
    see also Ephraim)
    Alternate spellings: Efrain [SP], Efren,
    Efron [HEB], Ephron
Eladio (el-LAW-dee-yoh or
    ee-LAW-dee-yoh or EL-lawd-yoh [SP])
Elbert (EL-burt)
Eldon (EL-den; see also Elton)
    Alternate spellings: Elden
Eldred (EL-drid)
Eldridge (EL-drij)
Elgin (EL-jin)
Eli (EE-ly or ELL-ee [HEB])
    Alternate spellings: Elly
Elian (EL-lee-yawn [SP], EE-lee-yawn)
Elias (EE-lee-yaws [HEB], el-LEE-yaws or
    eh-LEE-yes [SP], ee-LY-yes)
Eliezer (el-lee-YEZ-ur [HEB/AA], el-LEE-zur,
    el-LY-zur, el-lee-ZAIR or el-lee-THAIR
    [SP])
Elijah (el-LY-zhuh or uh-LY-juh [AA],
    el-lee-YAW-hoo [HEB])

Alternate spellings: Alijah, Eliyahu [HEB]
Eliseo (el-LEE-see-yoh, el-lee-ZAY-yoh
    [IT], el-lee-SAY-yoh [IT/SP],
    el-lee-THAY-yoh [SP])
Elisha (uh-LISH-uh or el-LY-shuh [AA],
    el-LEE-shuh [HEB])
Ellery (ELL-ur-ree)
Elliot (ELL-ee-yet)
    Alternate spellings: Elliott, Eliot
Ellis (EL-is)
Ellsworth (ELZ-wurth)
Elmer (EL-mur)
Elmo (EL-moh)
Elmore (EL-mor)
Eloy (EE-loi [BIB])
Elroy (EL-roi)
Elton (EL-ten; see also Eldon)
Elvin (EL-vin [CG])
Elvis (EL-viss [SCAN])
Elwin (EL-win)
    Alternate spellings: Elwyn
Elwood (EL-wood)
    Alternate spellings: Ellwood
Emerson (EM-ur-sen [GER])
Emery (EM-ur-ree [GER])
    Alternate spellings: Emory
Emiliano (em-eel-YAW-noh [SP],
    em-ee-lee-YAW-noh)
Emilio (em-MEE-lee-yoh [SP])
Emmanuel (ee-MAN-yoo-well [AA],
    ee-mawn-yoo-ELL [HEB],
    em-man-WELL [FR],
    ee-mawn-yoo-WELL or
    ee-man-WELL [SP])
    Alternate spellings: Emanuel,
    Immanuel
Emmett (EM-mit [GER/IR])
    Alternate spellings: Emmitt, Emmet
Ennis (EN-niss [IR])
Enrico (en-REE-koh [IT])
Enrique (en-REE-kay [SP])
Enzo (EN-zoh [IT])
Ephraim (ef-RYM or ef-ry-EEM [HEB],
    ef-ry-YEEM or EFF-rem [AA])
    Alternate spellings: Efrayim [HEB],
    Efraim, Efrem (see also Efrain)
Epifanio (ep-if-FAW-nee-yoh [SP])
Erasmo (eh-RAWS-moh or
    ee-RAWS-moh [SP])
Ernesto (air-NES-toh [IT/SP], air-NETH-toh
    [SP])
Esteban (es-TEB-awn or eth-TEV-awn [SP],
    ES-tuh-bawn, ES-tuh-vawn)
    Alternate spellings: Estevan

Estevan (ES-tuh-vawn)

Eugenio (ay-yoo-HEN-ee-yoh [SP])

Eusebio (ay-yoo-SEB-ee-yoh or
    ay-yoo-THEV-ee-yoh [SP])

Evan (EV-in)

Evans (EV-inz)

Everett (EV-ur-ret)
    Alternate spellings: Everette

Evert (EV-urt)

Ezekiel (ee-ZEE-kee-yell [AA],
    yuh-CHEZ-kel with guttural CH [HEB],
    ess-ay-KYL/eth-ay-KYL or
    ess-sy-KEEL/eth-y-KEEL [SP])
    Alternate spellings: Ezequiel,
    Yechezkel [HEB]

Ezra (EZ-ruh [HEB])

Fabian (FAY-bee-yen, faw-bee-AWN [FR])

Faron (FAIR-ren or FAIR-rohn [BR])

Federico (fed-air-EE-ko [IT])

Felipe (fel-LEE-pay [SP])

Felix (FEEL-iks, fel-LEEKS [SP], fay-LEEKS
    [FR])
    Alternate spellings: Felix [SP]

Felton (FELL-ten)

Fidel (fee-DELL [SP])

Finian (FIN-ee-yen [IR])
    Alternate spellings: Finnian

Fletcher (FLECH-ur)

Florencio (flor-REN-see-yoh or
    flor-REN-thee-yoh [SP])

Florentino (flor-ren-TEE-noh [IT])

Florian (flor-ree-YAWN [FR])

Floyd (FLOID)

Forrest (FOR-rest)
    Alternate spellings: Forest

Francesco (fran-CHESS-koh [IT])

Fred (FRED [GER])

Freddy (FRED-ee [GER])
    Alternate spellings: Freddie, Fredy

Frederick (FRED-ur-rik [GER],
    fray-day-REEK [FR])
    Alternate spellings: Frederic, Frédéric
    [FR]

Fredrick (FRED-rik [GER])
    Alternate spellings: Fredric

Freeman (FREE-men)

Furman (FUR-men)

Gabriel (GAY-bree-yell, gaw-bree-ELL or
    gaw-vree-ELL [HEB], gab-brrree-YELL
    [FR/SP/IT])
    Alternate spellings: Gavriel [HEB]

Garland (GAR-lend)

Garnett (GAR-net)
    Alternate spellings: Garnet

Garrett (GAIR-ret [CG])
    Alterative spellings: Garret, Garett

Garrison (GAIR-ris-sen)

Genaro (jen-NAR-roh [IT], hen-NAR-roh [SP])
    Alternate spellings: Gennaro

General (JEN-ur-rull)

German (JUR-men, her-MAWN [SP],
    zhair-MAN [FR])
    Alternate spellings: Germán [SP],
    Germain [FR]

Giuseppe (joo-SEP-pee [IT], joo-ZEP-pee)

Glendon (GLEN-den [IR])

Glenn (GLEN [CG])
    Alternate spellings: Glen, Glynn

Golden (GOHL-den)

Gordon (GOR-den)

Greg (GREG)
    Alternate spellings: Gregg

Gregorio (greg-OR-ree-oh [SP])

Gregory (GREG-ur-ree)
    Alternate spellings: Greggory

Hamilton (HAM-ill-ten)

Hansel (HAN-sell, HAWN-sell [GER/SCAN])

Härlan (HAR-len)
    Alternate spellings: Harland, Harlen

Harmon (HAR-men [GER])

Harrison (HAIR-ris-sen)

Hayden (HAY-den)
    Alternate spellings: Haden

Hector (HEK-tur, EK-tor [SP])
    Alternate spellings: Héctor [SP]

Helmer (HELL-mur [SCAN])

Henderson (HEN-dur-sen)

Henry (HEN-ree [GER], aw-REE with short
    N [FR])
    Alternate spellings: Henri [FR]

Herman (HUR-men [GER])
    Alternate spellings: Hermon,
    Hermann

Herschel (HUR-shell)
    Alternate spellings: Hershel

Hezekiah (hez-uh-KY-yuh,
    chiz-kee-YAW-hoo with guttural ch
    [HEB])
    Alternate spellings: Chizkiyahu [HEB]

Hilton (HILL-ten [BR])

Holden (HOHL-den)

Houston (HYOO-sten)
    Alternate spellings: Huston

Hyman (HY-men)

Ian (EE-yen, EYE-yen [BR])
Alternate spellings: Ean, Iain, Ion
Irvin (UR-ven)
Alternate spellings: Ervin
Isaac (EYE-zek, EET-zawk [HEB], is-HAWK
[AR])
Alternate spellings: Issac, Isaak,
Yitzchak [HEB]
Isaias (eye-ZAY-yes)
Israel (IZ-ree-yell, IZ-ray-yell [HEB],
iss-raw-EEL [AR], eess-RAY-yell or
eeth-RAY-yell [SP])
Alternate spellings: Yisrael [HEB]
Ivan (EYE-ven, ee-VAWN or
ee-BAWN [SP])

Jackson (JAK-sen)
Alternate spellings: Jaxon, Jaxson
Jaden (JAY-den [AA], yaw-DAWN or
yaw-DEEN [HEB])
Alternate spellings: Jayden, Jaiden,
Jadon [HEB], Jaydon, Jaeden, Jadyn,
Yadon or Jadin or Yadin [HEB]
Jalen (JAY-len [AA])
Alternate spellings: Jaylen, Jaylin,
Jaylan, Jaylon
Jared (JAIR-red, yar-RED [HEB])
Alternate spellings: Jarod, Jarred,
Jarrod, Jerrod, Jerod, Jerad, Jered,
Yared [HEB]
Jaron (JAIR-ren, yar-ROHN [HEB])
Alternate spellings: Jaren, Yaron [HEB]
Jarrett (JAIR-ret)
Alternate spellings: Jarret
Jason (JAY-sen)
Alternate spellings: Jayson, Jasen
Jed (JED)
Jedidiah (jed-did-DY-yuh,
yed-DEED-yaw [HEB])
Alternate spellings: Jedediah,
Jedidia, Yedidya [HEB]
Jeff (JEF)
Alternate spellings: Geoff
Jefferson (JEF-fur-sen)
Jeffrey (JEF-ree)
Alternate spellings: Jeffery, Geoffrey,
Jeffry, Jefferey
Jennings (JEN-eengz)
Jess (JESS)
Jesse (JES-see, ee-SHY [HEB])
Alternate spellings: Jessie, Jessy,
Yishai or Isai* [HEB]
Jett (JET [AA])
Joel (JOH-well, yoh-ELL [HEB],

zho-WELL [FR])
Alternate spellings: Joël [FR], Yoel [HEB]
Jordan (JOR-den, YAR-den [HEB])
Alternate spellings: Jordon, Jorden,
Yarden*
Joseph (JOH-sef, YOH-sef or yoh-SEF
[HEB], YOO-suf [AR], zho-ZEF [FR])
Alternate spellings: Josef, Yosef*,
Yusuf*
Judson (JUD-sen)
Julian (JOO-lee-yen, zhoo-lee-YAW with
short N [FR])
Alternate spellings: Julien
Julius (JOO-lee-yes)
Junius (JOON-yes, JOO-nee-yes)
Alternate spellings: Junious

Kalen (KAY-len)
Keaton (KEE-ten)
Keegan (KEE-gen)
Alternate spellings: Keagan, Kegan
Kelby (KEL-bee)
Kellen (KEL-in [CG])
Alternate spellings: Kellan
Kelly (KEL-lee)
Alternate spellings: Kelley
Kelsey (KEL-see)
Kelton (KEL-tun [CG])
Kelvin (KEL-vin [CG])
Ken (KEN)
Kendall (KEN-dull)
Alternate spellings: Kendal
Kendrick (KEN-drik)
Kenji (KEN-jee [JAP])
Kennedy (KEN-uh-dee [IR])
Kenneth (KEN-ith [CG])
Alternate spellings: Kennith
Kenny (KEN-ee [CG])
Alternate spellings: Kenney
Kent (KENT [WL])
Kenton (KEN-ten)
Kenya (KEN-yuh [AA])
Kenyatta (ken-YAW-tuh [AA])
Kenyon (KEN-yen)
Keon (KEE-yen [IR/PER], KEE-yawn [AA])
Alternate spellings: Keyon, Kian [IR/PER]

Landon (LAN-den)
Alternate spellings: Landen
Latrell (luh-TRELL [AA])
Laron (LAIR-ren, luh-RAWN [AA])
Lawrence (LOR-rens, lor-RAWS with
short N [FR], LOR-rens [GER])
Alternate spellings: Laurence [FR],

Lawerence, Lorenz [GER]
Lawson (LAW-sen)
Layton (LAY-ten [BR])
  Alternate spellings: Leighton
Leland (LEE-lend)
Lemuel (LEM-yoo-well [HEB])
Len (LEN)
  Alternate spellings: Lyn
Lenny (LEN-nee)
  Alternate spellings: Lennie
Leonard (LEN-urd [GER], lay-yoh-NAR [FR])
  Alternate spellings: Lenard, Léonard [FR]
Leroy (LEE-roi [AA], leh-RWAH [FR])
  Alternate spellings: Leeroy
Les (LES)
Leslie (LES-lee)
  Alternate spellings: Lesley
Lester (LES-tur)
Levi (LEE-vy or LEV-ee or LEE-vee [HEB])
Liam (LEE-yem [IR])
Lincoln (LEENG-ken)
Lionel (LY-null, lee-yoh-NELL [FR])
Lisandro (lee-SAWN-droh [SP])
Llewellyn (loo-WELL-in [WL])
Loden (LOH-den)
Logan (LOH-gen)
London (LUN-den)
Loren (LOR-ren)
  Alternate spellings: Lauren, Lorin,
  Loran (see also Lorne)
Lorenzo (loh-REN-zoh [SP])
Lowell (LOH-well)
Lucien (LOO-shen, loo-see-YEN [FR])
  Alternate spellings: Lucian
Lyman (LY-men)
Lyndon (LIN-den)

MacKenzie (muh-KEN-zee, mak-KEN-zee)
Maddox (MAD-eks)
  Alternate spelling: Mattox
Magnus (MAG-nes)
Mahlon (MAY-len, MAW-len)
Manuel (man-WELL [SP])
Marcel (mar-SELL [FR])
Marcelino (mar-say-LEE-noh or
  mar-thay-LEE-noh [SP],
  mar-chell-LEE-noh [IT])
  Alternate spellings: Marcellino [IT]
Marcellus (mar-SELL-us)
Marcelo (mar-SAY-yoh or mar-THAY-oh
  [SP], mar-CHELL-oh [IT])
  Alternate spellings: Marcello [IT]
Marion (MAIR-ree-yen)
Marlon (MAR-len)

Alternate spellings: Marlin, Marlyn
Marquez (MAR-kez or mar-KEZ,
  MAR-kess [SP])
  Alternate spellings: Márquez
Mason (MAY-sen)
Mekhi (mek-KY [AA])
Mel (MEL)
Melton (MEL-tun)
Melville (MEL-vill)
Melvin (MEL-vin [CG])
  Alternate spellings: Melvyn
Michael (MY-kel, mee-chy-ELL with
  guttural CH [HEB], mee-SHELL [FR])
  Alternate spellings: Micheal, Mikel,
  Michel, Michale, Michel [FR]
Miguel (mee-GEL [SP], mee-GWEL [AA])
Mikhail (mee-KHYL [RUS], MEE-ky-yell,
  mik-KAY-yell)
Milton (MIL-ten)
Misael (mee-SY-yell or mee-THY-yell [SP])
Modesto (moh-DESS-toh or
  moh-DETH-toh [SP])
Mohamed (moh-hawm-MUD or
  mo-HAM-med [AR])
  Alternate spellings: Mohammad,
  Mohammed, Muhammad
Moises (MOI-zess [HEB], moi-SES [SP])
Morgan (MOR-gen)
Moses (MOH-zess [HEB])
Myron (MY-ren)

Nathaniel (nuh-THAN-yell,
  naw-tawn-ELL [HEB])
  Alternate spellings: Nathanael,
  Nathanial, Netanel [HEB]
Ned (NED)
Neftali (nef-TAW-lee, NAWF-taw-lee [HEB])
  Alternate spellings: Naftali [HEB]
Nehemiah (nee-yuh-MY-yuh,
  neh-CHEM-ee-yuh with guttural CH
  [HEB])
  Alternate spellings: Nechemya or
  Nechemia [HEB]
Nels (NELZ)
Nelson (NEL-sen)
Nestor (NES-tur, NES-tor or NETH-tor [SP])
  Alternate spellings: Néstor [SP]
Newell (NOO-well)
Newman (NOO-men)
Newton (NOO-ten)
Nguyen (nig-GYOO-wen [VI])
Nigel (NY-jell [BR])
Nolan (NOH-len [CG])
  Alternate spellings: Nolen

Norman (NOR-men)
Normand (NOR-mend)
Norton (NOR-ten)

Odell (oh-DELL [AA/SCAN])
Olen (OH-len)
Alternate spellings: Olin, Olan
Oren (OR-ren [HEB/IR])
Alternate spellings: Orin, Orrin

Pedrick (PED-rik)
Pepe (PEP-pay, PAY-pay [SP])
Pernell (pur-NELL)
Peyton (PAY-ten)
Alternate spellings: Payton
Phelan (FAY-len, FWAY-lawn [IR])
Alternate spellings: Faelan, Faolan
Philias (FILL-ee-yes)
Phineas (FIN-ee-yes)
Alternate spellings: Finneas,
Phinnehas
Pietro (pee-YET-roh [IT], pee-YAY-troh)
Preston (PRES-ten)

Quentin (KWIN-ten, KWEN-tun, kwen-TE
with short N [FR])
Alternate spellings: Quenton, Quintin,
Quinten, Quinton
Quest (KWEST)

Radames (RAW-duh-mes [EGY],
RAD-uh-mes or RAD-uh-may [SP])
Rafael (RAF-ee-yell, raf-y-YELL,
rrraf-uh-YELL [FR], raw-faw-ELL [HEB/SP],
rrraw-FAY-yell [SP])
Alternate spellings: Raphael, Raphaël
Randall (RAN-dell)
Alternate spellings: Randal, Randell,
Randle
Reagan (RAY-gen, REE-gen)
Refugio (ref-FOO-hee-yoh [SP])
Reggie (REJ-ee)
Reginal (REJ-in-ul)
Reginald (REJ-in-uld [GER])
Remington (REM-eeng-ten)
Rémy (REM-ee, ray-MEE [FR])
Alternate spellings: Rémi
René (ren-NAY [FR])
Rex (REKS)
Rexford (REKS-furd, REKS-ford)
Reyes (RAY-yes, RRRAY-yes [SP])
Reynaud (rrren-NO [FR])
Reynold (REN-uld)
Rhett (RET [WL])

Riordan (REER-den, ROR-den,
ree-YOR-den [IR])
Roman (ROH-men)
Ronan (ROH-nen, ROH-nawn [IR])
Roosevelt (ROH-zuh-velt, ROOS-uh-velt)
Alternate spellings: Rosevelt
Rosendo (roh-ZEN-doh or
roh-THEN-doh [SP])
Roswell (RAWZ-well)
Rowan (ROH-wen)
Royal (ROI-yell)
Ruben (ROO-ben, ROO-ven or roo-
VAYN [HEB], roo-BEN or roo-VEN [SP])
Alternate spellings: Reuben, Rubin,
Rueben, Reuven or Ruvane [HEB],
Rubén [SP]
Russell (RUS-sell)
Alternate spellings: Russel
Ryan (RY-yen)
Rylan (RY-len)
Ryland (RY-lend)

Samuel (SAM-yoo-well, SAM-yool,
SHMOO-well [HEB], sam-WELL [IT/SP])
Alternate spellings: Shmuel [HEB]
Satchel (SACH-ell)
Sebastian (sub-BAS-chen,
sub-BAS-tee-yen, say-bas-tee-YAW
with short N [FR], say-baws-TAWN or
thay-vaws-TAWN [SP])
Alternate spellings: Sabastian,
Sebastien, Sébastien [FR], Sebastián [SP]
Selby (SELL-bee)
Selmer (SEL-mur [SCAN])
Seth (SETH, SHET [HEB])
Alternate spellings: Shet [HEB]
Shannon (SHAN-nen)
Alternate spellings: Shanon
Shelby (SHELL-bee)
Sheldon (SHELL-den)
Alternate spellings: Shelton
Silas (SY-less)
Soren (SOR-ren [SCAN])
Spencer (SPEN-sur)
Alternate spellings: Spenser
Stanton (STAN-ten)
Stefan (stef-FAWN [GER/FR])
Alternate spellings: Stephan, Stephon
Stetson (STET-sen)
Steven (STEE-ven)
Alternate spellings: Stephen,
Stephan, Stephon, Stevan
Sullivan (SUL-liv-en [CG])
Sven (SVEN [SCAN])

Syed (sy-YEED or SAY-yed [AR/AA], SY-yed
    [EI]; see also Zaid)
    Alternate spellings: Saeed, Said
Sylvan (SIL-ven)
Sylvester (sil-VES-tur)

Talmadge (TAL-mej)
Ted (TED)
Teddy (TED-ee)
Telly (TEL-ee)
Terrell (tuh-RELL [AA], TAIR-rill)
    Alternate spellings: Terrill
Terrence (TAIR-rens)
    Alternate spellings: Terrance, Terence
Tevin (TEV-in or TAY-vun)
    Alternate spellings: Tavon*
Thornton (THORN-ten)
Thurman (THUR-men)
Thurston (THURS-ten [SCAN])
Tillman (TIL-men)
Tobias (toh-BY-yes, toh-VY-yes or
    toh-VY-yuh [HEB])
    Alternate spellings: Toviya [HEB]
Torrance (TOR-rens)
Trek (TREK)
Trent (TRENT [GER])
Trenton (TREN-ten)
Trevon (TRAY-vun [AA], TREV-in)
    Alternate spellings: Travon, Trevin,
    Treven
Trevor (TREV-ur [CG])
    Alternate spellings: Trever
Treyton (TRAY-ten [AA])
Tristan (TRIS-ten [WL], trees-TAW with
    short N [FR], trees-TAWN or
    treeth-TAWN [SP])
    Alternate spellings: Tristen, Triston,
    Tristin, Trystan, Tristán [SP]
Tristian (TRIS-chen)
Truman (TROO-men [GER])
Tyrell (ty-RELL [AA])
    Alternate spellings: Tyrel
Tyson (TY-sen [AA])

Urban (UR-ben)
Uriel (YUR-ree-yell [HEB])

Valentin (val-en-TEEN [SP])
Valentine (VAL-en-tyn, vaw-lawn-TEEN
    [FR])
Vernell (VUR-null, vur-NELL)
Vester (VES-tur [GER])
Vicente (vee-SEN-tay or bee-THEN-tay
    [SP])

Vincent (VIN-sent, veh-SAW with short
    Ns [FR])
Vincenzo (vin-CHEN-zoh [IT])
Vinson (VIN-sen)

Walton (WALL-ten)
Wardell (wor-DELL)
Watson (WAHT-sen)
Webster (WEB-stur)
Weldon (WELL-den)
Wellington (WELL-eeng-ten)
Welton (WELL-ten)
Wendell (WEN-dull)
    Alternate spellings: Windell
Wes (WES)
Wesley (WES-lee)
    Alternate spellings: Westley
Weston (WES-ten)
Wilfred (WIL-fred)
Wilhelm (WIL-helm, VIL-helm [GER])
Wilson (WIL-sen)
Wilton (WIL-ten)
Winfred (WIN-fred [CG])
Winston (WIN-sten)
Winton (WIN-ten)
Wyatt (WY-yet)
Wyman (WY-men)

Yadiel (yaw-dee-YELL [SP])
Yarden (YAR-den [HEB])
    Alternate spellings: Jordan*, Jordon,
    Jorden
Ye (EE-yeh [CH])
Yosef (YO-sef or yo-SEF [HEB])

Zechariah (zek-kur-RY-uh,
    zuh-CHAR-ree-uh with guttural CH
    [HEB], zuk-uh-REE-yuh [AR])
    Alternate spellings: Zecharya [HEB]

■ LONG I (EYE OR Y) ■

Brian (BRY-yen [CG], BREE-yen [IR])
    Alternate spellings: Bryan, Brayan [SP],
    Bryon, Brien
Bryant (BRY-yent [CG])
Bryce (BRYS)
    Alternate spellings: Brice
Bryson (BRY-sen)
    Alternate spellings: Brycen
Byron (BY-ren)

Cael (KYL, KAYL [CG/HEB])

Alternate spellings: Cale*, Kale*, Kael
Carlyle (KAR-lyl)
Chaim (CHY-yem with guttural CH [HEB])
  Alternate spellings: Chayim
Clyde (KLYD [CG])
Cypress (SY-pris)
Cyrus (SY-russ, see-ROOS [PER])

Diamond (DY-mund [AA])

Efrain (eff-raw-EEN or EEF-rawn [HEB],
  EFF-ren [AA], eff-RA with short N [FR],
  eff-raw-EEN [SP], EE-fren or ef-RYN;
  see also Ephraim)
  Alternate spellings: Efrain [SP], Efren,
  Efron [HEB], Ephron
Eli (EE-ly or ELL-ee [HEB])
  Alternate spellings: Elly
Elian (EE-lee-yawn [SP])
Elias (EE-lee-yaws [HEB], el-LEE-yaws or
  eh-LEE-yes [SP], ee-LY-yes)
Eliezer (el-lee-YEZ-ur [HEB/AA], el-LEE-zur,
  el-LY-zur, el-lee-ZAIR or el-lee-THAIR
  [SP])
Elijah (el-LY-zhuh or uh-LY-juh [AA],
  el-lee-YAW-hoo [HEB])
  Alternate spellings: Alijah, Eliyahu [HEB]
Elisha (uh-LISH-uh or el-LY-shuh [AA],
  el-LEE-shuh [HEB])
Ephraim (eff-RYM or ef-ry-EEM [HEB],
  ef-ry-YEEM or EFF-rem [AA])
  Alternate spellings: Efrayim [HEB],
  Efraim, Efrem (see also Efrain)
Ezekiel (ee-ZEE-kee-yell [AA], yeh-CHEZ-kel
  with guttural CH [HEB], ess-ay-KYL/
  eth-ay-KYL or ess-sy-KEEL/
  eth-y-KEEL [SP])
  Alternate spellings: Ezequiel,
  Yechezkel [HEB]

Gaetano (gy-TAW-noh [IT], gy-TAWN [FR])
  Alternate spellings: Gaetane [FR]
Giles (JYLZ, ZHEEL [FR])
  Alternate spellings: Gilles [FR]
Guy (GY, GEE [FR])

Hezekiah (hez-uh-KY-yuh,
  chiz-kee-YAW-hoo with guttural ch
  [HEB])
  Alternate spellings: Chizkiyahu [HEB]
Hiram (HY-rem)
Hyman (HY-men)

Ian (EE-yen, EYE-yen [BR])

Alternate spellings: Ean, Iain, Ion
Ike (EYEK)
Ira (EYE-ruh [HEB])
Isaac (EYE-zek, EET-zawk [HEB], is-HAWK
  [AR])
  Alternate spellings: Issac, Isaak,
  Yitzchak [HEB]
Isai (EE-sy or ee-sy-YEE [BIB], ee-SHY [HEB])
  Alternate spellings: Yishai (see also
  Jesse)
Isaiah (eye-ZAY-yuh, is-shy-YAW or
  is-shy-YAW-hoo [HEB])
  Alternate spellings: Isiah, Izaiah,
  Yeshaya or Yeshayahu [HEB]
Isaias (eye-ZAY-yes)
Ishmael (ISH-mayl, eesh-my-ELL [HEB],
  iss-maw-EEL [AR])
  Alternate spellings: Yishmael [HEB]
Itai (EE-ty [HEB])
  Alternate spellings: Ittai
Ivan (EYE-ven, ee-VAWN or ee-BAWN
  [SP])
Ivory (EYE-vor-ree)

Jaime (JAY-mee, HY-may [SP])
  Alternate spellings: Jayme
Jair (JAY-yur [BIB], JAIR, yaw-EER or
  YAW-eer [HEB])
  Alternate spellings: Jere*, Yair [HEB],
  Yahir*
Jairo (HY-yeh-roh or HY-roh [SP])
Jedidiah (jed-did-DY-yuh,
  yed-DEED-yaw [HEB])
  Alternate spellings: Jedediah,
  Jedidia, Yedidya [HEB]
Jeremiah (jair-ruh-MY-yuh,
  yeer-mee-YAW-hoo [HEB])
  Alternate spellings: Yirmeyahu [HEB]
Josiah (joh-ZY-yuh, yoh-shee-YAW-hoo
  or yoh-SHEE-yuh [HEB])
  Alternate spellings: Yoshiyahu or
  Yoshiya [HEB]

Kai (KY [HW])
Kylan (KY-lin)
Kyle (KYL)
  Alternate spellings: Cael*
Kyler (KY-lur [SCAN])
Kyree (ky-REE [AA])

Levi (LEE-vy or LEV-ee or LEE-vee [HEB])
Lionel (LY-null, lee-yoh-NELL [FR])
Lyle (LYL, LY-yull)
Lyman (LY-men)

Makaio (maw-kaw-YEE-yoh or
    maw-KY-yoh [HW])
Malachi (MAL-uh-ky [IR], maw-law-CHEE
    with guttural CH [HEB])
    Alternate spellings: Malakai, Malachai
Mathias (muh-THY-yes)
Mattias (muh-TY-yes [HEB])
McKyle (mik-KYL [CG])
Mekhi (mek-KY [AA])
Meyer (MAY-ur or may-YEER [HEB], MY-ur)
    Alternate spellings: Meir
Micah (MY-kuh, MEE-chaw with guttural
    CH [HEB])
    Alternate spellings: Micha [HEB]
Michael (MY-kel, mee-chy-ELL with
    guttural CH [HEB], mee-SHELL [FR])
    Alternate spellings: Micheal, Mikel,
    Michel, Michale, Michel [FR]
Mike (MYK)
Mikhail (mee-KYL [RUS], MEE-ky-yell,
    mik-KAY-yell)
Miles (MYLZ, MY-yulz)
    Alternate spellings: Myles
Milo (MY-loh [GER])
Misael (mee-SY-yell or mee-THY-yell [SP])
Mordecai (MOR-dik-ky, mor-duh-CHY
    with guttural CH [HEB])
    Alternate spellings: Mordechai [HEB]
Myron (MY-ren)

Nehemiah (nee-yuh-MY-yuh,
    neh-CHEM-ee-yuh with guttural CH
    [HEB])
    Alternate spellings: Nechemya or
    Nechemia [HEB]
Niles (NYLZ [BRI])

Orion (or-RY-yun [AA])

Price (PRYS)

Rafael (RAF-ee-yell, raf-y-YELL,
    rrraf-uh-YELL [FR], raw-faw-ELL [HEB/SP],
    rrraw-FAY-yell [SP])
    Alternate spellings: Raphael, Raphaël
Riley (RY-lee [IR])
    Alternate spellings: Reilly, Rylee, Ryley
Ryan (RY-yen)
Ryder (RY-dur)
Ryker (RY-kur)
Rylan (RY-len)
Ryland (RY-lend)
Ryne (RYN [GER/IR/WL])

Silas (SY-less)
Simon (SY-mun [GRK], shee-MOHN [HEB],
    see-MAW with short N [FR])
    Alternate spellings: Shimon [HEB]
Skyler (SKY-lur)
    Alternate spellings: Skylar, Schuyler
Syed (sy-YEED or SAY-yed [AR/AA], SY-yed
    [EI]; see also Zaid)
    Alternate spellings: Saeed, Said

Titus (TYD-us)
Tobias (toh-BY-yes, toh-VY-yes or
    toh-VY-yuh [HEB])
    Alternate spellings: Toviya [HEB]
Ty (TY [AA])
Tyler (TY-lur)
    Alternate spellings: Tylor
Tyquan (ty-KWAHN [AA])
Tyree (ty-REE or TY-ree [AA])
Tyrell (ty-RELL [AA])
    Alternate spellings: Tyrel
Tyrese (ty-REES [AA])
Tyrone (ty-ROHN [AA/CG])
    Alternate spellings: Tyron
Tyshawn (TY-shawn or tuh-SHAWN or
    TEE-shawn [AA])
    Alternate spellings: Tshawn
Tyson (TY-sen [AA])

Wiley (WY-lee)
    Alternate spellings: Wylie
Wyatt (WY-yet)
Wylde (WYLD)
Wyman (WY-men)

Zachariah (zak-kur-RY-yuh,
    zuh-CHAR-ree-yuh with guttural CH
    [HEB], zuk-uh-REE-yuh [AR])
    Alternate spellings: Zecharya [HEB]
Zaid (ZAY-yid [AR], ZAYD, zy-YEED;
    see also Syed)
Zaire (zy-YEER [AA])
Zechariah (zek-kur-RY-uh,
    zuh-CHAR-ree-uh with guttural CH
    [HEB], zuk-uh-REE-yuh [AR])
    Alternate spellings: Zecharya [HEB]
Zion (ZY-yun [AA], tsee-YOHN [HEB])
    Alternate spellings: Tziyon

■ SHORT I (I) ■

PARTNER POINTER:
Short E, I, and U often
sound similar.

Abraham (AYB-ri-ham, awv-ruh-HAWM
  [HEB])
  Alternate spellings: Avraham [HEB]
Addison (ADD-is-sin)
Aditya (aw-DIT-yuh or aw-THIT-yuh [EI])
Adonis (uh-DAWN-iss, aw-DOH-nees [SP])
Alastair (AL-iss-tur [BR])
  Alternate spellings: Alistair, Allistair
Albin (AL-bin)
Alexis (uh-LEK-sis, aw-LEK-see or
  al-ek-SEES [FR])
Aloysius (al-oh-WISH-us)
Alvin (AL-vin [GER])
Alvis (AL-viss)
Anibal (ANN-nib-bull [GRK], aw-noo-BAWL
  [EI], AW-nee-bawl [IT], aw-NEE-bawl [SP])
Arden (AR-din)
Arlen (AR-lin [CG])
  Alternate spellings: Arlin, Arlan
Arlis (AR-lis)
Artis (ART-iss)
Arvid (AR-vid)
Arvil (AR-vil
  Alternate spellings: Arvel
Arvin (AR-vin [GER])
Atticus (AT-ik-us)
Austin (AWS-tin)
  Alternate spellings: Austyn, Austen

Basil (BAY-zill, BAZ-ill [BR])
Benedict (BEN-uh-dikt)
Benjamin (BEN-juh-min, bin-yaw-MEEN
  [HEB], ben-zhaw-ME with short N [FR]
  ben-haw-MEEN or ven-haw-MEEN [SP])
  Alternate spellings: Binyamin [HEB],
  Benjamín [SP]
Benton (BEN-tin)
Beryl (BAIR-rill [GRK/HEB])
  Alternate spellings: Beril
Bill (BILL)
Billy (BILL-ee [GER])
  Alternate spellings: Billie
Bishop (BISH-up)
Bixby (BIKS-bee)
Boris (BOR-riss)
Brandon (BRAN-din [CG])
  Alternate spellings: Branden,
  Brandyn, Brandan

Brannon (BRAN-in)
Brendan (BREN-din)
  Alternate spellings: Brenden,
  Brendon
Bridger (BRID-jur)
Britt (BRIT)
Broderick (BRAW-dur-rik [CG])
Bronson (BRAWN-sin)

Calvin (KAL-vin)
  Alternate spellings: Kalvin
Camden (KAM-din [CG])
Cassidy (KAS-sid-ee)
Cecil (SEE-sill, SESS-ill)
Cedric (SED-rik, SEED-rik)
  Alternate spellings: Cedrick, Sedrick
Chadrick (CHAD-rik)
Chadwick (CHAD-wik)
Chip (CHIP)
Chris (KRIS)
  Alternate spellings: Kris
Christian (KRIS-chen, KREE-stee-yawn
  or KREETH-tee-yawn [IT/SP],
  kree-stee-YAW with short N [FR])
  Alternate spellings: Cristian, Kristian
Christophe (KRIS-tawf)
  Alternate spellings: Christoff
Christopher (KRIS-toh-fur)
  Alternate spellings: Kristopher,
  Cristopher, Kristofer, Kristoffer,
  Cristofer
Cicero (SIS-ur-roh)
Clemens (KLEM-inz)
Cletus (KLEE-tis)
Cliff (KLIF)
Clifford (KLIF-urd)
Clifton (KLIF-ten)
Clint (KLINT)
Clinton (KLIN-ten)
Clovis (KLOH-viss [GER])
Colin (KAW-lin, KOH-lin [IR])
  Alternate spellings: Collin
Corbin (KOR-bin)
  Alternate spellings: Korbin
Crispin (KRIS-pin)
Cullen (KUL-lin [CG])
Curtis (KUR-tis)
  Alternate spellings: Kurtis, Curtiss
Cypress (SY-pris)
Cyril (SEER-ril, see-REEL [FR])
  Alternate spellings: Cyrille [FR]

Dallas (DAL-lis)
Dallin (DAL-lin)

Darren (DAIR-rin [CG])
   Alternate spellings: Darin, Darrin,
   Daron, Daren, Darron, Deron
Darwin (DAR-win)
David (DAY-vid, daw-VEED [HEB],
   dav-EED [FR])
Davis (DAY-vis)
Dedrick (DED-rik [AA])
Delvin (DEL-vin)
Dennis (DEN-iss)
   Alternate spellings: Denis*
Denton (DENT-in)
Denzil (DEN-zill [AA])
Derek (DAIR-rik [GER])
   Alternate spellings: Derrick, Derick,
   Derik, Darrick, Dereck, Deric
Derwin (DUR-win)
Destin (DES-tin)
Devin (DEV-in)
   Alternate spellings: Devon, Deven,
   Devan, Devyn
Dewitt (duh-WIT, DOO-wit)
Dick (DIK [GER])
Dickie (DIK-ee [GER])
Dillard (DILL-urd)
Dillion (DILL-ee-yun, DILL-yen)
Dimitri (dim-MEE-tree [RUS/FR])
   Alternate spellings: Dmitri
Dominic (DAW-min-ik, doh-mee-NEEK [FR])
   Alternate spellings: Dominick,
   Dominik, Doménic, Dominique,
   Domenick
Donovan (DAW-noh-vin [CG])
   Alternate spellings: Donavan
Duncan (DUN-kin [CG])
Dustin (DUS-tin)
Dylan (DIL-len [IR])
   Alternate spellings: Dillon, Dillan, Dylon

Edison (ED-is-sun)
Edwin (ED-win)
Eldred (EL-drid)
Eldridge (EL-drij)
Elgin (EL-jin)
Elisha (uh-LISH-uh or el-LY-shuh [AA],
   el-LEE-shuh [HEB])
Ellis (EL-is)
Elvin (EL-vin [CG])
Elvis (EL-viss [SCAN])
Elwin (EL-win)
   Alternate spellings: Elwyn
Emmett (EM-mit [GER/IR])
   Alternate spellings: Emmitt, Emmet
Ennis (EN-niss [IR])

Epifanio (ep-if-FAW-nee-yoh [SP])
Eric (AIR-rik [SCAN], air-REEK [FR])
   Alternate spellings: Erik, Erick, Erich,
   Aric
Erwin (UR-win)
Ethan (EE-thin, EE-tawn [HEB])
   Alternate spellings: Ethen, Eitan or
   Etan [HEB]
Eujin (YOO-jin [KOR])
Evan (EV-in)
Evans (EV-inz)
Ewan (YOO-win [SCOT])

Finian (FIN-ee-yen [IR])
   Alternate spellings: Finnian
Finley (FIN-lee [CG])
   Alternate spellings: Finlay, Findlay
Finn (FIN [IR])
   Alternate spellings: Fionn, Fynn
Finnegan (FIN-uh-gin [IR])
Fisher (FISH-ur)
Flynn (FLIN)
Francis (FRAN-sis)
   Alternate spellings: Frances
Frederick (FRED-ur-rik [GER],
   fray-day-REEK [FR])
   Alternate spellings: Frederic, Frédéric
   [FR]
Fredrick (FRED-rik [GER])
   Alternate spellings: Fredric
Friedrich (FREED-rik [GER])
Fritz (FRITS [GER])

Galen (GAY-lin [GRK])
   Alternate spellings: Gaylon
Galvin (GAL-vin [CG])
Gannon (GAN-in [CG])
Garrick (GAR-rik [BR], GAIR-rik)
Garrison (GAIR-ris-sen)
Gavin (GAV-in [WL])
   Alternate spellings: Gaven, Gavyn
Gideon (GID-ee-yun, GEED-ohn or
   geed-OHN [HEB])
   Alternate spellings: Gidon [HEB]
Gil (GILL [HEB])
   Alternate spellings: Gill
Gilbert (GIL-burt, zheel-BAIR [FR])
Gilberto (gil-BAIR-toh, hil-BAIR-toh or
   heel-VAIR-toh [SP])
Granville (GRAN-vill)
Griffin (GRIF-fin [WL])
Griffith (GRIF-fith [WL])
Gulliver (GUL-liv-ur)

Hamish (HAY-mish [SCOT])
Harris (HAIR-ris)
Harrison (HAIR-ris-sen)
Hilbert (HILL-burt)
Hillard (HILL-urd)
Hilliard (HILL-yurd)
Hilton (HILL-ten [BR])

Ishmael (ISH-mayl, eesh-my-ELL [HEB],
    iss-maw-EEL [AR])
    Alternate spellings: Yishmael [HEB]
Isidor (IZ-uh-dor [GRK], ee-see-DOR [FR])
    Alternate spellings: Isidore, Isador,
    Isadore
Ismael (IZ-mayl, ees-MAW-yell or
    eeth-MAW-yell [SP])
Israel (IZ-ree-yell, IZ-ray-yell [HEB],
    iss-raw-EEL [AR], eess-RAY-yell or
    eeth-RAY-yell [SP])
    Alternate spellings: Yisrael [HEB]

Jameson (JAY-mis-sun)
    Alternate spellings: Jamison
Jarvis (JAR-viss [GER])
Jedidiah (jed-did-DY-yuh,
    yed-DEED-yaw [HEB])
    Alternate spellings: Jedediah,
    Jedidia, Yedidya [HEB]
Jim (JIM)
Jimmy (JIM-ee)
    Alternate spellings: Jimmie
Joachim (wah-KEEM, JOH-wah-kim,
    zho-wah-SHE with short N [FR],
    yo-WAH-kim [GER], yuh-ho-wuh-KEEM
    or yow-wuh-KEEM [HEB])
    Alternate spellings: Joakim,
    Jehoiakim or Yehoyakim [HEB]
Justice (JUS-tis [AA])
    Alternate spellings: Justus
Justin (JUS-tin, zhoo-STE with short N [FR])
    Alternate spellings: Justyn, Justen,
    Juston

Keenan (KEE-nin [CG])
Kellen (KEL-in [CG])
    Alternate spellings: Kellan
Kelvin (KEL-vin [CG])
Kendrick (KEN-drik)
Kenneth (KEN-ith [CG])
    Alternate spellings: Kennith
Kevin (KEV-in [IR])
    Alternate spellings: Kevon, Keven
Kip (KIP)
Krishna (KRRRISH-nuh [EI])

Lindsey (LIN-zee)
    Alternate spellings: Lindsay
Linwood (LIN-wood)
    Alternate spellings: Lynwood
Louis (LOO-wiss [GER], loo-WEE [FR],
    loo-WEES [SP])
    Alternate spellings: Lewis, Luis [SP]
Lyndon (LIN-den)

Madison (MAD-iss-un)
Marquis (MAR-kwiss or mar-KEEZ or
    mar-KEES [AA], mar-KEE [FR], MAR-kus)
    Alternate spellings: Marquise,
    Marques, Marcus*, Markus
Martin (MAR-tin, mar-TA with short N
    [FR], mar-TEEN [SP])
    Alternate spellings: Martín [SP]
Marvin (MAR-vin)
Maurice (MOR-ris [BR], mor-REES [FR])
    Alternate spellings: Morris
Maverick (MAV-ur-rik)
Maxim (MAK-sim, mak-SEEM [RUS])
    Alternate spellings: Maksim
Maximilian (mak-sim-MIL-yen [GER],
    mak-see-meel-YA with short N [FR])
    Alternate spellings: Maximillian,
    Maximilien [FR]
Maximino (mak-sim-MEE-noh [SP])
Maximus (MAK-sim-us)
McArthur (mik-AR-thur [CG])
McCoy (mik-KOI [CG])
McKinley (mik-KIN-lee [CG])
McKyle (mik-KYL [CG])
Melville (MEL-vill)
Melvin (MEL-vin [CG])
    Alternate spellings: Melvyn
Merlin (MUR-lin [WL])
    Alternate spellings: Merlyn
Merrill (MAIR-rill)
Merritt (MAIR-rit)
Mervin (MUR-vin [WL])
    Alternate spellings: Mervyn
Mickey (MIK-ee)
Mikhail (mee-KHYL [RUS], MEE-ky-yell,
    mik-KAY-yell)
Milburn (MIL-burn)
Milford (MIL-furd)
Millard (MIL-lurd)
Miller (MIL-lur)
Milton (MIL-ten)
Mitch (MICH)
Mitchell (MICH-ull)
    Alternate spellings: Mitchel
Mordecai (MOR-dik-ky, mor-duh-CHY

with guttural CH [HEB])
Alternate spellings: Mordechai [HEB]
Mortimer (MOR-tim-ur)

Narciso (nar-SIS-oh, nar-SEE-soh or
    nar-THEE-thoh [SP], nar-CHEE-soh [IT])
Nathan (NAY-thin, nuh-TAWN [HEB])
    Alternate spellings: Nathen, Natan [HEB]
Nguyen (nig-GYOO-wen [VI])
Nicholas (NIK-ul-us, nee-koh-LAW [FR])
    Alternate spellings: Nicolas, Nickolas,
    Nikolas
Nicholaus (NIK-oh-lows or NICK-lows [GER])
    Alternate spellings: Nickolaus, Nicklaus
Nick (NIK)
Nicky (NIK-ee)
Nikhil (nik-KEEL [EI])
Nils (NILZ [SCAN])
Norris (NOR-ris)

Oliver (AW-liv-ur)
Orville (OR-vill)
    Alternate spellings: Orval, Orvil
Otis (OH-dis)
    Alternate spellings: Odis, Ottis
Owen (OH-win [IR])

Paris (PAIR-riss, pair-RRREE [FR])
Parrish (PAIR-rish)
Patrick (PAT-rik, PAR-rick or PAWD-rig [IR])
    Alternate spellings: Pádraig [IR]
Pedrick (PED-rik)
Percival (PUR-siv-ull [BR])
Phil (FILL)
Philias (FILL-ee-yes)
Phillip (FILL-ip, fee-LEEP [FR])
    Alternate spellings: Philip, Philippe [FR]
Phineas (FIN-ee-yes)
    Alternate spellings: Finneas,
    Phinnehas
Prince (PRINS)

Quentin (KWIN-ten, KWEN-tun, kwen-TE
    with short N [FR])
    Alternate spellings: Quenton, Quintin,
    Quinten, Quinton
Quincy (KWIN-see)
Quinn (KWIN [IR])

Reginal (REJ-in-ul)
Reginald (REJ-in-uld [GER])
Regis (REE-gis, ray-ZHEES [FR])
    Alternate spellings: Régis [FR]
Richard (RICH-urd, rrree-SHAR [FR])

Richie (RICH-ee)
Richmond (RICH-mund)
Ricky (RIK-ee)
    Alternate spellings: Rickey, Rickie, Ricki
Ridge (RIJ)
River (RIV-ur)
Rollin (RAW-lin)

Sheridan (SHAIR-rid-en [CG])
Sherrill (SHAIR-rill)
Sherwin (SHUR-win)
ShinIchi (shin-EE-chee [JAP])
Sid (SID)
Sidney (SID-nee)
    Alternate spellings: Sydney
Sigmund (SIG-mund [GER/SCAN]; see also
    Zigmund)
Sigurd (SIG-urd [SCAN])
Silvio (SIL-vee-yoh [IT/SP], THIL-bee-yoh [SP])
Sim (SIM)
Simeon (SIM-ee-yun [HEB])
Sincere (SIN-seer)
Smith (SMITH)
Sullivan (SUL-liv-en [CG])

Talon (TAL-in)
Tiernan (TEER-nin [CG])
Tillman (TIL-men)
Tim (TIM)
Timmy (TIM-ee)
    Alternate spellings: Timmie
Timothy (TIM-ith-ee, tee-moh-TAY [FR])
    Alternate spellings: Timmothy,
    Timothée [FR]
Tobin (TOH-bin)
Trinidad (TRIN-id-add, tree-nee-DAWD
    [SP])
Trinity (TRIN-it-ee)
Tristan (TRIS-ten [WL], trees-TAW with
    short N [FR], trees-TAWN or
    treeth-TAWN [SP])
    Alternate spellings: Tristen, Triston,
    Tristin, Trystan, Tristán [SP]
Tristian (TRIS-chen)

Ulises (yoo-LISS-seez, oo-LEE-says or
    oo-LEETH-ayth [SP])
    Alternate spellings: Ulysses

Verlin (VUR-lin)
Victor (VIK-tur, veek-TOR [FR], VEEK-tor
    or BEEK-tor [SP])
    Alternate spellings: Víctor [SP], Viktor
Vince (VINS)

Vincent (VIN-sent, veh-SAW with short
   Ns [FR])
Vincenzo (vin-CHEN-zoh [IT])
Vinson (VIN-sen)
Virgil (VUR-jil)
   Alternate spellings: Vergil
Vishnu (VISH-noo [EI])

Wallace (WALL-iss [CG])
Whitney (WIT-nee)
Wilbert (WIL-burt)
Wilbur (WIL-bur, VIL-bur [GER])
Wilburn (WIL-burn, VIL-burn [GER])
Wilford (WIL-furd)
Wilfred (WIL-fred)
Wilfredo (will-FRAY-doh [SP])
Wilfrid (WIL-frid)
Wilhelm (WIL-helm, VIL-helm [GER])
Will (WIL)
Willard (WIL-urd, VIL-urd [GER])
Willem (WIL-um [CG])
William (WIL-yum)
Williams (WIL-yumz)
Willie (WIL-ee)
Willis (WIL-iss)
Willy (WIL-ee)
Wilmer (WIL-mur, VIL-mur [GER])
Wilson (WIL-sen)
Wilton (WIL-ten)
Winfield (WIN-feeld, VIN-feeld [GER])
Winford (WIN-ford)
Winfred (WIN-fred [CG])
Winston (WIN-sten)
Winton (WIN-ten)

Zaid (ZAY-yid [AR], ZAYD, zy-YEED; see
   also Syed)
Zigmund (ZIG-mund; see also Sigmund)

■ LONG O (OH) ■

PARTNER POINTER:
Check the OI and OR lists, too.

Aaron (AIR-en, aw-har-ROHN [HEB],
   ar-ROHN [SP])
   Alternate spellings: Aron, Arron, Erin
   [IR], Aharon [HEB]
Adalberto (aw-dell-BAIR-toh [SP])
Adolfo (aw-DAWL-foh [IT/SP])
Adonis (uh-DAWN-iss, aw-DOH-nees [SP])
Alberto (awl-BAIR-toh [IT/SP])
Aldo (AWL-doh [GER/IT/SP])

Alejandro (aw-leh-HAWN-droh [SP])
Alessandro (aw-leh-SAWN-droh [IT])
Alexandro (al-eks-ZAN-droh,
   al-eks-ZAWN-droh)
Alfonso (al-FAWN-zoh [IT],
   awl-FAWN-soh [SP])
   Alternate spellings: Alphonso, Alfonzo
Alfredo (awl-FRAY-doh [IT/SP], al-FRAY-doh)
Alois (al-LOH-wees [GER])
Alonzo (uh-LAWN-zoh, aw-LOHN-soh [SP])
   Alternate spellings: Alonso
Aloysius (al-oh-WISH-us)
Álvaro (AWL-var-roh or AWL-bar-roh [SP])
Amado (aw-MAW-doh [SP])
Americo (aw-mair-EE-ko or
   aw-MAIR-ee-koh [IT/SP])
Amos (AY-mohs, AW-mohs [HEB])
Anastacio (aw-naw-STAW-see-oh [SP])
Angelo (AN-jell-oh, AWN-jell-oh [IT],
   AWN-hell-oh [SP])
Anselmo (awn-SELL-moh [IT/SP],
   awn-THELL-moh [SP])
Anton (AN-tun [AA], awn-TOHN [FR])
   Alternate spellings: Antone
Antonio (an-TOH-nee-yoh,
   awn-TOH-nee-yoh [IT/SP])
Arcadio (ar-CAW-dee-yoh)
Arlo (AR-loh)
Armando (ar-MAWN-doh [IT/SP])
Arnaldo (ar-NAWL-doh [IT/SP])
   Alternate spellings: Arnoldo*
Arno (AR-noh)
Arnoldo (ar-NOHL-doh [IT/SP],
   ar-NAWL-doh)
   Alternate spellings: Arnaldo*
Arnulfo (ar-NOOL-foh [SP])
Arturo (ar-TOO-roh [IT/SP])
Aurelio (or-REL-ee-yoh [SP])

Beau (BO [FR])
   Alternate spellings: Bo
Benicio (ben-EE-see-yoh or
   ven-EE-thee-yoh [SP])
Bernardo (bur-NAR-doh, bair-NAR-doh
   or vair-NAR-doh [SP])
Bienvenido (bee-yen-ben-EE-doh or
   vee-yen-ven-EE-doh [SP])
Braulio (BROH-lee-yoh, BROW-lee-yoh
   or VROW-lee-yoh [SP])
Brody (BROH-dee [CG])
   Alternate spellings: Brodie
Bruno (BROO-noh [GER/IT])

Calloway (KAL-oh-way)

Candelario (kan-dell-AR-ree-oh [SP])
Candido (KAWN-dee-doh or
    kan-DEE-doh [SP])
Carlo (KAR-loh [IT])
Carlos (KAR-lohs [SP])
Carmelo (kar-MEL-oh [IT/SP])
Celestino (sell-less-TEEN-oh or
    thell-leth-TEEN-oh [SP])
Cicero (SIS-ur-roh)
Claude (KLAWD, KLOHD [FR])
    Alternate spellings: Claud
Claudie (KLAW-dee, kloh-DEE [FR])
Claudio (KLAW-dee-yoh, KLOW-dee-yoh
    [IT/SP])
Cleo (KLEE-yoh, KLAY-oh [FR])
    Alternate spellings: Cléo
Clover (KLOH-vur)
Clovis (KLOH-viss [GER])
Cody (KOH-dee)
    Alternate spellings: Kody, Coty,
    Codey, Codie
Colby (KOHL-bee)
    Alternate spellings: Kolby
Cole (KOHL [CG])
    Alternate spellings: Kole
Coleman (KOHL-men [IR])
    Alternate spellings: Colman
Colin (KAW-lin, KOH-lin [IR])
    Alternate spellings: Collin
Colt (KOHLT)
Colton (KOHL-ten)
    Alternate spellings: Colten, Kolton
Columbus (koh-LUM-bus)
Cosmo (KOZ-moh)
Cristobal (kree-STOH-bawl or
    kreeth-TOH-vawl or
    kree-stoh-VAWL [SP])

Dakota (duh-KOH-tuh)
    Alternate spellings: Dakotah
Dangelo (DAN-jell-oh [AA])
Dario (DAR-ree-yoh, dar-REE-yoh [IT/SP])
Davion (DAY-vee-yohn or day-vee-YOHN
    [AA])
Deangelo (dee-YAN-jell-oh [AA/IT])
Delano (DEL-en-oh [CG])
Demarco (duh-MAR-koh)
Demario (duh-MAR-ree-yoh [AA])
Demetrios (duh-MEE-tree-yohs [GRK])
Dezso (DEZH-oh [HUN])
Diego (dee-YAY-goh [SP])
Dino (DEE-noh [IT])
Dionisio (dee-yoh-NEE-see-yoh or
    dee-yoh-NEE-thee-yoh [SP])

Django (JAYN-goh)
Domenico (doh-MEN-ee-koh [IT])
Domingo (doh-MEEN-goh [SP])
Donato (doh-NAW-toh [IT])
Donnell (DAW-nell, DOH-null [IR])
    Alternate spellings: Donal, Donell
Donovan (DAW-noh-vin [CG])
    Alternate spellings: Donavan

Edgardo (ed-GAR-doh [IT/SP])
Eduardo (ed-WAR-doh [IT/SP])
    Alternate spellings: Edwardo
Eino (AY-noh [SCAN])
Eladio (el-LAW-dee-yoh or
    ee-LAW-dee-yoh or EL-lawd-yoh [SP])
Eliseo (el-LEE-see-yoh, el-lee-ZAY-yoh [IT],
    el-lee-SAY-yoh [IT/SP], el-lee-THAY-yoh
    [SP])
Elmo (EL-moh)
Emiliano (em-eel-YAW-noh [SP])
Emilio (em-MEE-lee-yoh [SP])
Enrico (en-REE-koh [IT])
Enzo (EN-zoh [IT])
Epifanio (epp-if-FAW-nee-yoh [SP])
Erasmo (eh-RAWS-moh or
    ee-RAWS-moh [SP])
Ernesto (air-NES-toh [IT/SP], air-NETH-toh
    [SP])
Eugenio (ay-yoo-HEN-ee-yoh [SP])
Eusebio (ay-yoo-SEB-ee-yoh or ay-yoo-
    THEV-ee-yoh [SP])

Faustino (fow-STEEN-oh or fowth-
    TEEN-oh [SP])
Federico (fed-air-EE-ko [IT])
Fernando (fur-NAN-doh, fair-NAWN-doh
    [SP])
Florencio (flor-REN-see-yoh or
    flor-REN-thee-yoh [SP])
Florentino (flor-ren-TEE-noh [IT])
Fortunato (for-too-NAW-toh [IT/SP])
Francesco (fran-CHESS-koh [IT])
Francisco (fran-SEES-koh or
    fran-THEETH-koh [SP])

Gaetano (gy-TAW-noh [IT], gy-TAWN [FR])
    Alternate spellings: Gaetane [FR]
Gaston (GASS-tun [CG], gas-TOHN or
    gas-TAW with short N [FR])
Genaro (jen-NAR-roh [IT], hen-NAR-roh [SP])
    Alternate spellings: Gennaro
Geo (JEE-yoh)
Geraldo (hair-RAWL-doh [SP])
Gerardo (hair-RAR-doh [SP])

Giancarlo (jawn-KAR-lo [IT])

Gideon (GID-ee-yun, GEED-ohn or geed-OHN [HEB])
Alternate spellings: Gidon [HEB]

Gilberto (gil-BAIR-toh, hil-BAIR-toh or heel-VAIR-toh [SP])

Gino (JEE-noh [IT])

Giovanni (jee-yoh-VAW-nee or joh-VAW-nee [AA/IT])
Alternate spellings: Giovanny, Giovani, Jovani, Jovany, Jovanny, Jovanni

Golden (GOHL-den)

Gonzalo (gun-ZAW-loh, gohn-SAW-loh or gohn-THAW-loh [SP])

Gregorio (greg-OR-ree-oh [SP])

Grover (GROH-vur)

Guido (GWEE-doh [IT])

Guillermo (gee-YAIR-moh or YAIR-moh [SP])

Gustavo (goo-STAW-voh [IT/SP], gooth-TAW-boh [SP])

Heriberto (air-ree-BAIR-toh or air-ree-VAIR-toh [SP])

Herminio (air-MEE-nee-oh [SP])

Hidero (hee-DAIR-roh [JAP])

Hilario (ee-LAR-ree-yoh [SP])

Hilbert (HILL-burt)

Hipólito (ee-POH-lee-toh [SP])

Hobart (HO-bart)

Hobert (HO-burt)

Holden (HOHL-den)

Homer (HO-mur)

Hosea (ho-ZAY-yuh, ho-SHEE-yuh [HEB])
Alternate spellings: Hosheia

Hugo (HYOO-goh [GER], oo-GOH [SP])

Humberto (oom-BAIR-toh or oom-VAIR-toh [SP])

Ignacio (eeg-NAW-see-yoh or eeg-NAW-thee-yoh [SP])

Isidro (ee-SEE-droh or ee-THEE-droh [SP])

Jacinto (haw-SEEN-toh or haw-THEEN-toh [SP])

Jacob (JAY-kub, YAW-kohv [HEB], yaw-KOOB [AR])
Alternate spellings: Jakob, Yakov* or Yaakov [HEB], Yakoub* [AR]

Jacoby (juh-KOH-bee, JAY-kub-ee)
Alternate spellings: Jakobe, Jacobi

Jairo (HY-yeh-roh or HY-roh [SP])

Jarom (JAIR-rum, yar-ROHM [HEB])

Alternate spellings: Yarom [HEB]

Jaron (JAIR-ren, yar-ROHN [HEB])
Alternate spellings: Jaren, Yaron [HEB]

Jerome (jur-ROHM [AA], zhay-ROHM [FR])
Alternate spellings: Jérôme [FR]

Joachim (wah-KEEM, JOH-wah-kim, zho-wah-SHE with short N [FR], yo-WAH-kim [GER], yuh-ho-wuh-KEEM or yow-wuh-KEEM [HEB])
Alternate spellings: Joakim, Jehoiakim or Yehoyakim [HEB]

Joaquin (wah-KEEN, ho-wah-KEEN [SP], yuh-ho-wuh-CHEEN or yow-wuh-CHEEN with guttural CH [HEB])
Alternate spellings: Joaquin [SP], Jehoiachin or Yehoyachin [HEB]

Jody (JOH-dee)
Alternate spellings: Jodie

Joe (JOH)

Joel (JOHL, JOH-well, yoh-ELL [HEB], zho-WELL [FR])
Alternate spellings: Joël [FR], Yoel [HEB]

Joey (JOH-wee)

Johan (YOH-hawn [GER/SCAN])
Alternate spellings: Johann

Jomar (joh-MAR [BIB], juh-MAR [AA], OH-mar)
Alternate spellings: Omar*

Jonah (JOH-nuh, YOH-nuh [HEB])
Alternate spellings: Jona, Yona or Yonah [HEB]

Jonas (JOH-ness [GRK])

Jonathan (JAW-nuh-thin, yoh-nuh-TAWN [HEB])
Alternate spellings: Johnathan, Jonathon, Johnathon, Jonatan, Yonatan [HEB]

Jose (ho-ZAY, YO-see [HEB], ho-SAY or ho-THAY [SP])
Alternate spellings: José [SP]

Joseph (JOH-sef, YOH-sef or yoh-SEF [HEB], YOO-suf [AR], zho-ZEF [FR])
Alternate spellings: Josef, Yosef*, Yusuf*

Joshua (JAW-shoo-wuh, yuh-ho-SHOO-wuh [HEB])
Alternate spellings: Joshuah, Yehoshua [HEB]

Josiah (joh-ZY-yuh, yoh-shee-YAW-hoo or yoh-SHEE-yuh [HEB])
Alternate spellings: Yoshiyahu or Yoshiya [HEB]

Josué (ho-soo-WAY or ho-thoo-WAY [SP])

Jovan (joh-VAN or joh-VAWN [AA])
Julio (HOO-lee-yoh [SP])
Justo (HOOS-toh or HOOTH-toh [SP])

Kazuo (KAW-zoo-woh [JAP])
Kerouac (KAIR-roh-wak)
Kobe (KOH-bee [AA/HEB])
    Alternate spellings: Coby, Koby

Laszlo (LAZ-loh [HUN])
Lazaro (LAZ-uh-roh or luh-ZAR-oh [AA],
    law-ZAR-roh [IT])
Leo (LEE-yoh)
Leon (LEE-yawn [GER], lay-YAW with short
    N [FR], lay-YOHN [SP])
    Alternate spellings: Léon [FR], León [SP]
Leonard (LEN-urd [GER], lay-yoh-NAR [FR])
    Alternate spellings: Lenard, Léonard [FR]
Leonardo (lee-yoh-NAR-doh,
    lay-yoh-NAR-doh [SP])
Léonel (lay-yoh-NELL [FR])
Leopold (LEE-yup-old [GER],
    lay-yoh-POHLD [FR])
    Alternate spellings: Léopold [FR]
Leopoldo (lay-yoh-POHL-doh [IT/SP])
Lionel (LY-null, lee-yoh-NELL [FR])
Lisandro (lee-SAWN-droh [SP])
Loden (LOH-den)
Logan (LOH-gen)
Lonzo (LAWN-zoh [IT])
Lorenzo (loh-REN-zoh [SP])
Luciano (loo-CHAW-noh [IT],
    loo-see-YAWN-oh or
    loo-thee-YAWN-oh [SP])

Makaio (maw-kaw-YEE-yoh or
    maw-KY-yoh [HW])
Marcelino (mar-say-LEE-noh or
    mar-thay-LEE-noh [SP],
    mar-chell-LEE-noh [IT])
    Alternate spellings: Marcellino [IT]
Marcelo (mar-SAY-yoh or mar-THAY-oh
    [SP], mar-CHELL-oh [IT])
    Alternate spellings: Marcello [IT]
Marco (MAR-koh [IT/SP])
Marcos (MAR-kohs [SP])
Margarito (mar-gar-REE-toh [SP])
Mariano (mar-ree-YAWN-oh [IT])
Mario (MAR-ree-yoh [IT/SP])
Mateo (muh-TAY-yoh [SP])
    Alternate spellings: Matteo [IT]
Mauricio (mor-REE-see-yoh,
    mow-REE-see-yoh or
    mow-REE-thee-yoh [SP],

mow-REET-zee-yoh)
    Alternate spellings: Mauritzio [IT]
Maximino (mak-sim-MEE-noh [SP])
Maximo (mak-SEE-moh [SP])
Milo (MY-loh [GER])
Modesto (moh-DESS-toh or
    moh-DETH-toh [SP])
Moe (MOH)
Mohamed (moh-hawm-MUD or
    mo-HAM-med [AR])
    Alternate spellings: Mohammad,
    Mohammed, Muhammad
Monroe (mun-ROH [AA])
Monserrate (mohn-sair-RAWT [IT])
    Alternate spellings: Montserrat
Moses (MOH-zess [HEB])
Moshe (MOH-shuh or MOISH-uh [HEB])
    Alternate spellings: Mose, Moeshe

Napoleon (nuh-POH-lee-yen)
Narciso (nar-SIS-oh, nar-SEE-soh or
    nar-THEE-thoh [SP], nar-CHEE-soh [IT])
Nicholas (NIK-ul-us, nee-koh-LAW [FR])
    Alternate spellings: Nicolas, Nickolas,
    Nikolas
Nicholaus (NIK-oh-lows or NICK-lows [GER])
    Alternate spellings: Nickolaus, Nicklaus
Nico (NEE-koh [IT])
    Alternate spellings: Niko
Noah (NOH-wuh, NOH-wach with guttural
    CH [HEB], NOH with pronounced H [AR])
    Alternate spellings: Noach [HEB]
Noble (NOH-bull)
Noé (noh-WAY [FR], NOH-wee)
Nolan (NOH-len [CG])
    Alternate spellings: Nolen
Norberto (nor-BAIR-toh [IT/SP],
    nor-VAIR-toh [SP])
Nunzio (NOON-zee-yoh [IT])

Oakley (OHK-lee)
Obie (OH-bee [AA])
    Alternate spellings: Obi
Octavio (awk-TAW-vee-yoh or
    ohk-TAW-bee-yoh [SP])
Odell (oh-DELL [AA/SCAN])
Odie (OH-dee)
Okey (OH-kee)
Olaf (OH-lawf [SCAN])
Olen (OH-len)
    Alternate spellings: Olin, Olan
Omar (OH-mar or UM-ar [AR])
    Alternate spellings: Jomar*
Omari (oh-MAR-ree [AA])

Omarion (oh-MAR-ree-yawn or
uh-MAR-ree-yawn [AA])
Alternate spellings: Amarion
Omer (um-AIR or oh-MAIR [AR])
O'Neal (oh-NEEL)
Orlando (or-LAN-doh [AA], or-LAWN-doh
[SP])
Orlo (OR-loh)
Oswaldo (aws-VAWL-doh [IT/SP],
awth-BAWL-doh [SP])
Alternate spellings: Osvaldo, Osbaldo
Otis (OH-dis)
Alternate spellings: Odis, Ottis
Otto (AW-doh [GER])
Alternate spellings: Otho
Owen (OH-win [IR])

Pablo (PAW-bloh or PAWV-loh [SP])
Patricio (paw-TREE-see-yoh or
paw-TREE-thee-yoh [SP])
Patrizio (paw-TREET-zee-yoh [IT])
Pedro (PAYD-roh [SP])
Pietro (pee-YET-roh [IT], pee-YAY-troh)
Porfirio (por-FEER-ree-yoh [SP])
Primitivo (pree-MEE-tee-voh [SP])

Ramiro (rrraw-MEER-roh [SP])
Ramon (rrraw-MOHN [SP])
Raymundo (rrray-MOON-doh [SP])
Refugio (ref-FOO-hee-yoh [SP])
Reno (REE-noh)
Reynaldo (rrray-NAWL-doh [SP])
Alternate spellings: Reinaldo
Reynaud (rrren-NO [FR])
Ricárdo (rrrree-KAR-doh [SP])
Rico (REE-koh [IT/SP])
Rigoberto (ree-goh-BAIR-toh [SP])
Ringo (REEN-goh [JAP])
Rio (REE-yoh [SP])
Roberto (rrroh-BAIR-toh [SP], roh-BUR-toh)
Rocco (RAW-koh [IT])
Rodolfo (rrroh-DOHL-foh [IT/SP])
Rodrigo (rrroh-DREE-goh [IT/SP])
Roel (ROHL, ROH-well, RHOOL [SCAN])
Rogelio (rrroh-HELL-ee-yoh [SP])
Roger (RAW-jur [GER], rrroh-ZHAIR or
rrroh-ZHAY [FR])
Alternate spellings: Rodger
Rohan (ROH-han, rrroh-HAWN [EI])
Roland (ROH-lend [GER], rrroh-LAW with
short N [FR])
Alternate spellings: Rowland
Rolando (roh-LAN-doh, rrroh-LAWN-doh
[SP])

Rollo (RAW-loh)
Roman (ROH-men)
Romeo (ROH-mee-yoh,
rrroh-MAY-yoh [SP])
Ronaldo (rrroh-NAWL-doh [SP])
Ronan (ROH-nen, ROH-nawn [IR])
Roosevelt (ROH-zuh-velt, ROOS-uh-velt)
Alternate spellings: Rosevelt
Rosario (rrroh-SAR-ree-yoh or
rrroh-THAR-ree-yoh [SP])
Roscoe (RAW-skoh [SCAN])
Rosendo (roh-ZEN-doh or
roh-THEN-doh [SP])
Roshan (RRROH-shun [EI])
Rowan (ROH-wen)
Rudolph (ROO-dawlf, ROH-dawlf [GER],
roh-DAWLF [FR])
Alternate spellings: Rudolf, Rodolf
[GER], Rodolphe [FR]

Samson (SAM-sun, sheem-SHOHN [HEB])
Alternate spellings: Shimshon [HEB]
Sancho (SAWN-choh [SP])
Sandro (SAWND-roh [IT])
Santiago (sawn-tee-YAW-goh or
thawn-tee-YAW-goh [SP])
Santino (san-TEE-noh [IT])
Santo (SAWN-toh [IT])
Santos (SAWN-tohs [SP])
Sergio (SUR-jee-yoh, SAIR-jee-yoh or
SAIR-joh [IT], SAIR-hee-yoh or
THAIR-hee-yoh [SP])
Silvio (SIL-vee-yoh [IT/SP], THIL-bee-yoh [SP])
Sixto (SEEKS-toh [SP])
Sol (SOHL or THOHL [SP], SAWL)
Alternate spellings: Saul*
Solomon (SAW-loh-mun, SHLO-moh [HEB])
Alternate spellings: Shlomo [HEB]
Solon (SOH-lun [GRK])
Stone (STOHN)
Stoney (STOH-nee)

Teodoro (tay-yoh-DOR-roh [IT/SP])
Theo (THEE-yoh, TAY-yoh [FR])
Alternate spellings: Théo [FR]
Theodore (THEE-yuh-dor, tay-yoh-DOR
[FR])
Alternate spellings: Theadore,
Theodor, Théodore [FR]
Theron (THAIR-run [AA], TAIR-ren,
thair-ROHN)
Thomas (TAW-muss, TOH-maws [GER],
toh-MAW [FR], toh-MAWS [IR/SP])
Alternate spellings: Tomás

Timothy (TIM-ith-ee, tee-moh-TAY [FR])
  Alternate spellings: Timmothy,
  Timothée [FR]
Tito (TEE-toh [AA/IT/SP])
Tobias (toh-BY-yes, toh-VY-yes or
  toh-VY-yuh [HEB])
  Alternate spellings: Toviya [HEB]
Tobin (TOH-bin)
Toby (TOH-bee, toh-VEE [HEB])
  Alternate spellings: Tovi [HEB]
Tony (TOH-nee)
  Alternate spellings: Toney
Topher (TOH-fur)
Tyrone (ty-ROHN [AA/CG])
  Alternate spellings: Tyron

Virgilio (veer-JEE-lee-yoh [IT],
  veer-HEE-lee-yoh or
  beer-HEE-lee-yoh [SP])
Vito (VEE-toh [IT/SP], BEE-doh [SP])

Waino (VAY-noh [SCAN])
Waldo (WALL-doh, VAWL-doh [GER])
Wilfredo (will-FRAY-doh [SP])

Yakov (YAW-kohv [HEB])
  Alternate spellings: Yaakov, Jacob*,
  Jakob
Yosef (YO-sef or yo-SEF [HEB])

Zion (ZY-yun [AA], tsee-YOHN [HEB])
  Alternate spellings: Tziyon

■ SHORT O (AW OR AH) ■

PARTNER POINTER:
Check out the AR and OW lists, too.

Aaron (AIR-en, aw-har-ROHN [HEB],
  ar-ROHN [SP])
  Alternate spellings: Aron, Arron, Erin
  [IR], Aharon [HEB]
Abdiel (ab-DEEL [AA/AR]), awv-DEEL [HEB])
  Alternate spellings: Avdiel [HEB]
Abdul (ab-DULL or ab-DOOL or
  awb-DOOL [AR])
Abraham (AYB-ri-ham, awv-ruh-HAWM
  [HEB])
  Alternate spellings: Avraham [HEB]
Abram (AY-brum, aw-VRAWM [HEB])
  Alternate spellings: Avram [HEB]
Adalberto (aw-dell-BAIR-toh [SP])
Adam (AD-dum, aw-DAWM [HEB])

Adolfo (aw-DAWL-foh [IT/SP])
Adolph (AYD-awlf [GER], ad-DAWLF [FR])
  Alternate spellings: Adolphe [FR], Adolf
Adolphus (uh-DAWL-fus, ay-DAWL-fus)
Adonis (uh-DAWN-iss, aw-DOH-nees [SP])
Adrian (AY-dree-yen, , aw-DREE-yawn
  [SP], ad-ree-AW with short N [FR])
  Alternate spellings: Adrien [FR]
Adriel (AY-dree-yell, aw-dree-YELL [HEB])
Ahmad (AWH-mawd with pronounced H
  in middle [AR])
Ahmed (AWH-med with pronounced H
  in middle [AR])
Alden (AWL-den)
Aldo (AWL-doh [GER/IT/SP])
Aiejandro (aw-leh-HAWN-droh [SP])
Alessandro (aw-leh-SAWN-droh [IT])
Alexandre (al-eks-ZAWN-dray,
  al-ek-SAW-druh with short N [FR])
Alexandro (al-eks-ZAN-droh,
  al-eks-ZAWN-droh)
Alexis (uh-LEK-sis, aw-LEK-see or
  al-ek-SEES [FR])
Alfonso (al-FAWN-zoh [IT],
  awl-FAWN-soh [SP])
  Alternate spellings: Alphonso, Alfonzo
Alfredo (awl-FRAY-doh [IT/SP], al-FRAY-doh)
Ali (AW-lee or aw-LEE [AA/AR])
  Alternate spellings: Aali
Alma (AWL-muh)
Alonzo (uh-LAWN-zoh, aw-LONE-soh [SP])
  Alternate spellings: Alonso
Alphonse (al-FAWNS, al-FAWS with
  short N [FR])
Alton (AL-tun, AWL-tun)
Alva (AWL-vuh, AWL-buh [SP])
  Alternate spellings: Alvah
Álvaro (AWL-var-roh or AWL-bar-roh [SP])
Amado (aw-MAW-doh [SP])
Amador (AM-uh-dor, aw-maw-DOR [SP])
Americo (aw-mair-EE-ko or
  aw-MAIR-ee-koh [IT/SP])
Amir (aw-MEER [AR/HEB])
Amos (AY-mohs, AW-mohs [HEB])
Anastacio (aw-naw-STAW-see-oh [SP])
Andre (AWN-dray, awn-DRAY [FR])
  Alternate spellings: Andra, Andrée [FR]
Andrea (awn-DRAY-yuh [GRK/IT])
Andreas (awn-DRAY-yes [GRK])
Andrés (awn-DRAYS [SP])
Angel (AYN-jell, AWN-hell [SP])
  Alternate spellings: Ángel
Angelo (AN-jell-oh, AWN-jell-oh [IT],
  AWN-hell-oh [SP])

Anibal (ANN-nib-bull [GRK], aw-noo-BAWL [EI], AW-nee-bawl [IT], aw-NEE-bawl [SP])

Anselmo (awn-SELL-moh [IT/SP], awn-THELL-moh [SP])

Antoine (an-TWAHN, awn-TWAHN [FR])
Alternate spellings: Antwan, Antwon, Antione

Anton (AN-tun [AA], awn-TOHN [FR])
Alternate spellings: Antone

Antonio (an-TOH-nee-yoh, awn-TOH-nee-yoh [IT/SP])

Arcadio (ar-CAW-dee-yoh)

Archibald (AR-chee-bawld [GER])

Armand (ar-MAWND, ar-MAW with short N [FR])
Alternate spellings: Armond

Armando (ar-MAWN-doh [IT/SP])

Armani (ar-MAWN-ee)

Armstrong (ARMS-trawng)

Arnaldo (ar-NAWL-doh [IT/SP])
Alternate spellings: Arnoldo*

Arnav (ar-NAWV [EI/HEB])

Arnoldo (ar-NOHL-doh [IT/SP], ar-NAWL-doh)
Alternate spellings: Arnaldo*

Asher (ASH-ur, AW-shur [HEB])

Aubrey (AW-bree)

Audie (AW-dee)

August (AW-gest [GER], oh-GOOST [FR])
Alternate spellings: Auguste [FR]

Augustin (aw-GUS-tin, oh-goos-TEEN or ow-goh-STAW with short N [FR], aw-goo-STEEN or aw-gooth-TEEN [SP])
Alternate spellings: Agustin, Augustín [SP]
Alternate spellings: Augustine

Augustus (aw-GUS-tus)

Austin (AWS-tin)
Alternate spellings: Austyn, Austen

Bartholomew (bar-THAW-lum-yoo)

Benjamin (BEN-juh-min, bin-yaw-MEEN [HEB], ben-zhaw-ME with short N [FR] ben-haw-MEEN or ven-haw-MEEN [SP])
Alternate spellings: Binyamin [HEB], Benjamin [SP]

Bertrand (BURT-rend, bair-TRAW with short N [FR])

Bilal (bee-LAWL or bee-LAL [AR/EI])

Bob (BAWB)

Bobby (BAW-bee)
Alternate spellings: Bobbie

Brayden (BRAY-den [CG], BRAY-dawn [IR])
Alternate spellings: Braden, Braeden, Braydon, Braiden, Braedon, Bradyn

Brock (BRAWK)

Broderick (BRAW-dur-rik [CG])

Bronson (BRAWN-sin)

Candido (KAWN-dee-doh or kan-DEE-doh [SP])

Chauncey (CHAWN-see)

Christian (KRIS-chen, KREE-stee-yawn or KREETH-tee-yawn [IT/SP], kree-stee-YAW with short N [FR])
Alternate spellings: Cristian, Kristian

Christophe (KRIS-tawf)
Alternate spellings: Christoff

Claude (KLAWD, KLOHD [FR])
Alternate spellings: Claud

Claudie (KLAW-dee, kloh-DEE [FR])

Claudio (KLAW-dee-yoh, KLOW-dee-yoh [IT/SP])

Cleménce (klay-MAWS with short N [FR])

Clement (KLEM-ent, kluh-MENT, klay-MAW with short N [FR])
Alternate spellings: Clément [FR]

Colin (KAW-lin, KOH-lin [IR])
Alternate spellings: Collin

Connor (KAW-nur [IR])
Alternate spellings: Conner, Conor, Konnor

Conrad (KAWN-rad [GER])

Constantine (kawn-stan-TEEN [FR])

Crawford (KRAW-furd)

Cristobal (kree-STOH-bawl or kreeth-TOH-vawl or kree-stoh-VAWL [SP])

Dalton (DAWL-ten)

Damian (DAY-mee-yen, daw-mee-YAW with short N [FR])
Alternate spellings: Damien, Damion, Dameon

Dan (DAN, DAWN [HEB])

Dana (DAY-nuh, DAW-nuh [SP])

Dandre (DAWN-dray)

Daniel (DAN-yell, dawn-ee-YELL [HEB], dan-YELL [FR])
Alternate spellings: Danial

Dante (DAWN-tay [AA/IT])
Alternate spellings: Donte, Dontae, Donta

Daquan (duh-KWAHN [AA])
Alternate spellings: Dequan

David (DAY-vid, daw-VEED [HEB], dav-EED [FR])

Dawson (DAW-sen)

Deandre (dee-YAWN-dray [AA])

Alternate spellings: Deondre
Deepak (dee-PAWK [EI])
Dejuan (DAY-wan or duh-WAHN [AA])
Deon (dee-YAWN [AA])
   Alternate spellings: Dion, Deion
Deonte (dee-YAWN-tay [AA])
   Alternate spellings: Dionte
Deshawn (duh-SHAWN [AA])
   Alternate spellings: Dashawn, Deshaun
Devonte (duh-VAWN-tay [AA])
   Alternate spellings: Devante,
   Davonte, Devonta, Devontae
Dock (DAWK)
Dominic (DAW-min-ik, doh-mee-NEEK [FR])
   Alternate spellings: Dominick, Dominik,
   Domenic, Dominique, Domenick
Don (DAWN)
   Alternate spellings: Donn
Donal (DAW-null [IR], daw-NELL [AA])
Donald (DAWN-uld [CG])
Donato (doh-NAW-toh [IT])
Donnell (DAW-nell, DOH-null [IR])
   Alternate spellings: Donal, Donell
Donnie (DAWN-ee [CG])
   Alternate spellings: Donny
Donovan (DAW-noh-vin [CG])
   Alternate spellings: Donavan

Efrain (eff-raw-EEN or EEF-rawn [HEB],
   EFF-ren [AA], eff-RA with short N [FR],
   eff-raw-EEN [SP], EE-fren or ef-RYN;
   see also Ephraim)
   Alternate spellings: Efrain [SP], Efren,
   Efron [HEB], Ephron
Eladio (el-LAW-dee-yoh or
   ee-LAW-dee-yoh or EL-lawd-yoh [SP])
Elian (EL-lee-yawn [SP], EE-lee-yawn)
Elias (EE-lee-yaws [HEB], el-LEE-yaws or
   eh-LEE-yes [SP])
Elijah (el-LY-zhuh or uh-LY-juh [AA],
   el-lee-YAW-hoo [HEB])
   Alternate spellings: Alijah, Eliyahu [HEB]
Emiliano (em-eel-YAW-noh [SP],
   em-ee-lee-YAW-noh)
Emmanuel (ee-MAN-yoo-well [AA],
   ee-mawn-yoo-ELL [HEB],
   em-man-WELL [FR],
   ee-mawn-yoo-WELL or
   ee-man-WELL [SP])
   Alternate spellings: Emanuel,
   Immanuel
Enoch (EE-nuk, EE-nawk, chaw-NOCH
   with guttural CH [HEB])
   Alternate spellings: Chanoch [HEB]

Enos (EE-naws [HEB])
Epifanio (epp-if-FAW-nee-yoh [SP])
Erasmo (eh-RAWS-moh or
   ee-RAWS-moh [SP])
Esteban (es-TEB-awn or eth-TEV-awn
   [SP], ES-tuh-bawn, ES-tuh-vawn)
   Alternate spellings: Estevan
Ethan (EE-thin, EE-tawn [HEB])
   Alternate spellings: Ethen, Eitan or
   Etan [HEB]

Fabian (FAY-bee-yen, faw-bee-AWN [FR])
Ferdinand (FUR-din-and,
   FAIR-din-nawnd [GER],
   fair-dee-NAW with short ND [FR])
Fernand (fair-NAW with short ND [FR])
Fernando (fur-NAN-doh, fair-NAWN-doh
   [SP])
Fortunato (for-too-NAW-toh [IT/SP])
Foster (FAWS-tur)

Gabriel (GAY-bree-ell, gaw-bree-ELL or
   gaw-vree-ELL [HEB], gab-brrree-YELL
   [FR/SP/IT])
   Alternate spellings: Gavriel [HEB]
Gaetano (gy-TAW-noh [IT], gy-TAWN [FR])
   Alternate spellings: Gaetane [FR]
Gaston (GASS-tun [CG], gas-TOHN or
   gas-TAW with short N [FR])
Geraldo (hair-RAWL-doh [SP])
German (JUR-men, her-MAWN [SP],
   zhair-MAN [FR])
   Alternate spellings: Germán [SP],
   Germain [FR]
Giancarlo (jawn-KAR-lo [IT])
Gianni (jee-YAW-nee or JAWN-nee [IT])
   Alternate spellings: Johnny*, Johnnie,
   Johnie, Jonnie
Giovanni (jee-yoh-VAW-nee or
   joh-VAW-nee [AA/IT])
   Alternate spellings: Giovanny, Giovani,
   Jovani, Jovany, Jovanny, Jovanni
   Godfrey (GAWD-free [GER])
   Gonzalo (gun-ZAW-loh,
   gohn-SAW-loh or gohn-THAW-loh [SP])
   Guadalupe (gwah-duh-LOO-pay or
   gwah-THAW-loo-pay [SP])
   Gustave (GOO-stawv [GER/SCAN],
   goo-STAWV [FR])
   Alternate spellings: Gustav
Gustavo (goo-STAW-voh [IT/SP],
   gooth-TAW-boh [SP])

Hakeem (haw-KEEM or hak-EEM [AR])

Hamza (hum-ZAW [AR])
Hans (HAWNS [GER/SCAN])
Hansel (HAN-sell, HAWN-sell [GER/SCAN])
Hassan (HAW-sawn or haw-SAWN [AR])
Henry (HEN-ree [GER], aw-REE with short
  N [FR])
  Alternate spellings: Henri
Hernan (air-NAWN [SP])
Hezekiah (hez-uh-KY-yuh, chiz-kee-
  YAW-hoo with guttural ch [HEB])
  Alternate spellings: Chizkiyahu [HEB]
Hollis (HAW-lis)

Ibrahim (EEB-ruh-heem or EEB-ruh-him
  [AA], ee-braw-HEEM or ib-raw-HEEM
  [AR])
Ignacio (eeg-NAW-see-yoh or
  eeg-NAW-thee-yoh [SP])
Isaac (EYE-zek, EET-zawk [HEB], is-HAWK
  [AR])
  Alternate spellings: Issac, Isaak,
  Yitzchak [HEB]
Isaiah (eye-ZAY-yuh, is-shy-YAW or
  is-shy-YAW-hoo [HEB])
  Alternate spellings: Isiah, Izaiah,
  Yeshaya or Yeshayahu [HEB]
Ismael (IZ-mayl, ees-MAW-yell or
  eeth-MAW-yell [SP])
Israel (IZ-ree-yell, IZ-ray-yell [HEB],
  iss-raw-EEL [AR], eess-RAY-yell or
  eeth-RAY-yell [SP])
  Alternate spellings: Yisrael [HEB]
Ivan (EYE-ven, ee-VAWN or ee-BAWN [SP])

Jacinto (haw-SEEN-toh or
  haw-THEEN-toh [SP])
Jacob (JAY-kub, YAW-kohv [HEB],
  yaw-KOOB [AR])
  Alternate spellings: Jakob, Yakov* or
  Yaakov [HEB], Yakoub* [AR]
Jacques (ZHAWK [FR], HAW-kess [SP])
  Alternate spellings: Jaquez [SP]
Jaden (JAY-den [AA], yaw-DAWN or
  yaw-DEEN [HEB])
  Alternate spellings: Jayden, Jaiden,
  Jadon [HEB], Jaydon, Jaeden, Jadyn
  Yadon or Jadin or Yadin [HEB]
Jair (JAY-yur [BIB], JAIR, yaw-EER or
  YAW-eer [HEB])
  Alternate spellings: Jere*, Yair [HEB],
  Yahir*
Jamal (jum-AWL [AA], zhum-AYL or
  zhum-AWL [AR])
  Alternate spellings: Jamaal

Jan (YAWN, NYAWN [SCAN])
  Alternate spellings: Jann, Yann [FR]
Janis (jaw-NEES or YAW-nis [SCAN])
Javier (haw-vee-YAIR or haw-bee-YAIR
  [SP])
  Alternate spellings: Xavier*
Javion (JAY-vee-yawn or JAY-vee-yun [AA])
Javonte (juh-VAWN-tay [AA])
Jean (ZHAW with short N [FR], ZAWN [SCAN])
Jedidiah (jed-did-DY-yuh, yed-DEED-yaw
  [HEB])
  Alternate spellings: Jedediah,
  Jedidia, Yedidya [HEB]
Jeremiah (jair-uh-MY-uh,
  yeer-mee-YAW-hoo [HEB])
  Alternate spellings: Yirmeyahu [HEB]
Joachim (wah-KEEM, JOH-wah-kim,
  zho-wah-SHE with short N [FR],
  yo-WAH-kim [GER], ye-ho-wuh-KEEM
  or yow-wuh-KEEM [HEB])
  Alternate spellings: Joakim,
  Jehoiakim or Yehoyakim [HEB]
Joaquin (wah-KEEN, ho-wah-KEEN [SP],
  ye-ho-wuh-CHEEN with guttural CH
  [HEB])
  Alternate spellings: Joaquín [SP],
  Jehoiachin or Yehoyachin [HEB]
Johan (YOH-hawn [GER/SCAN])
  Alternate spellings: Johann
John (JAWN)
  Alternate spellings: Jon, Gian [IT]
Johnny (JAWN-ee)
  Alternate spellings: Johnnie, Johnie,
  Jonnie, Gianni*
Johnpaul (jawn-PAWL)
Johnson (JAWN-sen)
Jonathan (JAW-nuh-thin, yoh-nuh-TAWN
  [HEB])
  Alternate spellings: Johnathan,
  Jonathon, Johnathon, Jonatan,
  Yonatan [HEB]
Josh (JAWSH)
Joshua (JAW-shoo-wuh,
  ye-ho-SHOO-wuh [HEB])
  Alternate spellings: Joshuah,
  Yehoshua [HEB]
Josiah (joh-ZY-yuh, yoh-shee-YAW-hoo
  or yoh-SHEE-yuh [HEB])
  Alternate spellings: Yoshiyahu or
  Yoshiya [HEB]
Jovan (joh-VAN or joh-VAWN [AA])
Juan (HWAN [SP])
  Alternate spellings: Joan
Juwan (juh-WAHN [AA])

Kale (KAW-lay [HW], KAYL)
  Alternate spellings: Cale*, Cael*, Kael
Kazuo (KAW-zoo-oh [JAP])
Keanu (kee-YAWN-oo [HW])
Kenyatta (ken-YAW-tuh [AA])
Keon (KEE-yen [IR/PER], KEE-yawn [AA])
  Alternate spellings: Keyon, Kian [IR/PER]
Keshawn (kee-SHAWN [AA])
  Alternate spellings: Keyshawn
Khalid (kaw-LEED [AA], CHAW-leed with
  guttural CH or HAW-lid [AR])
Khalil (kaw-LEEL [AA], CHAW-leel with
  guttural CH [HEB/AR], HAW-leel [AR])
  Alternate spellings: Chalil [HEB], Halil,
  Hallil
Kieran (KEER-ren [CG], KEER-rawn [IR])
  Alternate spellings: Ciaran, Kyran [PER]
Kwame (KWAH-may [AA])

Lafayette (law-fee-YET, law-fy-YET,
  law-fay-YET)
Lamont (luh-MAWNT [AA/SCAN])
Lashawn (luh-SHAWN [AA])
Lawrence (LOR-rens, lor-RAWS with
  short N [FR], LOR-rens [GER])
  Alternate spellings: Laurence [FR],
  Lawerence, Lorenz [GER]
Lawson (LAW-sen)
Leon (LEE-yawn [GER], lay-YAW with short
  N [FR], lay-YOHN [SP])
  Alternate spellings: Léon [FR], León [SP]
Leroy (LEE-roy [AA], leh-RWAH [FR])
  Alternate spellings: Leeroy
Lisandro (lee-SAWN-droh [SP])
Lok (LAWK [CH])
Lon (LAWN)
Lonnie (LAW-nee)
  Alternate spellings: Lonny
Lonzo (LAWN-zoh [IT])
Luciano (loo-CHAW-noh [IT],
  loo-see-YAWN-oh or
  loo-thee-YAWN-oh [SP])

Mahlon (MAY-len, MAW-len)
Makaio (maw-kaw-YEE-yoh or
  maw-KY-yoh [HW])
Malachi (MAL-uh-ky [IR], maw-law-CHEE
  with guttural CH [HEB])
  Alternate spellings: Malakai, Malachai
Mariano (mar-ree-YAWN-oh [IT])
Masaaki (mas-SAW-aw-kee [JAP])
Milan (mee-LAWN [IT/RUS])
Mohamed (moh-hawm-MUD or
  mo-HAM-med [AR])

  Alternate spellings: Mohammad,
  Mohammed, Muhammad
Monserrate (mohn-sair-RAWT [IT])
  Alternate spellings: Montserrat
Montague (MAWN-tug-yoo)
Montana (mawn-TAN-nuh)
Monte (MAWN-tee)
  Alternate spellings: Monty
Montgomery (mawnt-GUM-ur-ree)
Mustafa (moo-STAW-fuh or
  moo-STUFF-uh [AR])

Najee (NAW-jee or naw-JEE [AA])
  Alternate spellings: Naji or Nagi [AR]
Nasir (NAW-seer or nuh-SEER or
  NAW-sur [AR])
Nathan (NAY-thin, nuh-TAWN [HEB])
  Alternate spellings: Nathen, Natan [HEB]
Nathaniel (nuh-THAN-yell, naw-tawn-ELL
  [HEB])
  Alternate spellings: Nathanael,
  Nathanial, Netanel [HEB]
  Neftali (nef-TAW-lee, NAWF-taw-lee
  [HEB])
  Alternate spellings: Naftali [HEB]
Noah (NOH-wuh, NOH-wach with
  guttural CH [HEB], NOH with
  pronounced H [AR])
  Alternate spellings: Noach [HEB]

Octavio (awk-TAW-vee-yoh or
  ohk-TAW-bee-yoh [SP])
Olaf (OH-lawf [SCAN])
Oliver (AW-liv-ur)
Ollie (AW-lee)
Osborne (AWZ-born [SCAN])
Oscar (AWS-kur [SCAN], aws-KAR or
  awth-KAR [SP])
Oswald (AWZ-wald)
Oswaldo (aws-VAWL-doh [IT/SP],
  awth-BAWL-doh [SP])
  Alternate spellings: Osvaldo, Osbaldo
Otto (AW-doh [GER])
  Alternate spellings: Otho

Pablo (PAW-bloh or PAWV-loh [SP])
Palmer (PAWL-mur, PAW-mur)
Pasquale (pass-KAL [FR], paw-skoo-WALL
  or pawth-KWALL [SP])
  Alternate spellings: Pascual [SP],
  Pasqual
Patrick (PAT-rik, PAR-rick or PAWD-rig [IR])
  Alternate spellings: Padraig [IR]
Paul (PAWL, POHL [FR])

Phelan (FAY-len, FWAY-lawn [IR])
Alternate spellings: Faelan, Faolan
Pranav (PRRRAW-nawv [EI])

Radames (RAW-duh-mes [EGY],
RAD-uh-mes or RAD-uh-may [SP])
Raekwon (ray-KWAHN [AA])
Rafael (RAF-ee-yell, raf-ee-YELL,
rrraf-uh-YELL [FR], raw-faw-ELL [HEB/SP],
rrraw-FAY-yell [SP])
Alternate spellings: Raphael, Raphaël
Raheem (ruh-HEEM or raw-HEEM [AA/AR])
Rahul (ruh-HOOL [AA], rrrraw-HOOL [EI])
Rakesh (rrraw-KESH [EI])
Raleigh (RAW-lee)
Alternate spellings: Rollie
Ram (RRRAWM [EI])
Ramiro (rrraw-MEER-roh [SP])
Ramón (rrraw-MOHN [SP])
Randolph (RAN-dawlf)
Raouf (raw-OOF [AR])
Rashad (ruh-SHAWD or ruh-SHAD [AA/AR])
Rashawn (ruh-SHAWN [AA/AR])
Alternate spellings: Rayshawn*
Rasheed (ruh-SHEED or raw-SHEED [AA/AR])
Raul (raw-OOL, rrraw-OOL [FR/SP])
Alternate spellings: Raoul, Rahul*
Ravi (RRRAW-vee [EI], RAW-vee [HEB])
Alternate spellings: Rafi [AR]
Raymond (RAY-mund [GER], rrray-MAW
with short N [FR])
Alternate spellings: Raymonde [FR]
Rayshawn (ray-SHAWN or ruh-SHAWN
[AA])
Alternate spellings: Rashawn*
Reynaldo (rrray-NAWL-doh [SP])
Alternate spellings: Reinaldo
Rob (RAWB)
Alternate spellings: Robb
Robbie (RAW-bee)
Alternate spellings: Robby
Robert (RAW-burt, rrroh-BAIR [FR])
Robin (RAW-bin)
Rocco (RAW-koh [IT])
Rock (RAWK)
Rocky (RAW-kee)
Rod (RAWD)
Roderick (RAW-dur-rik or RAWD-rik [GER])
Alternate spellings: Rodrick
Rodney (RAWD-nee)
Roger (RAW-jur [GER], rrroh-ZHAIR or
rrroh-ZHAY [FR])
Alternate spellings: Rodger
Rogers (RAW-jurz)

Rohan (ROH-han, rrroh-HAWN [EI])
Roland (ROH-lend [GER], rrroh-LAW with
short N [FR])
Alternate spellings: Rowland
Rolando (roh-LAN-doh,
rrroh-LAWN-doh [SP])
Rolf (RAWLF [GER/SCAN])
Rollin (RAW-lin)
Rollo (RAW-loh)
Ron (RAWN)
Ronald (RAW-nuld)
Ronaldo (rrroh-NAWL-doh [SP])
Ronan (ROH-nen, ROH-nawn [IR])
Ronnie (RAW-nee)
Alternate spellings: Ronny
Roscoe (RAW-skoh [SCAN])
Ross (RAWS [CG])
Roswell (RAWZ-well)
Rudolph (ROO-dawlf, ROH-dawlf [GER],
roh-DAWLF [FR])
Alternate spellings: Rudolf, Rodolf [GER],
Rodolphe [FR]

Salvador (sal-vaw-DOR or
thal-baw-DOR [SP])
Samir (saw-MEER or suh-MEER [AR])
Sancho (SAWN-choh [SP])
Sandro (SAWND-roh [IT])
Santiago (sawn-tee-YAW-goh or
thawn-tee-YAW-goh [SP])
Santo (SAWN-toh [IT])
Santos (SAWN-tohs [SP])
Sasha (SAW-shuh [GER/RUS], SASH-uh)
Alternate spellings: Sacha, Sascha
Saul (SAWL, shaw-OOL [HEB], saw-OOL or
thaw-OOL [SP])
Alternate spellings: Sol*, Shaul [HEB]
Savion (SAY-vee-yawn or say-vee-YAWN
[AA])
Scott (SKAWT)
Alternate spellings: Scot
Scottie (SKAW-tee)
Sean (SHAWN [IR])
Alternate spellings: Shawn, Shaun,
Shon, Shan [CH]
Sebastian (sub-BAS-chen,
sub-BAS-tee-yen, say-bas-tee-YAW
with short N [FR], say-baws-TAWN or
thay-vaws-TAWN [SP])
Alternate spellings: Sabastian,
Sebastien, Sébastien [FR], Sebastián [SP]
Semaj (suh-MAWJ [AA])
Alternate spellings: Samaj [EI]
Simon (SY-mun [GRK], shee-MOHN [HEB],

see-MAW with short N [FR])
Alternate spellings: Shimon [HEB]
Sol (SOHL or THOHL [SP], SAWL)
Alternate spellings: Saul*
Solomon (SAW-loh-mun, SHLO-moh [HEB])
Alternate spellings: Shlomo [HEB]
Stefan (stef-FAWN [GER/FR])
Alternate spellings: Stephan, Stephon

Tavion (TAY-vee-yawn or TAY-vee-yun [AA])
Tavon (TAY-vun or TAY-vawn [AA])
Alternate spellings: Tevon*, Tavin
Todd (TAWD)
Alternate spellings: Tod
Tom (TAWM)
Tommy (TAW-mee)
Alternate spellings: Tommie
Trevion (TRAY-vee-yun or
TRAY-vee-yawn [AA])
Trinidad (TRIN-id-add, tree-nee-DAWD
[SP])
Tristan (TRIS-ten [WL], trees-TAW with
short N [FR], trees-TAWN or
treeth-TAWN [SP])
Alternate spellings: Tristen, Triston,
Tristin, Trystan, Tristan [SP]
Tyquan (ty-KWAHN [AA])
Tyshawn (TY-shawn or tuh-SHAWN or
TEE-shawn [AA])
Alternate spellings: Tshawn

Valentine (VAL-en-tyn,
vaw-lawn-TEEN [FR])
Vaughn (VAWN [WL])
Alternate spellings: Von
Vidal (vee-DAWL or bee-DAWL [SP])
Vincent (VIN-sent, veh-SAW with short
Ns [FR])

Waldemar (WALL-duh-mar,
VAWL-duh-mar [GER/SCAN])
Alternate spellings: Valdemar [SCAN]
Waldo (WALL-doh, VAWL-doh [GER])
Wallace (WALL-iss [CG])
Wally (WALL-ee [CG])
Walker (WAH-kur)
Walter (WALL-tur, VAWL-tur [GER])
Walton (WALL-ten)
Washington (WASH-eeng-ten)
Watson (WAHT-sen)

Xavier (ZAY-vee-yur, ek-ZAY-vee-yur,
haw-vee-YAIR or haw-bee-YAIR [SP],
zav-YAY [FR])

Alternate spellings: Javier*, Xzavier,
Zavier

Yadiel (yaw-dee-YELL [SP])
Yahir (yaw-EER or YAW-eer [HEB])
Alternate spellings: Yair [HEB], Jair*
Yakoub (yaw-KOOB [AR])
Alternate spellings: Jacob*, Jakob
Yakov (YAW-kohv [HEB])
Alternate spellings: Yaakov, Jacob*,
Jakob

■ OI ■

PARTNER POINTER:
Check the long E, long O, and OR
lists, too.

Boyce (BOIS [GER])
Boyd (BOID [CG])

Cloyd (KLOID)
Coy (KOI)

Doyle (DOIL [CG])

Eloy (EE-loi [BIB])
Elroy (EL-roi)

Floyd (FLOID)
Foy (FOI [CG])

Hoyt (HOIT)

Leroy (LEE-roi [AA], leh-RWAH [FR])
Alternate spellings: Leeroy
Lloyd (LOID [WL])
Alternate spellings: Loyd
Loy (LOI)
Loyal (LOI-yull)

McCoy (mik-KOI [CG])
Moises (MOI-zess [HEB], moi-SES [SP])
Moshe (MOH-shuh or MOISH-uh [HEB])
Alternate spellings: Mose, Moeshe

Roy (ROI [CG])
Royal (ROI-yell)
Royce (ROIS)

Sawyer (SOI-yur)

Troy (TROI [CG])

■ OR ■

PARTNER POINTER:
Check the long O and OI lists, too.

Alford (AL-ford)
Amador (AM-uh-dor, aw-maw-DOR [SP])

Boris (BOR-riss)

Corbin (KOR-bin)
   Alternate spellings: Korbin
Cordell (kor-DELL [FR])
Corey (KOR-ree)
   Alternate spellings: Cory, Korey, Kory
Cormac (KOR-mak [IR])
Cornelius (kor-NEE-lee-yes
Cornell (kor-NELL [CG])
Cortéz (kor-TEZ [SP])
Courtney (KORT-nee)
   Alternate spellings: Cortney

Dorian (DOR-ree-yen)
Dorman (DOR-men)
Dorsey (DOR-see)

Elmore (EL-mor)

Florencio (flor-REN-see-yoh or
   flor-REN-thee-yoh [SP])
Florentino (flor-ren-TEE-noh [IT])
Florian (flor-ree-YAWN [FR])
Ford (FORD)
Forrest (FOR-rest)
   Alternate spellings: Forest
Fortunato (for-too-NAW-toh [IT/SP])

Gaylord (GAY-lord)
George (JORJ, ZHORZH [FR])
   Alternate spellings: Georges [FR]
Gordon (GOR-den)
Gregorio (greg-OR-ree-oh [SP])

Hector (HEK-tur, EK-tor [SP])
   Alternate spellings: Hector [SP]
Horace (HOR-ris)

Isidor (IZ-uh-dor [GRK], ee-see-DOR [FR])
   Alternate spellings: Isidore, Isador,
   Isadore
Ivory (EYE-vor-ree)

Jordan (JOR-den, YAR-den [HEB])
   Alternate spellings: Jordon, Jorden,

Yarden*
Jordy (JOR-dee)
Jorge (HOR-hay [SP])

Lawrence (LOR-rens, lor-RAWS with
   short N [FR], LOR-rens [GER])
   Alternate spellings: Laurence [FR],
   Lawerence, Lorenz [GER]
Loren (LOR-ren)
   Alternate spellings: Lauren, Lorin,
   Loran (see also Lorne)
Lorenzo (loh-REN-zoh [SP])
Lorne (LORN)

Maurice (MOR-ris [BR], mor-REES [FR])
   Alternate spellings: Morris
Mauricio (mor-REE-see-yoh,
   mow-REE-see-yoh or mow-REE-
   thee-yoh [SP], mow-REET-zee-yoh)
   Alternate spellings: Mauritzio [IT]
Maury (MOR-ree)
   Alternate spellings: Morry
Mordecai (MOR-dik-ky, mor-duh-CHY
   with guttural CH [HEB])
   Alternate spellings: Mordechai [HEB]
Morgan (MOR-gen)
Mortimer (MOR-tim-ur)
Morton (MOR-tun)

Nestor (NES-tur, NES-tor or NETH-tor
   [SP])
   Alternate spellings: Nestor [SP]
Norberto (nor-BAIR-toh [IT/SP],
   nor-VAIR-toh [SP])
Norman (NOR-men)
Normand (NOR-mend)
Norris (NOR-ris)
Norton (NOR-ten)
Norval (NOR-vull)
   Alternate spellings: Norville
Norwood (NOR-wood)

Ora (OR-ruh)
Oral (OR-rull)
Oran (OR-ran [IR])
Oren (OR-ren [HEB/IR])
   Alternate spellings: Orin, Orrin
Orie (OR-ree, or-REE [HEB])
Orion (or-RY-yun [AA])
Orlando (or-LAN-doh [AA], or-LAWN-doh
   [SP])
Orlo (OR-loh)
Orville (OR-vill)
   Alternate spellings: Orval, Orvil

Osborne (AWZ-born [SCAN])

Porfirio (por-FEER-ree-yoh [SP])
Porter (POR-tur)

Rexford (REKS-furd, REKS-ford)
Riordan (REER-den, ROR-den,
    ree-YOR-den [IR])
Rory (ROR-ree)

Salvador (sal-vaw-DOR or
    thal-baw-DOR [SP])
Salvatore (sal-vuh-TOR-ray [IT])
Seymour (SEE-mor)
Soren (SOR-ren [SCAN])
Storm (STORM)

Taurean (TOR-ree-yun [AA])
Teodoro (tay-yoh-DOR-roh [IT/SP])
Theodore (THEE-yuh-dor,
    tay-yoh-DOR [FR])
    Alternate spellings: Theadore,
    Theodor, Théodore [FR]
Thor (THOR [SCAN])
Thornton (THORN-ten)
Torrance (TOR-rens)
Tory (TOR-ree)
    Alternate spellings: Torrey
Tudor (TOO-dor [WL])

Victor (VIK-tur, veek-TOR [FR], VEEK-tor
    or BEEK-tor [SP])
    Alternate spellings: Victor [SP], Viktor
Vidor (VEE-dor [HUN])

Ward (WORD)
Wardell (wor-DELL)
Warner (WOR-nur, WAR-nur, VAR-nur [GER])
Winford (WIN-ford)

■ OW ■

PARTNER POINTER:
Check the short O and AR lists, too.

Augustin (aw-GUS-tin, oh-goos-TEEN or
    ow-goh-STAW with short N [FR],
    aw-goo-STEEN or aw-gooth-TEEN [SP])
    Alternate spellings: Agustin, Augustín
    [SP]
    Alternate spellings: Augustine

Braulio (BROH-lee-yoh, BROW-lee-yoh

    or VROW-lee-yoh [SP])
Brown (BROWN)

Claudio (KLAW-dee-yoh, KLOW-dee-yoh
    [IT/SP])

Faustino (fow-STEEN-oh or
    fowth-TEEN-oh [SP])

Howard (HOW-wurd)
Howell (HOW-well)

Joachim (wah-KEEM, JOH-wah-kim,
    zho-wah-SHE with short N [FR],
    yo-WAH-kim [GER], yuh-ho-wuh-KEEM
    or yow-wuh-KEEM [HEB])
    Alternate spellings: Joakim,
    Jehoiakim or Yehoyakim [HEB]
Joaquin (wah-KEEN, ho-wah-KEEN [SP],
    yuh-ho-wuh-CHEEN or
    yow-wuh-CHEEN with guttural CH
    [HEB])
    Alternate spellings: Joaquín [SP],
    Jehoiachin or Yehoyachin [HEB]

Klaus (KLOWS [GER])
    Alternate spellings: Claus

Mauricio (mor-REE-see-yoh,
    mow-REE-see-yoh or mow-REE-
    thee-yoh [SP], mow-REET-zee-yoh)
    Alternate spellings: Mauritzio [IT]

Nicholaus (NIK-oh-lows or NICK-lows [GER])
    Alternate spellings: Nickolaus,
    Nicklaus

Scout (SKOWT)

■ OO ■

PARTNER POINTER:
Check the UR list, too.

Abdul (ab-DULL or ab-DOOL or
    awb-DOOL [AR])
Abdullah (ab-DULL-uh [AR], ab-DOO-luh
    [AA])
Andrew (AND-roo)
Anibal (ANN-nib-bull [GRK], aw-noo-BAWL
    [EI], AW-nee-bawl [IT], aw-NEE-bawl [SP])
Arjun (AR-jun, ar-JOON) [EI]
Arnulfo (ar-NOOL-foh [SP])

Arturo (ar-TOO-roh [IT/SP])
August (AW-gest [GER], oh-GOOST [FR])
 Alternate spellings: Auguste [FR]

Bartholomew (bar-THAW-lum-yoo)
Booker (BOOK-ur)
Brook (BROOK)
Brooks (BROOKS)
Bruce (BROOS)
Bruno (BROO-noh [GER/IT])
Buford (BYOO-furd)
Butch (BOOCH)

Cooper (KOO-pur)
Cruz (KROOZ, KROOS or KROOTH [SP])
Cyrus (SY-russ, see-ROOS [PER])

Dewey (DOO-wee [WL])
Dewitt (duh-WIT, DOO-wit)
Drew (DROO)
Duke (DOOK)
Durwood (DUR-wood)

Elijah (el-LY-zhuh or uh-LY-juh [AA],
    el-lee-YAW-hoo [HEB])
 Alternate spellings: Alijah, Eliyahu
    [HEB]
Elwood (EL-wood)
 Alternate spellings: Ellwood
Emmanuel (ee-MAN-yoo-well [AA],
    ee-mawn-yoo-ELL [HEB],
    em-man-WELL [FR],
    ee-mawn-yoo-WELL or
    ee-man-WELL [SP])
 Alternate spellings: Emanuel,
    Immanuel
Eugene (yoo-JEEN, oo-ZHEN [FR])
Eugenio (ay-yoo-HEN-ee-yoh [SP])
Eujin (YOO-jin [KOR])
Eusebio (ay-yoo-SEB-ee-yoh or
    ay-yoo-THEV-ee-yoh [SP])
Ewan (YOO-win [SCOT])

Fortunato (for-too-NAW-toh [IT/SP])
Fu (FOO [CH])

Giuseppe (joo-SEP-pee [IT], joo-ZEP-pee)
Guadalupe (gwah-duh-LOO-pay or
    gwah-THAW-loo-pay [SP])
Gunther (GUN-thur, GOON-tur [GER])
Gustave (GOO-stawv [GER/SCAN],
    goo-STAWV [FR])
 Alternate spellings: Gustav
Gustavo (goo-STAW-voh [IT/SP],

    gooth-TAW-boh [SP])

Haywood (HAY-wood)
Hezekiah (hez-uh-KY-yuh,
    chiz-kee-YAW-hoo with guttural ch
    [HEB])
 Alternate spellings: Chizkiyahu [HEB]
Hoover (HOO-vur)
Houston (HYOO-sten)
 Alternate spellings: Huston
Hubert (HYOO-burt [GER], oo-BAIR [FR])
Huey (HYOO-wee [GER])
Hugh (HYOO [GER/IR])
Hugo (HYOO-goh [GER], oo-GOH [SP])
Humberto (oom-BAIR-toh or
    oom-VAIR-toh [SP])

Isaiah (eye-ZAY-yuh, is-shy-YAW or
    is-shy-YAW-hoo [HEB])
 Alternate spellings: Isiah, Izaiah,
    Yeshaya or Yeshayahu [HEB]

Jacob (JAY-kub, YAW-kohv [HEB],
    yaw-KOOB [AR])
 Alternate spellings: Jakob, Yakov* or
    Yaakov [HEB], Yakoub* [AR]
Jesús (hay-SOOS or hayth-OOTH [SP])
Jewell (JOO-well [AA])
 Alternate spellings: Jewel
Joseph (JOH-sef, YOH-sef or yoh-SEF [HEB],
    YOO-suf [AR], zho-ZEF [FR])
 Alternate spellings: Josef, Yosef*,
    Yusuf*
Joshua (JAW-shoo-wuh,
    ye-ho-SHOO-wuh [HEB])
 Alternate spellings: Joshuah,
    Yehoshua [HEB]
Josiah (joh-ZY-yuh, yoh-shee-YAW-hoo
    or yoh-SHEE-yuh [HEB])
 Alternate spellings: Yoshiyahu or
    Yoshiya [HEB]
Josué (ho-soo-WAY or ho-thoo-WAY [SP])
Judah (JOO-duh, ye-HOO-duh [HEB])
 Alternate spellings: Yehuda [HEB]
Jude (JOOD)
Jules (JOOLZ, ZHOOL [FR])
Julian (JOO-lee-yen, zhoo-lee-YAW with
    short N [FR])
 Alternate spellings: Julien
Julio (HOO-lee-yoh [SP])
Julius (JOO-lee-yes)
Jun (JOO-win [CH])
Junior (JOON-yur, JOO-nee-yur)
Junius (JOON-yes, JOO-nee-yes)

Alternate spellings: Junious
Justice (JUSS-tiss [AA])
  Alternate spellings: Justus
Justin (JUS-tin, zhoo-STE with short N [FR])
  Alternate spellings: Justyn, Justen, Juston
Justo (HOOS-toh or HOOTH-toh [SP])
Juwan (juh-WAHN or joo-WAHN [AA])

Kazuo (KAW-zoo-woh [JAP])
Keanu (kee-YAWN-oo [HW])

Lemuel (LEM-yoo-well [HEB])
Linwood (LIN-wood)
  Alternate spellings: Lynwood
Llewellyn (loo-WELL-in [WL])
Lou (LOO [GER])
  Alternate spellings: Lew
Louie (LOO-wee)
Louis (LOO-wiss [GER], loo-WEE [FR], loo-WEES [SP])
  Alternate spellings: Lewis, Luis [SP]
Luca (LOO-kuh [IT/HUN])
Lucas (LOO-kuss [GER/SCAN/SP], loo-KA [FR])
  Alternate spellings: Lukas
Luciano (loo-CHAW-noh [IT], loo-see-YAWN-oh or loo-thee-YAWN-oh [SP])
Lucien (LOO-shen, loo-see-YEN [FR])
  Alternate spellings: Lucian
Lucius (LOO-shus)
  Alternate spellings: Lucious
Ludwig (LOOD-wig, LOOD-vig [GER])
Luigi (loo-WEE-jee [IT])
Luke (LOOK)
  Alternate spellings: Luc [FR]
Lupe (LOO-pay [SP])
Luther (LOO-thur [GER])

Matthew (MATH-yoo [HEB])
  Alternate spellings: Mathew
Montague (MAWN-tug-yoo)
Mustafa (moo-STAW-fuh or moo-STUFF-uh [AR])

Newell (NOO-well)
Newman (NOO-men)
Newton (NOO-ten)
Nguyen (nig-GYOO-wen [VI])
Norwood (NOR-wood)
Nunzio (NOON-zee-yoh [IT])

Pasquale (pass-KAL [FR], paw-skoo-WALL or pawth-KWALL [SP])

Alternate spellings: Pascual [SP], Pasqual

Rahul (ruh-HOOL [AA], rrrraw-HOOL [EI])
Raouf (raw-OOF [AR])
Raul (raw-OOL, rrraw-OOL [FR/SP])
  Alternate spellings: Raoul, Rahul*
Raymundo (rrray-MOON-doh [SP])
Refugio (ref-FOO-hee-yoh [SP])
Roel (ROHL, ROH-well, RHOOL [SCAN])
Roosevelt (ROH-zuh-velt, ROOS-uh-velt)
  Alternate spellings: Rosevelt
Ruben (ROO-ben, ROO-ven or roo-VAYN [HEB], roo-BEN or roo-VEN [SP])
  Alternate spellings: Reuben, Rubin, Rueben, Reuven or Ruvane [HEB], Ruben [SP]
Ruby (ROO-bee)
Rudolph (ROO-dawlf, ROH-dawlf [GER], roh-DAWLF [FR])
  Alternate spellings: Rudolf, Rodolf [GER], Rodolphe [FR]
Rudy (ROO-dee [GER])
Rufus (ROO-fuss [BR])
Rupert (ROO-purt [BR/GER/SCAN])

Samuel (SAM-yoo-well, SAM-yool, SHMOO-well [HEB], sam-WELL [IT/SP])
  Alternate spellings: Shmuel [HEB]
Saul (SAWL, shaw-OOL [HEB], saw-OOL or thaw-OOL [SP])
  Alternate spellings: Sol*, Shaul [HEB]
Sherwood (SHUR-wood)
Stuart (STOO-wurt)
  Alternate spellings: Stewart

Truman (TROO-men [GER])
Tudor (TOO-dor [WL])

Ulises (yoo-LISS-seez, oo-LEE-says or oo-LEETH-ayth [SP])
  Alternate spellings: Ulysses

Vishnu (VISH-noo [EI])

Woodrow (WOOD-roh)
Woody (WOO-dee)

Yakoub (yaw-KOOB [AR])
  Alternate spellings: Jacob*, Jakob
Yul (YOOL [CH])
Yusuf (YOO-suf [AR])
Yuuji (YOO-oo-jee [JAP])

■ SHORT U (UH OR U) ■

PARTNER POINTER:
Short E, I, and U often sound similar. Please note that we are not including names that only end in "uh" on this list, because there are too many.

Abdul (ab-DULL or ab-DOOL or awb-DOOL [AR])
Abdullah (ab-DULL-uh [AR], ab-DOO-luh [AA])
Abraham (AYB-ri-ham, awv-ruh-HAWM [HEB])
    Alternate spellings: Avraham [HEB]
Abram (AY-brum, aw-VRAWM [HEB])
    Alternate spellings: Avram [HEB]
Adam (AD-dum, aw-DAWM [HEB])
Adelard (AD-uh-lard)
Adelbert (AD-dull-burt [GER], ad-dell-BAIR [FR])
Aditya (aw-DIT-yuh or aw-THIT-yuh [EI])
Adolphus (uh-DAWL-fus, ay-DAWL-fus)
Adonis (uh-DAWN-iss, aw-DOH-nees [SP])
Alonzo (uh-LAWN-zoh, aw-LOHN-soh [SP])
    Alternate spellings: Alonso
Amador (AM-uh-dor, aw-maw-DOR [SP])
Amari (uh-MAR-ree [AA])
Anton (AN-tun [AA], awn-TOHN [FR])
    Alternate spellings: Antone
Antony (AN-tun-ee)
Arjun (AR-jun, ar-JOON) [EI]
Arnold (AR-nuld [GER])
Augustin (aw-GUS-tin, oh-goos-TEEN or ow-goh-STAW with short N [FR], aw-goo-STEEN or aw-gooth-TEEN [SP])
    Alternate spellings: Agustin, Augustín [SP]
    Alternate spellings: Augustine
Augustus (aw-GUS-tus)

Barton (BAR-tun)
Bertram (BURT-rum)
Bishop (BISH-up)
Braxton (BRAK-stun)
Buck (BUK)
Bud (BUD)
Buddy (BUD-ee)
    Alternate spellings: Buddie
Buster (BUS-tur)
Buzz (BUZ [CG])

Campbell (KAM-bull)

Cheng (CHUNG [CH])
Chuck (CHUK)
Columbus (koh-LUM-bus)
Cullen (KUL-lin [CG])
Cyrus (SY-russ, see-ROOS [PER])

Dakota (duh-KOH-tuh)
    Alternate spellings: Dakotah
Darold (DAIR-ruld)
Darrell (DAIR-rull)
    Alternate spellings: Darryl, Daryl, Derrell, Daryle
Davon (DAY-vun [AA], DAV-in [IR])
    Alternate spellings: Davin
Delmas (DEL-muss)
Demarco (duh-MAR-koh)
Demarcus (duh-MAR-kuss [AA])
Demario (duh-MAR-ree-yoh [AA])
Demetrios (duh-MEE-tree-yohs [GRK])
Demetris (duh-MEE-tris [AA/GRK])
Demetrius (duh-MEE-tree-yes [GRK])
DeMond (duh-MAWND [AA])
Deshawn (duh-SHAWN [AA])
    Alternate spellings: Dashawn, Deshaun
Desmond (DEZ-mund [IR])
Devonte (duh-VAWN-tay [AA])
    Alternate spellings: Devante, Davonte, Devonta, Devontae
Dewayne (duh-WAYN or DWAYN [AA])
    Alternate spellings: Duwayne, Dwayne*, Duane, Dwain
Dewitt (duh-WIT, DOO-wit)
Diezel (DEE-zull)
Dillion (DILL-ee-yun, DILL-yen)
Donal (DAW-null [IR], daw-NELL [AA])
Donald (DAWN-uld [CG])
Donnell (DAW-nell, DOH-null [IR])
    Alternate spellings: Donal, Donell
Dudley (DUD-lee)
Duncan (DUN-kin [CG])
Dustin (DUS-tin)
Dusty (DUS-tee)

Edison (ED-is-sun)
Edmund (ED-mund)
    Alternate spellings: Edmond
Enoch (EE-nuk, EE-nawk, chaw-NOCH with guttural CH [HEB])
    Alternate spellings: Chanoch [HEB]
Esteban (es-TEB-awn or eth-TEV-awn [SP], ES-tuh-bawn, ES-tuh-vawn)
    Alternate spellings: Estevan

Fergus (FUR-gus, FAIR-ges [IR])

Ferguson (FUR-gus-sin)
Finnegan (FIN-uh-gin [IR])

Gaston (GASS-tun [CG], gas-TOHN or
     gas-TAW with short N [FR])
Gearld (GAIR-ruld)
     Alternate spellings: Gerald*, Garold,
     Gerold
General (JEN-ur-rull)
Gideon (GID-ee-yun, GEED-ohn or
     geed-OHN [HEB])
     Alternate spellings: Gidon [HEB]
Gonzalo (gun-ZAW-loh, gohn-SAW-loh
     or gohn-THAW-loh [SP])
Guadalupe (gwah-duh-LOO-pay or
     gwah-THAW-loo-pay [SP])
Gui (guh-WAY [CH])
Gulliver (GUL-liv-ur)
Gunnar (GUN-ur [SCAN])
     Alternate spellings: Gunner
Gunther (GUN-thur, GOON-tur [GER])
Gus (GUS [GER])

Hamza (hum-ZAW [AR])
Harold (HAIR-ruld [SCAN])
Haskell (HAS-kull)
Hezekiah (hez-uh-KY-yuh,
     chiz-kee-YAW-hoo with guttural ch
     [HEB])
     Alternate spellings: Chizkiyahu [HEB]
Hong (HUNG [CH])
Hudson (HUD-sen)
Humphrey (HUM-free [GER])
Hunter (HUN-tur)

Ibrahim (EEB-ruh-heem or EEB-ruh-him
     [AA], ee-braw-HEEM or ib-raw-HEEM
     [AR])
Ignatius (ig-NAY-shuss, ig-NAY-see-yus)
Isidor (IZ-uh-dor [GRK], ee-see-DOR [FR])
     Alternate spellings: Isidore, Isador,
     Isadore

Jabari (juh-BAR-ree [AA])
Jabreel (zhub-RRREEL [AR])
Jacari (juh-KAIR-ree or juh-KAR-ree or
     JAK-ur-ree)
Jacob (JAY-kub, YAW-kohv [HEB],
     yaw-KOOB [AR])
     Alternate spellings: Jakob, Yakov* or
     Yaakov [HEB], Yakoub* [AR]
Jacoby (juh-KOH-bee, JAY-kub-ee)
     Alternate spellings: Jakobe, Jacobi
Jaheim (juh-HEEM [AA/AR])

Alternate spellings: Jahiem, Jaheem
Jairo (HY-yuh-roh or HY-roh [SP])
Jaleel (jull-EEL [AA], zhul-EEL [AR])
Jamal (jum-AWL [AA], zhum-AYL or
     zhum-AWL [AR])
     Alternate spellings: Jamaal
Jamar (jum-MAR [AA])
Jamarcus (jum-MAR-kuss [AA])
Jamari (jum-MAR-ree [AA])
Jameson (JAY-mis-sun)
     Alternate spellings: Jamison
Jamil (jum-EEL or jum-ELL [AA],
     zhum-EEL [AR])
     Alternate spellings: Jamel
Jamir (jum-EER [AA])
Jarom (JAIR-rum, yar-ROHM [HEB])
     Alternate spellings: Yarom [HEB]
Javion (JAY-vee-yawn or JAY-vee-yun [AA])
Javon (JAY-vun [AA])
     Alternate spellings: Javen and Javan,
     Jevon
Javonte (juh-VAWN-tay [AA])
Jeremiah (jair-ruh-MY-yuh,
     yeer-mee-YAW-hoo [HEB])
     Alternate spellings: Yirmeyahu [HEB]
Jeremy (JAIR-ruh-mee)
     Alternate spellings: Jeramy, Jeremie,
     Jeromy, Jeremey, Jeramie
Jerrell (juh-RELL or JAIR-rell [AA])
     Alternate spellings: Jarrell, Jerel
Joachim (wah-KEEM, JOH-wah-kim,
     zho-wah-SHE with short N [FR],
     yo-WAH-kim [GER], yuh-ho-wuh-KEEM
     or yow-wuh-KEEM [HEB])
     Alternate spellings: Joakim,
     Jehoiakim or Yehoyakim [HEB]
Joaquin (wah-KEEN, ho-wah-KEEN [SP],
     yuh-ho-wuh-CHEEN or
     yow-wuh-CHEEN with guttural CH [HEB])
     Alternate spellings: Joaquín [SP],
     Jehoiachin or Yehoyachin [HEB]
Jomar (joh-MAR [BIB], juh-MAR [AA],
     OH-mar)
     Alternate spellings: Omar*
Jonathan (JAW-nuh-thin, yoh-nuh-TAWN
     [HEB])
     Alternate spellings: Johnathan,
     Jonathon, Johnathon, Jonatan,
     Yonatan [HEB]
Joshua (JAW-shoo-wuh,
     yuh-ho-SHOO-wuh [HEB])
     Alternate spellings: Joshuah,
     Yehoshua [HEB]
Judd (JUD)

Judge (JUDJ)
Judson (JUD-sen)
Justice (JUS-tis [AA])
    Alternate spellings: Justus
Justin (JUS-tin, zhoo-STE with short N [FR])
    Alternate spellings: Justyn, Justen,
    Juston
Juwan (juh-WAHN or joo-WAHN [AA])

Kadeem (kuh-DEEM [AA/AR])
Kamari (kuh-MAR-ee [AA])
Kareem (kuh-REEM [AA], kuh-RRREEM [AR])
Kelton (KEL-tun [CG])
Kendall (KEN-dull)
    Alternate spellings: Kendal
Kennedy (KEN-uh-dee [IR])

Lamar (luh-MAR [AA/GER])
Lamont (luh-MAWNT [AA/SCAN])
Latrell (luh-TRELL [AA])
Lashawn (luh-SHAWN [AA])
Lazaro (LAZ-uh-roh or luh-ZAR-oh [AA],
    law-ZAR-roh [IT])
Leopold (LEE-yup-old [GER],
    lay-yoh-POHLD [FR])
    Alternate spellings: Léopold [FR]
Levar (luh-VAR [AA])
Lionel (LY-null, lee-yoh-NELL [FR])
London (LUN-den)
Long (LUNG [CH])
Lucius (LOO-shus)
    Alternate spellings: Lucious

MacKenzie (muh-KEN-zee, mak-KEN-zee)
Malachi (MAL-uh-ky [IR], maw-law-CHEE
    with guttural CH [HEB])
    Alternate spellings: Malakai, Malachai
Malachy (MAL-uh-kee [IR])
Malcolm (MAL-kum [CG])
    Alternate spellings: Malcom
Malik (mul-EEK [AA], mal-EEK or MAL-ik
    or MUL-ik [AR])
Marcellus (mar-SELL-us)
Marcus (MAR-kus)
    Alternate spellings: Marquis*, Markus,
    Marques
Marshall (MAR-shull)
    Alternate spellings: Marshal, Marcial
Mateo (muh-TAY-yoh [SP])
    Alternate spellings: Matteo
Mathias (muh-THY-yes)
Mattias (muh-TY-yes [HEB])
Melton (MEL-tun)
Merton (MUR-tun)

Mitchell (MICH-ull)
    Alternate spellings: Mitchel
Montague (MAWN-tug-yoo)
Mordecai (MOR-dik-ky, mor-duh-CHY
    with guttural CH [HEB])
    Alternate spellings: Mordechai [HEB]
Morton (MOR-tun)

Nakia (nuh-KEE-yuh [AA])
Napoleon (nuh-POH-lee-yen)
Nasir (NAW-seer or nuh-SEER or
    NAW-sur [AR])
Nathan (NAY-thin, nuh-TAWN [HEB])
    Alternate spellings: Nathen, Natan [HEB]
Nathaniel (nuh-THAN-yell,
    naw-tawn-ELL [HEB])
    Alternate spellings: Nathanael,
    Nathanial, Netanel [HEB]
Nehemiah (nee-yuh-MY-yuh,
    neh-CHEM-ee-yuh with guttural CH
    [HEB])
    Alternate spellings: Nechemya or
    Nechemia [HEB]
Nicholas (NIK-ul-us, nee-koh-LAW [FR])
    Alternate spellings: Nicolas, Nickolas,
    Nikolas
Noble (NOH-bull)
Norval (NOR-vull)
    Alternate spellings: Norville

Omar (OH-mar or UM-ar [AR])
    Alternate spellings: Jomar*
Omer (um-AIR or oh-MAIR [AR])
Oral (OR-rull)

Paxton (PAK-stun)

Rafael (RAF-ee-yell, raf-y-YELL,
    rrraf-uh-YELL [FR], raw-faw-ELL [HEB/SP],
    rrraw-FAY-yell [SP])
    Alternate spellings: Raphael, Raphaël
Raheem (ruh-HEEM or raw-HEEM [AA/AR])
Rahul (ruh-HOOL [AA], rrrraw-HOOL [EI])
Ransom (RAN-sum)
Rashad (ruh-SHAWD or ruh-SHAD [AA/AR])
Rashawn (ruh-SHAWN [AA/AR])
    Alternate spellings: Rayshawn*
Rasheed (ruh-SHEED or raw-SHEED [AA/AR])
Raymon (RAY-mun)
    Alternate spellings: Ramón*
Raymond (RAY-mund [GER], rrray-MAW
    with short N [FR])
    Alternate spellings: Raymonde [FR]
Reginal (REJ-in-ul)

Reginald (REJ-in-uld [GER])
Richmond (RICH-mund)
Roosevelt (ROH-zuh-velt, ROO-suh-velt)
    Alternate spellings: Rosevelt
Rufus (ROO-fuss [BR])
Rush (RUSH)
Russ (RUS)
Russell (RUS-sell)
    Alternate spellings: Russel
Rusty (RUS-tee)

Salvatore (sal-vuh-TOR-ray [IT])
Sampath (SUM-put [EI])
Samson (SAM-sun, sheem-SHOHN [HEB])
    Alternate spellings: Shimshon [HEB]
Seamus (SHAY-muss [IR])
    Alternate spellings: Shamus
Sebastian (sub-BAS-chen,
    sub-BAS-tee-yen, say-bas-tee-YAW
    with short N [FR], say-baws-TAWN or
    thay-vaws-TAWN [SP])
    Alternate spellings: Sabastian,
    Sebastien, Sébastien [FR], Sebastián [SP]
Semaj (suh-MAWJ [AA])
    Alternate spellings: Samaj [EI]
Shamar (shum-MAR [AA])
    Alternate spellings: Shemar
Sigmund (SIG-mund [GER/SCAN]; see also
    Zigmund)
Simeon (SIM-ee-yun [HEB])
Simon (SY-mun [GRK], shee-MOHN [HEB],
    see-MAW with short N [FR])
    Alternate spellings: Shimon [HEB]
Solomon (SAW-loh-mun, SHLO-moh [HEB])
    Alternate spellings: Shlomo [HEB]
Solon (SOH-lun [GRK])
Sonny (SUN-ee)
Sullivan (SUL-liv-en [CG])
Sumner (SUM-nur)

Taurean (TOR-ree-yun [AA])
Tavon (TAY-vun or TAY-vawn [AA])
    Alternate spellings: Tevon*, Tavin
Terrell (tuh-RELL [AA], TAIR-rill)
    Alternate spellings: Terrill
Thaddeus (THAD-ee-yuss [GRK])
Theo (THEE-yoh, TAY-yoh [FR])
    Alternate spellings: Théo [FR]
Theodore (THEE-yuh-dor, tay-yoh-DOR
    [FR])
    Alternate spellings: Theadore,
    Theodor, Théodore [FR]
Theron (THAIR-run [AA], TAIR-ren,
    thair-ROHN)

Thomas (TAW-muss, TOH-maws [GER],
    toh-MAW [FR], toh-MAWS [IR/SP])
    Alternate spellings: Tomás
Titus (TYD-us)
Tremaine (truh-MAYN [AA/CG])
    Alternate spellings: Tremayne,
    Tremain
Trevion (TRAY-vee-yun or
    TRAY-vee-yawn [AA])
Trevon (TRAY-vun [AA], TREV-in)
    Alternate spellings: Travon, Trevin,
    Treven
Tucker (TUK-ur)

Waldemar (WALL-duh-mar,
    VAWL-duh-mar [GER/SCAN])
    Alternate spellings: Valdemar [SCAN]
Willem (WIL-um [CG])
William (WIL-yum)
Williams (WIL-yumz)

Zachariah (zak-kur-RY-yuh,
    zuh-CHAR-ree-yuh with guttural CH
    [HEB], zuk-uh-REE-yuh [AR])
    Alternate spellings: Zecharya [HEB]
Zechariah (zek-kur-RY-uh,
    zuh-CHAR-ree-uh with guttural CH
    [HEB], zuk-uh-REE-yuh [AR])
    Alternate spellings: Zecharya [HEB]
Zigmund (ZIG-mund; see also Sigmund)

■ UR ■

PARTNER POINTER:
Check the OO list, too.

Abner (AB-nur, AWV-nur [HEB])
    Alternate spellings: Avner [HEB]
Adelbert (AD-dull-burt [GER], ad-dell-BAIR
    [FR])
Alastair (AL-iss-tair or AL-iss-tur [BR])
    Alternate spellings: Alistair, Allistair
Albert (AL-burt [GER], al-BAIR [FR])
Alexander (al-eks-ZAN-dur)
    Alternate spellings: Alexzander
Anderson (AN-dur-sen)
Arthur (AR-thur [CG])
    Alternate spellings: Arther
Asher (ASH-ur, AW-shur [HEB])
Avery (AY-vur-ree)

Bernard (bur-NARD, bair-NAR [FR])
    Alternate spellings: Bernhard

Bernardo (bur-NAR-doh, bair-NAR-doh
  or vair-NAR-doh [SP])
Bernie (BUR-nee)
Bert (BURT [GER])
  Alternate spellings: Burt
Bertram (BURT-rum)
Bertrand (BURT-rend, bair-TRAW with
  short N [FR])
Booker (BOOK-ur)
Bradford (BRAD-furd)
Bridger (BRID-jur)
Broderick (BRAW-dur-rik [CG])
Buford (BYOO-furd)
Burdette (bur-DETT)
Burl (BURL)
Burley (BUR-lee)
Burnell (bur-NELL)
Burton (BUR-ten)
  Alternate spellings: Berton

Caesar (SEE-zur)
  Alternate spellings: Cesar*
Cameron (KAM-ur-ren, KAM-ren)
  Alternate spellings: Kameron,
  Camron, Kamron, Camren
Carter (KAR-tur)
Casper (KAS-pur [GER])
  Alternate spellings: Caspar, Kasper
Cedar (SEE-dur)
Cesar (SAY-sar/THAY-thar or SESS-
  ar/THE-thar [SP], SEE-zur)
  Alternate spellings: Caesar*
Chandler (CHAND-lur)
Chester (CHES-tur)
Christopher (KRIS-toh-fur)
  Alternate spellings: Kristopher,
  Cristopher, Kristofer, Kristoffer,
  Cristofer
Cicero (SIS-ur-roh)
Clifford (KLIF-urd)
Clover (KLOH-vur)
Connor (KAW-nur [IR])
  Alternate spellings: Conner, Conor,
  Konnor
Cooper (KOO-pur)
Crawford (KRAW-furd)
Curtis (KUR-tis)
  Alternate spellings: Kurtis, Curtiss

De (DUR [CH])
Delbert (DELL-burt)
Delmar (del-MAR, DEL-mur)
  Alternate spellings: Delmer*
Delmer (DEL-mur)

  Alternate spellings: Delmar*
Denver (DEN-vur)
Dermot (DUR-met [CG], DEER-mid [IR])
Derwin (DUR-win)
Dexter (DEK-stur)
Dillard (DILL-urd)
Dirk (DURK [GER])
Durward (DUR-wurd)
Durwood (DUR-wood)

Earl (URL [CG])
  Alternate spellings: Earle
Early (URL-ee)
  Alternate spellings: Earlie
Earnest (UR-nest [GER])
Edgar (ED-gur, ed-GAR [FR])
Edward (ED-wurd)
Elbert (EL-burt)
Eliezer (el-lee-YEZ-ur [HEB/AA], el-LEE-zur,
  el-LY-zur, el-lee-ZAIR or el-lee-THAIR
  [SP])
Ellery (ELL-ur-ree)
Ellsworth (ELZ-wurth)
Elmer (EL-mur)
Emerson (EM-ur-sen [GER])
Emery (EM-ur-ree [GER])
  Alternate spellings: Emory
Erling (UR-leeng)
Ernesto (air-NES-toh [IT/SP], air-NETH-toh
  [SP])
Ernie (UR-nee [GER])
Ernst (URNST [GER])
Erwin (UR-win)
Evert (EV-urt)

Ferdinand (FUR-din-and, FAIR-din-
  nawnd [GER], fair-dee-NAW with short
  ND [FR])
Fergus (FUR-gus, FAIR-ges [IR])
Ferguson (FUR-gus-sin)
Fernando (fur-NAN-doh, fair-NAWN-doh
  [SP])
Fisher (FISH-ur)
Fletcher (FLECH-ur)
Foster (FAWS-tur)
Frederick (FRED-ur-rik [GER],
  fray-day-REEK [FR])
  Alternate spellings: Frederic, Frederic
  [FR]
Furman (FUR-men)

Gardner (GARD-nur)
General (JEN-ur-rull)
Gerard (jur-RARD, zhay-RAR [FR])

Alternate spellings: Gérard [FR]
German (JUR-men, her-MAWN [SP],
    zhair-MAN [FR])
    Alternate spellings: Germán [SP],
    Germain [FR]
Gilbert (GIL-burt, zheel-BAIR [FR])
Gregory (GREG-ur-ree)
    Alternate spellings: Greggory
Grover (GROH-vur)
Gulliver (GUL-liv-ur)
Gunnar (GUN-ur [SCAN])
    Alternate spellings: Gunner
Gunther (GUN-thur, GOON-tur [GER])

Hayward (HAY-wurd)
Heber (HAY-bur, HEE-bur [BIB], ay-BAIR [IR])
Herb (HURB [GER])
Herbert (HUR-burt [GER], air-BAIR [FR])
Herman (HUR-men [GER])
    Alternate spellings: Hermon, Hermann
Herschel (HUR-shell)
    Alternate spellings: Hershel
Hilbert (HILL-burt)
Hillard (HILL-urd)
Hilliard (HILL-yurd)
Hobert (HO-burt)
Homer (HO-mur)
Hoover (HOO-vur)
Howard (HOW-wurd)
Hubert (HYOO-burt [GER], oo-BAIR [FR])
Hunter (HUN-tur)
Hurley (HUR-lee)

Irvin (UR-ven)
    Alternate spellings: Ervin
Irving (URV-eeng)

Jacari (juh-KAIR-ree or juh-KAR-ree or
    JAK-ur-ree)
Jagger (JAG-ur)
Jair (JAY-yur [BIB], JAIR, yaw-EER or
    YAW-eer [HEB])
    Alternate spellings: Jere*, Yair [HEB],
    Yahir*
Jasper (JAS-pur [BR])
Jefferson (JEF-fur-sen)
Jermaine (jur-MAYN [AA], zhur-MA [FR])
    Alternate spellings: Germaine,
    Jermain
Jerome (jur-ROHM [AA], zhay-ROHM [FR])
    Alternate spellings: Jérôme [FR]
Junior (JOON-yur, JOO-nee-yur)

Kermit (KUR-mit [CG])

Kerwin (KUR-win)
Kiefer (KEE-fur [CG])
    Alternate spellings: Keefer
Kirby (KUR-bee)
Kirk (KURK [SCAN])
Kurt (KURT [GER])
    Alternate spellings: Curt, Kirt
Kyler (KY-lur [SCAN])

Lambert (LAM-burt [GER], lam-BAIR [FR])
Lazarus (LAZ-ur-russ)
Leander (lee-YAN-dur)
Leonard (LEN-urd [GER], lay-yoh-NAR [FR])
    Alternate spellings: Lenard, Leonard [FR]
Lester (LES-tur)
Luther (LOO-thur [GER])

Major (MAY-jur)
Maverick (MAV-ur-rik)
Maynard (MAY-nurd, MAY-nard)
McArthur (mik-AR-thur [CG])
Merle (MURL)
    Alternate spellings: Murl, Merl, Mearl
Merlin (MUR-lin [WL])
    Alternate spellings: Merlyn
Merton (MUR-tun)
Mervin (MUR-vin [WL])
    Alternate spellings: Mervyn
Meyer (MAY-ur or may-YEER [HEB], MY-ur)
    Alternate spellings: Meir
Milburn (MIL-burn)
Milford (MIL-furd)
Millard (MIL-lurd)
Miller (MIL-lur)
Montgomery (mawnt-GUM-ur-ree)
Mortimer (MOR-tim-ur)
Murphy (MUR-fee)
Murray (MUR-ree)
    Alternate spellings: Murry

Nasir (NAW-seer or nuh-SEER or
    NAW-sur [AR])
Nestor (NES-tur, NES-tor or NETH-tor [SP])
    Alternate spellings: Néstor [SP]

Oliver (AW-liv-ur)
Oscar (AWS-kur [SCAN], aws-KAR or
    awth-KAR [SP])

Palmer (PAWL-mur, PAW-mur)
Parker (PAR-kur)
Percival (PUR-siv-ull [BR])
Percy (PER-see [BR])
Pernell (pur-NELL)

Pershing (PUR-sheeng)
Porter (POR-tur)

Rayburn (RAY-burn)
Rayford (RAY-furd)
Raynard (RAY-nurd, ray-NARD)
Rexford (REKS-furd, REKS-ford)
Richard (RICH-urd, rrree-SHAR [FR])
River (RIV-ur)
Robert (RAW-burt, rrroh-BAIR [FR])
Roberto (rrroh-BAIR-toh [SP], roh-BUR-toh)
Roderick (RAW-dur-rik or RAWD-rik [GER])
    Alternate spellings: Rodrick
Roger (RAW-jur [GER], rrroh-ZHAIR [FR])
    Alternate spellings: Rodger
Rogers (RAW-jurz, rrroh-ZHAY [FR])
Rupert (ROO-purt [BR/GER/SCAN])
Ryder (RY-dur)
Ryker (RY-kur)

Sanford (SAN-furd)
Sawyer (SOI-yur)
Selmer (SEL-mur [SCAN])
Serge (SURJ, SAIRZH [FR])
Sergei (SUR-gay or SAIR-gay [RUS])
    Alternate spellings: Serge
Sergio (SUR-jee-yoh, SAIR-jee-yoh or
    SAIR-joh [IT], SAIR-hee-yoh or
    THAIR-hee-yoh [SP])
Sherman (SHUR-men)
Sherwin (SHUR-win)
Sherwood (SHUR-wood)
Sigurd (SIG-urd [SCAN])
Skyler (SKY-lur)
    Alternate spellings: Skylar, Schuyler
Spencer (SPEN-sur)
    Alternate spellings: Spenser
Stanford (STAN-furd)
Sterling (STUR-leeng)
    Alternate spellings: Stirling
Stuart (STOO-wurt)
    Alternate spellings: Stewart
Sumner (SUM-nur)
Sylvester (sil-VES-tur)

Tanner (TAN-ur)
Taylor (TAY-lur)
    Alternate spellings: Tayler
Thatcher (THACH-ur)
Thurman (THUR-men)
Thurston (THURS-ten [SCAN])
Topher (TOH-fur)
Trevor (TREV-ur [CG])
    Alternate spellings: Trever

Tucker (TUK-ur)
Tudor (TOO-dor [WL], TOO-dur)
Turner (TUR-nur)
Tyler (TY-lur)
    Alternate spellings: Tylor

Urban (UR-ben)
Uriel (YUR-ree-yell [HEB])

Verl (VURL)
Verlin (VUR-lin)
Vern (VURN)
    Alternate spellings: Verne
Vernell (VUR-null, vur-NELL)
Vernie (VUR-nee)
Vernon (VUR-nen)
Vester (VES-tur [GER])
Victor (VIK-tur, veek-TOR [FR],
    VEEK-tor or BEEK-tor [SP])
    Alternate spellings: Victor [SP], Viktor
Virgil (VUR-jil)
    Alternate spellings: Vergil

Walker (WAH-kur)
Walter (WALL-tur, VAWL-tur [GER])
Warner (WOR-nur, WAR-nur, VAR-nur
    [GER])
Webster (WEB-stur)
Werner (WUR-nur, VUR-nur [GER])
    Alternate spellings: Verner
Wheeler (WEE-lur)
Wilbert (WIL-burt)
Wilbur (WIL-bur, VIL-bur [GER])
Wilburn (WIL-burn, VIL-burn [GER])
Wilford (WIL-furd)
Willard (WIL-urd, VIL-urd [GER])
Wilmer (WIL-mur, VIL-mur [GER])
Worth (WURTH)

Xavier (ZAY-vee-yur, eks-ZAY-vee-yur,
    haw-vee-YAIR or haw-bee-YAIR [SP],
    zav-YAY [FR])
    Alternate spellings: Javier*, Xzavier,
    Zavier

Yuri (YUR-ree [RUS])

Zachariah (zak-kur-RY-yuh,
    zuh-CHAR-ree-yuh with guttural CH
    [HEB], zuk-uh-REE-yuh [AR])
    Alternate spellings: Zecharya [HEB]
Zachary (ZAK-ur-ree)
    Alternate spellings: Zackary, Zachery,
    Zackery, Zakary

Zander (ZAN-dur)
    Alternate spellings: Xander
Zechariah (zek-kur-RY-uh, zuh-CHAR-
    ree-uh with guttural CH [HEB], zuk-uh-
    REE-yuh [AR])
    Alternate spellings: Zecharya [HEB]
Zhi (JUR [CH])

B, CH, D, F , G, H, J, K, L, M, N/NG, P, Q (KW), R, S, SH/ZH, T, TH, V, W, X (KS), Y, Z

Confused about how to pronounce it?
Consult the vowel lists.

■ B ■

PARTNER POINTER:
Check the P list, too.
Some Spanish speak-
ers pronounce "v" as
"b," so you will find
names like Olivia and
Virginia on this B list.

Abby
Abigail
Abrianna
Abril
Alba
Alberta
Albertha
Albertine
Albina
Amber
Annabella
Annabelle
Arabella
Aubrey

Babette
Bailey
Bambi
Barb
Barbara
Barbra
Beatrice
Beatrix
Becky
Belen
Belinda
Bella
Bellamy
Belle
Belva

Benita
Bennie
Berenice
Bernadette
Bernardine
Bernita
Berta
Bertha
Bertie
Beryl
Bess
Bessie
Beth
Bethel
Betsy
Bette
Bettina
Betty
Beulah
Beverly
Bianca
Billie
Birdie
Blair
Blanca
Blanche
Blossom
Blue
Bonita
Bonnie
Brandon
Brandy
Bree
Brenda
Brenna
Bria
Brianna
Brianne
Bridget
Brielle

Brigitte
Brisa
Britney
Brittany
Brooke
Brooklyn
Brunilda
Brynn
Buffy

Campbell
Clarabelle
Cybelle

Darby
Debbie
Deborah

Ebba
Ebony
Elba
Elizabeth
Erzsebet

Fabiola

Gabriel
Gabriela
Gabriella
Gabrielle

Ingeborg
Isabel
Isabela

Jovita

Kimberly

Libby

Liberty
Lisbet
Lizabeth
Lizbeth

Mabel
Maribel
Marybeth
Maybelle
Melba
Mirabelle

Octavia
Olivia

Phoebe

Reba
Rebecca
Robbie
Roberta
Robyn
Ruby

Sabina
Sabine
Sabrina
Sheba
Shelba
Shelby
Siobhan
Sybil

Tabitha
Toby

Valencia
Vera
Verona
Veronica
Vicenta
Victoria
Vilma
Viola
Virginia

■ CH ■

**PARTNER POINTER:
Check the J and
SH/ZH lists, too.**

Blanche

Cecilia
Celeste
Celestina
Celina
Chanda
Chandler
Chandra
Chanel
Charity
Charles
Charlie
Chasity
Chastity
Chaya
Chelsea
Cherie
Cherish
Cherry
China
Chiquita
Christian
Concetta

Felicita
Francesca

Gretchen

Lucia

Marcelina
Marcella
Michiko

Rachel

Satchel

Valencia
Vincenza

■ D ■

**PARTNER POINTER:
Check the T list, too.**

Ada
Addie
Addison
Adelaida
Adelaide
Adele

Adelia
Adelina
Adeline
Adrian
Adriana
Adrianna
Adrienne
Aida
Alda
Alejandra
Alessandra
Aleta
Alexandra
Alexandria
Alexandrie
Alfreda
Almeda
Alondra
Amanda
Andrea
Ardell
Ardella
Ardis
Ardith
Armida
Astrid
Audie
Audra
Audrey
Awilda

Belinda
Bernadette
Bernardine
Betty
Birdie
Brandon
Brandy
Brenda
Bridget
Brunilda

Cadence
Candace
Candida
Candy
Cassandra
Cassidy
Cedar
Chanda
Chandler
Chandra
Cinda
Cindy

Claudette
Claudia
Claudie
Claudine
Clotilde
Cody
Cordelia
Cordia
Cordie

Dagmar
Dagny
Daisy
Dakota
Dale
Dalia
Dallas
Damaris
Dana
Danelle
Danette
Dania
Danica
Daniela
Danielle
Danita
Danna
Daphne
Dara
Darby
Darcy
Darian
Darla
Darlene
Daryl
Dasia
Davin
Davina
Dawn
Dayana
Dean
Deann
Deanna
Deasia
Debbie
Deedee
Deepa
Deidre
Deirdre
Deja
Delaney
Delfina
Delia
Delilah

Delisa
Dell
Della
Delma
Delois
Delpha
Delphia
Delphine
Delta
Demetria
Demi
Deneen
Denise
Desiree
Dessie
Destiny
Devin
Dexter
Diamond
Diana
Diane
Dimple
Dina
Dionne
Dixie
Dolly
Dolores
Dominga
Dominique
Donna
Donnie
Dora
Dorcas
Doreen
Dori
Dorinda
Doris
Dorit
Dorotha
Dorothea
Dorothy
Dortha
Dorthy
Dottie
Dovie
Drew
Drucilla
Dulce
Dylan

Eda
Eddie
Eden
Edie

Edith
Edna
Edrie
Edwina
Elda
Eldora
Elfrieda
Elida
Emerald
Enid
Erlinda
Esmeralda
Esmerelda
Ettie
Eudora

Fernanda
Florida
Fonda
Freddie
Frida

Geraldine
Gerda
Gertie
Gertrude
Giada
Gladys
Glenda
Glynda
Golda
Golden
Goldia
Goldie
Greta
Gretel
Guadalupe
Gudrun
Gwendolyn

Hadley
Hattie
Haydee
Hayden
Hedwig
Heidi
Hettie
Hilda
Hilde
Hildegarde
Hildred
Hildur
Hulda

Ida
Idell
Idella
Imelda
India
Ingrid
Ireland
Isadora
Isadore

Jada
Jade
Jaden
Jetta
Jettie
Jodie
Jordan
Judith
Judy

Kayden
Kendall
Kendra
Kennedy
Khadijah

Ladonna
Lashanda
Lavada
Lawanda
Leandra
Leta
Lettie
Linda
Lindy
London
Lottie
Lourdes
Lucinda
Ludie
Lyda
Lydia

Maddalena
Madelena
Madeline
Madie
Madison
Madonna
Mafalda
Magdalen
Magdalena
Magdalene
Maida

Mandy
Matilda
Matilde
Maude
Maudie
Meadow
Melinda
Melody
Mercedes
Meredith
Migdalia
Mildred
Mindy
Miranda
Modesta

Nadia
Nadine
Naheed
Natividad
Nedra
Nelda
Nelida
Nereida
Neta
Nilda
Nydia

Odalys
Odell
Odessa
Odetta
Odette
Odie
Ouida

Patty
Providenci
Prudence

Randi
Rhoda
Rhonda
Rolanda
Rosalind
Rosalinda
Rosamond

Sade
Sadie
Sandra
Sandy
Shalonda
Shanda

Shandi
Sharonda
Shawanda
Shonda
Sidonie
Sigrid
Soledad
Sondra
Sudie
Sydney

Tawanda
Theda
Theodora
Trinidad
Trudy

Veda
Velda
Verda
Verla
Vida
Vita
Vonda

Wanda
Wendy
Wilda
Windy
Winifred

Yadira
Yarden
Yehudit
Yolanda

Zaida
Zelda
Zenda
Zetta
Zoraida

■ F ■

**PARTNER POINTER:
Check the T list, too.**

Afton
Alfreda
Alpha

Buffy

Christopher

Delfina
Delpha
Delphia
Delphine

Effie
Elfrieda
Estefania
Estefany

Fabiola
Fairy
Faith
Fallon
Fannie
Farrah
Fatima
Faye
Felicia
Felicita
Felicity
Felipa
Feng
Fern
Fernanda
Filomena
Fiona
Fleta
Flo
Flora
Florence
Florida
Florine
Florrie
Floy
Flynn
Fonda
Fran
Frances
Francesca
Francine
Francisca
Frankie
Freddie
Freya
Frida

Jennifer
Josefa
Josefina
Josephine

Mafalda

Ophelia

Philomena
Phoebe
Phoenix
Phyllis

Rafaela

Sophia
Sophie
Stephania
Stephanie

Tiffany

Winifred

■ **G** ■

**PARTNER POINTER:
Check the K, Q, and X
lists, too.**

Abigail
Agatha
Agnes
Agostina
Agustina
Altagracia
Augusta
Augustine

Brigitte

Dagmar
Dagny
Dominga

Gabriel
Gabriela
Gabriella
Gabrielle
Gail
Galilea
Garnett
Gay
Gayla
Gaynell
Gerda
Gertie

Gertrude
Gilda
Gillian
Gladys
Glenn
Glenda
Glenna
Glennie
Gloria
Glynda
Glynis
Golda
Golden
Goldia
Goldie
Grace
Gracie
Graciela
Gregoria
Greta
Gretchen
Gretel
Griselda
Guadalupe
Gudrun
Gui
Guinevere
Gussie
Gwen
Gwendolyn
Gwyneth

Hedwig
Helga
Hildegarde

Inga
Ingeborg
Ingrid

Logan

Magdalen
Magdalena
Magdalene
Maggie
Magnolia
Margaret
Margaretta
Margarita
Margie
Margit
Margo
Marguerite

Meg
Megan
Meghann
Migdalia
Milagros
Morgan

Olga

Peggy

Reagan

Sigrid

Teagan

Virgie

■ H ■

PARTNER POINTER:
Although some of
these names don't
have Hs in them, if
you break them down
phonetically, you will
hear the "huh" sound.

Alejandra
Amina
Amira
Anahi
Angel
Angela
Angeles
Angelica
Angelina
Angelita
Annika
Asia

Eugenia
Eugenie
Evangelina

Farrah

Hadley
Hailey
Hallie
Hannah
Harlene

Harley
Harmony
Harriet
Hassie
Hattie
Haven
Haydee
Hayden
Hazel
Heather
Heaven
Hedwig
Heidi
Helen
Helena
Helene
Helga
Henrietta
Henriette
Hermina
Hermine
Herminia
Hermione
Herta
Hester
Hettie
Hilda
Hilde
Hildegarde
Hildred
Hildur
Hillary
Hilma
Hiroko
Holly
Honey
Hong
Hope
Hortencia
Hortense
Hua
Hulda
Hunter

Jamila
Jessenia
Jesusa
Johanna
Josefa
Josefina
Jovita
Judith
Julia
Juliana

Khadijah
Khayla

Layla

Malia

Nadia
Naheed

Rayna
Roxana

Samara
Samira
Sarah
Sarahi
Soheila
Sonia

Virginia

Wilhelmina
Wilhelmine

Xia
Xiu

Yahaira
Yehudit

Zaida
Zoraida

■ J ■

PARTNER POINTER:
Check the CH and
SH/ZH lists, too.

Angel
Angela
Angeles
Angelia
Angelica
Angelina
Angeline
Angelique
Angelita
Angie
Anjali
Anjanette

Bridget	Jan	Josefina
	Jana	Josephine
Eugenia	Janae	Josette
Eugenie	Jane	Josie
Evangelina	Janelle	Joslyn
Evangeline	Janessa	Jothi
	Janet	Journey
Gemma	Janice	Jovita
Genesis	Janie	Joy
Geneva	Janine	Joyce
Genevieve	Janiya	Joycelyn
Genoveva	Jannie	Juana
George	Jasmine	Judith
Georgene	Jayla	Judy
Georgette	Jaylene	Julia
Georgia	Jazlyn	Juliana
Georgiana	Jean	Julianne
Georgianne	Jeanette	Julie
Georgie	Jeanine	Juliet
Georgina	Jeannie	Julissa
Geraldine	Jemima	June
Geralyn	Jen	Justice
Germaine	Jenna	Justina
Gia	Jennifer	Justine
Giada	Jenny	
Gianna	Jeri	Khadijah
Gigi	Jerline	
Gilda	Jerrica	Madge
Gillian	Jessenia	Marge
Gina	Jessica	Margie
Ginger	Jessie	Marjorie
Ginny	Jetta	Maryjane
Giovanna	Jettie	Maryjo
Gisela	Jewel	
Giselle	Jill	Nadia
	Jillian	
Imogene	Jimmie	Paige
	Jo	
Jacey	Joan	Regina
Jackie	Joanna	
Jaclyn	Jocelyn	Sage
Jacque	Jodie	Sugine
Jacqueline	Joelle	
Jada	Joellen	Tangela
Jade	Joetta	
Jaden	Joey	Virgie
Jaelyn	Johanna	Virginia
Jakayla	Johnnie	
Jalisa	Jolene	Yahaira
Jaliyah	Jolie	
James	Joni	Zhi
Jamie	Jordan	
Jamila	Joretta	
Jamya	Josefa	

■ K ■

PARTNER POINTER:
Check the G, Q,
and X lists, too.

Acacia
Aiko
Akiko
Akira
America
Angelica
Angelique
Annika

Becky
Bianca
Blanca
Brooklyn

Cadence
Calista
Callie
Cameron
Camilla
Camille
Campbell
Camry
Candace
Candida
Candy
Carina
Carissa
Carla
Carlene
Carlotta
Carly
Carma
Carmel
Carmela
Carmelita
Carmen
Carol
Carolann
Carolee
Carolina
Caroline
Carrie
Carson
Carys
Casey
Cassandra
Cassidy
Cassie

Catalina
Catherine
Catina
Charissa
Chiquita
Chloë
Chris
Chrissy
Christen
Christian
Christiana
Christina
Christine
Christopher
Christy
Ciara
Claire
Clara
Clarabelle
Clarice
Clarine
Clarissa
Claudette
Claudia
Claudie
Claudine
Clementina
Clementine
Clemmie
Cleo
Cleora
Cleta
Clotilde
Coco
Cody
Colette
Colleen
Concepcion
Concetta
Connie
Constance
Consuelo
Cora
Coral
Cordelia
Cordia
Cordie
Corina
Corinne
Corliss
Cornelia
Courtney
Creola
Cruz

Crystal

Dakota
Danica
Dominique
Dorcas

Electa
Emiko
Enriqueta
Erica

Francesca
Francisca
Frankie

Hedwig
Hiroko

Jackie
Jaclyn
Jacque
Jacqueline
Jakayla
Jerrica
Jessica

Kaitlyn
Kala
Kaliyah
Kalyn
Kami
Kaori
Kara
Karen
Kari
Karina
Karyme
Katarina
Kate
Kathaleen
Katharina
Kathleen
Kathlyn
Kathrine
Kathy
Katie
Katlin
Katrina
Kattie
Kay
Kaya
Kayden
Kayla

Kaylee
Kaylin
Kecia
Keely
Keiki
Keiko
Keisha
Keishla
Kelly
Kelsey
Kendall
Kendra
Kenna
Kennedy
Kenneth
Kenya
Kenyatta
Kenzie
Keshia
Khadijah
Khayla
Kiana
Kiara
Kiele
Kierra
Kim
Kimberly
Kinsey
Kirsten
Kirstie
Kitty
Kizzy
Kori
Krista
Kristen
Kya
Kyla
Kyle
Kylie

Lakeisha
Lakeshia
Laquita
Lilike
Lucrecia
Lyric

Mackenzie
Makayla
Malaika
Malika
Masako
McCoy
McKenna

Micah
Michael
Michaela
Michelina
Mickey
Miracle
Monica
Monique

Nakia
Nicola
Nicole
Nicolette
Nikita
Nikki

Octavia

Parker
Pinkie

Raquel
Rebecca
Rikki
Rivka

Scarlett
Scout
Sequoia
Shakira
Shameka
Shanika
Skye
Skyla
Skylar
Socorro

Tamika
Tamiko
Tomeka
Tomoko
Tuk Yoon

Unique

Veronica
Vicky
Victoria

Waleska

Yoko
Yoshiko
Yuka

■ **L** ■

Abigail
Abril
Adelaida
Adelaide
Adele
Adelia
Adelina
Adeline
Adella
Aileen
Ainsley
Aisling
Alana
Alani
Alanis
Alanna
Alba
Alberta
Albertha
Albertine
Albina
Alda
Aleah
Alejandra
Alessandra
Aleta
Alex
Alexa
Alexandra
Alexandria
Alexandrie
Alexia
Alexis
Alfreda
Ali
Alice
Alicia
Alina
Aline
Alisa
Alissa
Alize
Allie
Allison
Alma
Almeda
Alondra
Alpha
Alta
Altagracia
Altha
Althea

Alva
Alvera
Alverta
Alvina
Amalia
Amaryllis
Amelia
Amelie
Angel
Angela
Angeles
Angelia
Angelica
Angelina
Angeline
Angelique
Angelita
Anjali
Annabella
Annabelle
Annalise
Ansley
Apple
April
Arabella
Araceli
Ardell
Ardella
Arely
Ariel
Ariella
Arielle
Arlene
Arlie
Arvilla
Ashley
Ashlyn
Aurelia
Avlyn
Awilda
Ayla
Aylin

Bailey
Belen
Belinda
Bella
Bellamy
Belle
Belva
Beryl
Bethel
Beulah
Beverly

Billie
Blair
Blanca
Blanche
Blossom
Blue
Brielle
Brooklyn
Brunilda

Calista
Callie
Camilla
Camille
Campbell
Carla
Carlene
Carlotta
Carly
Carmel
Carmela
Carmelita
Carol
Carolann
Carolee
Carolina
Caroline
Catalina
Cecil
Cecile
Cecilia
Cecily
Ceil
Celeste
Celestina
Celestine
Celia
Celine
Celina
Chandler
Chandra
Chanel
Chantal
Chantel
Charla
Charlene
Charles
Charlie
Charlotte
Charolette
Chelsea
Cheryl
Chloë
Citlali

Claire
Clara
Clarabelle
Clarice
Clarine
Clarissa
Claudette
Claudia
Claudie
Claudine
Clementina
Clementine
Clemmie
Cleo
Cleora
Cleta
Clotilde
Colette
Colleen
Consuelo
Coral
Cordelia
Corliss
Cornelia
Creola
Crystal
Cybelle

Dale
Dalia
Dallas
Danelle
Daniela
Danielle
Darla
Darlene
Daryl
Delaney
Delfina
Delia
Delilah
Delisa
Dell
Della
Delma
Delois
Delpha
Delphia
Delphine
Delta
Dimple
Dolly
Dolores
Drucilla

Dulce	Ethel	Goldie
Dylan	Ethelene	Graciela
	Ethelyn	Gretel
Earlene	Eula	Griselda
Eileen	Eulalia	Guadalupe
Elaine	Eulalie	Gwendolyn
Elana	Evangelina	
Elba	Evangeline	Hadley
Elda	Evelyn	Hailey
Eldora	Evelyne	Hallie
Eleanor		Harlene
Eleanora	Fabiola	Harley
Electa	Fallon	Hazel
Elena	Felicia	Helen
Elfrieda	Felicita	Helena
Eliana Elida	Felicity	Helene
Elisa	Felipa	Helga
Elise	Filomena	Hilda
Elissa	Fleta	Hilde
Eliza	Flo	Hildegarde
Elizabeth	Flora	Hildred
Ella	Florence	Hildur
Ellamae	Florida	Hillary
Elle	Florine	Hilma
Ellen	Florrie	Holly
Ellie	Flossie	Hulda
Elma	Floy	
Elmira	Flynn	Idell
Elna		Idella
Elnora	Gabriel	Ila
Elois	Gabriela	Ilana
Eloisa	Gabriella	Iliana
Eloise	Gabrielle	Ilona
Elsa	Gail	Ilsa
Elsie	Galilea	Imelda
Elta	Gayla	Iola
Elva	Gaynell	Ireland
Elvera	Geraldine	Isabel
Elvia	Geralyn	Isabela
Elvira	Gilda	Itzel
Emelina	Gillian	Ivelisse
Emeline	Gisela	
Emerald	Giselle	Jaclyn
Emilia	Gladys	Jacqueline
Emilie	Glenda	Jaelyn
Emily	Glenn	Jakayla
Emmanuela	Glenna	Jalisa
Enola	Glennie	Jaliyah
Erlinda	Gloria	Jamila
Esmeralda	Glynda	Janelle
Esmerelda	Glynis	Jayla
Estella	Golda	Jazlyn
Estelle	Golden	Jerline
Estrella	Goldia	Jewel

Jill
Jillian
Jocelyn
Joelle
Joellen
Jolene
Jolie
Joslyn
Joycelyn
Julia
Juliana
Julianne
Julie
Juliet
Julissa

Kaitlyn
Kala
Kaliyah
Kalyn
Kathaleen
Kathleen
Kathlyn
Katlin
Kayla
Kaylee
Kaylin
Keely
Keishla
Kelly
Kelsey
Kendall
Khayla
Kiele
Kimberly
Kyla
Kyle
Kylie

Lacey
Ladonna
Laisha
Lakeisha
Lakeshia
Lana
Lanette
Laney
Laquita
Lara
Larissa
LaRue
Lashanda
Lashawn
Latanya

Latasha
Latonya
Latoya
Latrice
Laura
Laurel
Lauren
Lauretta
Laurette
Lavada
Lavera
Laverna
Laverne
Lavina
Lavinia
Lavonne
Lawanda
Lea
Leandra
Leanna
Leanne
Leatrice
Leena
Lei
Leigh
Leila
Leilani
Lelia
Lempi
Lena
Lennie
Lenora
Lenore
Leola
Leona
Leone
Leonor
Leonora
Leora
Leota
Lesia
Leslie
Lessie
Leta
Letha
Leticia
Letizia
Lettie
Lexi
Lexus
Leyna
Libby
Liberty
Liesel

Lila
Lilia
Liliana
Lilike
Lilla
Lilliam
Lillian
Lillith
Lilo
Lily
Lina
Linda
Lindsey
Lindy
Ling
Linnea
Linnie
Lisa
Lisbet
Lise
Lissa
Lissette
Litzy
Liv
Livia
Liz
Liza
Lizabeth
Lizbeth
Lizeth
Lizzie
Logan
Lois
Lola
Lolita
Loma
Lona
London
Lonnie
Lorelei
Lorena
Lorene
Lorenza
Loretta
Lori
Loriann
Lorna
Lorraine
Lottie
Lou
Louella
Louie
Louise
Lourdes

Lovie
Loyce
Luana
Luann
Lucero
Lucia
Luciena
Lucienne
Lucila
Lucille
Lucinda
Lucrecia
Lucy
Ludie
Luetta
Luisa
Lula
Lulu
Luna
Lupe
Lupita
Lura
Lurline
Luvenia
Luz
Lyda
Lydia
Lynette
Lynn
Lyric

Mabel
Maddalena
Madelena
Madeline
Mafalda
Magdalen
Magdalena
Magdalene
Magnolia
Makayla
Malaika
Maleah
Malia
Malika
Mallory
Malvina
Manuela
Marcelina
Marceline
Marcella
Marcelle
Maribel
Maricela

Mariel
Mariella
Marilee
Marilena
Marilyn
Marisol
Marla
Marlena
Marlene
Marley
Marlo
Marlyn
Marlys
Marvel
Maryellen
Marylou
Matilda
Matilde
Maybelle
Melanie
Melba
Melina
Melinda
Melisa
Meliss
Melissa
Mellie
Melody
Melva
Melvina
Merle
Merlene
Meryl
Michael
Michaela
Michelina
Michelle
Migdalia
Milagros
Mildred
Millicent
Millie
Mirabelle
Miracle
Molly
Mozella
Mozelle
Muriel
Myrtle

Natalia
Natalie
Nayeli
Nelda

Nelida
Nell
Nella
Nellie
Neyla
Nicola
Nicole
Nicolette
Nilda
Nilsa
Noelia
Noelle
Nola
Novella
Nyla

Odalys
Odell
Ola
Olene
Oleta
Olga
Oliana
Olina
Olive
Olivia
Olivie
Ollie
Opal
Ophelia
Oralia
Orla
Otilia
Ottilie
Ozella

Palma
Paloma
Pamela
Pamella
Paola
Paoletta
Paolina
Paula
Pauletta
Paulette
Paulina
Pauline
Pearl
Pearlie
Pearline
Penelope
Perla
Petranella

Philomena
Phyllis
Pilar
Polly
Presley
Priscila

Rachel
Rachelle
Rafaela
Raquel
Riley
Rilla
Rochelle
Rolanda
Rosalia
Rosalie
Rosalina
Rosalind
Rosalinda
Rosaline
Rosalyn
Rosella
Roselyn
Roslyn

Sailor
Sally
Salma
Salome
Satchel
Scarlett
Selena
Selma
Shalonda
Shayla
Shaylee
Sheila
Shelba
Shelby
Shelia
Shelly
Shelva
Sherlyn
Shirlene
Shirley
Skyla
Skylar
Soheila
Soledad
Starla
Stella
Suellen
Sybil

Sylvia
Sylvie

Talia
Tallulah
Tamela
Tami
Taylor
Tennille
Thelma
Theo
Theodora
Theola
Tillie
Twila
Tyler

Ursula

Valencia
Valentina
Valentine
Valeria
Valerie
Vallie
Velda
Vella
Velma
Velva
Verla
Verlie
Vernell
Vilma
Viola
Violet
Violetta
Violette

Waleska
Whitley
Wilda
Wilhelmina
Wilhelmine
Willa
Willamina
Willene
Willia
Willie
Willow
Wilma
Wylie

Yareli
Yolanda

Yoselin
Yuliana

Zelda
Zella
Zelma
Zoila
Zola
Zula
Zulma

■ M ■

Alma
Almeda
Amalia
Amanda
Amani
Amara
Amari
Amaris
Amaryllis
Amaya
Amber
Amelia
Amelie
America
Amie
Amina
Amiya
Amparo
Amy
Annamae
Annamarie
Annmarie
Armani
Armida
Autumn

Bambi
Bellamy
Blossom

Camilla
Camille
Cameron
Campbell
Camry
Carma
Carmel
Carmela
Carmelita
Carmen

Charmaine	James	Margaret
Clementina	Jamie	Margaretta
Clementine	Jamila	Margarita
Clemmie	Jamya	Marge
	Jemima	Margie
Dagmar	Jimmie	Margit
Damaris		Margo
Delma	Kami	Marguerite
Demetria	Karyme	Mari
Demi	Kim	Maria
Diamond	Kimberly	Mariah
Dimple		Mariam
Dominga	Lempi	Marian
Dominique	Lilliam	Mariana
	Loma	Marianne
Ellamae		Maribel
Elma	Mabel	Maricela
Elmira	Mackenzie	Marie
Emelina	Macy	Mariel
Emeline	Maddalena	Mariella
Emerald	Madelena	Marietta
Emerson	Madeline	Marilee
Emiko	Madge	Marilena
Emilia	Madie	Marilyn
Emilie	Madison	Marina
Emily	Madonna	Marisa
Emma	Mae	Marisol
Emmanuela	Maeve	Marissa
Emmie	Mafalda	Marita
Ermina	Magdalen	Maritza
Esmeralda	Magdalena	Marjorie
Esmerelda	Magdalene	Marla
	Maggie	Marlena
Fatima	Magnolia	Marlene
Filomena	Mai	Marley
	Maida	Marlo
Gemma	Mairwen	Marlyn
Germaine	Makayla	Marlys
Guillermina	Malaika	Marna
	Maleah	Marnie
Harmony	Malia	Marsha
Hermina	Malika	Marta
Hermine	Mallory	Martha
Herminia	Malvina	Martina
Hermione	Mamie	Marva
Hilma	Mammie	Marvel
	Mandy	Mary
Ima	Manuela	Marybeth
Imani	Mara	Maryellen
Imelda	Marcelina	Maryjane
Imogene	Marceline	Maryjo
Irma	Marcella	Marylou
Isamar	Marcelle	Masako
	Marci	Matilda

Matilde
Maude
Maudie
Maura
Maureen
Mavis
Maxie
Maxine
Maya
Maybelle
Mayme
Mayra
Mazie
McCoy
McKenna
Meadow
Meg
Megan
Melanie
Melba
Melina
Melinda
Melisa
Meliss
Melissa
Mellie
Melody
Melva
Melvina
Mercedes
Meredith
Merle
Merlene
Mertie
Meryl
Meta
Mia
Micah
Michael
Michaela
Michelina
Michelle
Michiko
Mickey
Migdalia
Milagros
Mildred
Millicent
Millie
Mimi
Mina
Mindy
Minerva
Ming

Minna
Minnie
Mirabelle
Miracle
Miranda
Mireya
Miriam
Mirta
Missouri
Missy
Misty
Mittie
Modesta
Moe
Moira
Molly
Mona
Monica
Monique
Monserrat
Montana
Morgan
Moriah
Mossie
Mozella
Mozelle
Muriel
Myra
Myrna
Myrtice
Myrtis
Myrtle

Naoma
Naomi
Natsumi
Neoma
Noemi
Norma

Oma
Omayra

Palma
Paloma
Pam
Pamela
Pamella
Philomena
Pomona

Ramona
Ramonita
Roma

Romaine
Romana
Rosamond
Rosemarie
Rosemary
Rumer

Salma
Salome
Samantha
Samara
Samira
Sammie
Selma
Shameka
Shamira
Simone
Soomie
Stormy
Summer

Tamara
Tamatha
Tamela
Tami
Tamia
Tamika
Tamiko
Tamra
Tatum
Thelma
Tomasa
Tomeka
Tommie
Tomoko

Uma

Velma
Vilma

Wilhelmina
Wilhelmine
Willamina
Wilma

Ximena
Xiomara

Yasmin
Yasmine
Yemima
Yumuna

Zelma
Zulma

■ **N/NG** ■

Abrianna
Addison
Adelina
Adeline
Adrian
Adriana
Adrianna
Adrienne
Afton
Agnes
Agnese
Agostina
Agustina
Aileen
Ainsley
Aisling
Alana
Alani
Alanis
Alanna
Albertine
Albina
Alejandra
Alessandra
Alexandra
Alexandria
Alexandrie
Alina
Aline
Allison
Alondra
Alvina
Amanda
Amani
Amina
Anahi
Anaïs
Anastasia
Anastasie
Andrea
Angel
Angela
Angeles
Angelia
Angelica
Angelina
Angeline
Angelique

Angelita
Angie
Anissa
Anita
Anitra
Aniya
Anjali
Anjanette
Anna
Annabella
Annabelle
Annalise
Annamae
Annamarie
Anne
Annetta
Annette
Annie
Annika
Annis
Annmarie
Antoinette
Antonetta
Antonette
Antonia
Antonietta
Antonina
Ansley
Anya
Ariana
Arianna
Arlene
Armani
Ashanti
Ashlyn
Ashton
Aspen
Assunta
Athena
Augustine
Autumn
Avlyn
Ayana
Ayanna
Aylin

Belen
Belinda
Benita
Bennie
Berenice
Bernadette
Bernardine
Bernita

Bethany
Bianca
Blanca
Blanche
Bonita
Bonnie
Brandon
Brandy
Brenda
Brenna
Brianna
Brianne
Britney
Brittany
Brooklyn
Brunilda
Brynn

Cadence
Cameron
Candace
Cándida
Candy
Carina
Carlene
Carmen
Carolina
Caroline
Carson
Catalina
Catherine
Catina
Celestina
Celestine
Celina
Celine
Chana
Chanda
Chandler
Chandra
Chanel
Chantal
Chantel
Charlene
Charmaine
Cheyenne
China
Christen
Christian
Christiana
Christina
Christine
Cinda
Cindy

Clarine
Claudine
Clementina
Clementine
Colleen
Concepcion
Concetta
Connie
Constance
Consuelo
Corina
Corinne
Cornelia
Courtney
Cynthia

Dagny
Dana
Danelle
Danette
Dania
Danica
Daniela
Danielle
Danita
Danna
Darian
Darlene
Davin
Davina
Dawn
Dayana
Dean
Deann
Deanna
Delaney
Delfina
Delphine
Deneen
Denise
Destiny
Devin
Diamond
Diane
Diana
Dina
Dionne
Dominga
Dominique
Donna
Donnie
Doreen
Dorinda
Dylan

Earlene
Ebony
Eden
Edna
Edwina
Eileen
Elaine
Elana
Eleanor
Eleanora
Elena
Eliana
Ellen
Elna
Elnora
Emelina
Emeline
Emerson
Emmanuela
Ena
Enid
Enola
Erin
Erlinda
Ermina
Erna
Ernestina
Ernestine
Esperanza
Essence
Estefania
Estefany
Ethelene
Ethelyn
Étienne
Eugenia
Eugenie
Eunice
Evangelina
Evangeline
Evelyn
Evelyne
Evon

Fallon
Fannie
Feng
Fern
Fernanda
Filomena
Fiona
Florence
Florine
Flynn

Fonda
Fran
Frances
Francesca
Francine
Francisca
Frankie

Garnett
Gaynell
Genesis
Geneva
Genevieve
Genoveva
Georgene
Georgiana
Georgianne
Georgina
Geraldine
Geralyn
Germaine
Gianna
Gillian
Gina
Ginger
Ginny
Giovanna
Glenn
Glenda
Glenna
Glennie
Glynda
Glynis
Gretchen
Gudrun
Guillermina
Guinevere
Gwen
Gwendolyn
Gwyneth

Hannah
Harlene
Harmony
Haven
Hayden
Heaven
Helen
Helena
Helene
Henrietta
Henriette
Hermina
Hermine

Herminia
Honey
Hong
Hortencia
Hortense
Hunter

Ilana
Iliana
Ilona
Imani
Imogene
Ina
India
Inez
Inga
Ingeborg
Ingrid
Iona
Ione
Ireland
Irene

Jaclyn
Jacqueline
Jaden
Jaelyn
Jan
Jana
Janae
Jane
Janelle
Janessa
Janet
Janice
Janie
Janine
Janiya
Jannie
Jasmine
Jaylene
Jazlyn
Jean
Jeanette
Jeanine
Jeannie
Jen
Jenna
Jennifer
Jenny
Jerline
Jessenia
Jillian
Joan

Joanna
Jocelyn
Joellen
Johanna
Johnnie
Jolene
Joni
Jordan
Josefina
Josephine
Joslyn
Journey
Joycelyn
Juana
Juanita
Juliana
Julianne
June
Justina
Justine

Kaitlyn
Kalyn
Karen
Karina
Katarina
Kathaleen
Katharina
Kathleen
Kathlyn
Kathrine
Katlin
Katrina
Kayden
Kaylin
Kendall
Kendra
Kenna
Kennedy
Kenneth
Kenya
Kenyatta
Kenzie
Kiana
Kinsey
Kirsten
Kristen

Ladonna
Lana
Lanette
Laney
Lashanda
Lashawn

Latanya
Latonya
Lauren
Laverna
Laverne
Lavina
Lavinia
Lavonne
Lawanda
Leandra
Leanna
Leanne
Leena
Lena
Lennie
Lenora
Lenore
Leona
Leone
Leonor
Leonora
Leyna
Liliana
Lillian
Lina
Linda
Lindsey
Lindy
Ling
Linnea
Linnie
Logan
Lona
London
Lonnie
Lorena
Lorene
Lorenza
Loriann
Lorna
Lorraine
Luana
Luann
Luciena
Lucienne
Lucinda
Luna
Lurline
Luvenia
Lynette
Lynn

Maddalena
Madelena

Madeline
Madison
Madonna
Magdalen
Magdalena
Magdalene
Magnolia
Mairwen
Malvina
Mandy
Manuela
Marcelina
Marceline
Marian
Mariana
Marianne
Marilena
Marilyn
Marina
Marlena
Marlene
Marlyn
Marna
Marnie
Martina
Maryellen
Maryjane
Maureen
Maxine
McKenna
Megan
Melanie
Melina
Melinda
Melvina
Merlene
Michelina
Millicent
Mina
Mindy
Minerva
Ming
Minna
Minnie
Miranda
Mona
Monica
Monique
Monserrat
Montana
Morgan
Myrna

Nadia

Nadine
Naheed
Nakia
Nan
Nancy
Nanette
Nannie
Naoma
Naomi
Natalia
Natalie
Natasha
Natividad
Natsumi
Nayeli
Nedra
Nelda
Nélida
Nell
Nella
Nellie
Neoma
Nereida
Neta
Nettie
Neva
Nevaeh
Neyla
Nia
Nicola
Nicole
Nicolette
Nikita
Nikki
Nilda
Nilsa
Nina
Nita
Nixie
Noelia
Noelle
Noemi
Nola
Nona
Nora
Noreen
Norma
Nova
Novella
Nyah
Nyasia
Nydia
Nyla

Olene
Oliana
Olina
Ona
Onie

Pansy
Paolina
Patience
Paulina
Pauline
Payton
Pearline
Penelope
Penny
Petranella
Philomena
Phoenix
Ping
Pinkie
Pomona
Princess
Providenci
Prudence

Queen
Queenie
Quinn

Ramona
Ramonita
Randi
Ranee
Raven
Rayna
Reagan
Regina
Rena
Renata
Renita
Renea
Renee
Reyna
Rezsin
Rhiannon
Rhonda
Rianna
Robyn
Rolanda
Romaine
Romana
Rona
Ronna
Ronnie

Rosalina
Rosalind
Rosaline
Rosalyn
Rosamond
Rosanna
Roseann
Roselyn
Rosina
Roslyn
Roxana
Roxanne
Rowan
Rowena
Ruthann
Ryan

Sabina
Sabine
Sabrina
Sanaa
Sandy
Sandra
Saniya
Santa
Santana
Santina
Santos
Sanya
Savannah
Selena
Serena
Serenity
Shalonda
Shana
Shanda
Shandi
Shani
Shania
Shanice
Shanika
Shaniqua
Shanita
Shannon
Shanta
Shante
Shanthi
Sharon
Shawn
Shawna
Shawanda
Shayna
Sheena
Sherlyn

Shirlene
Shonda
Shoshana
Sidonie
Sienna
Signe
Simone
Siobhan
Sondra
Sonia
Speranza
Spring
Stephania
Stephanie
Suellen
Sugine
Sunny
Sunshine
Susan
Susana
Suzanne
Sydney

Tana
Tangela
Tania
Tanisha
Taryn
Tatiana
Tawana
Tawanda
Tawny
Teagan
Tennie
Tennille
Tiana
Tiffany
Tina
Toni
Tonya
Trena
Trina
Trinidad
Trinity
Tristan
Tvuna

Una
Unique

Valencia
Valentina
Valentine
Vanessa
Vena

Venita
Venus
Verna
Vernell
Vernice
Vernie
Verona
Veronica
Vicenta
Vina
Vincenza
Vinnie
Virginia
Virginie
Vivian
Viviana
Vivienne
Von
Vonda
Vonnie

Wanda
Waneta
Wendy
Whitney
Wilhelmina
Wilhelmine
Willamina
Willene
Windy
Winifred
Winnie
Winona

Xena
Ximena

Yanira
Yarden
Yasmin
Yasmine
Yesenia
Yolanda
Yoselin
Yuliana
Yumuna
Yvonne

Zenda
Zina
Zona

■ P ■

PARTNER POINTER:
Check the B list, too.

Amparo
Apple
April
Aspen

Concepcion
Cypress

Deepa
Dimple

Esperanza

Felipa

Guadalupe

Hope

Lempi
Lupe
Lupita

Opal

Paige
Palma
Paloma
Pam
Pamela
Pamella
Pansy
Paola
Paoletta
Paolina
Paris
Parisa
Parker
Parvati
Pat
Patience
Patrica
Patrice
Patricia
Patrizia
Patsy
Patty
Paula
Pauletta

Paulette
Paulina
Pauline
Payton
Pearl
Pearlie
Pearline
Peggy
Penelope
Penny
Perla
Petra
Petranella
Pilar
Ping
Pinkie
Piper
Polly
Pomona
Poppy
Portia
Precious
Presley
Princess
Priscila
Providenci
Prudence
Pura

Speranza
Spring

■ Q ■

PARTNER POINTER:
Check the G, K, X,
and W lists, too.

Jacqueline

Laquita

Queen
Queenie
Quinn

Shaniqua

■ R ■

PARTNER POINTER:
This list shows names
with a hard R ("ruh")
sound. Check the AR,
AIR, OR, or UR lists for
names with soft Rs.

Abrianna
Abril
Adrian
Adriana
Adrianna
Adrienne
Akira
Alexandra
Alexandria
Alexandrie
Alfreda
Alondra
Altagracia
Amara
Amari
Amaris
Amaryllis
America
Amira
Amparo
Andrea
Anitra
April
Ara
Arabella
Araceli
Arely
Aria
Ariana
Arianna
Ariel
Ariella
Arielle
Arlie
Arrie
Astrid
Aubrey
Audra
Audrey
Aurea
Aurelia
Aurora
Aurore
Avery

Barbara
Barbra
Brandon
Brandy
Bree
Brenda
Brenna
Bria
Brianna
Brianne
Bridget
Brielle
Brigitte
Brisa
Britney
Brittany
Brooke
Brooklyn
Brunilda
Brynn

Cameron
Camry
Carina
Carissa
Carol
Carolann
Carolee
Carolina
Caroline
Carrie
Carys
Cassandra
Catherine
Ceres
Chandra
Charisse
Charissa
Charity
Charolette
Cherie
Cherry
Cherish
Cheryl
Chris
Chrissy
Christen
Christian
Christiana
Christina
Christine
Christopher
Christy
Ciara

Clara
Clarabelle
Clarice
Clarine
Clarissa
Cleora
Cora
Coral
Corina
Corinne
Creola
Cruz
Crystal
Christelle
Cypress

Damaris
Dara
Darian
Daryl
Deborah
Deidre
Deirdre
Demetria
Desiree
Dolores
Dora
Dorcas
Dori
Dorinda
Doris
Dorit
Dorotha
Dorothea
Dorothy
Drew
Drucilla

Edrie
Eleanora
Eldora
Elfrieda
Elmira
Elnora
Elvera
Elvira
Emerald
Enriqueta
Era
Erica
Erin
Eris
Esmeralda
Esmerelda

Esperanza
Estrella
Eudora
Eura

Fairy
Farrah
Flora
Florence
Florida
Florine
Florrie
Fran
Frances
Francesca
Francine
Francisca
Frankie
Freddie
Freya
Frida

Gabriel
Gabriela
Gabriella
Gabrielle
Geraldine
Geralyn
Gloria
Grace
Gracie
Graciela
Gregoria
Greta
Gretchen
Gretel
Griselda
Gudrun

Harriet
Henrietta
Henriette
Hildred
Hiroko

Ira
Irene
Iris
Isadora
Izora

Jeri
Jerrica
Joretta

Kaori
Kara
Karen
Kari
Karina
Karyme
Katarina
Katharina
Kathrine
Katrina
Kendra
Kiara
Kierra
Kori
Krista
Kristen

Lara
Larissa
LaRue
Latrice
Laura
Laurel
Lauren
Lauretta
Laurette
Leandra
Leatrice
Lenora
Leonora
Leora
Lorelei
Lorena
Lorene
Lorenza
Loretta
Lori
Loriann
Lorraine
Lucero
Lucrecia
Lura
Lyric

Mallory
Mara
Margaret
Margaretta
Margarita
Marguerite
Mari
Maria
Mariah
Mariam

Marian
Mariana
Marianne
Maribel
Maricela
Marie
Mariel
Mariella
Marietta
Marilee
Marilena
Marilyn
Marina
Marisa
Marisol
Marissa
Marita
Maritza
Marjorie
Mary
Marybeth
Maryellen
Maryjane
Maryjo
Marylou
Maura
Maureen
Mayra
Meredith
Meryl
Milagros
Mildred
Mirabelle
Miracle
Miranda
Mireya
Miriam
Missouri
Moira
Monserrat
Moriah
Muriel
Myra

Nedra
Nereida
Nora
Noreen

Omayra
Ora
Oralia

Paris

Parisa
Patrica
Patrice
Patricia
Patrizia
Petra
Petranella
Precious
Presley
Princess
Priscila
Providenci
Prudence
Pura

Rachel
Rachelle
Rae
Rafaela
Ramona
Ramonita
Randi
Ranee
Raquel
Raven
Rayna
Reagan
Reba
Rebecca
Reese
Regina
Rena
Renata
Renea
Renee
Renita
Ressie
Retha
Retta
Reva
Reyna
Rezsin
Rhea
Rhiannon
Rhoda
Rhonda
Rianna
Rikki
Riley
Rilla
Rita
Rivka
Robbie
Roberta

Robyn
Rochelle
Rocio
Rolanda
Roma
Romaine
Romana
Rona
Ronna
Ronnie
Rory
Rosa
Rosalia
Rosalie
Rosalina
Rosalind
Rosalinda
Rosaline
Rosalyn
Rosamond
Rosanna
Rosario
Rosaura
Rose
Roseann
Rosella
Roselyn
Rosemarie
Rosemary
Rosetta
Rosia
Rosina
Rosita
Roslyn
Rossie
Roxana
Roxanne
Roxie
Rowan
Rowena
Ruby
Rumer
Ruth
Ruthann
Ruthie
Ryan

Sabrina
Samara
Samira
Sandra
Sarah
Sarahi
Sarai

Sariah
Serena
Serenity
Shakira
Shamira
Shara
Sharon
Sharonda
Sheree
Sherita
Sherry
Shreya
Sigrid
Socorro
Speranza
Spring

Tamara
Tamra
Tara
Taryn
Teresa
Teresita
Teri
Theodora
Therese
Theresia
Thora
Thyra
Tiara
Tierra
Tori
Tracy
Tressa
Tressie
Treva
Trena
Trina
Trinidad
Trinity
Trisha
Trista
Tristan
Trudy
Tyra

Valeria
Valerie
Vera
Verona
Veronica
Victoria

Winifred

Xiomara

Yadira
Yahaira
Yanira
Yareli
Yaritza

Zara
Zaria
Zora
Zoraida

■ S ■

PARTNER POINTER:
Check the X and Z
lists, too, and if you
want, the SH/ZH list.

Addison
Agnes
Agostina
Agustina
Alanis
Alessandra
Alexis
Alice
Alicia
Alisa
Alissa
Allison
Altagracia
Amaris
Amaryllis
Anaïs
Anastasia
Anastasie
Angeles
Anissa
Annalise
Annis
Araceli
Ardis
Asia
Aspen
Assunta
Astrid
Augusta
Augustine
Avis

Beatrice
Berenice
Bess
Bessie
Betsy
Blossom
Brisa

Cadence
Calista
Candace
Carissa
Carson
Carys
Casey
Cassandra
Cassidy
Cassie
Cecil
Cecile
Cecilia
Cecily
Cedar
Ceil
Celeste
Celestina
Celestine
Celia
Celine
Celina
Ceres
Charissa
Charisse
Chasity
Chastity
Chelsea
Chris
Chrissy
Christen
Christian
Christiana
Christina
Christine
Christopher
Christy
Ciara
Cinda
Cindy
Citlali
Clarice
Clarissa
Concepcion
Constance
Consuelo

Corliss
Cruz
Crystal
Cybelle
Cynthia
Cypress

Dallas
Damaris
Darcy
Dasia
Deasia
Delisa
Delois
Denise
Dessie
Destiny
Dolores
Dorcas
Doris

Easter
Elisa
Elise
Elissa
Elois
Eloisa
Elsie
Emerson
Eris
Ernestina
Ernestine
Esmeralda
Esmerelda
Esperanza
Essence
Essie
Esta
Estefania
Estefany
Estella
Estelle
Esther
Estrella

Felicia
Felicity
Florence
Flossie
Frances
Francesca
Francine
Francisca

Genesis
Gladys
Glynis
Grace
Gracie
Graciela
Griselda
Gussie

Hassie
Hester
Hortencia
Hortense

Icie
Ilsa
Inez
Iris
Isabel
Isabela
Isadora
Isadore
Isamar
Isis
Ivelisse

Jacey
Jalisa
Janessa
Janice
Jasmine
Jessenia
Jessica
Jessie
Jesusa
Jocelyn
Josefa
Josefina
Josephine
Josie
Joyce
Joycelyn
Julissa
Justice
Justina
Justine

Kecia
Kelsey
Kirsten
Kirstie
Krista
Kristen

Lacey	Mossie	Sandy
Larissa	Myrtice	Saniya
Latrice	Myrtis	Santa
Leatrice		Santana
Lesia	Nancy	Santina
Leslie	Natsumi	Santos
Lessie	Nilsa	Sanya
Leticia	Nyasia	Sarah
Lexus		Sarahi
Lisa	Odalys	Sarai
Lisbet	Odessa	Sariah
Lise		Sasha
Lissa	Paris	Satchel
Lissette	Parisa	Savannah
Lois	Patience	Selena
Lourdes	Patrica	Selma
Loyce	Patrice	Sequoia
Lucero	Patricia	Serena
Lucia	Patsy	Serenity
Luciena	Phyllis	Scarlett
Lucienne	Precious	Scout
Lucila	Presley	Shanice
Lucille	Princess	Shasta
Lucinda	Priscila	Sidonie
Lucrecia	Providenci	Sienna
Lucy	Prudence	Sierra
Luisa		Signe
Luz	Reese	Sigrid
	Ressie	Simone
Macy	Rocio	Sister
Madison	Rosa	Sita
Marcelina	Rosalina	Skye
Marceline	Rosalinda	Skyla
Marcella	Rosaline	Skylar
Marcelle	Rosanna	Socorro
Marci	Rosario	Soheila
Maricela	Rosita	Soledad
Marisa	Rossie	Sondra
Marisol		Sonia
Marissa	Sabina	Sophia
Marlys	Sabine	Sophie
Masako	Sabrina	Soomie
Mavis	Sadie	Speranza
Melisa	Sage	Spring
Meliss	Sailor	Stacia
Melissa	Sally	Stacy
Mercedes	Salma	Starla
Milagros	Salome	Stella
Millicent	Samantha	Stephania
Missy	Samara	Stephanie
Misty	Samira	Stevie
Mitzi	Sammie	Stormy
Modesta	Sanaa	Sudie
Monserrat	Sandra	Sue

Suellen
Sugine
Summer
Sunny
Sunshine
Susan
Susana
Susie
Suzanne
Suzette
Sybil
Sydney
Sylvia
Sylvie

Teresa
Teresita
Tess
Tessa
Tessie
Therese
Theresia
Tomasa
Tracy
Tressa
Tressie
Trista
Tristan

Ursula

Valencia
Vanessa
Venus
Versie
Vesta
Vicenta

Waleska

Xiomara

Yasmin
Yasmine
Yesenia
Yoselin

Zoila

■ SH/ZH ■

**PARTNER POINTER:
Check the CH, J, S,
and Z lists, too.**

Acacia
Aisha
Aisling
Alicia
Anastasia
Angeline
Angelique
Asha
Ashanti
Ashley
Ashlyn
Ashton
Asia

Blanche
Brigitte

Chana
Chanda
Chandra
Chanel
Chantal
Chantel
Charissa
Charisse
Charla
Charlene
Charles
Charlotte
Charmaine
Charolette
Chaya
Chelsea
Cherie
Cherry
Cheryl
Cheyenne

Dasia
Deasia
Deja

Elizabeth
Erzsebet
Eugenie

Felicia

Genevieve
George
Georgene
Georgette
Georgianne
Germaine
Gigi
Giselle

Jacque
Jacqueline
Jean
Jeanette
Jeanine
Jennifer
Jocelyn
Joelle
Jolie
Josephine
Josette
Josie
Judith
Julianne
Julie
Juliet
Justine

Kecia
Keisha
Keishla
Keshia
Khadijah

Laisha
Lakeisha
Lakeshia
Lashanda
Lashawn
Latasha
Lesia
Leticia
Lucia
Lucrecia

Marsha
Michelina
Michelle

Natasha
Nyasia

Patience
Patricia
Portia

Precious	Sienna	Augusta
	Siobhan	Augustine
Rachel	Stacia	
Rachelle	Sunshine	Babette
Rezsin		Beatrice
Rochelle	Tanisha	Beatrix
	Tarsha	Benita
Sade	Tasha	Bernadette
Salome	Tisha	Bernita
Sasha	Trisha	Berta
Shakira	Tyesha	Bertha
Shalonda		Bertie
Shamira	Virginie	Betsy
Shana		Bette
Shanda	Xiomara	Bettina
Shandi		Betty
Shani	Yoshiko	Bonita
Shania		Bridget
Shanice	Zsa-zsa	Brigitte
Shanika		Britney
Shaniqua		Brittany
Shanita		
Shannon	■ T ■	Calista
Shanta		Carlotta
Shante	**PARTNER POINTER:**	Carmelita
Shanthi	**Check the D list, too.**	Catalina
Shara		Catherine
Sharon	Afton	Catina
Sharonda	Agatha	Celeste
Shasta	Agostina	Celestina
Shawn	Agustina	Celestine
Shawna	Alberta	Chantal
Shawanda	Albertine	Chantel
Shayla	Altagracia	Charity
Shaylee	Alverta	Charlotte
Shayna	Anastasia	Charolette
Shea	Anastasie	Chasity
Sheba	Angelita	Chastity
Sheena	Anita	Chiquita
Sheila	Anitra	Christen
Shelba	Anjanette	Christian
Shelby	Annetta	Christiana
Shelia	Annette	Christina
Shelly	Antoinette	Christine
Shelva	Antonetta	Christopher
Sheree	Antonette	Christy
Sherita	Antonia	Citlali
Sherlyn	Antonietta	Claudette
Sherry	Antonina	Clementina
Shirlene	Artie	Clementine
Shirley	Ashanti	Cleta
Shonda	Ashton	Clotilde
Shoshana	Assunta	Colette
Shreya	Astrid	Concetta

Constance	Jeanette	Margarita
Courtney	Jetta	Margit
Crystal	Joetta	Marguerite
	Joretta	Marietta
Dakota	Josette	Marita
Danette	Jothi	Maritza
Danita	Jovita	Marta
Delta	Juanita	Martina
Demetria	Judith	Matilda
Destiny	Juliet	Matilde
Dexter	Justice	Mertie
Dorit	Justina	Meta
Dottie	Justine	Mirta
		Mittie
Easter	Kaitlyn	Mitzi
Electa	Katarina	Modesta
Elizabeth	Kate	Monserrat
Elta	Katharina	Montana
Enriqueta	Katie	Myrtice
Ernestina	Katlin	Myrtis
Ernestine	Katrina	Myrtle
Erzsebet	Kattie	
Esta	Kenyatta	Natalia
Estefania	Krista	Natalie
Estefany	Kristen	Natasha
Estella		Natividad
Estelle	Lanette	Natsumi
Esther	Laquita	Neta
Estrella	Latanya	Nettie
Etha	Latasha	Nicolette
Étienne	Latonya	Nikita
Etta	Latoya	Nita
Ettie	Latrice	
	Lauretta	Octavia
Felicita	Laurette	Odetta
Felicity	Leatrice	Odette
Fleta	Leota	Oleta
	Leticia	Otilia
Garnett	Letizia	Ottilie
Georgette	Lettie	
Gertrude	Liberty	Paoletta
	Lillith	Parvati
Harriet	Lisbet	Pat
Henrietta	Lissette	Patrica
Henriette	Litzy	Patrice
Herta	Lizeth	Patricia
Hester	Loretta	Patrizia
Hortencia	Lottie	Patsy
Hortense	Luetta	Patty
Hunter	Lupita	Pauletta
	Lynette	Paulette
Itzel		Payton
Izetta	Margaret	Petra
	Margaretta	Petranella

	Tarsha	Twila
Ramonita	Tasha	Tyesha
Renata	Tatiana	Tyler
Renita	Tatum	Tyra
Retta	Tawana	
Rita	Tawanda	Valentina
Roberta	Tawny	Valentine
Rosetta	Taya	Venita
Rosita	Taylor	Vicenta
Ruth	Teagan	Victoria
Ruthie	Tennie	Violet
	Tennille	Violetta
Santa	Teresa	Violette
Santana	Teresita	Vita
Santina	Teri	
Santos	Tess	Waneta
Serenity	Tessa	Whitley
Scarlett	Tessie	Whitney
Scout	Thea	Wyatt
Shanita	Theo	
Shanta	Theodora	Yaritza
Shante	Therese	Yehudit
Shanthi	Theresia	Yetta
Shasta	Thyra	Yvette
Sherita	Tiana	
Sister	Tiara	Zetta
Sita	Tierra	
Stacia	Tiffany	
Stacy	Tillie	■ TH ■
Starla	Tina	
Stella	Tisha	**PARTNER POINTER:**
Stephania	Toby	**Although some**
Stephanie	Tomasa	**Spanish speakers**
Stevie	Tomeka	**pronounce "s" as "th,"**
Stormy	Tomoko	**we did not include**
Suzette	Tommie	**names with those "s"**
	Toni	**pronunciations on this**
Tabitha	Tonya	**list.**
Talia	Tori	
Tallulah	Toya	Agatha
Tamara	Tracy	Albertha
Tamatha	Tressa	Altha
Tamela	Tressie	Althea
Tami	Treva	Ardith
Tamia	Trena	Athena
Tamika	Trina	
Tamiko	Trinidad	Bertha
Tamra	Trinity	Beth
Tana	Trisha	Bethany
Tangela	Trista	Bethel
Tania	Tristan	
Tanisha	Trudy	Catherine
Tara	Tuk Yoon	Cynthia
Taryn	Tvuna	

Dorotha
Dorothea
Dorothy
Dortha
Dorthy

Edith
Elizabeth
Etha
Ethel
Ethelene
Ethelyn

Faith

Gwyneth

Heather

Judith

Kathaleen
Katharina
Kathleen
Kathlyn
Kathrine
Kathy
Kenneth

Letha
Lillith
Lizabeth
Lizbeth
Lizeth

Martha
Marybeth
Meredith

Retha
Ruth
Ruthann
Ruthie

Samantha

Tabitha
Tamatha
Thea
Theda
Thelma
Theo
Theodora
Theola

Thora
Thyra

■ V ■

**PARTNER POINTER:
Check the F list, too.
Some languages pro-
nounce "b" as "v," so
you will find names
like Abigail and
Blanca on this V list.**

Abigail
Abril
Alba
Alberta
Alva
Alvera
Alverta
Alvina
Arvilla
Ava
Avery
Avis
Avlyn

Barbara
Beatrice
Belva
Benita
Bernita
Berta
Beverly
Bianca
Blanca
Bonita

Davin
Davina
Deborah
Devin
Dovie

Elizabeth
Elva
Elvera
Elvia
Elvira
Eva
Evangelina
Evangeline
Eve

Evelyn
Evelyne
Evie
Evon

Gabriel
Gabriela
Gabriella
Geneva
Genevieve
Genoveva
Giovanna
Guinevere

Haven
Heaven
Hedwig

Isabel
Isabela
Iva
Ivelisse
Ivory
Ivy

Jovita

Lavada
Lavera
Laverna
Laverne
Lavina
Lavinia
Lavonne
Liv
Livia
Lovie
Luvenia

Maeve
Malvina
Marva
Marvel
Mavis
Melva
Melvina
Minerva

Natividad
Neva
Nevaeh
Nova
Novella

Octavia
Olive
Olivie
Olivia
Ova

Parvati
Providenci

Raven
Rebecca
Reva
Rivka

Savannah
Shelva
Siobhan
Stevie
Sylvia
Sylvie

Toby
Treva
Tvuna

Valencia
Valentina
Valentine
Valeria
Valerie
Vallie
Vanessa
Veda
Velda
Vella
Velma
Velva
Vena
Venita
Venus
Vera
Verda
Vernie
Verla
Verlie
Verna
Vernell
Vernice
Verona
Veronica
Versie
Vesta
Vicenta
Vicky

Victoria
Vida
Vilma
Vina
Vincenza
Vinnie
Viola
Violet
Violetta
Violette
Virgie
Virginia
Virginie
Vita
Viv
Vivia
Viva
Vivian
Viviana
Vivienne
Von
Vonda
Vonnie

Waleska
Wava
Wilda
Wilhelmina
Wilhelmine
Wilma

Yvette
Yvonne

■ W ■

PARTNER POINTER:
Although some of
these names don't
have Ws in them, if
you break them down
phonetically, you'll
hear the "wuh"
sound. Check the Q
list for names with a
"kwuh" sound, too.

Antoinette
Awilda

Chloë

Delois

Edwina
Elois
Eloisa
Eloise
Emmanuela

Guadalupe
Gui
Guinevere
Gwen
Gwendolyn
Gwyneth

Hedwig

Jewel
Joanna
Joelle
Joellen
Joetta
Joey
Johanna
Juana
Juanita

Lawanda
Lois
Louella
Louie
Louise
Luana
Luann
Luetta
Luisa

Mairwen
Manuela
Moe

Noelia
Noelle
Noemi

Ouida

Rowan
Rowena

Shawanda

Tawana
Tawanda

Twila

Waleska
Wanda
Waneta
Wava
Wei
Wendy
Whitley
Whitney
Wilda
Wilhelmina
Wilhelmine
Willa
Willamina
Willene
Willia
Willie
Willow
Wilma
Windy
Winifred
Winnie
Winona
Wyatt
Wylie

Zoë

∎ X (KS) ∎

PARTNER POINTER:
Check the G, K, Q, S,
and Z lists, too.

Alex
Alexa
Alexandra
Alexandria
Alexandrie
Alexia
Alexis

Beatrix

Dexter
Dixie

Exie

Jacqueline

Lexi

Lexus

Maxie
Maxine

Nixie

Phoenix

Roxana
Roxanne
Roxie

Shaniqua

∎ Y ∎

PARTNER POINTER:
This list shows names
that use Y as a conso-
nant. Although some
of these names don't
have Ys in them, if
you break them down
phonetically, you'll
hear the "yuh" sound.
For names that use Y
as a vowel, check the
long E, long I, or
short I lists.

Aaliyah
Abrianna
Adelia
Adrian
Adriana
Adrianna
Adrienne
Agnese
Aida
Aisha
Aleah
Alexia
Althea
Amalia
Amaya
Amelia
Amiya
Anaïs
Anastasia
Andrea
Angelia
Aniya

Antonia
Antonietta
Anya
Aria
Ariana
Arianna
Ariel
Ariella
Arielle
Asia
Aurea
Aurelia
Ayana
Ayanna

Beatrice
Beatrix
Beulah
Bianca
Bria
Brianna
Brianne
Brielle

Cecilia
Chaya
Cheyenne
Ciara
Cleo
Cleora
Concepcion
Cordelia
Cordia
Cornelia
Creola
Cynthia

Dalia
Dania
Daniela
Danielle
Darian
Dasia
Dayana
Deann
Deanna
Deasia
Delia
Delphia
Demetria
Diana
Diane
Dolores
Dorothea

Eleanor
Eleanora
Eliana
Elvia
Emilia
Estefania
Estrella
Étienne
Eudora
Eugenia
Eugenie
Eula
Eulalia
Eulalie
Eura
Eunice

Fabiola
Fiona
Freya

Gabriel
Gabriela
Gabriella
Gabrielle
Galilea
Georgiana
Georgianne
Gia
Giada
Gianna
Giovanna
Gloria
Goldia
Graciela
Gregoria
Guillermina

Harriet
Henrietta
Henriette
Herminia
Hermione
Hortencia

Iliana
India
Iola
Iona
Ione
Irma

Jamya

Janiya
Jemima
Jessenia
Jillian
Jocelyn
Johanna
Jordan
Josefa
Judith
Julia
Juliana
Julianne
Juliet

Kaliyah
Kaori
Kecia
Keiki
Kenya
Kenyatta
Keshia
Kiana
Kiara
Kierra
Kya

Laisha
Lakeshia
Latanya
Latonya
Latoya
Lavinia
Lea
Leandra
Leanna
Leanne
Leatrice
Lelia
Leola
Leona
Leone
Leonor
Leonora
Leora
Leota
Lesia
Leticia
Letizia
Lilia
Liliana
Lilike
Lilla
Lilliam
Lillian

Linnea
Linnie
Livia
Loriann
Lucia
Luciena
Lucienne
Lucrecia
Luvenia
Lydia

Magnolia
Mairwen
Maleah
Malia
Maria
Mariah
Mariam
Marian
Mariana
Marianne
Mariel
Mariella
Marietta
Maryellen
Maya
Mia
Michaela
Migdalia
Mireya
Miriam
Moriah
Muriel

Nadia
Nakia
Naoma
Naomi
Natalia
Nayeli
Neoma
Nevaeh
Nyah
Nyasia
Nydia

Octavia
Oliana
Olivia
Ophelia
Oralia
Otilia

Patricia

Patrizia

Rafaela
Renea
Rhiannon
Rianna
Rocio
Rosalia
Rosario
Rosia
Ryan

Saniya
Sanya
Sariah
Sequoia
Shania
Shelia
Shreya
Sienna
Sierra
Soheila
Sonia
Sophia
Stacia
Stephania
Sylvia

Talia
Tamia
Tania
Tatiana
Taya
Thea
Theo
Theodora
Theola
Theresia
Tiana
Tiara
Tierra
Tonya
Toya
Tuk Yoon
Tyesha

Unique

Valencia
Valeria
Victoria
Viola
Violet
Violetta

Violette
Virginia
Vivia
Vivian
Viviana
Vivienne

Willia
Wyatt

Xiomara
Xia
Xiu

Yadira
Yahaira
Yanira
Yarden
Yareli
Yaritza
Yasmin
Yasmine
Yehudit
Yemima
Yesenia
Yetta
Yoko
Yolanda
Yoselin
Yoshiko
Yuliana
Yuka
Yumuna

Zaida
Zaria

■ Z ■

PARTNER POINTER:
Check the S, X, and
SH/ZH lists, too.

Agnese
Ainsley
Alexandra
Alexandria
Alize
Anastasia
Anastasie
Angeles
Ansley

Ceres
Charisse
Charles
Chelsea

Daisy
Denise
Desiree

Elise
Eliza
Elizabeth
Elois
Eloise
Elsa
Esmeralda
Esmerelda

Gisela
Giselle
Griselda

Hazel

Inez
Isabel
Isabela
Isadora
Isadore
Itzel
Izetta
Izora

James
Jasmine
Jazlyn
Josephine
Josette
Joslyn

Kenzie
Kinsey
Kizzy

Letizia
Liesel
Lindsey
Lisbet
Lise
Lissette
Litzy
Liz
Liza
Lizabeth

Lizbeth
Lizeth
Lizzie
Lorenza
Louise
Lucrecia
Luisa

Mackenzie
Marisa
Maritza
Mazie
Mercedes
Missouri
Mozella
Mozelle

Ozella

Pansy
Patrizia

Rosa
Rosalia
Rosalie
Rosalind
Rosaline
Rosalyn

Rosamond
Rosanna
Rosaura
Rose
Roseann
Rosella
Roselyn
Rosemarie
Rosemary
Rosetta
Rosia
Rosina
Rosita
Roslyn

Signe
Speranza
Stacia
Susan
Susana
Susie
Suzanne
Suzette

Teresa
Therese

Vincenza

Xena

Yaritza
Yasmin
Yasmine
Yoselin

Zaida
Zara
Zaria
Zelda
Zella
Zelma
Zenda
Zetta
Zina
Zita
Zoë
Zoila
Zola
Zona
Zora
Zoraida
Zsa-zsa
Zula
Zulma

CONSONANT NAMES FOR BOYS

B, CH, D, F, G, H, J, K, L, M, N/NG, P, Q (KW), R, S, SH/ZH, T, TH, V, W, X (KS), Y, Z

Confused about how to pronounce it?
Consult the vowel lists.

■ B ■

PARTNER POINTER:
Check the P list, too.
Some Spanish speak-
ers pronounce "v" as
"b" so you will find
names like Álvaro and
Victor on this B list.

Abdiel
Abdul
Abdullah
Abe
Abel
Abner
Abraham
Abram
Adalberto
Adelbert
Albert
Alberto
Albin
Alva
Álvaro
Ambrose
Anibal
Archibald
Aubrey

Bailey
Baron
Barrett
Barry
Barney
Bart
Bartholomew
Barton
Basil

Beau
Ben
Benedict
Benicio
Benito
Benjamin
Bennett
Benny
Benton
Bernard
Bernardo
Bernie
Bert
Bertram
Bertrand
Beryl
Bienvenido
Bilal
Bill
Billy
Bishop
Bixby
Blaine
Blair
Blaise
Blake
Bob
Bobby
Booker
Boris
Boyce
Boyd
Brad
Bradford
Bradley
Brady
Brandon
Brandt
Brannon

Braulio
Braxton
Brayden
Brendan
Brennan
Brent
Brenton
Brett
Brian
Bridger
Britt
Brock
Broderick
Brody
Bronson
Brook
Brooks
Brown
Bruce
Bruno
Bryant
Bryce
Bryson
Buck
Bud
Buddy
Buford
Burdette
Burl
Burley
Burnell
Burton
Buster
Butch
Buzz
Byron

Caleb
Campbell

Colby
Columbus
Corbin
Cristobal

Darby
Delbert

Elbert
Esteban
Eusebio

Fabian

Gabe
Gabriel
Gilbert
Gilberto
Gustavo

Heber
Herb
Herbert
Heriberto
Hilbert
Hobart
Hobert
Hubert
Humberto

Ibrahim
Ivan

Jabari
Jabreel
Jacob
Jacoby
Javier

Kelby
Kirby
Kobe

Lambert

Milburn

Najib
Noble
Norberto

Obie
Octavio
Osborne

Oswaldo

Pablo

Rayburn
Rigoberto
Rob
Robbie
Robert
Roberto
Robin
Ruben
Ruby

Salvador
Sebastian
Selby
Shelby
Silvio

Tobias
Tobin
Toby

Urban

Vicente
Victor
Vidal
Virgilio
Vito

Webster
Wilbert
Wilbur
Wilburn

Xavier

Yakoub

■ CH ■

**PARTNER POINTER:
Check the J and
SH/ZH lists, too.**

Arch
Archibald
Archie

Butch

Cecilio
Chad
Chadrick
Chadwick
Chance
Chandler
Chaney
Charles
Charlie
Chase
Chauncey
Chaz
Cheng
Chesley
Chester
Chet
Chip
Christian
Chuck

Fletcher
Francesco

Luciano

Marcelino
Marcelo
Mitch
Mitchell

Narciso

Richard
Richie
Richmond

Sancho
Satchel
Sebastian
ShinIchi

Thatcher
Tristian

Vincenzo

■ D ■

**PARTNER POINTER:
Check the T list, too.**

Abdiel
Abdul

Abdullah
Adalberto
Adam
Addison
Adelard
Adelbert
Aditya
Adolfo
Adolph
Adolphus
Adonis
Adrian
Adriel
Ahmad
Ahmed
Aidan
Alden
Aldo
Alejandro
Alessandro
Alexander
Alexandre
Alexandro
Alfred
Alfredo
Alford
Amado
Amador
Anderson
Andre
Andrea
Andreas
Andrés
Andrew
Andy
Arcadio
Archibald
Ardell
Arden
Armand
Armando
Arnaldo
Arnold
Arnoldo
Arvid
Audie

Benedict
Bernard
Bernardo
Bertrand
Bienvenido
Boyd
Brad

Bradford
Bradley
Brady
Brandon
Brayden
Brendan
Bridger
Broderick
Brody
Bud
Buddy
Buford
Burdette

Cade
Caden
Camden
Candelario
Candido
Cassidy
Cedar
Cedric
Chad
Chadrick
Chadwick
Chandler
Claude
Claudie
Claudio
Cleveland
Clifford
Cloyd
Clyde
Cody
Conrad
Cordell
Crawford

Dakota
Dale
Dallas
Dallin
Dalton
Damian
Damon
Dan
Dana
Dandre
Dane
Dangelo
Daniel
Danny
Dante
Daquan

Darby
Darian
Dario
Darius
Darold
Darnell
Darrell
Darren
Darwin
Dashiell
Dave
Davey
David
Davion
Davis
Davon
Dawson
Dax
Dayton
De
Dean
Deandre
Deangelo
Declan
Dedrick
Dee
Deepak
Dejuan
Delano
Delbert
Dell
Delmar
Delmas
Delmer
Delton
Delvin
Demarco
Demarcus
Demario
Demetris
Demetrios
Demetrius
DeMond
Dempsey
Denis
Dennis
Denny
Denton
Denver
Denzel
Denzil
Deon
Deonte
Derek

Dermot
Derwin
Deshawn
Desmond
Destin
Devin
Devonte
Dewayne
Dewey
Dewitt
Dexter
Dezso
Diamond
Dick
Dickie
Diego
Diezel
Dillard
Dillion
Dimitri
Dino
Dionisio
Dirk
Dock
Dominic
Domingo
Domenico
Don
Donal
Donald
Donato
Donnell
Donnie
Donovan
Dorian
Dorman
Dorsey
Doug
Douglas
Doyle
Drake
Draven
Drew
Dudley
Duke
Duncan
Durward
Durwood
Dustin
Dusty
Dwayne
Dwight
Dylan

Ed
Eddie
Edgar
Edgardo
Edison
Edmund
Edsel
Edward
Edwin
Eduardo
Eladio
Eldon
Eldred
Eldridge
Elwood

Federico
Ferdinand
Floyd
Ford
Fred
Freddy
Frederick
Fredrick
Friedrich

Gardner
Garfield
Garland
Gaylord
Gearld
Gerald
Geraldo
Gerard
Gerardo
Gideon
Glendon
Godfrey
Golden
Gordon
Grady
Guadalupe
Guido

Harding
Hardy
Harold
Hayden
Hayward
Haywood
Henderson
Hidero
Hillard
Hilliard

Holden
Howard
Hudson

Isidor
Isidro

Jade
Jaden
Jared
Jed
Jedidiah
Jody
Jordan
Jordy
Judah
Judd
Jude
Judge
Judson

Kadeem
Kendall
Kendrick
Kennedy
Khalid

Ladarius
Laddie
Landon
Leander
Leland
Leonard
Leonardo
Leopold
Leopoldo
Linwood
Lisandro
Lloyd
Loden
London
Ludwig
Lyndon

Maddox
Madison
Maynard
Milford
Millard
Modesto
Mohamed
Mordecai

Ned

Normand
Norwood

Odell
Odie
Orlando
Oswald
Oswaldo
Otis
Otto

Paddy
Patrick
Pedrick
Pedro

Radames
Rand
Randall
Randolph
Randy
Rashad
Rasheed
Rayford
Raymond
Raymundo
Raynard
Reid
Reginald
Reinhold
Rexford
Reynaldo
Reynold
Ricardo
Richard
Richmond
Riordan
Rod
Roderick
Rodney
Rodolfo
Rodrigo
Roland
Rolando
Ronald
Ronaldo
Rosendo
Rudolph
Rudy
Ryder
Ryland

Salvador
Sandro

Sandy
Sanford
Shad
Sheldon
Sheridan
Sherwood
Sid
Sidney
Sigmund
Sigurd
Stanford
Syed

Tad
Ted
Teddy
Tedros
Teodoro
Thad
Thaddeus
Theodore
Titus
Todd
Trinidad
Tudor

Vidal
Vidor
Vito

Wade
Waldemar
Waldo
Ward
Wardell
Weldon
Wendell
Wilford
Wilfred
Wilfredo
Wilfrid
Willard
Winfield
Winford
Winfred
Woodrow
Woody
Wylde

Yadiel
Yarden

Zaid
Zander

Zigmund

■ F ■

**PARTNER POINTER:
Check the V list, too.**

Adolfo
Adolph
Adolphus
Alf
Alfie
Alfonso
Alfred
Alfredo
Alford
Alpha
Alphonse
Arnulfo

Bradford
Buford

Christophe
Christopher
Cliff
Clifford
Clifton
Crawford

Efrain
Ephraim
Epifanio

Fabian
Faron
Farrell
Faustino
Federico
Felipe
Felix
Felton
Ferdinand
Fergus
Ferguson
Fermin
Fernand
Fernando
Fidel
Finley
Finn
Finnegan
Finian

Fisher
Fletcher
Florencio
Florentin
Florian
Floyd
Flynn
Fortunato
Foster
Foy
Francesco
Francis
Francisco
Frank
Frankie
Franklin
Franz
Fred
Freddy
Frederick
Fredrick
Freeman
Friedrich
Fritz
Fu
Furman

Garfield
Godfrey
Griffin
Griffith

Humphrey

Jeff
Jefferson
Jeffrey
Joseph

Kiefer

Lafayette
Leif

Milford
Murphy
Mustafa

Neftali

Olaf

Phelan
Phil

Philias
Phillip
Phineas
Phoenix
Porfirio

Rafael
Ralph
Randolph
Raouf
Rayford
Refugio
Rexford
Rodolfo
Rolf
Rudolph
Rufus

Sanford
Stanford
Stefan

Topher

Wilford
Wilfred
Wilfredo
Wilfrid
Winfield
Winford
Winfred

Yosef
Yusuf

■ **G** ■

PARTNER POINTER:
Check the K, Q,
and X lists, too.

Angus
August
Augustin
Augustus

Craig

Diego
Django
Domingo
Doug
Douglas

Edgar
Edgardo

Fergus
Ferguson
Finnegan

Gabe
Gabriel
Gaetano
Gage
Gale
Galen
Galvin
Gannon
Gardner
Garfield
Garland
Garnett
Garrett
Garrick
Garrison
Garth
Gary
Gaston
Gavin
Gaylord
Gearld
Geary
Gerhard
Gideon
Gil
Gilbert
Gilberto
Glendon
Glenn
Godfrey
Golden
Gonzalo
Gordon
Grady
Graham
Grant
Granville
Grayson
Green
Greg
Gregorio
Gregory
Griffin
Griffith
Grover
Guadalupe
Gui

Guido
Guillermo
Gulliver
Gunnar
Gunther
Gus
Gustave
Gustavo
Guy

Hugo

Ignacio
Ignatius

Jagger

Keegan

Logan
Ludwig

Magnus
Margarito
Miguel
Montague
Montgomery
Morgan

Nguyen

Patrick

Reagan
Regis
Rigoberto
Ringo
Rodrigo

Santiago
Sergei
Sigmund
Sigurd

Zigmund

■ H ■

PARTNER POINTER:
Although some of
these names don't
have Hs in them, if
you break them down
phonetically, you'll
hear the "huh" sound.

Aaron
Abraham
Ahmad
Ahmed
Alejandro
Angel
Angelo

Benjamin

Elijah
Eugenio

Genaro
Geraldo
Gerardo
German
Gilberto
Graham

Hakeem
Hal
Hallie
Hamilton
Hamish
Hamza
Hank
Hans
Hansel
Harding
Hardy
Harlan
Harley
Harmon
Harold
Harris
Harrison
Harry
Harvey
Haskell
Hassan
Hayden
Hayward
Haywood

Heath
Heber
Hector
Helmer
Henderson
Henry
Herb
Herbert
Herman
Herschel
Hezekiah
Hidero
Hilbert
Hillard
Hilliard
Hilton
Hiram
Hobart
Hobert
Holden
Hollis
Homer
Hong
Hoover
Horace
Hosea
Houston
Howard
Howell
Hoyt
Hubert
Hudson
Huey
Hugh
Hugo
Humphrey
Hunter
Hurley
Hyman

Ibrahim
Isaac

Jacinto
Jacques
Jahelm
Jaime
Jairo
Javier
Jeremiah
Jesús
Joachim
Joaquin
Johan
Jorge

Jose
Joshua
Josiah
Josué
Juan
Judah
Julio
Justo

Khalid
Khalil

Mohamed

Noah

Raheem
Rahul
Refugio
Reinhold
Rogelio
Rohan

Sergio

Virgilio

Wilhelm

Xavier

■ **J** ■

PARTNER POINTER:
Check the CH and
SH/ZH lists, too.

Angel
Angelo
Arjun

Benjamin
Bridger

Dangelo
Deangelo
Django

Eldridge
Elgin
Elijah
Eugene
Eujin

Gage
Geary
General
Genaro
Gene
Geo
George
Gerald
Gerard
German
Giancarlo
Gianni
Giles
Gino
Giovanni
Giuseppe

Jabari
Jacari
Jace
Jack
Jackie
Jackson
Jacob
Jacoby
Jade
Jaden
Jagger
Jaheim
Jaime
Jair
Jake
Jaleel
Jalen
Jamal
Jamar
Jamarcus
Jamari
James
Jameson
Jamie
Jamil
Jamir
Janis
Jara
Jared
Jaron
Jarom
Jarrett
Jarvis
Jason
Jasper
Javion
Javon

Javonte
Jay
Jazz
Jed
Jedidiah
Jeff
Jefferson
Jeffrey
Jennings
Jere
Jeremiah
Jeremy
Jermaine
Jerome
Jerrell
Jerry
Jess
Jesse
Jett
Jewell
Jim
Jimmy
JJ
Joachim
Jody
Joe
Joel
Joey
John
Johnny
Johnpaul
Johnson
Jomar
Jonah
Jonas
Jonathan
Jordan
Jordy
Joseph
Josh
Joshua
Josiah
Jovan
Judah
Judd
Jude
Judge
Judson
Jules
Julian
Jun
Junior
Junius
Justice

Justin
Juwan

Kenji

Luigi

Major

Najee
Nigel

Reggie
Reginal
Reginald
Ridge
Roger
Rogers

Sage
Semaj
Serge
Sergio

Talmadge

Virgil
Virgilio

Yuuji

Zhi

■ K ■

PARTNER POINTER:
Check the G, Q,
and X lists, too.

Akeem
Alec
Americo
Atticus

Benedict
Blake
Booker
Brock
Broderick
Brook
Brooks
Buck

Cade
Caden
Cael
Cale
Caleb
Calloway
Calvin
Camden
Cameron
Campbell
Candelario
Candido
Cannon
Carl
Carlo
Carlos
Carlton
Carlyle
Carmelo
Carmen
Carmine
Carnell
Carson
Carter
Casey
Cash
Casimir
Cason
Casper
Cassidy
Cedric
Chadrick
Chadwick
Chris
Christ
Christian
Christien
Christophe
Christopher
Chuck
Clarence
Clark
Claude
Claudie
Claudio
Clay
Clayton
Clem
Clémence
Clemens
Clement
Cleo
Cleon
Cletus

Cleve
Cleveland
Cliff
Clifford
Clifton
Clint
Clinton
Clover
Clovis
Cloyd
Clyde
Cody
Colby
Cole
Coleman
Colin
Colt
Colton
Columbus
Connor
Conrad
Constantine
Cooper
Corbin
Cordell
Corey
Cormac
Cornelius
Cornell
Cortéz
Cosmo
Courtney
Coy
Craig
Crawford
Crispin
Cristobal
Cruz
Cullen
Curtis

Dakota
Declan
Dedrick
Deepak
Demarco
Demarcus
Derek
Dick
Dickie
Dirk
Dock
Domenico
Dominic

Drake	Keegan	MacKenzie
Duke	Keenan	Makaio
Duncan	Keith	Malachi
	Kelby	Malachy
Enoch	Kellen	Malcolm
Enrico	Kelly	Malik
Enrique	Kelsey	Marco
Eric	Kelton	Marcos
Ezekiel	Kelvin	Marcus
	Ken	Mark
Federico	Kendall	Marquez
Francesco	Kendrick	Marquis
Francisco	Kenji	Masaaki
Frank	Kennedy	Maverick
Frankie	Kenneth	McArthur
Franklin	Kenny	McCoy
Frederick	Kent	McKinley
Fredrick	Kenton	McKyle
Friedrich	Kenya	Mekhi
	Kenyatta	Micah
Garrick	Kenyon	Michael
Giancarlo	Keon	Mickey
	Kermit	Mike
Hakeem	Kerouac	Mikhail
Hank	Kerry	Mordecai
Haskell	Kerwin	
Hector	Keshawn	Nakia
Hezekiah	Kevin	Nicholas
	Khalid	Nicholaus
Ike	Khalil	Nick
Isaac	Kiefer	Nicky
	Kiel	Nico
Jacari	Kieran	Nikhil
Jack	King	
Jackie	Kip	Oakley
Jackson	Kirby	Octavio
Jacob	Kirk	Okey
Jacoby	Klaus	Oscar
Jacques	Kobe	
Jake	Krishna	Parker
Jamarcus	Kurt	Pasquale
Joachim	Kwame	Patrick
Joaquin	Kylan	Pedrick
	Kyle	
Kadeem	Kyler	Raekwon
Kai	Kyree	Rakesh
Kale		Ricardo
Kalen	Lincoln	Ricky
Kamari	Lok	Rico
Kane	Luca	Rocco
Kareem	Lucas	Rock
Kazuo	Luke	Rocky
Keanu		Roderick
Keaton	Mack	Roscoe

Ryker

Scott
Scottie
Scout
Shaquille
Skyler

Tariq
Trek
Tucker

Victor

Walker

Yakoub
Yakov

Zachariah
Zachary
Zack
Zechariah
Zeke

■ L ■

Abdiel
Abdul
Abdullah
Abel
Adalberto
Adelard
Adelbert
Adolfo
Adolph
Adolphus
Adriel
Al
Alan
Alastair
Albert
Alberto
Albin
Alden
Aldo
Alec
Alejandro
Alessandro
Alex
Alexander
Alexandre
Alexandro

Alexis
Alf
Alfie
Alfonso
Alfred
Alfredo
Alford
Ali
Alma
Alois
Alonzo
Aloysius
Alpha
Alphonse
Alton
Alva
Álvaro
Alvie
Alvin
Alvis
Angel
Angelo
Anibal
Ansel
Anselmo
Archibald
Ariel
Ardell
Arlen
Arlie
Arlis
Arlo
Arnaldo
Arnold
Arnoldo
Arnulfo
Arvil
Ashley
Aurelio
Axel

Bailey
Bartholomew
Basil
Beryl
Bilal
Bill
Billy
Blaine
Blair
Blaise
Blake
Bradley
Braulio

Burl
Burley
Burnell

Cael
Cale
Caleb
Calloway
Calvin
Candelario
Carl
Carlo
Carlos
Carlton
Carlyle
Carmelo
Carnell
Cecil
Cecilio
Celestino
Chandler
Charles
Charlie
Chesley
Clarence
Clark
Claude
Claudie
Claudio
Clay
Clayton
Clem
Clémence
Clemens
Clement
Cleo
Cleon
Cletus
Cleve
Cleveland
Cliff
Clifford
Clifton
Clint
Clinton
Clover
Clovis
Cloyd
Clyde
Colby
Cole
Coleman
Colin
Colt

Colton	Eliezer	Giles
Columbus	Elijah	Glendon
Cordell	Eliseo	Glenn
Cornelius	Elisha	Golden
Cornell	Ellery	Gonzalo
Cristobal	Elliot	Guadalupe
Cullen	Ellis	Gulliver
Cyril	Ellsworth	
	Elmer	Hal
Dale	Elmo	Hallie
Dallas	Elmore	Hamilton
Dallin	Eloy	Hansel
Dalton	Elroy	Harlan
Dangelo	Elton	Harley
Daniel	Elvin	Harold
Darold	Elvis	Haskell
Darnell	Elwin	Helmer
Darrell	Elwood	Herschel
Dashiell	Émil	Hilario
Deangelo	Emiliano	Hilbert
Declan	Emilio	Hillard
Delano	Emmanuel	Hilliard
Delbert	Erling	Hilton
Dell	Errol	Hipólito
Delmar	Ezekiel	Holden
Delmas		Hollis
Delmer	Farrell	Howell
Delton	Felipe	Hurley
Delvin	Felix	
Denzel	Felton	Ishmael
Denzil	Fidel	Ismael
Diezel	Finley	Israel
Dillard	Fletcher	
Dillion	Florencio	Jabreel
Donal	Florentino	Jaleel
Donald	Florian	Jalen
Donnell	Floyd	Jamal
Douglas	Flynn	Jamil
Doyle	Franklin	Jerrell
Dudley		Jewell
Dylan	Gabriel	Joel
	Gale	Jules
Earl	Galen	Julian
Early	Galvin	Julio
Edsel	Garland	Julius
Eladio	Gaylord	
Elbert	Gearld	Kale
Eldon	General	Kalen
Eldred	Gerald	Kelby
Eldridge	Geraldo	Kellen
Elgin	Giancarlo	Kelly
Eli	Gil	Kelsey
Elian	Gilbert	Kelton
Elias	Gilberto	Kelvin

Kendall	Lindsey	Mel
Khalid	Linwood	Melton
Khalil	Lionel	Melville
Kiel	Lisandro	Melvin
Klaus	Llewellyn	Merle
Kylan	Lloyd	Merlin
Kyle	Loden	Merrill
Kyler	Logan	Michael
	Lok	Miguel
Lacy	Lon	Mikhail
Ladarius	London	Milan
Laddie	Long	Milburn
Lafayette	Lonnie	Miles
Lamar	Lonzo	Milford
Lambert	Loren	Millard
Lamont	Lorenzo	Miller
Lance	Lorne	Milo
Landon	Lou	Milton
Lane	Louie	Misael
Lanny	Louis	Mitchell
Laron	Lowell	
Larry	Loy	Napoleon
Lars	Loyal	Nathaniel
Lashawn	Luca	Neftali
Laszlo	Lucas	Neil
Latrell	Luciano	Nels
Lawrence	Lucien	Nelson
Lawson	Lucius	Newell
Layton	Ludwig	Nicholas
Lazaro	Luigi	Nicholaus
Lazarus	Luke	Nigel
Leamon	Lupe	Nikhil
Leander	Luther	Niles
Lee	Lyle	Nils
Leif	Lyman	Noble
Leland	Lyndon	Nolan
Lemuel		
Len	Mahlon	Oakley
Lenny	Malachi	Odell
Leo	Malachy	Olaf
Leon	Malcolm	Olen
Leonard	Malik	Oliver
Leonardo	Manley	Ollie
Léonel	Manuel	O'Neal
Leopold	Marcel	Oral
Leopoldo	Marcelo	Orlando
Leroy	Marcelino	Orlo
Les	Marcellus	Orville
Leslie	Marlon	Oswald
Lester	Marshall	Oswaldo
Levar	Maximilian	
Levi	Maxwell	Pablo
Liam	McKinley	Palmer
Lincoln	McKyle	Pasquale

Paul
Percival
Pernell
Phelan
Phil
Philias
Phillip

Rafael
Rahul
Raleigh
Ralph
Randall
Randolph
Raul
Reginal
Reginald
Reinhold
Reynaldo
Reynold
Riley
Rodolfo
Roel
Rogelio
Roland
Rolando
Rolf
Rollin
Rollo
Ronald
Ronaldo
Roswell
Royal
Rudolph
Russell
Rylan
Ryland

Sal
Salvador
Salvatore
Samuel
Satchel
Selby
Selmer
Shaquille
Sheldon
Sherrill
Silas
Silvio
Skyler
Sol
Solomon
Solon

Stanley
Sterling
Sullivan
Sylvan
Sylvester

Talmadge
Talon
Taylor
Telly
Terrell
Tillman
Tyler
Tyrell

Ulises
Uriel

Val
Valentin
Valentine
Verl
Verlin
Vernell
Vidal
Virgil
Virgilio

Waldemar
Waldo
Walker
Wallace
Wally
Walter
Walton
Wardell
Waylon
Weldon
Wellington
Welton
Wendell
Wesley
Wheeler
Wilbert
Wilbur
Wilburn
Wiley
Wilford
Wilfred
Wilfredo
Wilfrid
Wilhelm
Will
Willard

Willem
William
Williams
Willie
Willis
Willy
Wilmer
Wilson
Wilton
Wylde

Yadiel
Yul

■ M ■

Abraham
Abram
Adam
Ahmad
Ahmed
Akeem
Alma
Amado
Amador
Amari
Ambrose
Americo
Amir
Amos
Anselmo
Armand
Armando
Armani
Armstrong

Bartholomew
Benjamin
Bertram

Camden
Cameron
Campbell
Carmelo
Carmen
Carmine
Chaim
Clem
Clémence
Clemens
Clement
Coleman
Columbus

Cormac
Cosmo

Damian
Damon
Delmar
Delmas
Delmer
Demarco
Demarcus
Demario
Demetrios
Demetris
Demetrius
DeMond
Dempsey
Dermot
Desmond
Diamond
Dimitri
Domenico
Domingo
Dominic
Dorman

Edmund
Elmer
Elmo
Elmore
Emerson
Emery
Émil
Emiliano
Emilio
Emmanuel
Emmett
Ephraim
Erasmo

Fermin
Freeman
Furman

German
Graham
Guillermo

Hakeem
Hamilton
Hamish
Hamza
Harmon
Helmer
Herman

Herminio
Hiram
Homer
Humberto
Humphrey
Hyman

Ibrahim
Ishmael
Ismael

Jaheim
Jaime
Jamal
Jamar
Jamarcus
Jamari
James
Jameson
Jamie
Jamil
Jamir
Jarom
Jeremiah
Jeremy
Jermaine
Jerome
Jim
Jimmy
Joachim
Jomar

Kadeem
Kamari
Kareem
Kermit
Kwame

Lamar
Lambert
Lamont
Leamon
Lemuel
Liam
Lyman

Mack
MacKenzie
Maddox
Madison
Magnus
Mahlon
Major
Makaio

Malachi
Malachy
Malcolm
Malik
Manley
Manny
Manuel
Marcel
Marcellus
Marcelo
Marco
Marcos
Marcus
Margarito
Mariano
Mario
Marion
Mark
Marlon
Marquez
Marquis
Marshall
Martin
Marty
Marvin
Masaaki
Mason
Mateo
Mathias
Matt
Matthew
Mattias
Maurice
Mauricio
Maury
Maverick
Max
Maxie
Maxim
Maximilian
Maximino
Maximo
Maximus
Maxwell
Maynard
McArthur
McCoy
McKinley
McKyle
Mekhi
Mel
Melton
Melville
Melvin

Merle
Merlin
Merrill
Merritt
Merton
Mervin
Meyer
Micah
Michael
Mickey
Miguel
Mike
Mikhail
Milan
Milburn
Miles
Milford
Millard
Miller
Milo
Milton
Ming
Misael
Mitch
Mitchell
Modesto
Moe
Mohamed
Moises
Monroe
Monserrate
Montague
Montana
Monte
Montgomery
Mordecai
Morgan
Mortimer
Morton
Moses
Moshe
Murphy
Murray
Mustafa
Myron

Nehemiah
Newman
Norman
Normand

Omar
Omari
Omarion

Omer

Palmer
Primitivo

Radames
Raheem
Ram
Ramiro
Ramón
Ramsey
Ransom
Raymon
Raymond
Raymundo
Remington
Rémy
Richmond
Roman
Romeo

Sam
Samir
Sammy
Sampath
Samson
Samuel
Seamus
Selmer
Semaj
Seymour
Shamar
Sherman
Sim
Simeon
Simon
Smith
Solomon
Storm
Sumner

Talmadge
Thomas
Thurman
Tillman
Tim
Timmy
Timothy
Tom
Tommy
Tremaine
Truman

Waymon

Wilhelm
Willem
William
Williams
Wilmer
Wyman

Zigmund

■ **N/NG** ■

Aaron
Abner
Adonis
Adrian
Aidan
Alan
Albin
Alden
Alejandro
Alessandro
Alexander
Alexandre
Alexandro
Alonzo
Alphonse
Alton
Alvin
Anastacio
Anderson
Andre
Andrea
Andreas
Andrés
Andrew
Andy
Angel
Angelo
Angus
Anibal
Ansel
Anselmo
Anthony
Antoine
Anton
Antonio
Antony
Arden
Arjun
Arlen
Armand
Armando
Armani

Armstrong
Arnaldo
Arnav
Arne
Arno
Arnold
Arnoldo
Arnulfo
Arvin
Ashton
Augustin
Austin

Barney
Baron
Barton
Ben
Benedict
Benicio
Benito
Benjamin
Bennett
Benny
Benton
Bernard
Bernardo
Bernie
Bertrand
Bienvenido
Blaine
Brandon
Brandt
Brannon
Braxton
Brayden
Brendan
Brennan
Brent
Brenton
Brian
Bronson
Brown
Bruno
Bryant
Bryson
Burnell
Burton
Byron

Caden
Calvin
Camden
Cameron
Candelario

Candido
Cannon
Carlton
Carmen
Carmine
Carnell
Carson
Cason
Celestino
Chance
Chandler
Chaney
Chauncey
Cheng
Christian
Christien
Clarence
Clayton
Clémence
Clemens
Clement
Cleon
Cleveland
Clifton
Clint
Clinton
Coleman
Colin
Colton
Connor
Conrad
Constantine
Cornelius
Cornell
Courtney
Crispin

Dallin
Dalton
Damian
Damon
Dan
Dana
Dandre
Dane
Dangelo
Daniel
Danny
Dante
Daquan
Darian
Darnell
Darrell
Darren

Darwin
Davion
Davon
Dawson
Dayton
Dean
Deandre
Deangelo
Declan
Dejuan
Delano
Delton
Delvin
DeMond
Denis
Dennis
Denny
Denton
Denver
Denzel
Denzil
Deon
Deonte
Derwin
Deshawn
Desmond
Destin
Devin
Devonte
Dewayne
Diamond
Dillion
Dino
Dionisio
Django
Domenico
Domingo
Dominic
Don
Donal
Donald
Donato
Donnell
Donnie
Donovan
Dorian
Dorman
Draven
Duncan
Dustin
Dwayne
Dylan

Earnest

Easton
Edison
Edmund
Edwin
Efrain
Einar
Eino
Eldon
Elgin
Elian
Elton
Elvin
Elwin
Emerson
Emiliano
Emmanuel
Ennis
Enoch
Enos
Enrico
Enrique
Enzo
Epifanio
Erling
Ernesto
Ernie
Ernst
Erwin
Esteban
Estevan
Ethan
Eugene
Eugenio
Eujin
Evan
Evans
Ewan

Fabian
Faron
Faustino
Felton
Ferdinand
Ferguson
Fermin
Fernand
Fernando
Finian
Finley
Finn
Finnegan
Florencio
Florentino
Florian

Flynn
Fortunato
Francesco
Francis
Francisco
Frank
Frankie
Franklin
Franz
Freeman
Furman

Gaetano
Galen
Galvin
Gannon
Gardner
Garnett
Garrison
Gaston
Genaro
Gene
General
German
Giancarlo
Gianni
Gideon
Gino
Giovanni
Glendon
Glenn
Golden
Gonzalo
Gordon
Grant
Granville
Grayson
Green
Griffin
Gunnar
Gunther

Hamilton
Hamish
Hank
Hans
Hansel
Harding
Harlan
Harmon
Harrison
Hassan
Hayden
Henderson

Henry
Herman
Herminio
Hernan
Hilton
Holden
Hong
Houston
Hudson
Hunter
Hyman

Ian
Ignacio
Ignatius
Irvin
Irving
Ivan

Jacinto
Jackson
Jaden
Jalen
Jameson
Jan
Janis
Jaron
Jason
Javion
Javon
Javonte
Jean
Jefferson
Jennings
Jermaine
Joaquin
Johan
John
Johnny
Johnpaul
Johnson
Jonah
Jonas
Jonathan
Jordan
Jovan
Juan
Judson
Julian
Jun
Junior
Junius
Justin
Juwan

Kalen
Kane
Keanu
Keaton
Keegan
Keenan
Kellen
Kelton
Kelvin
Ken
Kendall
Kendrick
Kenji
Kennedy
Kenneth
Kenny
Kent
Kenton
Kenya
Kenyatta
Kenyon
Keon
Kerwin
Keshawn
Kevin
Kieran
King
Krishna
Kylan

Lamont
Lance
Landon
Lane
Lanny
Laron
Lashawn
Lawrence
Lawson
Layton
Leamon
Leander
Leland
Len
Lenny
Leon
Leonard
Leonardo
Léonel
Leopold
Lincoln
Lindsey
Linwood
Lionel

Lisandro
Loden
Logan
Lon
London
Long
Lonnie
Lonzo
Loren
Lorenzo
Lorne
Luciano
Lucien
Lyman
Lyndon

MacKenzie
Madison
Magnus
Mahlon
Manley
Manny
Manuel
Marcelino
Mariano
Marion
Marlon
Martin
Marvin
Mason
Maximilian
Maximino
Maynard
McKinley
Melton
Melvin
Merlin
Merton
Mervin
Milan
Milburn
Milton
Ming
Monroe
Monserrate
Montague
Montana
Monte
Montgomery
Morgan
Morton
Myron

Najee

Najib
Nakia
Napoleon
Narciso
Nash
Nasir
Nat
Nate
Nathan
Nathaniel
Ned
Neftali
Nehemiah
Neil
Nels
Nelson
Nestor
Newell
Newman
Newton
Nguyen
Nicholas
Nicholaus
Nick
Nicky
Nico
Nigel
Nikhil
Niles
Nils
Noah
Noble
Noé
Nolan
Norberto
Norman
Normand
Norris
Norton
Norval
Norwood
Nunzio

Olen
Omarion
O'Neal
Oran
Oren
Orion
Orlando
Osborne
Owen

Paxton

Pernell
Pershing
Peyton
Phelan
Phineas
Phoenix
Ping
Pranav
Preston
Prince

Quentin
Quincy
Quinn

Raekwon
Rand
Randall
Randolph
Randy
Ransom
Rashawn
Rayburn
Raymon
Raymond
Raymundo
Raynard
Rayshawn
Reagan
Reginal
Reginald
Reinhold
Reino
Remington
René
Reno
Reynaldo
Reynaud
Reynold
Richmond
Ringo
Riordan
Robin
Rodney
Rohan
Roland
Rolando
Rollin
Roman
Ron
Ronald
Ronaldo
Ronan
Ronnie

Rosendo
Roshan
Rowan
Ruben
Ryan
Rylan
Ryland
Ryne

Samson
Sancho
Sandro
Sandy
Sanford
Santiago
Santino
Santo
Santos
Savion
Sean
Sebastian
Shane
Shannon
Sheldon
Sheridan
Sherman
Sherwin
Shing
Shinichi
Sidney
Sigmund
Simeon
Simon
Sincere
Solomon
Solon
Sonny
Soren
Spencer
Stan
Stanford
Stanley
Stanton
Stefan
Sterling
Stetson
Steven
Stone
Stoney
Sullivan
Sumner
Sven
Sylvan

Talon
Tanner
Taurean
Tavion
Tavon
Terrence
Tevin
Theron
Thornton
Thurman
Thurston
Tiernan
Tierney
Tillman
Tobin
Tony
Torrance
Tremaine
Trent
Trenton
Trevion
Trevon
Treyton
Trinidad
Trinity
Tristan
Tristian
Truman
Turner
Tyquan
Tyrone
Tyshawn
Tyson

Urban

Valentin
Valentine
Van
Vance
Vaughn
Verlin
Vern
Vernell
Vernie
Vernon
Vicente
Vince
Vincent
Vincenzo
Vinson
Vishnu

Waino

Walton
Warner
Washington
Watson
Waylon
Waymon
Wayne
Weldon
Wellington
Welton
Wendell
Werner
Weston
Whitney
Wilburn
Wilson
Wilton
Winfield
Winford
Winfred
Winston
Winton
Wyman

Yarden

Zander
Zane
Zigmund

■ P ■

PARTNER POINTER:
Check the B list, too.

Bishop

Casper
Chip
Cooper
Crispin
Cypress

Deepak
Dempsey

Epifanio

Felipe

Giuseppe
Guadalupe

Hipólito

Jasper
Johnpaul

Kip

Leopold
Leopoldo
Lupe

Napoleon

Pablo
Pacey
Paddy
Palmer
Paris
Parker
Parrish
Pasquale
Pat
Patricio
Patrick
Patrizio
Patsy
Paul
Pax
Paxton
Pedrick
Pedro
Pepe
Percival
Percy
Pernell
Perry
Pershing
Pete
Peter
Peyton
Pierce
Pierre
Pietro
Ping
Porfirio
Porter
Pranav
Preston
Price
Primitivo
Prince

Rupert

Sampath
Spencer

■ Q (KW) ■

PARTNER POINTER:
Check the G, K, X,
and W lists, too.

Daquan

Kwame

Marquis

Pasquale

Quentin
Quest
Quincy
Quinn

Raekwon

Tyquan

■ R ■

PARTNER POINTER:
This list shows names
with a hard R ("ruh")
sound. Check the AR,
AIR, OR, or UR lists for
names with soft Rs.

Aaron
Abraham
Abram
Adrian
Adriel
Alejandro
Alessandro
Alexandre
Alexandro
Alfred
Alfredo
Álvaro
Amari
Ambrose
Americo
Andre
Andrea

Andreas
Andrés
Andrew
Ari
Ariel
Arturo
Aubrey
Aurelio
Avery

Baron
Barrett
Barry
Bertram
Bertrand
Beryl
Boris
Brad
Bradford
Bradley
Brady
Brandon
Brandt
Brannon
Braulio
Braxton
Brayden
Brendan
Brennan
Brent
Brenton
Brett
Brian
Bridger
Britt
Brock
Broderick
Brody
Bronson
Brook
Brooks
Brown
Bruce
Bruno
Bryant
Bryce
Bryson
Byron

Cameron
Candelario
Cedric
Chadrick
Chris

Christ
Christian
Christien
Christophe
Christopher
Cicero
Clarence
Conrad
Corey
Craig
Crawford
Crispin
Cristobal
Cruz
Cypress
Cyril
Cyrus

Darian
Dario
Darius
Darold
Darrell
Darren
Deandre
Dedrick
Demario
Demetrios
Demetris
Demetrius
Derek
Dimitri
Dorian
Drake
Draven
Drew

Efrain
Eldred
Eldridge
Ellery
Elroy
Emery
Enrico
Enrique
Ephraim
Erasmo
Eric
Errol
Everett
Ezra

Faron
Farrell

Federico
Florencio
Florentino
Florian
Forrest
Francesco
Francis
Francisco
Frank
Frankie
Franklin
Franz
Fred
Freddy
Frederick
Fredrick
Freeman
Friedrich
Fritz

Gabriel
Garrett
Garrick
Garrison
Gearld
Geary
Genaro
General
Gerald
Geraldo
Gerard
Gerardo
Godfrey
Grady
Graham
Grant
Granville
Grayson
Green
Greg
Gregorio
Gregory
Griffin
Griffith
Grover

Harold
Harris
Harrison
Harry
Henri
Henry
Heriberto
Hidero

Hilario
Hiram
Horace

Ibrahim
Ira
Isidro
Israel
Ivory

Jabari
Jabreel
Jacari
Jairo
Jamari
Jara
Jared
Jarrett
Jaron
Jarom
Jeffrey
Jeremiah
Jeremy
Jerome
Jerrell
Jerry

Kamari
Kareem
Kendrick
Kerouac
Kerry
Kieran
Krishna
Kyree

Ladarius
Laron
Larry
Latrell
Lawrence
Lazaro
Lazarus
Leroy
Lisandro
Loren
Lorenzo

Margarito
Mariano
Mario
Marion
Maurice
Mauricio

Maury
Maverick
Merrill
Merritt
Monroe
Monserrate
Montgomery
Murray
Myron

Norris

Omari
Omarion
Ora
Oral
Oran
Oren
Orie
Orion

Paris
Parrish
Patricio
Patrick
Patrizio
Pedrick
Pedro
Perry
Pietro
Porfirio
Pranav
Preston
Price
Primitivo
Prince

Radames
Raekwon
Rafael
Raheem
Rahul
Rakesh
Raleigh
Ralph
Ram
Ramiro
Ramón
Ramsey
Rand
Randall
Randolph
Randy
Ransom

Rashad
Rashawn
Rasheed
Raouf
Raul
Ravi
Ray
Rayburn
Rayford
Raymon
Raymond
Raymundo
Raynard
Rayshawn
Reagan
Reese
Reid
Refugio
Reggie
Reginal
Reginald
Regis
Reinhold
Reino
Remington
Rémy
René
Reno
Rex
Rexford
Reyes
Reynaldo
Reynaud
Reynold
Rhett
Ricardo
Richard
Richie
Richmond
Ricky
Rico
Ridge
Rigoberto
Riley
Ringo
Rio
Riordan
River
Rob
Robbie
Robert
Roberto
Robin
Rocco

Rock
Rocky
Rod
Roderick
Rodney
Rodolfo
Rodrigo
Roel
Rogelio
Roger
Rogers
Rohan
Roland
Rolando
Rolf
Rollin
Rollo
Roman
Romeo
Ron
Ronald
Ronaldo
Ronan
Ronnie
Roosevelt
Rory
Rosario
Roscoe
Rosendo
Roshan
Ross
Roswell
Rowan
Roy
Royal
Royce
Ruben
Ruby
Rudolph
Rudy
Rufus
Rupert
Rush
Russ
Russell
Rusty
Ryan
Ryder
Ryker
Rylan
Ryland
Ryne

Salvatore

Sandro
Sheridan
Sherrill
Soren

Tariq
Taurean
Tavares
Tedros
Teodoro
Terrell
Terrence
Terry
Theron
Torrance
Tory
Trace
Tracy
Travis
Trek
Tremaine
Trent
Trenton
Trevion
Trevon
Trevor
Trey
Treyton
Trinidad
Trinity
Tristan
Tristian
Troy
Truman
Tyree
Tyrell
Tyrese
Tyrone

Uriel

Wilfred
Wilfredo
Wilfrid
Winfred
Woodrow

Yuri

Zachariah
Zachary
Zechariah

■ S ■

PARTNER POINTER:
Check the X and Z
lists, too, and if you
want, the SH/ZH list.

Addison
Adolphus
Adonis
Alastair
Alessandro
Alexis
Alois
Aloysius
Alphonse
Alvis
Amos
Anastacio
Anderson
Andreas
Andres
Angus
Ansel
Anselmo
Arlis
Armstrong
Artis
Asa
Atticus
August
Augustin
Augustus
Austin

Benicio
Boris
Boyce
Brooks
Bruce
Bryce
Bryson
Buster

Caesar
Carlos
Carson
Casey
Cason
Casper
Cassidy
Cecil
Cecilio
Cedar

Cedric
Celestino
Cesar
Chance
Chase
Chauncey
Chesley
Chester
Chris
Christ
Christian
Christien
Christophe
Christopher
Cicero
Clarence
Clémence
Cletus
Clovis
Columbus
Constantine
Cornelius
Crispin
Cristobal
Cruz
Curtis
Cypress
Cyril
Cyrus

Dallas
Darius
Davis
Dawson
Delmas
Demarcus
Demetrios
Demetris
Demetrius
Dempsey
Denis
Dennis
Destin
Dionisio
Dorsey
Douglas
Dustin
Dusty

Earnest
Easton
Edison
Edsel
Elias

Eliseo
Ellis
Elvis
Ennis
Enos
Erasmo
Ernesto
Ernst
Esteban
Eusebio
Ezekiel

Faustino
Fergus
Ferguson
Florencio
Forrest
Foster
Francesco
Francis
Francisco
Franz
Fritz

Garrison
Gaston
Giuseppe
Gonzalo
Grayson
Gus
Gustave
Gustavo

Hans
Hansel
Harris
Harrison
Haskell
Hassan
Henderson
Hollis
Horace
Houston
Hudson

Ignacio
Isaac
Isai
Isaiah
Isaias
Ishmael
Isidor
Isidro
Ismael

Israel

Jace
Jacinto
Jackson
Jacques
Jamarcus
Jameson
Janis
Jarvis
Jasper
Jason
Jefferson
Jess
Jesse
Jesús
Jonas
Jose
Josué
Judson
Julius
Junius
Justice
Justin
Justo

Kelsey
Klaus

Lacy
Ladarius
Lance
Lawrence
Lawson
Lazarus
Les
Leslie
Lester
Lisandro
Louis
Lucas
Luciano
Lucien
Lucius

Madison
Magnus
Marcel
Marcelino
Marcellus
Marcelo
Marcos
Marcus
Marquis

Masaaki	Russ	Solomon
Mason	Russell	Solon
Mathias	Rusty	Sonny
Mattias		Soren
Maurice	Sage	Spencer
Mauricio	Sal	Stacy
Maximus	Salvador	Stan
Misael	Salvatore	Stanford
Modesto	Sam	Stanley
Moises	Samir	Stanton
Monserrate	Sammy	Stefan
Moses	Sampath	Sterling
Mustafa	Samson	Stetson
	Samuel	Steve
Narciso	Sancho	Steven
Nasir	Sandro	Stevie
Nelson	Sandy	Stone
Nestor	Sanford	Stoney
Nicholas	Santiago	Storm
Nicholaus	Santino	Stuart
Norris	Santo	Sullivan
	Santos	Sumner
Oscar	Satchel	Sven
Oswaldo	Sasha	Syed
Otis	Saul	Sylvan
	Savion	Sylvester
Pacey	Sawyer	
Paris	Scott	Tavares
Pasquale	Scottie	Tedros
Patricio	Scout	Terrence
Patsy	Sebastian	Thaddeus
Percival	Selby	Thomas
Percy	Selmer	Thurston
Philias	Semaj	Titus
Phineas	Serge	Tobias
Pierce	Sergei	Torrance
Preston	Sergio	Trace
Price	Seth	Tracy
Prince	Seymour	Travis
	Shad	Tristan
Quest	Sid	Tristian
Quincy	Sidney	Tyrese
	Sigmund	Tyson
Radames	Sigurd	
Ransom	Silas	Ulises
Reese	Silvio	
Regis	Sim	Vester
Reyes	Simeon	Vicente
Rosario	Simon	Vince
Roscoe	Sincere	Vincent
Rosendo	Sixto	Vincenzo
Ross	Skyler	Vinson
Royce	Smith	
Rufus	Sol	Wallace

Watson
Webster
Wes
Wesley
Weston
Willis
Wilson
Winston

Yosef
Yusuf

Zion

■ SH/ZH ■

**PARTNER POINTER:
Check the CH, J, S,
and Z lists, too.**

Aloysius
Asher
Ashley
Ashton

Benjamin
Bishop

Cash
Casimir
Charles

Dashiell
Deshawn
Dezso

Elijah
Elisha
Eugene

Fisher

George
Gerard
German
Gilbert
Giles

Hamish
Herschel
Hosea

Ignatius

Isai
Isaiah
Ishmael

Jabreel
Jacques
Jaleel
Jamal
Jamil
Jean
Jermaine
Jerome
Jesse
Joachim
Joel
Joseph
Josh
Joshua
Josiah
Jules
Julian
Justin

Keshawn
Krishna

Lashawn
Lucien
Lucius

Marshall
Michael
Moshe

Najib
Nash

Parrish
Pershing

Rakesh
Rashad
Rashawn
Rasheed
Rayshawn
Regis
Richard
Roger
Roshan
Rush

Samson
Samuel
Sasha

Saul
Seamus
Sean
Serge
Seth
Shad
Shamar
Shane
Shannon
Shaquille
Shea
Shelby
Sheldon
Sheridan
Sherman
Sherrill
Sherwin
Sherwood
Shing
ShinIchi
Simon

Tyshawn

Vishnu

Washington

■ T ■

**PARTNER POINTER:
Check the D list, too.**

Adalberto
Adelbert
Aditya
Alastair
Albert
Alberto
Alton
Anastacio
Antoine
Anton
Antonio
Antony
Armstrong
Art
Artie
Artis
Arturo
Ashton
Atticus
August

Augustin
Augustus
Austin

Barrett
Bart
Barton
Benedict
Benito
Bennett
Benton
Bert
Bertram
Bertrand
Brandt
Braxton
Brent
Brenton
Brett
Britt
Bryant
Burton
Buster

Carlton
Carter
Celestino
Chester
Chet
Christ
Christian
Christien
Christophe
Christopher
Clayton
Clement
Clifton
Clint
Clinton
Colt
Colton
Constantine
Cortéz
Courtney
Cristobal
Curtis

Dakota
Dalton
Dante
Dayton
Delbert
Delton
Demetrios

Demetris
Demetrius
Denton
Deonte
Dermot
Destin
Devonte
Dewitt
Dexter
Dimitri
Donato
Dustin
Dusty
Dwight

Earnest
Easton
Elbert
Elliot
Elton
Emmett
Ernesto
Ernst
Esteban
Ethan
Everett
Evert

Faustino
Felton
Florentino
Forrest
Fortunato
Foster
Fritz

Gaetano
Garnett
Garrett
Gaston
Gerhard
Gilbert
Gilberto
Grant
Gustave
Gustavo

Hamilton
Hector
Herbert
Heriberto
Hilbert
Hipolito
Hobart

Hobert
Houston
Hoyt
Hubert
Humberto
Hunter

Itai

Jacinto
Jarrett
Javonte
Jett
Jonathan
Justice
Justin
Justo

Keaton
Kent
Kenton
Kenyatta
Kermit
Kurt

Lafayette
Lambert
Lamont
Latrell
Layton
Lester

Margarito
Martin
Marty
Matt
Mattias
Melton
Merritt
Merton
Milton
Modesto
Monserrate
Montague
Montana
Monte
Montgomery
Mortimer
Morton
Mustafa

Nat
Nate
Nathan

Nathaniel
Neftali
Nestor
Newton
Norberto
Norton

Octavio

Pat
Patricio
Patrick
Patrizio
Patsy
Pete
Peter
Peyton
Pietro
Porter
Primitivo

Quentin
Quest

Remington
Rhett
Rigoberto
Robert
Roberto
Rupert
Rusty

Salvatore
Sampath
Santiago
Santino
Santo
Santos
Scott
Scottie
Scout
Sebastian
Sixto
Stacy
Stan
Stanford
Stanley
Stanton
Stefan
Sterling
Stetson
Steve
Steven
Stevie
Stone

Stoney
Storm
Stuart
Sylvester

Tad
Talmadge
Talon
Tanner
Tariq
Tate
Taurean
Tavares
Tavion
Tavon
Taye
Taylor
Ted
Teddy
Tedros
Telly
Teodoro
Terrell
Terrence
Terry
Tevin
Theo
Theodore
Theron
Thomas
Thornton
Thurston
Tiernan
Tierney
Tillman
Tim
Timmy
Timothy
Tito
Titus
Tobias
Tobin
Toby
Todd
Tom
Tommy
Tony
Topher
Torrance
Tory
Trace
Tracy
Travis
Trek
Tremaine

Trent
Trenton
Trevion
Trevon
Trevor
Trey
Treyton
Trinidad
Trinity
Tristan
Tristian
Troy
Truman
Tucker
Tudor
Turner
Ty
Tyler
Tyquan
Tyree
Tyrell
Tyrese
Tyrone
Tyshawn
Tyson

Valentin
Valentine
Vester
Vicente
Victor
Vincent
Vito

Walton
Watson
Webster
Wellington
Welton
Wyatt

■ TH ■

PARTNER POINTER:
Although some
Spanish speakers
pronounce "s" as
"th," we did not
include names with
those "s" pronuncia-
tions on this list. Both
pronunciations
appear on the S list.

Aditya
Anthony
Arthur

Bartholomew

Ellsworth
Ethan

Garth
Griffith
Gunther

Heath

Jonathan

Keith
Kenneth

Luther

Mathias
Matthew
McArthur

Nathan
Nathaniel

Seth
Smith

Thad
Thaddeus
Thatcher
Theo
Theodore
Theron
Thor
Thornton
Thurman
Thurston
Timothy

Worth

■ V ■

**PARTNER POINTER:
Check the F list, too.
Some languages
pronounce "b" as "v"
so you will find names
like Abraham and
Bernardo on this V list.**

Abdiel
Abel
Abner
Abraham
Abram
Alva
Álvaro
Alvie
Alvin
Alvis
Arnav
Arvid
Arvil
Arvin
Avery

Benicio
Benito
Benjamin
Bernardo
Bienvenido
Braulio

Caleb
Calvin
Cleve
Cleveland
Clover
Clovis
Cristobal

Dave
Davey
David
Davion
Davis
Davon
Delvin
Denver
Devin
Devonte
Donovan
Draven

Elvin
Elvis
Esteban
Eusebio
Evan
Evans
Everett
Everette
Evert

Gabriel
Galvin
Gavin
Gilberto
Giovanni
Granville
Grover
Gulliver
Gustave
Gustavo

Harvey
Heriberto
Hoover
Humberto

Irvin
Irving
Ivan
Ivory

Jacob
Jarvis
Javier
Javion
Javon
Javonte
Jovan

Kelvin
Kevin

Levar
Levi
Ludwig

Marvin
Maverick
Melville
Melvin
Mervin

Norberto
Norval

Octavio
Oliver
Orville
Oswaldo

Pablo
Percival
Pranav
Primitivo

Ravi
River
Roosevelt
Ruben

Salvador
Salvatore
Savion
Sebastian
Silvio
Steve
Steven
Stevie
Sullivan
Sven
Sylvan
Sylvester

Tavares
Tavion
Tavon
Tevin
Tobias
Toby
Travis
Trevion
Trevon
Trevor

Val
Valentin
Valentine
Van
Vance
Vaughn
Verl
Verlin
Vern
Vernell
Vernie
Vernon
Vester
Vicente
Victor

Vidal
Vidor
Vince
Vincent
Vincenzo
Vinson
Virgil
Virgilio
Vishnu
Vito

Waino
Waldemar
Waldo
Walter
Warner
Werner
Wilbur
Wilburn
Wilhelm
Willard
Wilmer
Winfield

Xavier

Yakov

■ W ■

PARTNER POINTER:
Although some of
these names don't
have Ws in them, if
you break them down
phonetically, you'll
hear the "wuh"
sound. Check the Q
list for names with a
"kwuh" sound, too.

Alois
Aloysius
Antoine

Calloway
Chadwick

Darwin
Dejuan
Dewayne
Dewey
Dewitt

Durward
Durwood
Dwayne
Dwight

Edward
Edwin
Eduardo
Ellsworth
Elwin
Elwood
Emmanuel
Erwin
Ewan

Guadalupe
Gui
Guido

Hayward
Haywood
Howard
Howell

Jewell
Joachim
Joaquin
Joel
Joey
Joshua
Josué
Juan
Juwan

Kazuo
Kerwin
Kwame

Lemuel
Llewellyn
Louie
Louis
Lowell
Ludwig
Luigi

Manuel
Maxwell
Miguel

Newell
Nguyen
Noah
Noé

Norwood

Oswald
Oswaldo
Owen

Phelan

Raekwon
Roel
Rowan

Samuel
Sherwin
Sherwood
Stuart

Wade
Waino
Waldemar
Waldo
Walker
Wallace
Wally
Walter
Walton
Ward
Wardell
Warner
Washington
Watson
Waylon
Waymon
Wayne
Webster
Weldon
Wellington
Welton
Wendell
Werner
Wes
Wesley
Weston
Wheeler
Whitney
Wilbert
Wilbur
Wilburn
Wiley
Wilford
Wilfred
Wilfredo
Wilfrid
Wilhelm

Will
Willard
Willem
William
Williams
Willie
Willis
Willy
Wilmer
Wilson
Wilton
Winfield
Winford
Winfred
Winston
Winton
Woodrow
Woody
Worth
Wyatt
Wylde
Wyman

■ X (KS) ■

PARTNER POINTER:
Check the G, K, Q, S,
and Z lists, too.

Alex
Alexander
Alexandre
Alexandro
Alexis
Axel

Bixby
Braxton
Brooks

Dax
Dexter

Felix

Jackson

Maddox
Max
Maxie
Maxim
Maximilian
Maximino

Maximo
Maximus
Maxwell

Pax
Paxton
Phoenix

Rex
Rexford

Sixto

Xavier

■ Y ■

PARTNER POINTER:
**This list shows names
that use Y as a conso-
nant. Although some
of these names don't
have Ys in them, if
you break them down
phonetically, you'll
hear the "yuh" sound.
For names that use Y
as a vowel, check the
long E, long I, or
short I lists.**

Aditya
Adrian
Adriel
Anastacio
Andreas
Antonio
Arcadio
Ariel
Aurelio

Bartholomew
Benicio
Benjamin
Bienvenido
Brian
Bryant
Buford

Candelario
Cecilio
Christian
Christien

Claudio
Cornelius

Damian
Darian
Dario
Darius
Deandre
Deangelo
Demario
Demetrios
Demetrius
Deon
Deonte
Diamond
Diego
Dillion
Dionisio
Dorian

Eladio
Elian
Elias
Eliezer
Eliseo
Elliot
Emiliano
Emmanuel
Ephraim
Epifanio
Eugene
Eugenio
Eujin
Eusebio
Ewan
Ezekiel

Fabian
Finian
Florencio
Florian

Gabriel
Geo
Gianni
Gideon
Giovanni
Gregorio

Herminio
Hezekiah
Hilario
Hilliard
Hosea
Hubert

Huey
Hugh
Hugo

Ian
Ignacio
Ignatius
Isai
Isaiah
Isaias
Ishmael
Ismael
Israel

Jair
Jairo
Jan
Javier
Javion
Jedidiah
Jeremiah
Joachim
Joaquin
Joel
Johan
Jonah
Jonathan
Jordan
Joseph
Joshua
Josiah
Judah
Julian
Julio
Julius
Junior
Junius

Keanu
Kenya
Kenyatta
Kenyon
Keon

Ladarius
Lafayette
Lemuel
Leo
Leon
Leonard
Leonardo
Léonel
Leopold
Leopoldo
Liam

Lionel
Loyal
Luciano
Lucien

Makaio
Mariano
Mario
Marion
Mateo
Mathias
Mattias
Mauricio
Maximilian
Meyer
Michael
Mikhail
Misael

Nakia
Napoleon
Nathaniel
Neftali
Nehemiah
Nguyen

Octavio
Omarion
Orion

Patricio
Patrizio
Philias
Phineas
Pierre
Pietro
Porfirio

Rafael
Refugio
Reyes
Rio
Riordan
Rogelio
Romeo
Rosario
Royal
Ryan

Samuel
Santiago
Savion
Sawyer
Sebastian
Sergio

Silvio
Simeon
Syed

Taurean
Tavion
Teodoro
Thaddeus
Theo
Theodore
Tobias
Trevion

Ulises
Uriel

Virgilio

Wyatt

Xavier

Yadiel
Yahir
Yakoub
Yakov
Yarden
Ye
Yosef
Yul
Yuri
Yusuf
Yuuji

Zachariah
Zaid
Zaire
Zechariah
Zion

■ Z ■

PARTNER POINTER:
Check the S, X, and
SH/ZH lists, too.

Alexander
Alexandre
Alexandro
Alfonso
Alonzo
Ambrose

Basil
Blaise

Caesar
Casimir
Cesar
Charles
Chaz
Chesley
Clemens
Cortéz
Cosmo
Cruz

Denzel
Denzil
Desmond
Diezel

Eliezer
Eliseo
Ellsworth
Enzo
Evans
Ezekiel
Ezra

Franz

Giles
Giuseppe
Gonzalo

Hamza
Hezekiah
Hosea

Isaac
Isaiah
Isaias
Isidor
Ismael
Israel
Izzy

James
Jazz
Jean
Jennings
Jose
Joseph
Josiah
Jules

Kazuo

Lars
Laszlo
Lazaro
Lazarus
Lindsey
Lonzo
Lorenzo

MacKenzie
Marquez
Marquis
Mauricio
Miles
Moises
Moses

Nels
Niles
Nils
Nunzio

Osborne
Oswald

Patrizio

Ramsey
Rogers
Roosevelt
Rosendo
Roswell

Ulises

Vincenzo

Williams

Xavier

Zachariah
Zachary
Zack
Zaid
Zaire
Zander
Zane
Zechariah
Zeke
Zion
Zigmund

RHYTHM-BASED NAMES FOR GIRLS

Confused about how to pronounce it?
Consult the vowel lists.

■ TROCHEE ■

One heavily stressed syllable
followed by one
unstressed syllable.

BEAT BAROMETER:
Trochaic first names
(DA-da) can sound
good with any type of
surname. You might
especially like these
names if your last
name is a trochee,
dactyl, or one syllable.

Abby	Amber	Barbra
Abril	Amie	Becky
Ada	Amy	Bella
Addie	Angel	Belva
Afton	Angie	Bennie
Agnes	Anna	Berta
Aida	Annie	Bertha
Aiko	Annis	Bertie
Aileen	Ansley	Beryl
Ainsley	Anya	Bessie
Aisha	Apple	Bethel
Aisling	April	Betsy
Alba	Ara	Betty
Alda	Ardell	Beulah
Alex	Ardis	Billie
Ali	Ardith	Birdie
Alice	Arlie	Blanca
Allie	Arrie	Blossom
Alma	Artie	Bobbie
Alpha	Asha	Bonnie
Alta	Ashley	Brandon
Altha	Ashlyn	Brandy
Alva	Ashton	Brenda
	Asia	Brenna
	Aspen	Bria
	Astrid	Bridget
	Aubrey	Brisa
	Audie	Britney
	Audra	Brooklyn
	Audrey	Buffy
	Autumn	
	Ava	Cadence
	Avis	Callie
	Avlyn	Campbell
	Ayla	Camry
	Aylin	Candace
		Candy
	Bailey	Carla
	Bambi	Carly

Carma	Dallas	Elba
Carmen	Dana	Elda
Carol	Dania	Ella
Carrie	Danna	Ellen
Carson	Dara	Ellie
Carys	Darby	Elma
Casey	Darcy	Elna
Cassie	Darla	Elsa
Cecil	Daryl	Elsie
Cedar	Dasia	Elta
Ceres	Davin	Elva
Chana	Debbie	Emma
Chanda	Deedee	Emmie
Chandler	Deepa	Ena
Chandra	Deidre	Enid
Charla	Deirdre	Era
Charlie	Déja	Erin
Charlotte	Della	Eris
Chaya	Delma	Erna
Chelsea	Delpha	Essence
Cherie	Delta	Essie
Cherry	Dessie	Esta
Cherish	Dexter	Esther
Cheryl	Devin	Etha
China	Diamond	Ethel
Chloë	Dimple	Etta
Chrissy	Dina	Ettie
Christen	Dionne	Eula
Christian	Dixie	Eura
Christy	Dolly	Eunice
Ciara	Donna	Eva
Cinda	Donnie	Eve
Cindy	Dora	Evie
Clara	Dorcas	Evon
Claudie	Dori	Exie
Clemmie	Doris	
Cleo	Dorit	Fairy
Cleta	Dortha	Fallon
Coco	Dorthy	Fannie
Cody	Dottie	Farrah
Connie	Dovie	Fatima
Constance	Dulce	Fleta
Cora	Dylan	Flora
Coral		Florence
Cordie	Easter	Florrie
Corliss	Ebba	Flossie
Courtney	Eddie	Fonda
Crystal	Eda	Frances
Christelle	Eden	Frankie
Cypress	Edie	Freddie
	Edith	Freya
Dagmar	Edna	Frida
Dagny	Edrie	
Daisy	Effie	Garnett

Gayla
Gemma
Georgia
Georgie
Gerda
Gertie
Gertrude
Gia
Giada
Gianna
Gigi
Gilda
Gina
Ginger
Ginny
Gladys
Glenda
Glenna
Glennie
Glynda
Glynis
Golda
Golden
Goldie
Gracie
Greta
Gretchen
Gretel
Gudrun
Gussie
Gwyneth

Hadley
Hailey
Hallie
Hannah
Harley
Hassie
Hattie
Haven
Haydee
Hayden
Hazel
Heather
Heaven
Hedwig
Heidi
Helga
Helen
Helene
Herta
Hester
Hettie
Hilda

Hilde
Hildred
Hildur
Hilma
Holly
Honey
Hortense
Hulda
Hunter

Icie
Ida
Ila
Ilsa
Ima
Ina
Inga
Ingrid
Ira
Ireland
Iris
Irma
Isamar
Isis
Itzel
Iva
Ivy

Jacey
Jackie
Jaclyn
Jacque
Jada
Jaden
Jaelyn
Jamie
Jana
Janet
Janice
Janie
Jannie
Jasmine
Jayla
Jazlyn
Jeannie
Jenna
Jenny
Jeri
Jessie
Jetta
Jettie
Jewel
Jimmie
Jocelyn

Jodie
Joey
Johnnie
Jolie
Joni
Jordan
Josie
Joslyn
Jothi
Journey
Judith
Judy
Julie
Justice

Kaitlyn
Kala
Kalyn
Kami
Kaori
Kara
Karen
Kari
Kathlyn
Kathrine
Kathy
Katie
Katlin
Kattie
Kaya
Kayden
Kayla
Kaylee
Kaylin
Kecia
Keely
Keiki
Keiko
Keisha
Keishla
Kelly
Kelsey
Kendall
Kendra
Kenna
Kenneth
Kenya
Kenzie
Keshia
Khayla
Kiara
Kiele
Kinsey
Kirsten

Kirstie	Lois	Maudie
Kitty	Lola	Maura
Kizzy	Loma	Maxie
Kori	Lona	Mavis
Kristen	London	Maya
Kya	Lonnie	Mayra
Kyla	Lorene	Mazie
Kylie	Lori	Meadow
	Lorri	Melba
Lacey	Lorna	Mellie
Lana	Lottie	Melva
Laney	Louie	Mertie
Lara	Lourdes	Meryl
Laura	Lovie	Meta
Laurel	Lucia	Mia
Lauren	Lucy	Micah
Layla	Ludie	Michael
Lea	Lula	Michelle
Leena	Lulu	Mickey
Leila	Luna	Mildred
Lempi	Lupe	Millie
Lena	Lura	Mimi
Lennie	Lyda	Mina
Lesia	Lyric	Mindy
Leslie		Minna
Lessie	Mabel	Minnie
Leta	Macy	Mirta
Letha	Madie	Missy
Lettie	Maggie	Misty
Lexi	Maida	Mittie
Lexus	Mairwen	Mitzi
Leyna	Mamie	Moe
Libby	Mammie	Moira
Liesel	Mandy	Molly
Lila	Mara	Mona
Lilla	Marci	Morgan
Lillith	Margaret	Mossie
Lilo	Margie	Myra
Lily	Margit	Myrna
Lina	Margo	Myrtis
Linda	Mari	Myrtle
Lindsey	Marla	
Lindy	Marley	Naheed
Linnie	Marlo	Nancy
Lisa	Marlyn	Nannie
Lisbet	Marlys	Naomi
Lise	Marna	Nedra
Lissa	Marnie	Nelda
Litzy	Marsha	Nella
Liza	Marta	Nellie
Lizbeth	Martha	Neta
Lizeth	Marva	Nettie
Lizzie	Marvel	Neva
Logan	Mary	Neyla

Nia	Princess	Saniya
Nikki	Prudence	Santa
Nilda	Pura	Santos
Nilsa		Sanya
Nina	Queenie	Sarah
Nita		Sasha
Nixie	Rachel	Satchel
Nola	Randi	Scarlett
Nona	Ranee	Selma
Nora	Raven	Shana
Norma	Rayna	Shanda
Nova	Reagan	Shandi
Nyah	Reba	Shani
Nyla	Rena	Shannon
	Ressie	Shanta
Odie	Retha	Shanthi
Ola	Retta	Shara
Olga	Reva	Sharon
Olive	Reyna	Shasta
Ollie	Rezsin	Shawna
Oma	Rhea	Shayla
Ona	Rhoda	Shaylee
Onie	Rhonda	Shayna
Opal	Rikki	Sheba
Ora	Riley	Sheena
Orla	Rilla	Sheila
Ouida	Rita	Shelba
Ova	Rivka	Shelby
	Robbie	Shelly
Palma	Robyn	Shelva
Pansy	Roma	Sherlyn
Paola	Rona	Sherry
Paris	Ronna	Shirley
Parker	Ronnie	Shonda
Patience	Rory	Shreya
Patsy	Rosa	Signe
Patty	Roselyn	Sigrid
Paula	Roslyn	Sister
Payton	Rossie	Sita
Pearlie	Roxie	Skyla
Peggy	Rowan	Skylar
Penny	Ruby	Sondra
Perla	Rumer	Sonia
Petra	Ruthie	Soomie
Phoebe	Ryan	Sophie
Phoenix		Stacia
Phyllis	Sadie	Stacy
Pinkie	Sailor	Starla
Piper	Sally	Stella
Polly	Salma	Stevie
Poppy	Sammie	Stormy
Portia	Sanaa	Sudie
Precious	Sandy	Sugine
Presley	Sandra	Summer

Sunny
Sunshine
Susan
Susie
Sybil
Sydney
Sylvie

Tami
Tamia
Tamra
Tana
Tania
Tara
Taryn
Tarsha
Tasha
Tatum
Tawny
Taya
Taylor
Teagan
Tennie
Teri
Tessa
Tessie
Thea
Theda
Thelma
Theo
Thora
Thyra
Tillie
Tina
Tisha
Toby
Tommie
Toni
Tonya
Tori
Toya
Tracy
Tressa
Tressie
Treva
Trena
Trina
Trisha
Trista
Tristan
Trudy
Tuk Yoon
Twila
Tyler

Tyra

Uma
Una

Vallie
Veda
Velda
Vella
Velma
Velva
Vena
Venus
Vera
Verda
Vernie
Verla
Verlie
Verna
Versie
Vesta
Vicky
Vida
Vilma
Vina
Vinnie
Virgie
Vita
Viva
Vonda
Vonnie

Wanda
Wava
Wendy
Whitley
Whitney
Wilda
Willa
Willie
Willow
Wilma
Windy
Winnie
Wyatt
Wylie

Xena
Xiu

Yarden
Yasmin
Yehudit
Yetta

Yoko
Yuka

Zaida
Zara
Zelda
Zella
Zelma
Zenda
Zetta
Zina
Zita
Zoe
Zoila
Zola
Zona
Zora
Zsa-zsa
Zula
Zulma

■ IAMB ■

*One unstressed syllable
followed by a heavy
stressed syllable.*

**BEAT BAROMETER:
Iambic first names
(da-DA) go well with
iambic, anapestic,
and middle-accented
surnames.**

Abril
Adele
Agatha
Agnes
Agnese
Aileen
Ali
Alice
Aline
Alize
Amie
Annette
Annis
Arlene
Aurore

Babette
Belen
Berenice

Bettina
Brianne
Brigitte
Brielle

Camille
Carlene
Carmel
Catherine
Cecile
Celeste
Celine
Ceres
Chanel
Chantal
Chantel
Charisse
Charlene
Charmaine
Cherie
Cheyenne
Chloë
Christen
Christine
Clarice
Clarine
Claudette
Claudie
Claudine
Clemmie
Clotilde
Colette
Colleen
Constance
Corinne
Crystal
Cybelle

Danelle
Danette
Danielle
Darcy
Darlene
Deann
Delphine
Demi
Deneen
Denise
Diane
Dina
Dionne
Doreen

Earlene

Eileen
Elaine
Elise
Estelle
Esther

Farrah
Florence
Florine
Francine

Gaynell
Georgene
Georgette
Germaine
Gigi
Giselle
Gui

Harlene
Hermine
Hua

Idell
Inez
Ione
Irene
Itzel

Jacqueline
Janae
Janelle
Janice
Janine
Jasmine
Jaylene
Jeanette
Jeanine
Jerline
Joelle
Jolene
Jolie
Josette
Josie
Judith
Julie
Justine

Karyme
Kathleen
Kathrine
Katie

Lanette

Laquita
LaRue
Lashawn
Latrice
Laurette
Laverne
Lavonne
Leanne
Lenore
Leonor
Lisbet
Lissette
Lizbeth
Lizeth
Lorene
Lorraine
Louise
Luann
Lucille
Lucy
Lurline
Lynette

Marcelle
Margit
Margo
Marie
Marlene
Matilde
Maureen
Maxine
Maybelle
McCoy
Meliss
Merlene
Michelle
Miriam
Monique
Mozelle
Myrtice

Nadine
Nanette
Nicole
Noelle
Noreen

Odell
Odette
Olene

Paris
Patrice
Paulette

Pauline
Pearline
Pilar

Rachel
Rachelle
Ranee
Raquel
Rena
Renea
Renee
Rochelle
Romaine
Roseann
Roxanne
Ruthann

Sabine
Sade
Salome
Sanaa
Sarai
Shanice
Shanta
Shante
Sharon
Shelva
Sheree
Shirlene
Sigrid
Simone
Siobhan
Sophie
Suzanne
Suzette
Sybil
Sylvie

Tennille
Therese
Tristan

Unique

Vernell
Vernice

Willene

Xia

Yasmin
Yasmine
Yvette

Yvonne

Zoe

■ DACTYL ■

*One heavily stressed syllable
followed by two
unstressed syllables.*

**BEAT BAROMETER:
Dactylic first names
(DA-da-da) sound
good with any type of
surname. You might
especially like these
names if your last
name is a trochee,
dactyl, or one syllable.**

Aaliyah
Abigail
Addison
Adelaide
Adeline
Adrian
Agatha
Aisha
Akiko
Aleah
Allison
Amaris
Amina
Amira
Amiya
Andrea
Angela
Angeles
Aniya
Annabelle
Annamae
Annika
Arely
Aria
Ariel
Asia
Aurea
Avery

Barbara
Beatrice
Beatrix
Bellamy

Bethany
Beverly
Brittany

Cameron
Cándida
Carolee
Caroline
Cassidy
Catherine
Cecily
Celia
Charity
Charolette
Chasity
Chastity
Christopher
Clarabelle
Claudia
Clementine
Cordia
Cynthia

Dalia
Damaris
Dania
Danica
Darian
Dasia
Dayana
Deborah
Delia
Desiree
Destiny
Dorotha
Dorothy

Ebony
Eleanor
Elena
Eliana
Ellamae
Elois
Eloise
Elvia
Emeline
Emerald
Emerson
Emiko
Emilie
Emily
Erica
Ernestine
Erzsebet

Ethelyn
Evelyn

Fatima
Florida

Gabriel
Genesis
Genevieve
Geralyn
Gillian
Gloria
Goldia
Guinevere
Gwendolyn

Harmony
Harriet
Hildegarde
Hillary
Hiroko

Imogene
India
Ingeborg
Isabel
Isadore
Ivory

Jacqueline
Jalisa
Jennifer
Jerrica
Jessica
Jillian
Jocelyn
Joycelyn
Julia
Juliet

Kaliyah
Kecia
Kennedy
Keshia
Kimberly

Leatrice
Lelia
Leonor
Lesia
Liberty
Lilia
Lilike
Lilliam

Lillian
Livia
Lizabeth
Lorelei
Lydia

Madeline
Madison
Magdalen
Mairwen
Malia
Malika
Mallory
Margaret
Mariam
Marian
Maribel
Mariel
Marilee
Marilyn
Marjorie
Masako
Melanie
Melody
Meredith
Michiko
Millicent
Minerva
Mirabelle
Miracle
Miriam
Monica
Muriel

Nadia
Naomi
Natalie
Natsumi
Nayeli
Nélida
Nicola
Nydia

Pamela
Parvati

Rayna
Rhiannon
Rosalie
Rosalind
Rosaline
Rosalyn
Rosamond
Roselyn

Rosemary
Rosia

Salome
Shakira
Sheila
Shelia
Sidonie
Sonia
Stacia
Stephanie
Sylvia

Tabitha
Talia
Tamara
Tamatha
Tamela
Tamia
Tamiko
Tangela
Tiffany
Tomoko
Trinidad
Trinity

Ursula

Valentine
Valerie
Violet
Vivia
Vivian

Willia
Winifred

Yoselin
Yoshiko
Yumuna

■ ANAPEST ■

*Two unstressed syllables
followed by one heavy
stressed syllable.*

**BEAT BAROMETER:
Anapestic first names
(da-da-DA) sound best
with surnames that are
iambs, anapests, or
accented in the middle.**

Abigail
Adelaide
Adeline
Adrienne
Albertine
Allison
Amelie
Angeline
Angelique
Anjanette
Annabelle
Annalise
Annmarie
Antoinette
Antonette
Ariel
Arielle
Augustine

Beatrice
Beatrix
Bernadette
Bernardine

Carolann
Caroline
Celestine
Christian
Clarabelle
Clementine

Desiree
Dominique

Elana
Eleanor
Eloise
Emeline
Emilie
Ethelene
Etienne
Eugenie
Eulalie
Evangeline
Evelyne

Gabriel
Gabrielle
Genevieve
Georgianne
Geraldine

Henriette

Irene
Isabel
Isadore
Ivelisse

Jacqueline
Jennifer
Jocelyn
Josefa
Josephine
Julianne
Juliet

Kathaleen

Leatrice
Leone
Loriann
Lucienne

Madeline
Magdalene
Marceline
Marguerite
Marianne
Maribel
Mariel
Marisol
Marybeth
Maryjane
Maryjo ·
Marylou
Melanie
Michael
Mirabelle
Monserrat
Moriah

Natalie
Nicolette

Odalys
Olivie

Parisa
Penelope

Rosaline
Rosemarie

Salome
Sidonie
Soledad
Stephanie

Trinidad

Valentine
Valerie
Violette
Virginie
Vivienne

Wilhelmine

■ ONE-SYLLABLE ■

**Beat barometer:
One-syllable first
names sound best
with iambic, anapestic,
or middle-accented
surnames. If your sur-
name is one syllable,
you can use a one-
syllable first name to
create a spondee of
two equally heavy
stresses (DA DA). You
might also like these
punchy little names if
your surname is long
or unusual.**

Anne

Barb
Belle
Bess
Beth
Bette
Blair
Blanche
Blue
Bree
Brooke
Brynn

Ceil
Charles
Chris
Claire
Cruz

Dale
Dawn
Dean

Dee
Dell
Drew

Elle
Eve

Faith
Faye
Feng
Fern
Flo
Floy
Flynn
Fran

Gail
Gay
George
Glenn
Grace
Gwen

Hong
Hope

Jacque
Jade
James
Jan
Jane
Jean
Jen
Jill
Jo
Joan
Joy
Joyce
June

Kate
Kay
Kim
Kyle

Lei
Leigh
Ling
Lise
Liv
Liz
Lou
Lourdes
Loyce

Lulu
Luz
Lynn

Madge
Mae
Maeve
Mai
Marge
Maude
Mayme
Meg
Merle
Mimi
Ming
Moe

Nan
Nell

Paige
Pam
Pat
Pearl
Ping

Queen
Quinn

Rae
Reese
Rose
Ruth

Sage
Scout
Shawn
Shea
Skye
Spring
Sue

Tess

Viv
Von

Wei

Zhi
Zsa-zsa*

*String together two one-syllable names to make a spondee, as in the French pronunciations of Lulu, Mimi, and any other equally-stressed repetitive name.

■ MIDDLE-STRESSED ■

BEAT BAROMETER: Middle-accented first names (da-DA-da or da-DA-da-da or da-da-DA-da) can match any type of surname. You might especially like these longer names if your last name is a trochee or one syllable.

Aaliyah
Abrianna
Acacia
Adelia
Adella
Adelaida
Adelina
Adriana
Adrianna
Agnese
Agostina
Agustina
Aida
Aisha
Akira
Alana
Alanna
Alani
Alanis
Alberta
Albertha
Albina
Aleah
Alejandra
Alessandra
Aleta
Alexa
Alexandra
Alexandria
Alexia

Alexis
Alfreda
Alicia
Alina
Alisa
Alissa
Alize
Almeda
Alondra
Altagracia
Althea
Alvera
Alverta
Alvina
Amanda
Amalia
Amani
Amara
Amari
Amaris
Amaryllis
Amaya
Amelia
America
Amina
Amira
Amiya
Amparo
Anahi
Anaïs
Anastasia
Andrea
Angela
Angeles
Angelia
Angelica
Angelina
Angelita
Anissa
Anita
Anitra
Aniya
Anjali
Annabella
Annetta
Annika
Antonetta
Antonia
Antonietta
Antonina
Anya
Arabella
Araceli
Ardella

Arely
Ariana
Arianna
Ariella
Armani
Armida
Arvilla
Ashanti
Assunta
Athena
Augusta
Aurea
Aurelia
Aurora
Awilda
Ayana
Ayanna

Belinda
Benita
Bernita
Bettina
Beulah
Bianca
Bonita
Brianna
Brunilda

Calista
Camilla
Candida
Carina
Carissa
Carlotta
Carmela
Carmelita
Carolina
Cassandra
Catalina
Catina
Cecilia
Celeste
Celestina
Charissa
Chiquita
Christiana
Christina
Ciara
Citlali
Clarissa
Clementina
Cleora
Clotilde
Concepcion

Concetta
Consuelo
Cordelia
Corina
Cornelia
Creola

Dakota
Damaris
Daniela
Danita
Davina
Dayana
Deanna
Deasia
Deborah
Delaney
Delilah
Delisa
Delfina
Delois
Delphia
Demetria
Diana
Dominga
Dorinda
Dorothea
Drucilla

Edwina
Elana
Eleanora
Electa
Elena
Eldora
Elfrieda
Eliana
Elida
Elisa
Elissa
Eliza
Elizabeth
Elmira
Elnora
Elois
Eloisa
Elvera
Elvia
Elvira
Emelina
Emilia
Emmanuela
Enola
Enriqueta

Erlinda
Ermina
Ernestina
Esmeralda
Esmerelda
Esperanza
Estefania
Estefany
Estella
Estrella
Eudora
Eugenia
Eulalia
Eulalie
Evangelina

Fabiola
Fatima
Felicia
Felicity
Felipa
Fernanda
Filomena
Fiona
Florida
Francesca
Francisca

Gabriela
Gabriella
Galilea
Geneva
Genoveva
Georgiana
Georgina
Giada
Gianna
Giovanna
Gisela
Graciela
Gregoria
Griselda
Guadalupe
Guillermina

Helena
Henrietta
Hermina
Herminia
Hermione
Hortencia

Idella
Ilana

Iliana
Ilona
Imani
Imelda
Iola
Iona
Ione
Irene
Isabela
Isadora
Isamar
Izetta
Izora

Jakayla
Jalisa
Jaliyah
Jamila
Jamya
Janessa
Janiya
Jemima
Jessenia
Jesusa
Joanna
Jocelyn
Joellen
Joetta
Johanna
Joretta
Josefa
Josefina
Jovita
Juana
Juanita
Juliana
Julissa
Justina

Kaliyah
Karina
Karyme
Katarina
Katharina
Katrina
Keiki
Kenyatta
Khadijah
Kiana
Kiara
Kiele
Kierra

Ladonna

Laisha
Lakeisha
Lakeshia
Larissa
Lashanda
Latanya
Latasha
Latonya
Latoya
Laura
Lauretta
Lavada
Lavera
Laverna
Lavina
Lavinia
Lawanda
Leandra
Leanna
Leilani
Lenora
Leola
Leona
Leone
Leonora
Leora
Leota
Leticia
Letizia
Liliana
Linnea
Lolita
Lorena
Lorenza
Loretta
Louella
Luana
Lucero
Lucia
Luciena
Lucila
Lucinda
Lucrecia
Luetta
Luisa
Lupita
Luvenia

Mackenzie
Maddalena
Madelena
Madonna
Mafalda
Magdalena

Magnolia
Makayla
Malaika
Maleah
Malia
Malika
Malvina
Manuela
Marcelina
Marcella
Margaretta
Margarita
Maria
Mariah
Mariana
Maricela
Mariella
Marietta
Marilena
Marina
Marisa
Marissa
Marita
Maritza
Marlena
Marlene
Martina
Maryellen
Matilda
Matilde
McKenna
Melina
Melinda
Melisa
Melissa
Melvina
Mercedes
Michaela
Michelina
Migdalia
Milagros
Miranda
Mireya
Missouri
Modesta
Montana
Moriah
Mozella

Nakia
Naoma
Naomi
Natalia
Natasha

Nayeli
Nélida
Neoma
Nereida
Nevaeh
Nicola
Nikita
Noelia
Noemi
Novella
Nyasia

Octavia
Odalys
Odessa
Odetta
Oleta
Oliana
Olina
Olivia
Omayra
Ophelia
Oralia
Otilia
Ottilie
Ozella

Paloma
Pamella
Paola
Paoletta
Paolina
Parisa
Patrica
Patricia
Patrizia
Pauletta
Paulina
Penelope
Petranella
Philomena
Pomona
Priscila
Providenci

Rafaela
Ramona
Ramonita
Rebecca
Regina
Renata
Renita
Renea
Rhiannon

Rianna
Roberta
Rocio
Rolanda
Romana
Rosalia
Rosalina
Rosalinda
Rosanna
Rosario
Rosaura
Rosella
Rosetta
Rosina
Rosita
Roxana
Rowena

Sabina
Sabrina
Salome
Samantha
Samara
Samira
Saniya
Santana
Santina
Sarahi
Sariah
Savannah
Selena
Sequoia
Serena
Serenity
Shakira
Shalonda
Shameka
Shamira
Shaniqua
Shania
Shanika
Shanita
Sharonda
Shawanda
Shelia
Sherita
Shoshana
Sidonie
Sienna
Sierra
Socorro
Soheila
Sonia
Sophia

Speranza
Stephania
Suellen
Susana

Tabitha
Talia
Tallulah
Tamara
Tamela
Tamika
Tania
Tanisha
Tatiana
Tawana
Tawanda
Teresa
Teresita
Theodora
Theola
Theresia
Tiana
Tiara

Tierra
Tomasa
Tomeka
Tvuna
Tyesha

Valencia
Valentina
Valeria
Vanessa
Venita
Verona
Veronica
Vicenta
Victoria
Vincenza
Viola
Violetta
Virginia
Viviana

Waleska
Waneta

Wilhelmina
Willamina
Winona

Xiomara
Ximena

Yadira
Yahaira
Yanira
Yareli
Yaritza
Yehudit
Yemima
Yesenia
Yolanda
Yoselin
Yuliana

Zaida
Zaria
Zoraida

RULE-BREAKERS

THESE NAMES ARE four syllables long with the accent at the end, which doesn't quite fit any of our poetic patterns. But if we break down their rhythms, we can see that they're really just two names—two iambs or a trochee and an iamb—stitched together. If you have a somewhat simple iambic surname, these names might just be a great match.

Adelaide (uh-DELL-uh-**YEED** [FR])—two iambs
Alexandrie (al-LEK-saw-**DREE** with short N [FR])—two iambs
Anastasie (ANN-aw-staw-**ZEE** [FR])—trochee and iamb
Annamarie (ANN-uh-muh-**REE**, AW-nuh-maw-**REE** [FR])—trochee and iamb
Eleanor (el-LAY-yoh-**NOR** [FR])—two iambs
    Alternate spellings: Eleanore, Elinor, Elinore, Elenor, Eleonore [FR]
Felicita (fel-EE-chee-**TAW** [IT])—two iambs
Natividad (naw-TEE-vee-**DAWD** [SP])—two iambs

Trochee, Iamb, Dactyl, Anapest, One-syllable, Middle-stressed

Confused about how to pronounce it?
Consult the vowel lists.

■ TROCHEE ■

One heavily stressed syllable
followed by one
unstressed syllable.

BEAT BAROMETER:
Trochaic first names
(DA-da) can sound
good with any type of
surname. You might
especially like these
names if your last
name is a trochee,
dactyl, or one syllable.

Aaron	Alva	Austin
Abel	Alvie	Axel
Abner	Alvin	
Abram	Alvis	Bailey
Adam	Ambrose	Barney
Adolph	Amos	Baron
Ahmad	Andre	Barrett
Ahmed	Andrew	Barry
Aidan	Andy	Barton
Alan	Angel	Basil
Albert	Angus	Bennett
Albin	Ansel	Benny
Alden	Anthony	Benton
Aldo	Anton	Bernie
Alec	Archie	Bertram
Alex	Arden	Bertrand
Alfie	Ari	Beryl
Alfred	Arjun	Billy
Alford	Arlen	Bishop
Ali	Arlie	Bixby
Alma	Arlis	Bobby
Alpha	Arlo	Booker
Alton	Armstrong	Boris
	Arne	Bradford
	Arno	Bradley
	Arnold	Brady
	Arthur	Brandon
	Artie	Brannon
	Artis	Braxton
	Arvid	Brayden
	Arvil	Brendan
	Arvin	Brennan
	Asa	Brenton
	Asher	Brian
	Ashley	Bridger
	Ashton	Brody
	Aubrey	Bronson
	Audie	Bruno
	August	Bryant

Bryson
Buddy
Buford
Burley
Burton
Buster
Byron

Caden
Caesar
Caleb
Calvin
Camden
Campbell
Cannon
Carlo
Carlos
Carlton
Carlyle
Carmen
Carmine
Carson
Carter
Casey
Casimir
Cason
Casper
Cecil
Cedar
Cedric
Cesar
Chadrick
Chadwick
Chaim
Chandler
Chaney
Charlie
Chauncey
Chesley
Chester
Christian
Christien
Christophe
Clarence
Claudie
Clayton
Clemens
Clement
Cleo
Cleon
Cletus
Cleveland
Clifford
Clifton

Clinton
Clover
Clovis
Cody
Colby
Coleman
Colin
Colton
Connor
Conrad
Cooper
Corbin
Corey
Cormac
Cosmo
Courtney
Crawford
Crispin
Cruz
Cullen
Curtis
Cypress
Cyri
Cyrus

Dallas
Dallin
Dalton
Damon
Dana
Dandre
Dangelo
Daniel
Danny
Dante
Darby
Darold
Darrell
Darren
Darwin
Dashiell
Davey
David
Davis
Davon
Dawson
Dayton
Declan
Dedrick
Dejuan
Delbert
Delmar
Delmas
Delmer

Delton
Delvin
Dempsey
Denis
Dennis
Denny
Denton
Denver
Denzel
Denzil
Derek
Dermot
Derwin
Desmond
Destin
Devin
Dewey
Dewitt
Dexter
Dezso
Diamond
Dickie
Diezel
Dillard
Dillion
Dino
Django
Donal
Donald
Donnell
Donnie
Dorman
Dorsey
Douglas
Draven
Dudley
Duncan
Durward
Durwood
Dustin
Dusty
Dylan

Early
Earnest
Easton
Eddie
Edgar
Edmund
Edsel
Edward
Edwin
Eduardo
Efrain

Einar	Friedrich	Harry
Eino	Furman	Harvey
Elbert		Haskell
Eldon	Galen	Hassan
Eldred	Galvin	Hayden
Eldridge	Gannon	Hayward
Elgin	Gardner	Haywood
Eli	Garfield	Heber
Ellis	Garland	Hector
Ellsworth	Garnett	Helmer
Elmer	Garrett	Henry
Elmo	Garrick	Herbert
Elmore	Gary	Herman
Eloy	Gaston	Herschel
Elroy	Gavin	Hilbert
Elton	Gaylord	Hillard
Elvin	Gearld	Hilliard
Elvis	Geary	Hilton
Elwin	Geo	Hiram
Elwood	Gerald	Hobart
Emmett	Gerhard	Hobert
Ennis	German	Hobert
Enoch	Gianni	Holden
Enos	Gideon	Hollis
Enzo	Gilbert	Homer
Ephraim	Gino	Hoover
Eric	Glendon	Horace
Erling	Godfrey	Houston
Ernie	Golden	Howard
Errol	Gordon	Howell
Erwin	Grady	Hubert
Eujin	Graham	Huey
Evan	Granville	Hugo
Evans	Grayson	Hudson
Evert	Griffin	Hunter
Ewan	Griffith	Humphrey
Ezra	Grover	Hurley
	Guido	Hyman
Faron	Guillermo	
Farrell	Gunnar	Ian
Felix	Gunther	Ira
Felton	Gustave	Irvin
Fergus		Irving
Finley	Hallie	Isaac
Fisher	Hamilton	Isai
Fletcher	Hamish	Ishmael
Forrest	Hansel	Ismael
Foster	Harding	Itai
Francis	Hardy	Ivan
Frankie	Harlan	Izzy
Franklin	Harley	
Freddy	Harmon	Jackie
Fredrick	Harold	Jackson
Freeman	Harris	Jacob
		Jacques

Jaden	Kelsey	Logan
Jagger	Kelton	London
Jaime	Kelvin	Lonnie
Jair	Kendall	Lonzo
Jairo	Kendrick	Loren
Jalen	Kenji	Louie
Jamie	Kenneth	Louis
Janis	Kenny	Lowell
Jara	Kenton	Loyal
Jared	Kenya	Luca
Jarrett	Kenyon	Lucas
Jarom	Keon	Lucien
Jaron	Kermit	Lucius
Jarvis	Kerry	Ludwig
Jason	Kerwin	Lupe
Jasper	Kevin	Luther
Javon	Khalil	Lyle
Jeffrey	Kiefer	Lyman
Jennings	Kieran	Lyndon
Jerrell	Kirby	
Jerry	Kobe	Maddox
Jesse	Krishna	Magnus
Jewell	Kwame	Mahlon
Jimmy	Kylan	Major
JJ	Kyler	Malcolm
Jody		Malik
Joel	Lacy	Manley
Joey	Laddie	Manny
Johan	Lambert	Marco
Johnny	Landon	Marcos
Johnson	Lanny	Marcus
Jonah	Laron	Marlon
Jonas	Larry	Marquez
Jordan	Laszlo	Marquis
Jordy	Lawrence	Marshall
Jorge	Lawson	Martin
Jose	Layton	Marty
Joseph	Leamon	Marvin
Judah	Leander	Mason
Judson	Leland	Matthew
Jun	Lenny	Maurice
Junior	Leo	Maury
Junius	Leon	Maxie
Justice	Leonard	Maxim
Justin	Leroy	Maxwell
Justo	Leslie	Maynard
	Lester	Melton
Kalen	Levi	Melville
Keaton	Liam	Melvin
Keegan	Lincoln	Merlin
Keenan	Lindsey	Merrill
Kelby	Linwood	Merritt
Kellen	Lionel	Merton
Kelly	Loden	Mervin

Meyer	Omar	Raynard
Micah	Ora	Reagan
Michael	Oral	Reggie
Mickey	Oran	Regis
Milburn	Oren	Reinhold
Miles	Orie	Reino
Milford	Orlo	Rémy
Millard	Orville	Reno
Miller	Osborne	Rexford
Milo	Oscar	Reyes
Milton	Oswald	Reynold
Mitchell	Otis	Richie
Moises	Otto	Richmond
Monte	Owen	Ricky
Morgan		Rico
Morton	Pablo	Riley
Moses	Pacey	Ringo
Moshe	Paddy	Rio
Murphy	Palmer	Riordan
Murray	Paris	River
Myron	Parker	Robbie
	Parrish	Robert
Najee	Patrick	Robin
Nasir	Patsy	Rocco
Nathan	Paxton	Rocky
Nathaniel	Pedrick	Roderick
Neil	Pedro	Rodney
Nelson	Pepe	Roel
Nestor	Percy	Roger
Newell	Perry	Rogers
Newman	Pershing	Rohan
Newton	Peter	Roland
Nicholaus	Peyton	Rollin
Nicky	Phelan	Rollo
Nico	Phillip	Roman
Nigel	Phoenix	Ronald
Noah	Porter	Ronan
Noble	Pranav	Ronnie
Noé	Preston	Rory
Nolan		Roscoe
Norman	Quentin	Roshan
Normand	Quincy	Roswell
Norris		Rowan
Norton	Raleigh	Royal
Norval	Ramsey	Ruben
Norwood	Randall	Ruby
	Randolph	Rudolph
Oakley	Randy	Rudy
Obie	Ransom	Rufus
Odie	Ravi	Rupert
Okey	Rayburn	Russell
Olaf	Rayford	Rusty
Olen	Raymon	Ryan
Ollie	Raymond	Ryder

Ryker
Rylan
Ryland

Sammy
Sampath
Samson
Samuel
Sancho
Sandro
Sandy
Sanford
Santo
Santos
Satchel
Sasha
Sawyer
Scottie
Seamus
Selby
Selmer
Sergei
Seymour
Shannon
Shelby
Sheldon
Sherman
Sherrill
Sherwin
Sherwood
Sidney
Sigmund
Sigurd
Silas
Simon
Sincere
Sixto
Skyler
Solomon
Solon
Sonny
Soren
Spencer
Stacy
Stanford
Stanley
Stanton
Sterling
Stetson
Steven
Stevie
Stoney
Stuart
Sumner

Syed
Sylvan

Talmadge
Talon
Tanner
Tariq
Tavon
Taylor
Teddy
Tedros
Telly
Terrell
Terrence
Terry
Tevin
Thatcher
Theo
Theron
Thomas
Thornton
Thurman
Thurston
Tiernan
Tierney
Tillman
Timmy
Tito
Titus
Tobin
Toby
Tommy
Tony
Topher
Torrance
Tory
Tracy
Travis
Trenton
Trevon
Trevor
Treyton
Tristan
Tristian
Truman
Tucker
Tudor
Turner
Tyler
Tyshawn
Tyson

Urban

Valentine
Verlin
Vernie
Vernon
Vester
Victor
Vidor
Vincent
Vinson
Virgil
Vishnu
Vito

Waino
Waldo
Walker
Wallace
Wally
Walter
Walton
Warner
Watson
Waylon
Waymon
Webster
Weldon
Welton
Wendell
Werner
Wesley
Weston
Wheeler
Whitney
Wilbert
Wilbur
Wilburn
Wiley
Wilford
Wilfred
Wilfrid
Wilhelm
Willard
Willem
William
Williams
Willie
Willis
Willy
Wilmer
Wilson
Wilton
Winfield
Winford
Winfred

Winston
Winton
Woodrow
Woody
Wyatt
Wyman

Yahir
Yakov
Yarden
Ye
Yosef
Yuri
Yusuf

Zaid
Zander
Zigmund
Zion

■ IAMB ■

*One unstressed syllable
followed by a
heavy stressed syllable.*

BEAT BAROMETER:
Iambic first names
(da-DA) go well with
iambic, anapestic, and
middle-accented sur-
names.

Aaron
Abdiel
Abdul
Abel
Abram
Adam
Adolph
Akeem
Alan
Albert
Alfred
Ali
Alphonse
Amir
Andre
Andrés
Antoine
Anton
Ardell
Arjun

Armand
Arnav
August

Bernard
Bertrand
Bilal
Burdette
Burnell

Carnell
Clémence
Clement
Cordell
Cornell
Cortéz
Cyril
Cyrus

Daniel
Daquan
Darnell
Deepak
Dejuan
Delmar
DeMond
Denis
Denzel
Deon
Deshawn
Dewayne
Dewitt

Efrain
Émil
Enoch
Ephraim
Eric
Eugene

Felix
Fermin
Fernand

Gaetano
Gaston
Gerard
German
Gideon
Gilbert
Gui
Gustave

Hakeem

Hamza
Heber
Herbert
Hernan
Hubert
Hugo

Isaac
Isai

Jabreel
Jaden
Jaheim
Jair
Jaleel
Jamal
Jamar
Jamil
Jamir
Janis
Jared
Jarom
Jaron
Jermaine
Jerome
Jerrell
Jesse
Jesús
Joachim
Joaquin
Joel
Johnpaul
Jomar
Jose
Joseph
Jovan
Justin
Juwan

Kadeem
Kareem
Keshawn
Khalid
Khalil
Kyree

Lamar
Lambert
Lamont
Laron
Lashawn
Latrell
Lawrence
Leon

Leroy
Levar
Louis
Lucas

Malik
Manuel
Marcel
Marquez
Marquis
Maurice
Maxim
McKyle
McCoy
Mekhi
Meyer
Michael
Miguel
Mikhail
Milan
Monroe

Najee
Najib
Nasir
Nathan
Nikhil
Noé

Odell
Omer
O'Neal
Orie
Oscar

Paris
Pasquale
Pernell
Phillip
Pierre

Raekwon
Raheem
Rahul
Rakesh
Ramón
Raouf
Rashad
Rashawn
Rasheed
Raul
Raymond
Raynard
Rayshawn

Regis
Rémy
René
Reynaud
Richard
Robert
Roger
Rohan
Roland
Ruben
Rudolph

Samir
Samson
Samuel
Saul
Semaj
Shamar
Shaquille
Simon
Stefan

Tariq
Terrell
Theron
Thomas
Tremaine
Tristan
Tyquan
Tyree
Tyrell
Tyrese
Tyrone
Tyshawn

Vernell
Victor
Vidal
Vincent

Wardell

Xavier

Yahir
Yakoub
Yosef

Zaire
Zion

■ DACTYL ■

*One heavily stressed
syllable followed by two
unstressed syllables.*

**BEAT BAROMETER:
Dactylic first names
(DA-da-da) sound
good with any type of
surname. You might
especially like these
names if your last
name is a trochee,
dactyl, or one syllable.**

Abraham
Addison
Adelard
Adelbert
Adrian
Adriel
Alastair
Álvaro
Amador
Anderson
Angelo
Anibal
Antony
Archibald
Ariel
Atticus
Avery

Benedict
Benjamin
Braulio
Broderick

Calloway
Cameron
Candido
Casimir
Cassidy
Christian
Christopher
Cicero
Claudio

Damian
Darian
Dario
Darius
Davion

Delano
Dillion
Dominic
Donovan
Dorian

Edison
Eladio
Elian
Elias
Ellery
Elliot
Emerson
Emery
Esteban
Everett

Fabian
Ferguson
Finian
Finnegan
Frederick

Gabriel
Garrison
General
Gideon
Gregory
Gulliver

Harrison
Henderson

Ibrahim
Isidor
Ivory

Jacari
Jacoby
Jairo
Jameson
Javion
Jefferson
Jeremy
Joachim
Jonathan
Joshua
Julian
Julio
Julius
Junior
Junius

Kazuo

Kennedy
Kerouac

Lazaro
Lazarus
Lemuel
Leopold

Madison
Malachi
Malachy
Mario
Marion
Maverick
Maximus
Mikhail
Montague
Mordecai
Mortimer

Neftali
Nicholas
Nicholaus
Nunzio

Oliver

Percival
Philias
Phineas

Radames
Rafael
Reginal
Reginald
Remington
Roderick
Romeo
Roosevelt

Samuel
Savion
Sergio
Sheridan
Silvio
Simeon
Solomon
Sullivan

Taurean
Tavion
Thaddeus
Theodore
Timothy

Trevion
Trinidad
Trinity

Uriel

Waldemar
Washington
Wellington

Xavier

Yuuji

Zachary

■ ANAPEST ■

*Two unstressed syllables
followed by one heavy
stressed syllable.*

BEAT BAROMETER:
**Anapestic first names
(da-da-DA) sound
best with surnames
that are iambs,
anapests, or accented
in the middle.**

Aaron
Abraham
Adelbert
Adrian
Adriel
Alexis
Amador
Anibal
Ariel
Augustin

Benjamin

Christian
Christien
Constantine
Cristobal

Damian
Daniel
Davion
Dominic

Efrain
Eliezer
Emmanuel
Ephraim
Ezekiel

Fabian
Ferdinand
Florian
Frederick

Gabriel

Ibrahim
Isai
Isaiah
Ishmael
Isidor
Israel

Javier
Joachim
Joaquin
Jonathan
Josué
Julian

Lafayette
Leonard
Léonel
Leopold
Lionel
Lucien

Malachi
Michael
Mohamed
Monserrate
Mordecai

Nathaniel
Nicholas

Pasquale

Rafael

Savion
Sebastian

Theodore
Timothy
Trinidad
Trinity

Tristian

Valentin
Valentine

Xavier

Yadiel

■ ONE-SYLLABLE ■

**BEAT BAROMETER:
One-syllable first
names sound best with
iambic, anapestic, or
middle-accented
surnames. If your
surname is one sylla-
ble, you can use a one-
syllable first name to
create a spondee of
two equally heavy
stresses (DA DA). You
might also like these
punchy little names if
your surname is long
or unusual.**

Abe
Al
Alf
Arch
Arne
Art

Bart
Beau
Ben
Bert
Bill
Blaine
Blair
Blaise
Blake
Bob
Boyce
Boyd
Brad
Brandt
Brent
Brett
Britt
Brock

Brook
Brooks
Brown
Bruce
Bryce
Buck
Bud
Burl
Butch
Buzz

Cade
Cael
Cale
Carl
Cash
Chad
Chance
Charles
Chase
Chaz
Cheng
Chet
Chip
Chris
Christ
Chuck
Clark
Claude
Clay
Clem
Cleve
Cliff
Clint
Cloyd
Clyde
Cole
Colt
Coy
Craig
Cruz

Dale
Dan
Dane
Dave
Dax
De
Dean
Dee
Dell
Dewayne
Dick
Dirk

Dock	Jack	Loy
Don	Jacques	Luke
Doug	Jade	Lyle
Doyle	Jair	
Drake	Jake	Mack
Drew	James	Mark
Dudley	Jan	Matt
Duke	Jay	Max
Dwayne	Jazz	Mel
Dwight	Jean	Merle
	Jed	Mike
Earl	Jeff	Miles
Ed	Jere	Ming
Ernst	Jess	Mitch
	Jett	Moe
Finn	Jim	
Floyd	JJ	Nash
Flynn	Joe	Nat
Ford	Joel	Nate
Foy	John	Ned
Frank	Josh	Neil
Franz	Juan	Nels
Fred	Judd	Nick
Fritz	Jude	Niles
Fu	Judge	Nils
	Jules	Noah
Gabe		
Gage	Kai	Pat
Gale	Kale	Paul
Garth	Kane	Pax
Gene	Keith	Pete
George	Ken	Phil
Gil	Kent	Pierce
Giles	Kiel	Ping
Glenn	King	Price
Graham	Kip	Prince
Grant	Kirk	
Green	Klaus	Quest
Greg	Kurt	Quinn
Gus	Kyle	
Guy		Ralph
	Lance	Ram
Hal	Lane	Rand
Hank	Lars	Ray
Hans	Lee	Reese
Heath	Leif	Reid
Herb	Len	Rex
Hong	Les	Rhett
Hoyt	Lloyd	Ridge
Hugh	Lok	Rob
	Lon	Rock
Ike	Long	Rod
	Lorne	Roel
Jace	Lou	Rolf

Ron
Ross
Roy
Royce
Rush
Russ
Ryne

Sage
Sal
Sam
Saul
Scott
Scout
Sean
Serge
Seth
Shad
Shane
Shea
Shing
Sid
Sim
Smith
Sol
Stan
Steve
Stone
Storm
Sven

Tad
Tate
Taye
Ted
Thad
Thor
Tim
Todd
Tom
Trace
Trek
Trent
Trey
Troy
Ty

Val
Van
Vance
Vaughn
Verl
Vern
Vince

Wade
Ward
Wayne
Wes
Will
Worth
Wylde

Yul

Zack
Zaid
Zane
Zeke
Zhi

*String two one-syllable names together to make a spondee, as in JJ, JR, TJ, CC, or any initial nickname.

■ MIDDLE-STRESSED ■

BEAT BAROMETER: Middle-accented first names (da-DA-da or da-DA-da-da or da-DA-da) can match any type of surname. You might especially like these longer names if your last name is a trochee or one syllable.

Abdullah
Adalberto
Aditya
Adolfo
Adolphus
Adonis
Adrian
Alberto
Alejandro
Alessandro
Alexander
Alexandre
Alexandro
Alexis

Alfonso
Alfredo
Alois
Alonzo
Aloysius
Amado
Amari
Americo
Anastacio
Andrea
Andreas
Anibal
Anselmo
Antonio
Arcadio
Armando
Armani
Arnaldo
Arnoldo
Arnulfo
Arturo
Augustin
Augustus
Aurelio

Bartholomew
Benicio
Benito
Bernardo
Bienvenido

Candelario
Candido
Carmelo
Cecilio
Celestino
Columbus
Cornelius
Cristobal

Dakota
Dario
Deandre
Deangelo
Demarco
Demarcus
Demario
Demetrios
Demetris
Demetrius
Deonte
Devonte
Diego
Dimitri

Dionisio
Domenico
Domingo
Donato

Edgardo
Eladio
Elias
Eliezer
Elijah
Eliseo
Elisha
Emiliano
Emilio
Emmanuel
Enrico
Enrique
Epifanio
Erasmo
Ernesto
Esteban
Eugenio
Eusebio
Ezekiel

Faustino
Federico
Felipe
Fernando
Florencio
Florentino
Fortunato
Francesco
Francisco

Gaetano
Genaro
Geraldo
Gerardo
Giancarlo
Gianni
Gilberto
Giovanni
Giuseppe
Gonzalo
Gregorio
Guadalupe
Guillermo
Gustavo

Heriberto
Herminio
Hezekiah
Hidero

Hilario
Hipólito
Hosea
Humberto

Ignacio
Ignatius
Isaiah
Isaias
Ismael
Israel

Jabari
Jacari
Jacinto
Jacoby
Jamarcus
Jamari
Javonte
Jedidiah
Jeremiah
Joachim
Joshua
Josiah
Judah

Kamari
Keanu
Kenyatta

Ladarius
Lazaro
Leonardo
Leopoldo
Lisandro
Llewellyn
Lorenzo
Luciano
Luigi

MacKenzie
Makaio
Marcelino
Marcellus
Marcelo
Margarito
Mariano
Masaaki
Mateo
Mathias
Mattias
Mauricio
Maximilian
Maximino

Maximo
McArthur
McKinley
Mikhail
Misael
Modesto
Mohamed
Montana
Montgomery
Mustafa

Nakia
Napoleon
Narciso
Nathaniel
Neftali
Nehemiah
Nguyen
Norberto

Octavio
Omari
Omarion
Orion
Orlando
Oswaldo

Patricio
Patrizio
Pietro
Porfirio
Primitivo

Rafael
Ramiro
Raymundo
Refugio
Reynaldo
Ricardo
Rigoberto
Roberto
Rodolfo
Rodrigo
Rogelio
Rolando
Romeo
Ronaldo
Rosario
Rosendo

Salvador
Salvatore
Santiago
Santino

Sebastian	Tobias	Virgilio
ShinIchi		
Sylvester	Ulises	Wilfredo
Tavares	Vicente	Zachariah
Teodoro	Vincenzo	Zechariah

RULE-BREAKERS

THESE NAMES ARE four syllables long with the accent at the end, which doesn't quite fit any of our poetic patterns. But if we break down their rhythms, we can see that they're really just two names—two iambs or a trochee and an iamb—stitched together. If you have a somewhat simple iambic surname, these names might just be a great match.

Emmanuel (ee-MAWN-yoo-**ELL** [HEB], ee-MAWN-yoo-**WELL** [SP])—two iambs
Alternate spellings: Emanuel, Immanuel
Joachim (yuh-HO-wuh-**KEEM** [HEB])—two iambs
Alternate spellings: Joakim, Jehoiakim or Yehoyakim [HEB]
Joaquin (yuh-HO-wuh-**CHEEN** with guttural CH [HEB])—two iambs
Alternate spellings: Joaquin [SP], Jehoiachin or Yehoyachin [HEB]
Maximilian (MAK-see-meel-**YA** with short N [FR])—trochee and iamb
Alternate spellings: Maximillian, Maximilien [FR]
Sebastian (say-BAS-tee-**YAW** with short N [FR])—two iambs
Alternate spellings: Sabastian, Sebastien, Sebastien [FR], Sebastián [SP]

CROSSOVER NAMES

If you and your spouse want a name that represents two or more ethnic backgrounds, then you need a crossover—that is, a name that's recognized by different cultures. For instance, Annika is commonly used in Scandinavian and Arabic countries, and it's also popular with African-American families, although it might sound different among each group. As you'll see from the phonetic spellings, Marina is pronounced roughly the same way in many languages, whereas Anastasia and Michaela sound different in Hebrew or Italian, Russian or Greek.

Girls

Adelaide (ADD-uh-layd [GER], add-eh-LED or uh-dell-uh-EED [FR])

Adella (uh-DELL-uh [GER], aw-DELL-aw [IT/SP], aw-DEE-luh or AW-dill-uh [AR])

Agatha (AG-uh-thuh, AW-guh-tuh [IT], ag-GAT [FR])

Akira (uh-KEER-uh [AA/SCOT])

Alisa (uh-LEE-suh, aw-LEE-saw [HEB/SP], aw-LEE-thaw [SP])

Amaya (uh-MY-yuh, aw-MY-yaw [SP])

Amie (em-MAY or aw-MEE [FR], AW-mee [HEB], AY-mee)

Anastasia (aw-naw-STAW-zee-yuh or aw-naw-STAW-zhuh [RUS], ann-uh-STAY-shuh, aw-naw-STAW-see-yuh [IT], aw-naw-staw-SEE-yuh [GRK])

Annalise (ann-uh-LEES [GER/FR])

Annika (AW-nik-uh or ANN-ik-uh [SCAN], aw-NEE-kuh [AA] with pronounced H at end [AR])

Ariana (ar-ree-YAW-nuh [HEB/IT])

Ariel (AIR-ree-yell, AR-ree-yell, ar-ree-YELL [HEB/FR])

Armani (ar-MAW-nee [AA/IT])

Beatrice (BEE-yuh-triss, bay-yuh-TREES [FR/SP], vay-yuh-TRITH [SP])

Beatrix (BEE-yuh-triks [GER/SCAN], bay-yuh-TREEKS [IT])

Bettina (bet-TEE-nuh [GER], bet-TEEN with sustained N [FR])

Bridget (BRID-jid or BRID-jet [IR])

Carina (kar-EE-nuh [IT/SP], kuh-RIN-uh [SCAN])

Carmela (kar-MELL-uh [HEB], karrr-MELL-aw [IT/SP])

Carolina (kair-oh-LY-nuh, kar-oh-LEE-nuh [GER/IT/SP])

Cassandra (kuh-SAN-druh [GRK], kaw-SAWN-draw or kaw-THAWN-draw [SP])

Cecilia (se-SEE-lee-yuh [IT/SP], che-CHEE-lee-uh [IT], the-THEE-lee-yuh [SP])

Celeste (sell-EST, chell-ESS-teh [IT], say-LEST [FR])

Celia (SEE-lee-yuh or THEE-lee-yuh [SP])

Chantel (shawn-TELL, shan-TELL [AA/FR])

Chaya (SHY-yuh, CHY-yuh [HEB/EI])

Chloë (KLOH-wee [GRK], kloh-WAY [FR])

Ciara (see-YAR-ruh, kee-YAR-ruh [IT], KEER-ruh [IR])

Claire (KLAIR [IR], KLAIRRR [FR])

Clotilde (kloh-TIL-dee or kloh-TIL-duh [GER], kloh-TEELD [FR], kloh-TEEL-deh [IT])

Corinne (kor-REEN [GRK/FR])

Dalia (DAW-lee-yuh [HEB], DAL-lee-yuh [SCAN])

Danelle (dan-NELL [FR], daw-NELL [HEB])

Dania (DAN-ee-yuh, DAY-nee-yuh, duh-NEE-yuh or duh-NY-yuh [AA], DAWN-yuh or DAW-nee-yuh [HEB])

Daniela (dan-YELL-uh [IT], dawn-YELL-uh [HEB/SP])

Danielle (dan-YELL [FR], dawn-YELL [HEB])

Darcy (DAR-see [IR], dar-SEE [FR])

Darlene (dar-LEEN [BR/FR])

Dasia (DAY-zhuh [AA], DAY-shuh [GRK/RUS], DAY-see-yuh)

Davina (duh-VEE-nuh, daw-VEE-nuh [HEB/IT])

Deneen (duh-NEEN [AA/IR])
Dionne (DEE-yawn [AA], dee-YAW with
    short N [FR/GRK])
Dori (DOR-ree [GRK/HEB])

Edna (ED-nuh [HEB/SP])
Eliana (el-lee-AW-nuh [IT/SP],
    ELL-ee-aw-nuh [HEB]; see also Iliana)
Elise (ee-LEES, el-LEES [GER], ay-LEEZ [FR])
Elizabeth (el-LIZ-uh-beth, el-lee-SHEE-
    vuh [HEB], el-lee-zuh-BET [FR])
Esther (ESS-tur, ess-TAIR [FR/HEB])
Eugenie (yoo-JEE-nee, yoo-JAY-nee,
    ay-yoo-HAY-nee [SP], oo-zhay-NEE [FR])
Eve (EEV, EV [FR], CHAW-vuh [HEB])

Fatima (FAW-tim-uh or FAWT-muh [AR],
    fat-EE-muh [IT])

Gabriel (GAY-bree-ell, gaw-bree-ELL or
    gaw-vree-ELL [HEB], gab-brrree-YELL
    [FR/SP/IT])
Gabriela (gaw-bree-YELL-uh [SP],
    gab-ree-YELL-uh,
    gaw-vree-ELL-uh [HEB])
Gabriella (gab-ree-YELL-uh [IT],
    gaw-vree-ELL-uh [HEB])
Genevieve (JEN-uh-veev [CG],
    zhen-uh-vee-YEV or zhawn-vee-YEV
    [FR])
Gigi (JEE-jee [IT], zhee-ZHEE [FR])
Griselda (griz-ELL-duh [GER],
    gree-SELL-duh or gree-THELL-duh [SP])

Hannah (HAN-nuh, HAW-nuh,
    CHAW-naw with guttural CH [HEB],
    hen-NUH with pronounced H at end
    [AR])
Helga (HEL-guh [SCAN], ELL-gah [SP])
Henriette (hen-ree-YET [GER], aw-ree-YET
    with short N [FR])
Hilda (HIL-duh [HEB/SCAN])

Irene (eye-REEN, ee-RAY-nuh [HUN],
    ee-REN or ee-ray-NAY [FR])
Irma (UR-muh [GER], YEER-muh [IT],
    EER-muh [SP])
Isabel (IZ-uh-bell, ee-zaw-BELL [FR],
    EE-saw-bell or ee-saw-BELL or
    ee-thuh-VELL [SP])

Jasmine (JAZ-min, jass-MEEN,
    JAS-oo-meen [JAP]), yaz-MEEN [AR],
    yass-MEEN [HEB/PER])

Jean (JEEN [CG], ZHAN [FR])
Jeanette (jen-NET [CG], zhan-NET [FR])
Jeanine (jen-NEEN [CG], zhan-NEEN [FR])
Jennifer (JEN-nif-ur [WL], zheh-nee-FAIR
    [FR])
Jessenia (jes-SAY-nee-yuh,
    jes-SEN-ee-yuh, yes-SEE-nuh [AR],
    hes-SAY-nee-yuh or
    he-THAY-nee-yuh [SP])
Judith (JOO-dith, zhoo-DEET [FR],
    YOO-dit or yuh-HOO-dit [HEB])

Kaliyah (KAW-lee-yuh or kuh-LEE-yuh
    [AA], kaw-LEE-yuh [HW])
Kaya (KY-yuh [NA/SCAN/JAP], KAY-yuh)
Kayla (KAY-luh or KY-luh [IR])
Kiara (kee-YAR-ruh [IT], KEER-ruh [IR])

Leila (LEE-luh, LAY-luh [AR/HEB/PER])
Leone (lee-YOH-nee [GER], lay-yoh-NEE
    [FR])
Lise (LEE-zuh [GER], LEEZ [FR], LEE-suh)
Luana (loo-WAH-nuh [GER/HW],
    loo-WAN-uh [IT])
Lucia (LOO-shuh, loo-CHEE-yuh [IT/SCAN],
    loo-SEE-yuh or loo-THEE-yuh [SP])
Luisa (loo-WEEZ-uh [IT], loo-WEES-uh
    [GER/SP], loo-WEETH-uh)
Lulu (LOO-LOO [AR/FR])

Maida (MAY-duh [BR/GRK])
Makayla (muh-KAY-luh or mak-KAY-luh
    [CG/SP])
Malia (maw-LEE-yuh [HW/AA],
    muh-LEE-haw [AR], MAW-lee-yuh)
Malika (MEL-ik-uh or mal-EE-kuh [AR],
    MAW-lee-kuh [EI/HUN], muh-LY-kuh [AA])
Mara (MAR-raw [HEB/IT], MAIR-ruh)
Mariel (MAIR-ree-yell, MAR-ree-yell [GER],
    mair-ree-YELL [FR])
Marina (mar-REE-naw [IT/GER/GRK/RUSS/SP])
Matilda (mat-TIL-duh [GER], mat-TEELD-deh
    [IT])
Matilde (mat-TIL-dee, mat-TEELD [FR],
    mat-TEEL-day [SP], mat-TIL-duh [GER])
Maya (MY-yuh [EI/GRK/NA])
Michaela (mik-ELL-uh or mik-y-YELL-uh
    [IT], muh-KAY-luh, mee-chy-ELL-uh
    with guttural CH [HEB])
Mina (MEE-nuh [JAP/IT/SP])
Muriel (MUR-ree-yell [CG/HEB])

Nadia (NAW-dee-yuh, NAW-dee-yah
    with pronounced H at end [AR],

NAD-ee-yuh [IT])

Naomi (nay-YOH-mee or NOH-mee [HEB], ny-YOH-mee, NAW-oh-mee [JAP])

Natalie (NAD-uh-lee, naw-taw-LEE [HEB], nat-tal-LEE [FR])

Nereida (nair-RAY-duh [SP/GRK])

Nina (NEE-nuh [AR/FR/HEB/IT/RUS/SP], NY-nuh)

Nita (NEE-tuh [HEB/SP])

Noemi (no-WEM-ee, noh-WAY-mee, noh-way-MEE [IT/FR/SP])

Nora (NOR-ruh [AR/GR/HEB/IR])

Noreen (nor-REEN [AR/IR])

Nyah (NEE-yuh or NY-yuh [AA])

Odell (oh-DELL [AA/IR])

Ola (OH-luh [HEB/SCAN])

Olga (OHL-gaw [GER/SP])

Patricia (pat-RISH-uh, pat-REES-ee-yuh [FR/SP], pat-REE-thee-yuh [SP])

Phoebe (FEE-bee [FR/GRK])

Phoenix (FEE-niks [AA/GRK])

Rachel (RAY-chell, ruh-CHELL with guttural CH [HEB], raw-SHELL [FR])

Rafaela (raff-ay-YELL-uh, raff-eye-ELL-uh [IT], raw-fuh-ELL-uh [HEB/SP])

Raquel (rrrak-ELL [FR/SP])

Rebecca (reb-EK-uh, RIV-kuh [HEB], reb-AY-kuh [SP])

Rhea (REE-yuh [GRK], RAY-yuh)

Roma (ROH-muh [HEB/IT])

Rona (ROH-nuh [CG/HEB])

Rosina (roh-ZEE-nuh [CG/IT])

Roxana (rawk-SAW-nuh, rawk-SAN-nuh, rohk-SAW-naw or rohk-THAW-naw [SP], ruk-SAW-nah with pronounced H at end [AR])

Salma (SAL-muh, SAWL-maw [HEB/SP], THAWL-maw [SP], SUL-mah with pronounced H at end [AR])

Salome (sal-LOH-mee, SAW-loh-may, suh-LOHM, SAL-loh-may [BR], saw-loh-MAY [FR], shaw-LOHM [HEB])

Sasha (SAW-shuh [GER/RUS], SASH-uh)

Selma (SEL-muh [GER/SCAN/SP])

Shawn (SHAWN [IR])

Shayla (SHAY-luh [AA/CG], SHY-luh)

Shaylee (SHAY-lee [AA/CG])

Sheila (SHEE-luh [CG], SHAY-hell-uh [PER], SHAY-luh, SHY-luh)

Sigrid (SIG-rid [SCAN], see-GREED [FR])

Sonia (SOHN-yaw [IT/HEB/RUS/SP], soh-NEE-yaw or thoh-NEE-yaw [SP], SOHN-nee-yuh with pronounced H at end [AR], SAWN-yuh [RUS])

Sophia (soh-FEE-yuh [GRK/IT/SP], thoh-FEE-yuh [SP])

Sophie (SOH-fee [GRK], soh-FEE [FR])

Stephanie (STEF-uh-nee [GRK], stay-faw-NEE [FR])

Tamara (TAM-uh-ruh, tuh-MAR-ruh [AR/EI], tuh-MAIR-ruh [AA], tuh-MAR [HEB], TAW-mar-ruh [RUS])

Tara (TAR-ruh [IR/CG], TAIR-ruh, TARRR-raw [EI])

Toya (TOY-yuh [AA/JAP/SCAN])

Tristan (TRIS-ten [WL], trees-TAW with short N [FR], trees-TAWN or treeth-TAWN [SP])

Tyra (TY-ruh [SCAN/AA])

Una (OO-nuh [IR/IT], YOO-nuh)

Winona (win-OH-nuh [BR/NA])

Yadira (yad-DEER-ruh [HEB/SP])

Yanira (yan-NEER-raw [AA/GRK/HEB/SP])

Yesenia (yess-SAY-nee-yuh, yee-SEN-ee-yuh or ye-THEN-ee-yuh [SP], yes-SEE-nuh [AR])

Yuliana (yoo-lee-YAWN-uh [SP/RUS])

Zina (ZY-nuh, ZEE-nuh [AR])

Zoe (ZOH-wee [GRK/HEB], zoh-WAY [FR])

Zoraida (zoh-RAY-duh with pronounced H at end [AR], zor-RY-duh [SP])

Zsa-zsa (ZHAW-zhaw [HUN], ZAW-ZAW)

Boys

Aaron (AIR-en, aw-haw-ROHN [HEB], aw-ROHN [SP])

Abel (AY-bell, AW-vell [HEB], aw-BELL [SP])

Adelbert (AD-dull-burt [GER], ad-dell-BAIR [FR])

Adolph (AYD-awlf [GER], ad-DAWLF [FR])

Adrian (AY-dree-yen, , aw-DREE-yawn [SP], ad-ree-AW with short N [FR]))

Aidan (AY-den [IR], ED-in [HEB])

Alan (AL-len [CG], al-LE with short N [FR])

Albert (AL-burt [GER], al-BAIR [FR])

Aldo (AWL-doh [GER/IT/SP])

Andrea (awn-DRAY-yuh [GRK/IT])

Anibal (ANN-nib-bull [GRK], aw-noo-BAWL [EI], AW-nee-bawl [IT])

Ariel (AIR-ree-yell, AR-ree-yell, ar-ree-YELL [HEB/FR])

Arnav (ar-NAWV [EI/HEB])

August (AW-gest [GER], oh-GOOST [FR])

Augustin (aw-GUS-tin, oh-goos-TEEN or ow-goh-STAW with short N [FR], aw-goo-STEEN or aw-gooth-TEEN [SP])

Benjamin (BEN-juh-min, bin-yaw-MEEN [HEB], ben-zhaw-ME with short N [FR] ben-haw-MEEN or ven-haw-MEEN [SP])

Beryl (BAIR-rill [GRK/HEB])

Bilal (bee-LAWL or bee-LAL [AR/EI])

Bruno (BROO-noh [GER/IT])

Cael (KYL, KAYL [CG/HEB])

Cale (KAYL [CG/HEB])

Christian (KRIS-chen, KREE-stee-yawn or KREETH-tee-yawn [IT/SP], kree-stee-YAW with short N [FR])

Cordell (kor-DELL [FR])

Dante (DAWN-tay [AA/IT])

David (DAY-vid, daw-VEED [HEB], dav-EED [FR])

Davon (DAY-vun [AA], DAV-in [IR])

Deangelo (dee-YAN-jell-oh [AA/IT])

Demetris (duh-MEE-tris [AA/GRK])

Dimitri (dim-MEE-tree [RUS/FR])

Donal (DAW-null [IR], daw-NELL [AA])

Efrain (eff-raw-EEN or EEF-rawn [HEB], EFF-ren [AA], eff-RA with short N [FR], eff-raw-EEN [SP], EE-fren or ef-RYN; see also Ephraim)

Elias (EE-lee-yaws [HEB], el-LEE-yaws or eh-LEE-yes [SP])

Eliezer (el-lee-YEZ-ur [HEB/AA], el-LEE-zur, el-LY-zur, el-lee-ZAIR or el-lee-THAIR [SP])

Emmanuel (ee-MAN-yoo-well [AA], ee-mawn-yoo-ELL [HEB], em-man-WELL [FR], ee-mawn-yoo-WELL or ee-man-WELL [SP])

Emmett (EM-mit [GER/IR])

Ezekiel (ee-ZEE-kee-yell [AA], yeh-CHEZ-kel with guttural CH [HEB], ess-ay-KYL/eth-ay-KYL or ess-sy-KEEL/eth-y-KEEL [SP])

Felix (FEEL-iks, fel-LEEKS [SP], fay-LEEKS [FR])

Ferdinand (FUR-din-and, FAIR-din-nawnd [GER], fair-dee-NAW with short ND [FR])

Gabriel (GAY-bree-ell, gaw-bree-ELL or gaw-vree-ELL [HEB], gab-brrree-YELL [FR/SP/IT])

Gaston (GASS-tun [CG], gas-TOHN or gas-TAW with short N [FR])

Giovanni (jee-yoh-VAW-nee or joh-VAW-nee [AA/IT])

Gustave (GOO-stawv [GER/SCAN], goo-STAWV [FR])

Henry (HEN-ree [GER], aw-REE with short N [FR])

Herbert (HUR-burt [GER], air-BAIR [FR])

Hubert (HYOO-burt [GER], oo-BAIR [FR])

Hugo (HYOO-goh [GER], oo-GOH [SP])

Israel (IZ-ree-yell, IZ-ray-yell [HEB], iss-raw-EEL [AR], eess-RAY-yell or eeth-RAY-yell [SP])

Jacques (ZHAWK [FR], HAW-kess [SP])

Jan (YAWN, NYAWN [SCAN])

Joachim (wah-KEEM, JOH-wah-kim, zho-wah-SHE with short N [FR], yo-WAH-kim [GER], ye-ho-wuh-KEEM or yow-wuh-KEEM [HEB])

Joaquin (wah-KEEN, ho-wah-KEEN [SP], ye-ho-wuh-CHEEN with guttural CH [HEB])

Joel (JOH-well, yoh-ELL [HEB], zho-WELL [FR])

Jose (ho-ZAY, YO-see [HEB], ho-SAY or ho-THAY [SP])

Joseph (JOH-sef, YOH-sef or yoh-SEF [HEB], YOO-suf [AR], zho-ZEF [FR])

Keon (KEE-yen [IR/PER], KEE-yawn [AA])

Kieran (KEER-ren [CG], KEER-rawn [IR])

Lamar (luh-MAR [AA/GER])

Lambert (LAM-burt [GER], lam-BAIR [FR])

Lamont (luh-MAWNT [AA/SCAN])

Lawrence (LOR-rens, lor-RAWS with short N [FR], LOR-rens [GER])

Leon (LEE-yawn [GER], lay-YAW with short N [FR], lay-YOHN [SP])

Leonard (LEN-urd [GER], lay-yoh-NAR [FR])

Leopold (LEE-yup-old [GER], lay-yoh-POHLD [FR])
Leroy (LEE-roy [AA], leh-RWAH [FR])
Louis (LOO-wiss [GER], loo-WEE [FR])
Luca (LOO-kuh [IT/HUN])
Lucas (LOO-kuss [GER/SCAN/SP], loo-KA [FR])

Martin (MAR-tin, mar-TA with short N [FR], mar-TEEN [SP])
Maximilian (mak-sim-MIL-yen [GER], mak-see-meel-YA with short N [FR])
Michael (MY-kel, mee-chy-ELL with guttural CH [HEB], mee-SHELL [FR])
Milan (mee-LAWN [IT/RUS])

Odell (oh-DELL [AA/SCAN])
Oren (OR-ren [HEB/IR])
Orlando (or-LAN-doh [AA], or-LAWN-doh [SP])
Oscar (AWS-kur [SCAN], aws-KAR or awth-KAR [SP])

Radames (RAW-duh-mes [EGY], RAD-uh-mes or RAD-uh-may [SP])
Rafael (RAF-ee-yell, raf-ee-YELL, rrraf-uh-YELL [FR], raw-faw-ELL [HEB/SP], rrraw-FAY-yell [SP])
Rahul (ruh-HOOL [AA], rrrraw-HOOL [EI])
Raul (raw-OOL, rrraw-OOL [FR/SP])
Ravi (RRRAW-vee [EI], RAW-vee [HEB])
Raymond (RAY-mund [GER], rrray-MAW with short N [FR])
Ruben (ROO-ben, ROO-ven or roo-VAYN [HEB], roo-BEN or roo-VEN [SP])

Rudolph (ROOD-awlf, ROH-dawlf [GER], roh-DAWLF [FR])
Ryne (RYN [GER/IR/WL])

Samuel (SAM-yoo-well, SAM-yool, SHMOO-well [HEB], sam-WELL [IT/SP])
Sasha (SAW-shuh [GER/RUS], SASH-uh)
Saul (SAWL, shaw-OOL [HEB], saw-OOL or thaw-OOL [SP])
Sean (SHAWN [IR])
Sebastian (sub-BAS-chen, sub-BAS-tee-yen, say-bas-tee-YAW with short N [FR], say-baws-TAWN or thay-vaws-TAWN [SP])
Simon (SY-mun [GRK], shee-MOHN [HEB], see-MAW with short N [FR])
Stefan (stef-FAWN [GER/FR])
Syed (sy-YEED or SAY-yed [AR/AA], SY-yed [EI]; see also Zaid)

Thomas (TAW-muss, TOH-maws [GER], toh-MAW [FR], toh-MAWS [IR/SP])
Tito (TEE-toh [AA/IT/SP])
Tremaine (truh-MAYN [AA/CG])
Tristan (TRIS-ten [WL], trees-TAW with short N [FR], trees-TAWN or treeth-TAWN [SP])
Tyrone (ty-ROHN [AA/CG])

Xavier (ZAY-vee-yur, eks-ZAY-vee-yur, haw-vee-YAIR or haw-bee-YAIR [SP], zav-YAY [FR])

EXTRAS
AND RESOURCES

This chapter offers a few extras parents may want to consider when naming their child.

The Pros and Cons of Unusual Names

"Everyone wants to find a name that's different, but not too different," says baby name expert Cleveland Kent Evans, an associate psychology professor at Bellevue University in Nebraska. Thanks to today's technology, people who want to avoid giving their kids a common name can look up potential candidates on the Internet and avoid anything in the top ten. "For the first time in history, the top fifty names account for less than fifty percent of boys born each year, and for less than forty percent of girls," says Evans. "The common names now are going to turn over quicker, and the new fashions sound like the old fashions." Classics like Kate and Daniel are suddenly appealing again because they're actually less common than trendy chart-toppers like Madison (#3) and Ethan (#6). Old-fashioned boys' names like Asa and Ezra (Paul Reiser's son) are on the rise, too, so it seems inevitable that Hazel, Zelda, and Mabel (Tracy Ullman's daughter) will soon mount a comeback.

So how do you know which way to go—traditional or unusual? Let's take a look at the pluses and minuses.

ODD NAME OUT

If you like names like Brunilda, Django, Hedwig, and Clover, Cari Clark has one piece of advice. "Don't do it!" she shouts. "It takes a tremendous amount of time out of your life to have to constantly spell, pronounce, and explain your name."

Clark should know. Growing up Cari Bilyeu, she felt like an odd girl out among a sea of Susans, Debbies, and Cathys. "I didn't know any other Caris when I was a kid, especially spelled the way I was," she says, "so whenever I wanted to buy those little license plates, I could never find my name. Even now, I have at least two credit cards with Carl on them." Her advice is that, especially with an unusual last name, simpler is better. "You're blessing your child with something that will be his fingerprint the rest of his life," she explains. "If you go with a time-tested name, you really can't go wrong, but you're taking a chance when you cook something up on your own. Some of these names sound like pharmaceutical products!"

Indeed, Allegra was a beautiful Spanish name meaning joy . . . until the allergy medicine came out. Not surprisingly, Kermit and Grover were popular boys' names in the 1960s, but when *Sesame Street* hit the airwaves, they dropped out of sight.

ODD NAME IN

By the time your kids are in school, it's likely the teacher will have to know how to pronounce Xavier, Eliezer, Mekhi, Sanaa, Karyme, and Aaliyah, to mention just a few. Kids will be so used to so-called *different* names, they won't bother teasing each other about them. (Of course, they'll undoubtedly find something else!) Eventually, employers will get used to asking for proper spellings and pronunciations as well, so an unusual name can be yet another way for your child to stand out while also fitting in.

This "anything goes" mindset is certainly subject to geographic and cultural influences, however. Where we live in the San Francisco/Berkeley area of California, we know of children named Scout, Bixby, Finnegan, Beatrix, Tallulah, Wylie, Phoenix, Whisper, Rip, Itai, Faelan, Cypress, Cedar, Sequoia, Ceres, and Satchel. Although those kids might get puzzled stares in Michigan or Wyoming, here their names get compliments.

Although theories abound that people will associate certain names with positive or negative characteristics (like Tiffany with dumb blondes and Jacqueline with elegance), there has been just as much research to show that those preconceived notions hold only until we meet a person by that name who doesn't fit the stereotype. The truth is, the more you hear odd names, the less odd they sound. Remember, your child's name should be something that you won't mind saying dozens of times a day. So don't be afraid to be a trendsetter. Pick something you love and let the rest of the world catch on later.

Initial Power

Initials are another nickname option that can be fun when your children are young and can still seem classy when they're adults. It's nice if the phonemes match, like JJ (double long A sounds) for Jasper James or PG (double long Es) for Paul George, making them memorable enough to stick with people. And if your child prefers his middle name, he can always go the one-initial route of F. Scott Fitzgerald and T. Coraghessan Boyle.

In fact, while you're considering initials, think about monograms, too. Franklin Alexander Tucker is a fine name, except that the poor chap's initials spell FAT, while lucky little Jade Olivia Yoo spells JOY. This may seem trivial, but it has some scientific backing: A 1998 University of California study showed that men with positive monograms like ACE, VIP, and WIN live an average of five years longer than those whose initials spell something neutral or nothing at all. (And by the way, those with decidedly negative initials such as PIG, RAT, BUM, or DIE passed away nearly three years younger than the neutral group.) So why not give your child every advantage?

Pet Names

You can use our system to name your pets, too. Now you're probably thinking that pets are known by first names alone—but haven't you noticed how the veterinarian dubs Fido with your surname? Some pets even have first and last names on their ID tags. We know of dogs named Zoe Zuckerbrot (matching Zs), Beau Wool-Baum (matching B in Baum and long O sound similar to OO in Wool), and Clara Kaplan (matching Ks, Ls, and short As). Of course, you can always make up a last name for your four-legged friend, as in Harris the Cat, matching short A phonemes, or Ollie Dog, matching short O sounds.

Spelling Counts

Your child will be writing his name countless times in the years to come. So before you fill out the birth certificate, ask yourself, how easy is it to misspell this name? Does it seem awkward or stand out just enough? Does it look pretty or too flowery? How will it come across on a resume? Written in lights? Hanging on the door of the oval office?

Star Babies

Celebrities tend to be more adventurous with their names, launching trends that give the rest of us permission to follow suit. Thanks to Demi, Woody, and Gwyneth, names like Scout, Satchel, and even Apple will undoubtedly make the top 1000 list in the next few years. Here are some of the more original celebrity baby name choices, and how they match their surnames:

- **Apple Blythe Allison Martin** (Gwyneth Paltrow and Chris Martin). Apple Martin has a nice trochaic rhythm to it and the middle names (the first names of grandmas on both sides) tie it together phonetically: The P and L in Apple matches the B and L in Blythe; the short A and L in Apple matches the short A and L in Allison; and the short I in Allison matches the short I in Martin. Hopefully Gwyneth and Chris anticipated the inevitable Apple Martini jokes. For their next child, maybe they'll go with another theme name, Austin Martin.
- **Coco Riley Arquette** (Courteney Cox-Arquette and David Arquette). Coco Arquette might sound like too much alliteration for some people, but Courteney obviously likes the phonetic echoes in her own name. Since Arquette features the AR sound, a sibling could be Dario to use the same "-o" ending as Coco. Or, to stay in the food world, they might like Olive, with a short O vowel similar to the AR sound.
- **Nevaeh Sandoval** (Sonny Sandoval). Nevaeh matches the N and V in Sandoval, and the rhythm is nice, too: da-DA-da DA-da-da. Since Nevaeh is heaven spelled backwards, Sandoval

might want to rearrange the same letters again for siblings Evenah and Vehena.

○ **Rumer Glenn Willis, Scout LaRue Willis, and Tallulah Belle Willis** (Demi Moore and Bruce Willis). This celebrity couple set the pace for interesting names among the Hollywood set in the 1980s—Rumer was named for British novelist Rumer Godden, Scout for *To Kill a Mockingbird*, and Tallulah for the actress Tallulah Bankhead—but how do their choices match their surname? Willis is a pretty simple surname, so the unconventional first names probably help the girls stand out. We like how they paired different syllables in the first and middle names, and how the S in Scout matches the S in Willis. But the four L sounds in Tallulah Belle Willis are a little over-the-top.

○ **Jasper Armstrong Marsalis** (Wynton Marsalis). Okay, we're partial to the name Jasper since we have one of our own, but this is an especially good match of the prominent short As in JASS-pur and mar-SAL-iss. Plus, the middle and last name feature the AR sound and the Ss tie all three names together. Louis Armstrong's surname adds an artistic touch in the middle. Kelly and Don Johnson took the alliteration route with their son, Jasper Johnson, whose middle name Breckenridge also features a J sound.

○ **Carys Zeta Douglas** (Catherine Zeta Jones and Michael Douglas). Carys comes from the Welsh "caru" which means "to love" and reflects Zeta Jones's Welsh heritage. The first and last name have the same "-s" ending, which is a no-no for some people, but in this case it's not difficult to pronounce and it's broken up by the "-a" ending in the middle name: If she's like her mother, she'll go by all three names.

○ **Scarlet Rose Stallone** (Sylvester Stallone and Jennifer Flavin). Nice matching of S, L, and long O sounds between the first, middle, and last names. Plus, "scarlet rose" is very colorful.

○ **Audrey Caroline McGraw** (Faith Hill and Tim McGraw). Audrey McGraw has a short O phonetic echo and pairs a trochee with an iamb: DA-da da-DA.

○ **Braeden Cooper Sorbo** (Sam and Kevin Sorbo). The repeating B/P sounds tie these three names together nicely. To avoid a sibling with the same first initial, the Sorbos might like Piper or Libby.

○ **Lourdes Maria Ciccone Leon** (Madonna and Carlos Leon) and Rocco Ritchie (Madonna and Guy Ritchie). The material mom likes alliteration, but she's also got a sentimental side. Lourdes was named as a tribute to Madonna's mother, who died before fulfilling her dream of visiting Lourdes, France, where the Virgin Mary (a.k.a. Madonna) appeared in 1858. Plus, Lola and Rocco have that long O in common.

○ **Dexter Dean Keaton** (Diane Keaton). These boy names sound even better for a girl, and the three names tie together beautifully, thanks to the repeating D/Ts in Dexter, Dean, and Keaton, the long Es in Dean and Keaton, and the K/Xs in Dexter and Keaton.

○ **Eja Lange** (Shania Twain and Mutt Lange). Pronounced like Asia, this is a lovely long A match, and it's an interesting name with a unique spelling.

○ **Jaden Christopher Syre Smith** and **Willow Camille Reign Smith** (Will Smith and Jada Pinkett Smith). Obviously the Smiths wanted Jaden to pay tribute to Jada and Willow to pay tribute to Will. The Fresh Prince even has another son from a previous marriage who follows that tradition, Willard Smith III. The middle names are probably family placeholders, since they don't offer much in the way of flow, but Willow Smith has a short I phonetic echo and Jaden and Willow are trochaic so they go together.

Where to Go for More

The point of this book is to teach you a method for finding a first name that sounds good with your last name, but it cannot be all things to all people—we simply didn't have the room to put in every name from every language. Our intent was to help you avoid going through those other books with more than 20,000 names in them. We didn't want to overstuff our lists just to make them longer and overstuff your brains in the process. Your brains work plenty hard already with a new babe on the way.

So consider the names here as inspiration to go out and find your own name, if you so desire. Our sound-and-rhythm matching system will work with any culturally specific name, but since the first names we use are drawn from the 1000 most popular baby names in the United States, readers with international origins may want to seek supplementary name lists elsewhere.

As we have stated in the preceding chapters, you can also seek out new name ideas by turning to foreign dictionaries and maps, hobby and trade periodicals, and family friends and relatives. Now that you know what we've taught you, go out in the world and apply the matching technique to any name you come across.

Finally visit our website, www.theperfectbabyname.com for lots more baby-naming tips, stories, and the complete name lists with pronunciations and alternate spellings.

Reaction

Adrienne – Shoot E, N, R
Lexi
Scarlett – Shoot E, R
Tess – Shoot E

Annika – Shoot I, K, N